Engaging with Chaucer

Engaging with Chaucer

Practice, Authority, Reading

Edited by
C.W.R.D. Moseley

berghahn
NEW YORK · OXFORD
www.berghahnbooks.com

Published in 2021 by
Berghahn Books
www.berghahnbooks.com

© 2021 Berghahn Books

Originally published as two special issues of *Critical Survey:*
Volume 29, issue 3 (2017) and Volume 30, issue 3 (2018).

Library of Congress Cataloging-in-Publication Data

Library of Congress Control Number: 2020942893

British Library Cataloguing in Publication Data

A catalogue record for this book is available from the British Library

ISBN 978-1-78920-999-0 hardback
ISBN 978-1-78920-971-6 paperback
ISBN 978-1-78920-476-6 ebook

Contents

Introduction
'The craft so long to lerne...'
C.W.R.D. Moseley
1

Chapter 1
'And gret wel Chaucer whan ye mete'
Chaucer's Earliest Readers, Addresses and Audiences
Sebastian Sobecki
13

Chapter 2
Unhap, Misadventure, Infortune
Chaucer's Vocabulary of Mischance
Helen Cooper
21

Chapter 3
Chaucer's Tears
Barry Windeatt
34

Chapter 4
In Appreciation of Metrical Abnormality
Headless Lines and Initial Inversion in Chaucer
Ad Putter
55

Chapter 5
Blanche, Two Chaucers and the Stanley Family
Rethinking the Reception of The Book of the Duchess
Simon Meecham-Jones
77

Chapter 6
'Tu Numeris Elementa Ligas'
The Consolation of Nature's Numbers in Parlement of Foulys
C.W.R.D. Moseley
104

Chapter 7   134
Troilus and Criseyde **and the 'Parfit Blisse of Love'**
Simone Fryer-Bovair

Chapter 8   159
Hateful Contraries in 'The Merchant's Tale'
John M. Fyler

Chapter 9   193
String Theory and 'The Man of Law's Tale'
Where is Constancy?
William A. Quinn

Chapter 10   211
The Pardoner's Passing and How It Matters
Gender, Relics and Speech Acts
Alex da Costa

Chapter 11   233
'Double Sorrow'
The Complexity of Complaint in Chaucer's Anelida and Arcite
and Henryson's Testament of Cresseid
Jacqueline Tasioulas

Index   249

Introduction

'The craft so long to lerne...'

C.W.R.D. Moseley

As I write, it seems to many that we are living at a time of unprece-dented social, political, moral, epistemological and environmental uncertainty. And that was before the Coronavirus hit. It seems we are moving into – or are already in – what some historians call a General Crisis. That term was first used of the seventeenth century,[1] but that time of radical upheaval is not the only one in human history that can be documented and so described. Chaucer was himself living through just such a period,[2] when ancient cer-tainties and assumptions seemed fundamentally unstable, when society seemed to be sliding into irresolvable war and chaos, and the weather was reliably unreliable as climate worsened across the entire globe. Gaunt Famine stalked every happy harvest. Dame Fortune seemed to be at her most unpredictable – indeed, Helen Cooper's essay in this collection on the single word 'hap' and its cognates demonstrates beyond argument how much this issue, and what it might mean, mattered to Chaucer. Perhaps ancient voices from that anxious time may have something to say which we might find helpful in our own.

Notes for this section begin on page 11.

Tot homines, quot sententiae: like the birds in *The Parlement of Foulys*, readers of Chaucer over the long centuries have argued many things about his work, and about him, often wholly consistently in themselves, but frequently from incompatible standpoints. As in that poem, we know there is something to learn, but we cannot be sure we know how to do it. There have been many different ideas of Chaucer as poet, and indeed of what a poet is. The many images, in every sense, of Chaucer himself that have been constructed[3] often tell us as much about the constructor as about the constructed. Simon Meecham-Jones' essay below suggests that the lack of early witnesses for *The Book of the Duchess* may be indicative of some family embarrassment, even disappointment, with it as a conventional elegy that could be used in the yearly commemorations of Blanche which John of Gaunt instituted. But its eventual appearance, and the company it keeps, in three mid-fifteenth century MSS, all of which are anthologies and two of which are also the earliest witnesses for the *Hous of Fame*, suggest that perceptions of 'Chaucer' as well as of his work are being actively qualified, for collecting poems into a MS for, or as specified by, a patron is an act of choice. Indeed, this essay suggests that the compilation of one of the MSS may be a symptom of dynastic rivalries in those turbulent years of Henry VI. If so, it is a material example of people adjusting their Chaucers to fit their own agendas. Later, more brashly, the radically anti-fraternal 'Plowman's Tale', originally from around 1400, was printed as Chaucer's in 1532[4] by Thynne, with a new prologue linking it to the Canterbury pilgrimage. This deliberately suggests that Chaucer, now effectively central in a new *English* (as distinct from Latin or French) canon,[5] held the impeccable proto-Reformist views that would now be expected of one in such a position. He is now too important to be left to the opposition, and the challenges he would surely have posed to the certainties on either side of the religious divide are simply ignored. John Speed's engraving 'The Progenie of Geffrey Chaucer' in Speght's *The Workes of our Antient and Lerned English Poet, Newly Printed* (London, 1598) seeks to claim both historical accuracy for the portrait[6] and also to insert Chaucer into an aristocratic lineage which includes Henry VII and his own great-grandson Edmund de la Pole, Duke of Suffolk – an interesting gentrification of a writer and his craft which would have mystified Chaucer's diffident, de-authorising, *persona*, and perhaps the poet himself as well. Just how diversely readers over the centuries have conceptualised Chaucer's writing and the man behind it is admirably demonstrated in Caroline Spurgeon's and Derek Brewer's work.[7] More publicly-visible instances which both reflect and in turn affect ideas of the man might be Burne-Jones' 1864 stained glass panel,[8] which mediates the varying sunlight into a pensive poet, straight out of a sort of 'Legend of Good Poets', contemplating a daisy in a fashion just short of the greenery-yallery,[9] or, some decades later (1900), the serious figure with the steady gaze in the memorial window by Charles Eamer Kemp in the north aisle of Southwark Cathedral.[10]

Canonisation, moreover, not infrequently detaches the myth of the man from his work completely. As time passes that myth may well become dominant outside the academy. For there is an ineradicable (it seems) legend (perhaps first evidenced by Pope's juvenile 'Imitation of Chaucer')[11] of the cheerful roly-poly poet who went on pilgrimages and left merely a fund of stories, mostly memorable for the risqué ones – ignore everything else more demanding.[12] This myth can, moreover, sell. First staged in March 1968, a musical, *The Canterbury Tales*, with Neville Coghill's lyrics and music by John Hawkins and Richard Hill, played for over 2000 performances on the London stage to many to whom 'Chaucer' was only a name, a signifier, for a certain vision of England, like advertisers in that same decade using a picture of a hail-fellow-well-met actor dressed up as Henry VIII waving a half-eaten chicken drumstick in order to sell mass-produced oven-ready chickens. The musical was considered, for the time, very bawdy: the Lord Chamberlain's censorship of the theatre had just ended. *Plus ça change*: Richard Lloyd Playscripts[13] currently offers a script for

> *The Canterbury Tales*... Six of the best, funniest, and bawdiest of Chaucer's tales... There's nothing quite like *The Canterbury Tales* to put the present-day observer in touch with the ordinary lives of our medieval forbearers... These stories convey the gritty reality of life in Medieval England, combining into one boisterous and hilarious portrait of ordinary folk preoccupied with petty jealousies, mundane squabbles, and simple pleasures – all conveying really how little the English people have changed during 600 intervening years.[14]

Well, six hundred years is not a long time in human history, and we need not bother too much about the semantics.

'Engaging' in this book's title can have the sense of 'enter into conflict with',[15] and certainly Chaucer offers many challenges to the way people think and to their assumptions. He has never lacked serious readers, and writers, engaging with his work and making space for themselves in what they saw as a high tradition stemming from him. This is both challenge and, to use Harold Bloom's word, anxiety. For example, in *The Prelude, or, Growth of a Poet's Mind* (1805), 278ff., Wordsworth subtly links himself, now a poet claiming a high calling, but then an undergraduate in Cambridge, to the canonical authority of Milton, Spenser, and

> Beside the pleasant Mill of Trompington
> I laugh'd with Chaucer, in the hawthorn shade,
> Heard him, while birds were warbling, tell his tales
> Of amorous passion

His interest lasted, and his respect broadened. While Dorothy read aloud 'The Miller's Tale' to William and Mary by the fire at Grasmere on Boxing Day 1801 – a domestic scene of some interest – William was currently working seriously on modernisations of tales from Chaucer and part of *Troilus and Criseyde*. We ourselves still read, write and argue about Chaucer. Why? After all, the crass neophilia that rules so much of our culture would readily dismiss as of no importance – 'relevance'? – to us the work of someone who lived in a world of assumptions and behaviour immeasurably and unknowably different from ours, and was, moreover, white, male and very dead for over six hundred years. What is it about him? The simplest answers to my question may be the best: he is fun – very important, for rational pleasure is one of the proper pursuits of mankind; and because he is fun – I do not mean funny – he draws us into engaging with his thoughts, with the many voices he uses, and thus challenges our intelligence and questions our certainties, just as his were challenged and questioned by what he read. His journey of unknowing and ours join up. For it is a truism that great writing – great art of any kind, indeed – transcends the conventions and contexts of its time, and Chaucer, indeed, has outlasted many -isms, his work silently criticising those who blunt their critical tools on what he wrote. By any standards his was a coruscating intellect, and he was also a meticulous craftsman, as Ad Putter's essay in this volume demonstrates. But in addition his poetry can also be immensely moving in that inexplicable way that defeats all analysis. He gives us a line, if we will listen to him, on this puzzle of being human, and despite the long time between the light he saw and ours, he articulates the human imperatives. Dryden remarked, in his Preface to the *Fables* (1700): '...mankind is ever the same, and nothing is lost out of nature, though everything is altered.' Even so: making out of quotidian normality poetry that lasts is an art that requires the agile processing skills of a great poet as well as the skills of his attentive readers. Both are worth exploring.

The vagaries of critical fashion, New or not, have taken us on tours of various Fallacies, Intentional, Authorial and even perhaps Narratorial; they have taken us through long arguments proving that arguments prove nothing and that all language can discuss is itself. What was intended as a lens can easily become a filter. Yet the whirligig of Time seems now to have brought some of us to believe in the Resurrection of the Author[16] – though not without a wholly welcome re-emphasis that the different stances and capacities of readers affect the poem that they see. In the welter of critical cleverness, it is so easy quietly to forget that authors, real people, existed, and they wrestled with the intractability of language: we are dealing with a unique vision of one person in one temporal context. Writers developed different ideas and perspectives as they grew older, they read books, and sometimes they misunderstood them – or saw what they wanted to see. And they said what they wanted to say in that serious game with an audience or reader – whose taste they understood and with whom they could leave a lot unsaid.

So Chaucer speaks to us with peculiar sharpness in our confused and conflicted post-modern world with news from that other country we call the past. This might be one reason why it is high folly *not* to teach him to the young, and why, when you do, they respond so enthusiastically. The Middle Ages had much more in common with modernism, indeed with our own uncertainties, than with the confidence of the nineteenth century when so much spadework was done in recovering and re-examining many of the materials we now value. The mediaevals shared our itchy unease about what constitutes truth in statement, or the reliability of knowledge; they anticipated the non-naturalistic representation of time in the polychronic conventions of some visual art; the sophistication of *entrelace* makes the narration of Scandi-*noir* TV series like *The Bridge* seem like child's play. In the Luttrell Psalter horses climb (apparently cheerfully, to judge from their expression) out of one plane into the side margin. As Helen Cooper has remarked, the mediaevals 'delighted in Picasso-esque clashes of perspective', and in playing with aspectuality,[17] where contradictory things can both be true. Chaucer delights in de-authorising the act of authorship, as in *Troilus and Criseyde*, or in presenting us with unreliable *personae* as guides to his problematic fictional worlds. He has no trouble in Sternely moving between different storytelling/narratorial levels, or different implied audiences, even within the same tale.[18] Just so the Man of Law can be sniffy about the poems by his own author he has 'read' – but that author is also a fictional character in the same narrative space/time as himself (*Canterbury Tales*, II 46ff.); just so Justinus cites the Wife of Bath, or the fictional Parson condemns fiction: 'Thou getest fable noon ytold for me...' (*CT* X. 31ff.)

Chaucer's poems remain, challenging the effectiveness of whatever tools we bring to them, and ultimately, like all great art, they remain inexhaustible and beyond the categorising and diminishing reach of changing fashion or taste. Just as Chaucer implies the provisionality of his poetry, so we accept the provisionality of our reading. The poems read us, one might say, as well as the other way round. All we can do is hope one day 'to fare / The bet, and thus to rede [we] nyl nat spare'.[19]

Chaucer the real Author had real people who were real readers, and he released his poems, as he himself says (e.g. *Troilus and Criseyde*, V. 1786ff.), into a future he knew would be different from the mental and physical world in which he lived. Robert Henryson in the opening stanzas of *The Testament of Cresseid* allows us a glimpse of one of those new worlds. Sebastian Sobecki's chapter reminds us forcefully not only of the nexus of relationships, even the minutiae of place, within which Chaucer himself worked, but also the dynamics of the early circulation of his work. For if it be true, as suggested above, that poems 'read' the readers, how readers read – both physically and conceptually – are important concerns and ones to which Chaucer himself seems to have been alert. My own essay on the form and structure of *The Parlement of Foulys* argues for Chaucer being quite aware that the poem as it might be heard – indeed, performed – and the poem as read are quite different things, and that he makes that tension, contradiction even, part of the issues the poem discusses. If there be any force in this argument, it suggests that other poems, and not only of Chaucer, might also be fruitfully re-examined on these terms.

The whole point about stories, poems, is that they say what cannot be said. Humans are not the only intelligent creatures on this planet, but so far as we know we are the only species that makes sense of the world by telling each other stories about it: *homo sapiens sapiens*, but also *homo sapiens narrans*. A pupil of mine, a mature student who had been a ballet dancer, when once asked what her dance had meant, replied, 'If I could say what my dance meant, I would not have needed to dance it'. Exactly. What does *Troilus and Criseyde* 'mean'? or *King Lear?* To Conrad's Marlow, 'the meaning of an episode was not inside like a kernel but outside enveloping the tale which brought it out only as a glow brings out a haze, in the likeness of one of those misty haloes that sometimes are made visible by the spectral illumination of moonshine.'[20] The experience is the meaning. To understand – but we never shall – that experience and how it works is one of the tasks of criticism. That must mean that grappling with verbal texture and semantics – the figures in the dance – are important: indeed, they are the only road we have towards apprehending the mystery at the heart. And they can give a pretty fair line on areas of the author's concern. Ad Putter's elegant essay shows how what some might see as a very technical exploration of prosody can genuinely illuminate not only Chaucer's meticulous command of sonic effects, but also the conceptual intricacies of Chaucer's work, and the way those effects enhance the semantic patterns and structures – and how they are read. Too many people now read poetry with tin ears, and the sophisticated music of Chaucer's verse is a far more complex and considered thing than most realise. (I try to imagine those two highly competent readers like the Wordsworths reading Chaucer in their strong Cumberland accents.) Readers who do not hear Chaucer's poetry in their heads, or indeed who do not read it aloud, miss so much of its pleasure and wit. I suspect that Chaucer, when reading aloud himself, was a master of timing and inflection. Ad Putter's essay reminds us, too, of what we, alas, have not: Chaucer's youthful 'enditynges of worldly vanite... many a songe and many a leccherous lay' presuppose a musical/metrical talent which the verse we *do* have, of his late twenties and after, develops and hones into something bravura.

I have already noted how Helen Cooper's lucid and thought-provoking exploration across the canon of that single concept, 'hap', demonstrates just how intellectually and emotionally charged this issue was for Chaucer all through the intellectual and literary career of which we can have knowledge.[21] Indeed, 'Fortune's sharp adversitee', the topsyturviness to which things are liable, leads to an extraordinary interest – in *Troilus and Criseyde*, in 'The Knight's Tale' and others of the *Canterbury Tales*, the *Hous of Fame*, for example – in what *can* be relied on: to take the line somewhat out of context, can we be reassured that 'Trouthe thee shall deliver, it is no drede'?[22]

But what *is* 'trouthe'? That word, and the broadly related concepts it can signify, clearly mattered to Chaucer in the turbulence of his world. In the Prologue to the *Canterbury Tales,* 'The Knight's Tale', and *Troilus and Criseyde*, Chaucer uses 'Trewe' 46 times, and 'trouthe' 64. But it has many shades of meaning. As something like 'integrity', it is the key characteristic of Troilus, 'trewe as stiel.' (V. 831) In that poem, moreover, Chaucer rhymes 'trouthe' with 'routhe' – 'compassion' – no less than 18 times, thus setting up a provocative if understated dialogue between the two concepts. Yet 'trouthe' also implies certainty, knowledge, reliability,[23] and it could be argued that the whole of *The Hous of Fame* is an essay on how and what we *can* know, and on how 'true' that knowledge can be. The *aporia* with which that poem closes – well, what *could* that man of 'gret auctoritee' have said, when the poem has subverted all authority and certainty in history, narrative, speech, language? Perhaps the *aporia* of silence is that to which all our knowledge and cleverness, our poems, ultimately lead.

These are not comfortable ideas. We can be quite sure that if we can read Chaucer in this way, his contemporaries and successors could also. (And, after all, we can reach even further back: there is little in modern uncertainties about language, utterance and culture which is not anticipated in, for example, Augustine or Aristotle.) And that worry about authority, knowledge, and interpretation, which seems to run like a *leitmotif* through his work, is also for a long time part of the very long shadow he casts, just as much as is the rhetorical and linguistic dexterity for which his immediate successors praise him. Jacqueline Tasioulas' exploration of one of the very greatest of late mediaeval poems, Henryson's *Testament of Cresseid*, leads us straight into a consideration of how a poet could make room for himself under that complex shadow, indeed profit from it, use it. Henryson's poem has not a nonce intertextuality, but a serious engagement with how a very great poem *can* be read, with the counter-story it does not tell but which it implies, and with some of Chaucer's own great themes: the nature of knowing, authority and 'truth', and the key issue of fortune and human responsibility. It is to that very issue of the conflicts inherent in any 'authority' to which John M. Fyler's essay draws attention: 'The Merchant's Tale', *Troilus and Criseyde* and *The Testament of Cresseid* may seem miles apart, but they share the same uneasiness about literary authority, precedent and the possibility of certainty in anything – indeed, in language itself. Is seeing believing? William A. Quinn's essay also explores indeterminacy and ambiguity as qualities radical to 'The Man of Law's Tale', examining some points of fracture in the narrative where Chaucer's fictional cosmos might slide for different readers into alternative realities. Ambiguity in every sense underlies Alex da Costa's exploration of the implications of how the Pardoner is presented, and the uneasy relation between accident and substance opens up a new and powerful historical/cultural perspective, especially relevant as we re-examine concepts of gender and performativity. By contrast, John Fyler's detailed and thoughtful discussion shows the attractiveness and exegetical value, too, of a critical approach where we agree to take to take the fiction at its word, surrender to its illusion, and give the narrator an intimate and organic relationship to his or her tale. Indeed, it could be argued that Chaucer himself began ironically to play with the fruitfulness of this idea, when he took *decorum* to new and extraordinary heights with 'The Pardoner's Prologue and Tale.'[24]

But 'trewe as stiel...'[25] – does Troilus search for that which is always just beyond the finding – as in *Hous of Fame,* or *Parlement of Foulys?* Is that where 'trouthe' lies? Is the Ladder of Love, ascending from the romantic to the inenarrable divine the key, as it was for Dante?[26] The seven great Boethian stanzas that preface Book III of *Troilus and Criseyde,* or Theseus' speech (again drawing from Boethius) at the end of 'The Knight's Tale' might suggest so. But even as Castiglione's Bembo has his hearers rapt with his hymn to the ascent of the soul from love of created things to love of the Uncreated at the end of Book III of *Il Cortegiano* (1528), his rhapsody is undercut by the misogyny and plausible cynicism of Morello da Ortona. So too Chaucer never allows us an authorised, easy answer one way or the other. Simone Bovair's approach to one of the greatest poems about human love in Western literature explores what Chaucer might have meant by (and, perhaps more interestingly, how he might have valued) what we call 'romantic' love and its associated emotions – for the poem also includes the voice of Pandarus. The question of how they can be depicted – for the depiction hides as much as it reveals – is also an issue. For

> ...in forme of speche is change
> Withinne a thousand yeer, and wordes tho
> That hadden prys, now wonder nyce and straunge
> Us thinketh hem; and yet they spake hem so
> And spedde as wel in love as men now do. (*Troilus and Criseyde,* II, 22–8)

As so often, there is much we cannot know... even what the signs of emotion and body language or emotion, which we might think we recognise and understand, might actually mean. What is the significance of Arveragus' weeping? ('The Franklin's Tale', V (F) 1478–1479). Or the Prioress' tears (*CT*, I (A) 144). Barry Windeatt's 'Chaucer's Tears', which examines the unusually emphasised and detailed emotionalism – even if sometimes with moments of delicate comedy and irony – which Chaucer gives especially to his heroines, addresses the question of how the lost translation of Pseudo-Origen's *De Maria Magdalena*, which Chaucer claims among his early works (Prologue to *Legend of Good Women*, F 427–8), might have affected his treatment of weeping. The tears of 'routhe' might be more complex than they seem at first.

'Trouthe is the hiehst thing man may kepe.' However ironically and problematically framed Arveragus' words to Dorigen may be – for 'with that word he brast anon to wepe' – the issues of integrity, and compassion, which the lines focus are faced by every person in every age:

'How shall a man judge what to do in such times?'
'As he has ever judged,' said Aragorn. 'Good and ill have not changed since yesteryear; nor are they one thing among Elves and Dwarves and another among Men. It is a man's part to discern them, as much in the Golden Wood as in his own house.'[27]

One value of reading old poets – besides simply pleasure, too often forgotten when we are being highminded and academic – is that they remind us that they faced these problems too, and their response may help us to cultivate our own moral and intellectual gardens the better.

This collection of essays is humble homage to a toweringly great poet. It also acknowledges the intellectual excitement, challenge and pleasure on so many levels that readers individually owe to him. Chaucer was the child of a specific cultural episteme, the heir of its imperatives and priorities; he lived in a world where many things were unimaginably and unknowably different from our own experience. But his work, his reaction to that world, changed the way that people could think of themselves – and that is true of all great writers, our spiritual ancestors, even if they are not even mere names to the majority of people. For they have helped make the world, and the language (in every sense) we ourselves take for granted. Unfolding what we *can* know of how Chaucer worked and could have thought –

'the craft so longe to lerne' – can be intensely rewarding and never ending, as anyone who teaches knows, for *both* teacher *and* taught. Engaging with his poems still has the capacity to change the way we can see, and grapple with the fundamental questions of knowledge, understanding, beauty and pleasure. And truth.

C.W.R.D. Moseley teaches in the Faculty of English at the University of Cambridge, and has been Director of Studies in English for several colleges of the university as well as Program Director of the university's International Summer Schools in English Literature and Shakespeare.

Notes

1. Geoffrey Parker and Lesley M. Smith, eds., *The General Crisis of the Seventeenth Century*, (London: Taylor and Francis, 1997).
2. Bruce M.S. Campbell, *The Great Transition: Climate, Disease and Society in the Late Medieval World* (Cambridge: Cambridge University Press, 2016).
3. The discussion of the early visual representations of Chaucer by Sonia Drimmer stresses how complex their semiotics can be: see *The Art of Allusion: Illuminators and the Making of English Literature, 1403–1476* (Philadelphia: University of Pennsylvania Press, 2019): see pp. 53–84, 'Chaucer's Manicule.'
4. *The workes of Geffray Chaucer newly printed, with dyuers workes whiche were never in print before* (London: printed by Thomas Godfrey, 1532). *The Plowman's Tale* dates from within a few years of *Piers the Plowman's Crede*, another poem of satire and complaint of Lollard cast which piggybacks on the prestige and reputation of a much more complex, profound and subtle poem. It is tempting to suggest that the *Plowman's Tale* might indicate how one early reader at least perceived Chaucer's incomplete *Canterbury Tales*.
5. The witness of (for example) John Skelton in *Philip Sparrow* (612ff., 677ff, 787ff.) is indicative, but even more so is John Bale's *Illustrium majoris Britanniae scriptorum, hoc est, Angliae, Cambriae, ac Scotiae Summarium* (Ipswich and Wesel for John Overton, 1548, 1549.) The cultural and ideological importance of this work is discussed in my article, 'Shakespeare and the English Canon', *Early Modern Culture Online*, 8 (forthcoming).
6. 'The true portraiture of GEFFREY CHAUCER the famous English poet, as by THOMAS OCCLEVE is described who liued in his time and was his Scholar.'
7. *Five Hundred Years of Chaucer Criticism and Allusion, 1357–1900*, (London: Cambridge University Press, 1925); Derek Brewer, *Chaucer: The Critical Heritage*, 2 vols, (London: Routledge and Kegan Paul, 1978).
8. 'Chaucer Asleep', from a series of six panels 'based on *Goode Wimmin*', by Sir Edward Burne-Jones, in the Victoria and Albert Museum: http://collections.vam.ac.uk/item/O8453/panel-burne-jones-edward (accessed 24 August 2020).

9. And thus makes dominant the *persona* of the Prologue to the *Legend of Good Women*, rather than the shrewd operator who was diplomat, Collector of Customs, and Knight of the Shire in the radical Wonderful Parliament of 1386.

10. The window was unveiled by Alfred Austin, Poet Laureate.

11. *Pope: Poetical Works*, ed. Herbert Davis (London: Oxford University Press 1966), p. 229. The squib does not enhance his reputation.

12. A fossil of this weighting remains, I suggest, in the practice in so many Collected Works of Chaucer of starting with *The Canterbury Tales* rather than printing his work in probable date order, which would give a far more nuanced picture of his development to the new reader.

13. http://richardlloydplayscripts.com/script/the-canterbury-tales/ (accessed 15 June 2020).

14. Contrast John Dryden's desire to make Chaucer respectable in an age of periwigs and *politesse:* '...I have confined my choice [in the *Fables,* (1700)] to such tales of Chaucer as savour nothing of immodesty. If I had desired more to please than to instruct, the Reeve, the Miller, the Shipman, the Merchant, the Sumner, and, above all, the wife of Bath, in the prologue to her tale, would have procured me as many friends and readers, as there are beaux and ladies of pleasure in the town. But I will no more offend against good manners.' (This almost anticipates the line Alec Guinness speaks as the old parson in Hamer's *Kind Hearts and Coronets* (1949) about the stained glass in his church: 'I always say it has all the exuberance of Chaucer with none of his concomitant crudities.')

15. OED, 'engage', sense 8.

16. See J.C. Carlier [C.T. Watts], 'Roland Barthes's Resurrection of the Author and Redemption of Biography'. *Cambridge Quarterly*, 29 (4) (2000), pp. 386–393.

17. The notion that truth is not singular is a key concept in physics, as Einstein proposed. William Empson, in *Seven Types of Ambiguity*, (London: Chatto & Windus, 1930) followed, developing Wittgenstein's insight that both truths cannot be seen at one and the same time – a proposition he memorably demonstrated using the duck/rabbit image of Gestalt psychology. Jonathan Bate, in *The Genius of Shakespeare* (London: Macmillan, 1997), p. 327, fruitfully applies this tool to Shakespeare. Chaucer himself would well have been aware of the Scholastic insight that a 'fact' is dependent both on the thing perceived and on the perceiver.

18. Cf. A.C. Spearing, *Textual Subjectivity* (Oxford: Oxford University Press, 2005), 101–36.

19. *Parlement of Fowlis*, 699.

20. *Heart of Darkness* (London: Penguin, 2007[1899]), 6.

21. Much we cannot know: we can be quite certain that, as with Shakespeare, much has been lost, especially of the work of Chaucer's youth and early manhood.

22. *Truth – Balade de Bon Conseyl*, 7.

23. *Middle English Dictonary*, senses 9,10,11a.

24. Cf. my discussion in C.W.R.D. Moseley (ed), *Chaucer: The Pardoner's Tale* (Harmondsworth: Penguin, 1989), pp. 39–49.

25. *Troilus and Criseyde*, V. 831.

26. L'amor che muove il sole e l'altre stelle (*Paradiso* XXXIII.145).

27. J.R.R. Tolkien, *The Lord of the Rings* (London, 1955) III, Chapter 2.

Chapter 1

'And gret wel Chaucer whan ye mete'
Chaucer's Earliest Readers, Addressees and Audiences

Sebastian Sobecki

Little can be said with any certainty about the earliest reception of Chaucer's works. We do not really know how his writings were experienced. Were the poems enjoyed in silence by individual readers who may or may not have mouthed the words as they were moving their fingers along each line? Or were his works read aloud to groups of eager listeners, as is suggested by the celebrated frontispiece illumination in the copy of *Troilus and Criseyde* in Cambridge Corpus Christi College, MS 61?[1] Where and when, in which locations and on what occasions, did Chaucer's readers first experience his poetry? If some of his works were performed, were these readings punctuated by interjections or even topical exchanges? Were his earliest audiences socially diverse?

Often the best answers are afforded by diligent manuscript work, the painstaking combing through often multiple interrelated versions of a text in an attempt to learn more about the process of copying, assembling, correcting and annotating medieval texts. Scribes are therefore the earliest readers of medieval texts we encounter.

Notes for this section begin on page 19.

A good deal can be gleaned by observing their craft. A scribe may copy the same work on a number of occasions, and his hand can appear in other texts, too. Scribal mistakes, self-corrections and countless other palaeographical practices open up a window into the sophisticated and arcane world of professional copyists. Yet for all their significance, scribes are not readers in a typical sense, of course: they interfere with texts; they interpret and censure, elaborate and forget, interpolate and confuse, update and condense. As valuable a source of textual knowledge as they are, scribes are not necessarily representative of other categories of medieval audiences. Their engagement with a text may be intimate yet ultimately intermediary; they are not recipients but handlers.

As far as we know, no single manuscript containing Chaucer's known works can be dated to his lifetime, although it is not impossible that the Ellesmere *Canterbury Tales*, now San Marino, Huntington Library MS EL 26 C9, might have been started before 1400, the year in which Chaucer probably died. But we *do* know that Chaucer was read during his lifetime. Some of the evidence is circumstantial and some of it has reached us in the form of other poets' use of Chaucer's work before 1400. This article will attempt to take stock of what we know about Chaucer's earliest audiences, that is, about uses of and references to his work made during his lifetime.[2] Such a fixed chronological boundary is useful in the sense that the consumption of secular literature usually was limited to defined social circles or particular circulation networks. At a time when writers interacted with one another and with their audiences through their writings, the biological availability of a writer represented an opportunity for exchange. Literary conventions were differently configured during a period where writers did not call themselves authors, where willed anonymity was the default condition of texts, where retractions relied for their effect on the intentional fallacy, and where the death of the writer became the birth of the author.

As concerns Chaucer's earliest readers, one of the most exciting finds in recent years was Martha Carlin's discovery that Thomas Spencer, a scrivener from Southwark and member of the London scriveners' company, used 'a certain book called *Troylous*' to repay a debt in 1394.[3] In all probability, *Troylous* is Chaucer's *Troilus and Criseyde*, not least because Spencer was closely acquainted with John Brynchele, another Southwark resident and later clerk who, according to his will of 1420, was one of the earliest known owners of a copy of *The Canterbury Tales*.[4] Two Chancery clerks were also known to have owned a copy of the work. In his will of 1419, Richard Sotheworth left his fellow Chancery clerk John Stopyndon 'quendam librum meum de Canterbury Tales'.[5]

A second set of readers can be inferred from the probable addressees of some of Chaucer's shorter poems. The envoy to 'Truth', also known as 'Balade de Bon Conseyl', is directed at a certain 'Vache':

> Therfore, thou Vache, leve thyn old wrecchednesse;
> Unto the world leve now to be thral.
> Crye him mercy, that of his hy goodnesse
> Made thee of noght, and in especial
> Draw unto him, and pray in general
> For thee, and eek for other, hevenlich mede;
> And trouthe thee shal delivere, it is no drede.[5]

The addressee in question is in all likelihood Sir Philip de la Vache (d. 1408), a courtier and later Garter knight.[6] The narrator's gentle moralizing even suggests a certain degree of intimacy between the speaker and the persona of the recipient. At any rate, as the poem's dedicatee, de la Vache can be safely counted among Chaucer's earliest audiences.

By the same token, the addressees of Chaucer's two 'Lenvoys', to 'Scogan' and 'Bukton' respectively, belong among Chaucer's first readers. The Scogan of the first poem is usually believed to be Henry Scogan (d. 1407), lord of the manor of Haviles from 1391. Scogan was a squire in Richard II's household and later tutor to the future Henry V and his brothers.[7] A poet himself, Scogan even receives a hypothetical speaking part in the poem:

> But wel I wot, thow wolt answere and saye,
> 'Lo, olde Grisel lyst to ryme and playe!'
> Nay, Scogan, say not so, for I m'excuse —
> God helpe me so! — in no rym, dowteles[8]

With medieval poems frequently invoking allusions to their own performativity, a speaking part is more than a literary trope: Scogan's persona and person are summoned at the same time, making him both a part of the audience and of the poem. The third of Chaucer's lyrics with a named addressee is the 'Lenvoy de Chaucer a Bukton'. The 'My maister Bukton' of the first line of the poem is Sir Peter Bukton (d. 1414), a knight and politician.[9]

It is difficult to assess how many of Chaucer's other dedicatees or addressees can be counted among his earliest readers and listeners.

While it is probable that John of Gaunt and his household were familiar with *The Book of the Duchess*, a work likely composed to commemorate the death of John's wife Blanche, it is more difficult to ascertain whether Richard II, the nominal addressee of 'Lak of Stedfastnesse' ever saw the pontificating envoy dedicated to him:

> *Lenvoy to King Richard*
> O prince, desyre to be honourable,
> Cherish thy folk and hate extorcioun.
> Suffre nothing that may be reprevable
> To thyn estat don in thy regioun.
> Shew forth thy swerd of castigacioun,
> Dred God, do law, love trouthe and worthinesse,
> And wed thy folk agein to stedfastnesse.[10]

By the same token, the ironic though earnest 'Complaint of Chaucer to His Purse', written as a request to the recently crowned Henry IV in the hope that the new monarch would pay Chaucer's arrears, was probably not meant for its famous dedicatee. Although the poem may have reached neither the king's eyes nor his ears, it surely ended up in the hands of some royal administrator since the records show that payments to Chaucer later resumed. Other names, such as Chaucer's surmised son 'Lyte Lowys', who appears as the addressee of the poet's *Treatise on the Astrolabe*, can be added to Chaucer's earliest audience, though in this case not of poetry but of scientific prose. And if 'Chaucer's Wordes unto Adam, His Owne Scriveyn' was indeed written by Chaucer, then the scribe Adam named here (whether his surname was Pinkhurst or not) is another early, if allegedly careless, reader and copyist.

Chaucer's contemporary poets certainly belong to the earliest documented audience of his works, and there have been new developments in this field, too. The trilingual poet John Gower (d. 1408), a leading English writer, appears to have had personal dealings with Chaucer in 1378, when he was charged with the power of attorney by Chaucer ahead of a continental voyage.[11] While it is not clear whether their relationship was personal or professional at this point in time, by the late 1380s, when Gower composed his best-known English work, the *Confessio Amantis*, he refers to Chaucer by name in the earliest version of the work:

> And gret wel Chaucer whan ye mete,
> As mi disciple and mi poete:
> For in the floures of his youthe

In sondri wise, as he wel couthe,
Of Ditees and of songes glade,
The whiche he for mi sake made,
The lond fulfild is overal:
Whereof to him in special
Above alle othre I am most holde.[12]

Chaucer reciprocates this praise, at about the same time, in the penultimate stanza of his *Troilus*, when he extols (or perhaps gently mocks) Gower's virtues:[13]

O moral Gower, this book I directe
To the and to the, philosophical Strode,
To vouchen sauf, ther nede is, to correcte,
Of youre benignites and zeles goode.[14]

Gower is of course not the only addressee of this stanza. 'Philosophical Strode', the second name mentioned here, is not a certain identification. It may be Ralph Strode, an Oxford logician and Latin poet.[15] He may also be the same man as the London lawyer who was Common Serjeant of the City of London from 1373 to 1385 and Standing Counsel until his death in 1387.[16] Documentary evidence shows that Chaucer knew the London Strode, and it is likely that both Strodes are one and the same person.[17]

In line with Chaucer's wish for the *Troilus* to 'go' into the world and be disseminated,[18] there is indeed evidence that this poem, together with his translation of Boethius's *Consolation of Philosophy*, circulated during his lifetime. In addition to the scribe Adam, the scrivener Spencer and the poets Gower and Strode, another writer must have enjoyed access to this work: Thomas Usk, the undersheriff for London who was executed during the purges of the Merciless Parliament in 1388. Usk borrows from Chaucer's *Troilus* in his *Testament of Love*. Usk's prose work anticipates the fifteenth-century praise uttered by Lydgate and other admirers, and at one stage he refers to Chaucer as the 'noble philosophical poete in Englisshe' who has made a 'treatise' of 'Troylus', identified a few lines later as 'the *Boke of Troylus*'.[19]

The courtier, poet and follower of John Wyclif, Sir John Clanvowe (d. 1391), also belongs to this group of Chaucer's earliest readers. Clanvowe's *The Book of Cupide*, composed in the late 1380s or early 1390s, harks back to the Knight's Tale and the *Legend of Good Women*.[20] There may of course have been other English writers who had read or heard Chaucer's works during his lifetime – John

Walton or William Langland are possible candidates – but their knowledge of Chaucer's works before 1400 cannot be ascertained with the same confidence or, at least, high degree of probability as that of the individuals listed above.

Then there is also the influential French poet Eustache Deschamps (1340–1406) from whom Chaucer frequently borrows. Deschamps wrote a ballade dedicated to Chaucer, in which he celebrates the English writer as 'grant translateur, Geffroy Chaucier', largely for the latter's translation of the *Romance of the Rose*.[21] The French poet must therefore have seen a copy of Chaucer's translation, though it is doubtful that he would have been able to read it. Chaucer's friend Sir Lewis Clifford (d. 1404) is said by Deschamps to have delivered the French ballade to Chaucer, probably in 1386.[22] It is therefore not unlikely that Clifford may have had access to Chaucer's translation of the *Romance*.

A final consideration belongs to the role of Thomas Hoccleve (d. 1426), poet and privy seal clerk. Hoccleve was certainly one of Chaucer's earliest posthumous readers, borrowing frequently from his predecessor and addressing him as 'the firste fyndere of our fair langage' in his longest work, the *Regement of Princes*.[23] Simon Horobin has recently argued that, based on instances of Hoccleve's hand, the production of the Hengwrt and Ellesmere manuscripts of *The Canterbury Tales* was overseen and conducted by Hoccleve himself.[24] Horobin suggests that Hoccleve may have acquired Chaucer's papers after his death in 1400,[25] but it is not impossible that Hoccleve had access to these materials earlier, during Chaucer's lifetime. After all, there is no evidence that Chaucer was working on *The Canterbury Tales* in the years immediately preceding his death, particularly if he lost interest in the project or if his health did not permit him to continue. Hoccleve, then, may have been not only Chaucer's first editor but also one of Chaucer's last readers during his lifetime.

Sebastian Sobecki is Professor of Medieval English Literature and Culture at Groningen University. His first book, *The Sea and Medieval English Literature* (Brewer), appeared in 2008, and his second monograph, *Unwritten Verities: The Making of England's Vernacular Legal Culture, 1463–1549* (Notre Dame University Press) in 2015. He is working on *The Material Politics of England's Fifteenth-Century*

Literature (Oxford University Press) and completing two volumes of a new edition of Hakluyt's *Principal Navigations* (Oxford University Press), as well as co-editing three books: *Medieval English Travel* (Oxford University Press), with Anthony Bale; *A Companion to John Skelton* (Brewer), with John Scattergood; and, with Candace Barrington, *The Cambridge Companion to Medieval Law and Literature* (Cambridge University Press). His articles have appeared in *Speculum*, *Studies in the Age of Chaucer*, *Renaissance Studies*, *The English Historical Review*, *The Chaucer Review*, *The Library*, *New Medieval Literatures* and *The Review of English Studies*, among others.

Notes

1. On the frontispiece, see Joyce Coleman, 'Where Chaucer Got His Pulpit: Audience and Intervisuality in the *Troilus and Criseyde* Frontispiece', *Studies in the Age of Chaucer: The Yearbook of the New Chaucer Society* 32 (2010): 103–128.
2. For further reading on Chaucer's early audiences, see Richard Firth Green, 'Women in Chaucer's Audience', *The Chaucer Review* 18 (1983): 146–154; Dieter Mehl, 'The Audience of Chaucer's *Troilus and Criseyde*', in *The Audience of Chaucer's Troilus and Criseyde*, ed. Beryl Rowland (London: Allen and Unwin 1974), 173–189; A.S.G. Edwards, 'The Early Reception of Chaucer and Langland', *Florilegium* 15 (1998): 1–22; Julia Boffey and A.S.G. Edwards, 'Manuscripts and Audience', in *A Concise Companion to Chaucer*, ed. Corinne Saunders (Oxford: Blackwell, 2006), 34–50; Paul Strohm, *The Poet's Tale: Chaucer and the Year That Made The Canterbury Tales* (London: Profile, 2015); Paul Strohm, *Social Chaucer* (Cambridge, MA: Harvard University Press, 1989).
3. Martha Carlin, 'Thomas Spencer, Southwark Scrivener (d. 1428): Owner of a Copy of Chaucer's *Troilus* in 1394?', *The Chaucer Review* 49, no. 4 (2015): 387.
4. Ibid., 393–394.
5. Malcolm Richardson, 'The Earliest Known Owners of Canterbury Tales MSS and Chaucer's Secondary Audience', *The Chaucer Review* 25, no. 1 (1990): 17–32.
5. Ll. 21–28. All quotations from Chaucer's works are taken from Larry D. Benson, *The Riverside Chaucer* (Oxford: Oxford University Press, 1987).
6. On this poem and its probable dedicatee, see Craig E. Bertolet, 'Chaucer's Envoys and the Poet-Diplomat', *The Chaucer Review* 33, no. 1 (1998): 75ff; V.J. Scattergood, 'Chaucer's Curial Satire: The "Balade de Bon Conseyl"', *Hermathena*, no. 133 (1982): 29–45.
7. John Scattergood, 'Old Age, Love and Friendship in Chaucer's Envoy to Scogan', *Nottingham Medieval Studies* 35 (1991): 92; Douglas Gray, 'Scogan, Henry (c.1361–1407)', *Oxford Dictionary of National Biography* (Oxford, 2004), http://www.oxforddnb.com.proxy-ub.rug.nl/view/article/24847 (accessed 13 October 2016).
8. Ll. 34–37. On 'Lenvoy de Chaucer a Scogan', see Alfred David, 'Chaucer's Good Counsel to Scogan', *The Chaucer Review* 3, no. 4 (1969): 265–274; Scattergood, 'Old Age, Love and Friendship'; Robert Epstein, 'Chaucer's Scogan and Scogan's

Chaucer', *Studies in Philology* 96, no. 1 (1999): 1–21; and Richard P. Horvath, 'Chaucer's Epistolary Poetic: The Envoys to Bukton and Scogan', *The Chaucer Review* 37, no. 2 (20 December 2002): 173–189.

9. On this poem, see John Scattergood, '"Chaucer a Bukton" and Proverbs', *Nottingham Medieval Studies* 31 (1987): 98; Lawrence Besserman, 'Chaucer's Envoy to Bukton and "Truth" in Biblical Interpretation: Some Medieval and Modern Contexts', *New Literary History* 22, no. 1 (1991): 177–197; Horvath, 'Chaucer's Epistolary Poetic'.
10. Ll. 22–28.
11. Martin M. Crow and Clair C. Olson, *Chaucer Life-Records* (Oxford: Clarendon Press, 1966), 54.
12. Book VIII, ll. 2941–2949, quoted from John Gower, *The English Works of John Gower II*, ed. George Campbell Macaulay, vol. 2, repr. 1969, EETS E.S. (London: Oxford University Press, 1901), 466.
13. In addition, some readers have argued that the Man of Law in *The Canterbury Tales* is modelled on Gower (the critical discussion is summarized in Benson, *The Riverside Chaucer*, 854).
14. Book V, ll. 1856–1859.
15. Benson, *The Riverside Chaucer*, 1058, note to ll. 1856–1859.
16. Ibid.
17. On this identification, see Rodney Delasanta, 'Chaucer and Strode', *The Chaucer Review* 26, no. 2 (1991): 205–218.
18. Book V, l. 1786.
19. Thomas Usk, *The Testament of Love*, ed. R. Allen Shoaf (Kalamazoo, MI: Medieval Institute Publications 1998), Book 3, chapter 4, 266–267. On Usk's use of Chaucer, see also Benson, *The Riverside Chaucer*, 1020; and Marion Turner, '"Certaynly His Noble Sayenges Can I Not Amende": Thomas Usk and *Troilus and Criseyde*', *The Chaucer Review* 37, no. 1 (2002): 26–39; Edwards, 'The Early Reception of Chaucer and Langland', 3.
20. On Clanvowe, see Lee Patterson, 'Court Politics and the Invention of Literature: The Case of Sir John Clanvowe', in *Culture and History, 1350–1600: Essays on English Communities, Identities, and Writing*, ed. David Aers (Detroit: Wayne State University Press, 1992), 7–41; Andrew Cole, *Literature and Heresy in the Age of Chaucer* (Cambridge Studies in Medieval Literature) (Cambridge: Cambridge University Press, 2008); Sir John Clanvowe, *The Works of Sir John Clanvowe*, ed. John Scattergood (Cambridge: Brewer, 1975).
21. Elizaveta Strakhov, 'Tending to One's Garden: Deschamps's "Ballade to Chaucer" Reconsidered', *Medium Aevum* 85, no. 2 (2016): 236–258.
22. Benson, *The Riverside Chaucer*, 1060.
23. Thomas Hoccleve, *The Regiment of Princes*, ed. Charles Ramsay Blyth (Kalamazoo, MI: Medieval Institute Publications 1999), l. 4978.
24. Simon Horobin, 'Thomas Hoccleve: Chaucer's First Editor?', *The Chaucer Review* 50, no. 3 (2015): 228–250.
25. Ibid., 24.

Chapter 2

Unhap, Misadventure, Infortune
Chaucer's Vocabulary of Mischance

Helen Cooper

That Chaucer was profoundly interested in the workings of chance and fortune is evident to any reader of his work. Less immediately obvious is the range of vocabulary he employs to describe and discuss these issues. He uses every word available to him, and invents a handful more as well, and this wide vocabulary for random events is deployed with marked care and subtlety. Of other contemporary Middle English poets, only John Gower shows a comparable habit of referring to Fortune, but he rarely develops the concept into an argument, and he is much more sparing of synonyms when it comes to bad fortune.[1] There was an increasing interest in the fourteenth century in such issues. Images of Fortune turning her wheel were beginning to multiply at a striking rate, and the contemporary debates over predestination extended far enough down into the non-clerical imagination for Chaucer to be able to include a reference to them in the 'Nun's Priest's Tale', even if he puts it into the mouth of a cleric.

Issues concerning providence and astrological determinism, predestination and free will, fortune as arbitrary and as following an inexorable pattern, the lack of poetic (or any) justice in this world and a belief in God's ordering appear in poem after poem of Chaucer's, from the *Book of the Duchess* to the end of his career. This fascination may be one reason – perhaps even the main reason, though we have no way of knowing – why he chose to translate Boethius's *Consolation of Philosophy*, the great late-Classical work that debates just those questions. Boethius casts himself as a prisoner (which he indeed was) conducting a dispute with a personification of Philosophy, who argues that despite all appearances to the contrary, God does in fact exercise control over the world through providential ordering. Divine knowledge does not exclude the possibility of an individual's exercise of free will; true happiness can never be found within the instability of this world; and Fortune is no more than an imperfect intermediary between God and humankind, imperfect not least because mere mortals cannot see past it to the just and righteous workings of the divine order. The form of the work gives Boethius himself a way of dramatizing, making more vivid, a debate that is essentially within his own mind, between his own doubts and his answers to those doubts, and it is clear who wins. Philosophy, moreover, being a personification rather than a person, has objectivity and authority on her side, to set against the prisoner's anxieties – anxieties that remain individual despite being shared with everyone who has ever felt a sense of unfairness at what is happening to them.

Although references to fortune figure in Chaucer's work even before he encountered Boethius, and the 'Monk's Tale' is concerned with little else, his most searching explorations of these concerns appear in the 'Knight's Tale' and *Troilus and Criseyde*. Palamon and Arcite are convinced that the gods are out to torment them despite their own innocence. Palamon, left in prison after Arcite has been released, rebels against the fixed fate prescribed by the gods, and demands,

> What governance is in this prescience
> That giltelees tormenteth innocence? (*CT* I.1313–1314)[2]

Arcite, free but therefore deprived of the sight of Emily, laments that people (not least himself) are unable to see how 'purveiaunce of God, or of Fortune' may be providing for them better than they are able to comprehend (I.1252). Despite the two young men being effectively doubles of each other, one loses the battle but wins the lady, while the other wins the battle but dies – a way of resolving both the love triangle that governs the plot of the tale and the quarrel of the planetary gods, but which flagrantly breaches poetic justice. Both knights' speeches against fate and fortune derive from Boethius's Prisoner, and although Theseus, at the end of the tale, is allowed an assertion of divine providence analogous to Philosophy's (*CT* I.2987–3015), there is rather little sense that the issue has actually been settled. *Troilus* is pervaded by references to the instability of Fortune, not least because many of the events are represented as being beyond the characters' control: the events of history, in the shape of the Trojan war, intervene to frustrate the protagonists' own hopes, and the disposition of the stars and planets is also cited at key moments. Troilus is notoriously given a lengthy debate with himself, again closely based on the *Consolation*, as to whether God's foreknowledge amounts to inexorable destiny; and he decides that it does. There is no reason to believe that such speeches necessarily represent Chaucer's own views, just as the Prisoner's speeches represent only one side of the debate Boethius conducts with himself. It is notable, however – and an important clue as to how such passages should be read – that when Chaucer's characters seem to be getting things wrong, or are not seeing far enough, he borrows words for them from the insufficiently enlightened Prisoner, or, in the case of Troilus's soliloquy on predestination, from Philosophy when she is expounding men's errors; whereas when they are getting things right (as at the start of Theseus's closing speech, or Troilus's hymn to love, III.1744–71), he draws on the arguments and insights assigned to Philosophy. How far either the characters or the readers, or indeed Chaucer himself, might actually be convinced by these more positive arguments remains more open. Fiction, and not least Chaucer's fiction, presents possibilities for emotional empathy that disputation does not, and there is no doubt about the pain these characters suffer.

Chaucer has the reputation of being a genial poet, a reputation curiously at odds with his readiness to write about misfortune and death. The darker side of his thinking is also carried through in his vocabulary, in particular in his readiness to use, or on occasion coin, privatives – the grammatical term for negative prefixes: in his Middle English, dis-, in-, un- or mis-. These vary in both etymology and in implication. Dis- and in- (with variants des- and im-) are used in this negative sense almost entirely for words of romance origin (French or Latin): 'desordinat' (*CT* X.415), 'instable' (variant, *CT* IV.2057).

They imply a simple negative, as does the Old English–derived un-. 'Untrouthe' (eleven instances as a noun across the *Works*, plus many more of 'untrue') is clearly a morally wrong falling away from the ethical standard of 'trouthe'; Troilus's inability to 'unloven' Criseyde (*TC* V.1698), even when he knows she is unfaithful, is a painful adherence to an untenable ideal. As in those examples, 'un-' is used most often with words of similarly Old English etymology, but it appears fairly often too with romance-derived words, sometimes as an alternative to 'in-': 'unstable' (*TC* III.820). 'Mis-' has a dual etymology, from both Old English and romance, and Chaucer regularly uses it for words of either linguistic origin. It may function as a direct negative, but it more often carries a meaning of something going astray, amiss (which itself has a different derivation). Sometimes these usages indicate departures from what is correct rather than what is morally right: one should not 'mysmetre' verse (a neologism, *Troilus* V.1796); 'myswandering' (another neologism, *Boece* II pr. 8, 29; III pr. 2, 23–4) and 'misturn' (*Boece* III pr. 3, 8) describe a mistaken turning aside from the right way, the making of an erroneous choice but without the full moral culpability of 'untrouthe'. Where the vocabulary of chance is concerned, the root words themselves – fortune, hap, aventure, chance, cas – are superficially neutral, and in the instance of 'cas' remain so, but it is striking how often Chaucer adds privative prefixes that turn the meanings of the first four of those words towards the dangerous, the unfair or unjust.

The speeches of Boethius's Philosophy are packed with the vocabulary of fortune, but she will not countenance the idea of chance at all. When the Prisoner asks, 'Yif thou wenest that hap be anything, what is it?', she replies:

> Yif any wyght diffynisse hap in the manere, that is to seyn that 'hap is bytydynge ibrought forth by foolisshe moevynge and by no knyttynge of causes,' I conferme that hap nis right naught in no wise; and I deme al outrely that hap nis ... but an idel word, withouten any significacioun of thing. (*Boece* V pr. 1, 31–38)

'Hap', in the sense of a random event, an event without a cause, can have no meaning, for nothing can have 'his beynge of naught' (44); and when the Prisoner asks for more help as to the nature of 'hap or elles aventure of fortune', Philosophy goes on to explain why 'fortuit hap' always has causes. She offers a different definition, that 'hap' is the result of unknown causes that come together for a different purpose from that originally intended (her key example is the chance finding of buried gold), but which 'descendeth fro the welle of purveaunce that ordeyneth alle thingis in hir places and in hir tymes' (94–96). The Prisoner is prepared to accept that, but he then goes on to ask about the question of free will that Chaucer will borrow for Troilus; and just as Troilus does not accept the tenor of the argument (he cuts it short with a despairing denial), Chaucer rarely promotes the providential argument about chance, whether in the mouths of the characters within his narratives or those of his surrogate narrators or in his own unmediated voice.[3] The main exception is the short poem *Fortune*, discussed below, though whether the 'Pleintif' of that poem is the spokesperson for Chaucer's own views is impossible to tell. In theory, the arguments should be the same whether the discussion concerns good fortune or bad, but Philosophy gives a strong positive spin to the affective quality of her argument by choosing an example of good fortune, the finding of the gold. The rioters of the 'Pardoner's Tale' believe they have been given their own heap of gold by 'Fortune' (*CT* VI.779), but it is certainly not fortune in the sense that they intend the term. Fortune in Chaucer is always ready to turn to the bad, to 'infortune', and fortune is not going to feel the same to those who suffer its consequences rather than profiting from them.

'Fortune' is the term of Chaucer's that is least naturalized. It entered the language around 1300, so it was not new, but most of his usages of the word carry a strong sense of personification, of the goddess Fortuna: she is an active agent, not a signifier for a random event. This is in marked contrast to the way Gower uses the word, where 'fortune' is generally a common noun indicating little more than that something happens. The element of personification in Chaucer is emphasized by the fact that the word typically appears with an initial ff-, the standard form for a capital F, and is carried over thus into modern editions. The great majority of those usages occur in just two texts – the *Boece*, where it has some claim to be the principal subject, and the 'Monk's Tale', which is explicitly about historical or supposedly historical figures who fell from Fortune's wheel; the 'Knight's Tale' comes in a strong third.[4] The Monk introduces his series of tragedies with a definition of the genre by precisely that image, of men (they are all men except one) falling from the high degree in which they stood (*CT* VII.1991–1994), and the individual tales all illustrate that process. The stories may have individual morals (don't trust your wife, VII.2092), but their universal moral is,

'Who may truste on Fortune any throwe?' (VII.2136). In many other writers' stories of the hostility of fortune, including Boccaccio's *De casibus virorum illustrium*, the model on which the 'Monk's Tale' is based, these falls are associated with divine justice – the appropriate downfall of the wicked or over-mighty. It is worth noting that the word for 'fall' here, *casus*, is the same term that Boethius uses for Chaucer's 'hap'[5]: a word that is apparently neutral and is often used simply in the sense of an event, what befalls, but the root verb *cadere* means to fall as well as to befall, and that process of falling governs the whole *de casibus* tradition. In the 'Monk's Tale', however, in contrast to Boccaccio, the victims are frequently virtuous, or at least with no greater reason for their fall than they are at the top of the wheel: Hercules, Zenobia, Peter of Spain, Peter of Cyprus, Julius Caesar. Even Ugolino, whom Dante places in the lowest circle of hell, is turned by Chaucer into the victim of false accusation (*CT* VII.2415–2417). The same apparent innocence is true of most of his other characters who find themselves suffering at the hands of Fortune: Troilus, Palamon and Arcite, Griselda (*CT* IV.756 – though in her case Fortune has a great deal less to do with her suffering than does Walter). This mismatch between desert and outcome emphasizes the chance element of the concept in moral terms, while doing nothing to remove the sense of inevitability, that those who are at the top of the wheel, or who count themselves happy, are bound to suffer. Chaucer's antonym for 'fortune' is 'infortune', bad fortune, not normally with any sense of personification or agency (the sole exception is *TC* IV.185: 'infortune it wolde' that the people want the exchange of Criseyde). 'Infortune' is also what the unfortunate planets will bring, as in 'the infortune of Marte' ('Knight's Tale', *CT* I.2021), again a usage that emphasizes inevitability, not randomness. The word 'misfortune' entered the language only some decades after Chaucer's death, but he was ready enough to coin other 'mis-' terms ('miswandering' and 'misweyes', each used twice in *Boece*). Perhaps he avoided coining 'misfortune' too because the form would imply fortune going astray rather than leading to disaster, so lessening that element of necessity in the turning of the wheel. 'Infortune' is more decisive, and makes a different philosophical point.

The degree of negativity attaching to other common nouns for random events varies considerably. 'Chance' is the one that is most likely to be linked to a privative, to turn out badly. Chaucer has sixteen instances of 'chance', of which three collocate with 'good', mostly in exclamations (as in 'God yeve thee good chaunce!'), and one with 'sorry'. The rest of the usages are context-dependent, though that context is by no means always optimistic. Against those sixteen occurrences of 'chance' are set forty-seven usages of 'mischance', many again in the course of ill-wishing. The contrast with Gower here is at its most striking: he has sixty-three instances of 'chance', but none at all for 'mischance' – a ratio that again underlines the pressure towards ill omen in Chaucer's work. One of Chaucer's usages is a personification (Mischance sits in the middle of Mars's temple, *CT* I.2009), and the words with which the term collocates include hell, women (*CT* VII.2062), peril, woe, fortune and disease. In the *ABC*, the devil threatens to overcome the soul 'in his lystes of mischaunce' (85), a decidedly more sinister theatre of battle than the lists of the 'Knight's Tale'. Even when God is being adjured to send good chance or mischance, however, there is rarely any sense of inevitability about it, as there tends to be with fortune, nor of Providence either; 'chance' is perhaps the closest Chaucerian equivalent to 'luck', which does not enter the language until the mid fifteenth century. 'Luck', however, tends to be associated in the first instance in modern English with good luck, though with some dependence on the idiom at issue ('Just my luck' is negative); Chaucer's 'chance' is an altogether riskier business.

'Hap', as both verb and noun, is perhaps the least marked of Chaucer's words for chance, the word most likely to be used casually: it had been around in the language for longest, and looks as if it should be the equivalent of the modern 'happen' (a form Chaucer also uses). Even here, however, things are not quite so simple, as his choice of the noun for the debate on chance between the Prisoner and Philosophy demonstrates. It is often used as one of a pair, where its accompanying synonym or collocating term emphasizes its explicit quality of randomness: his narrative poems are full of phrases such as 'fall or hap', 'hap or fortune', 'of aventure happed hire', 'it happede hym *par cas*' or '*par chaunce*'. *Boece* is especially full of such doublings, though here the associated words often serve to define the precise nature of the 'hap' in question with more philosophical exactitude than in the narratives: 'hap or elles aventure', 'hap and fortune', 'O sodeyn hap! O thou Fortune instable!', 'th ordre of destine, and of sodeyn hap'. The word only rarely contains a positive prognosis. In the *Book of the Duchess*, 'hap' as a noun pairs with 'grace' and 'blisse' (*BD* 810, 1039), but the Man in Black himself notes that things didn't turn out well. It has two privative forms, 'unhap' and 'mishap', the second functioning as a verb as well as a noun, with nine occurrences between them: only a fraction of his uses of 'hap', but enough to pressure the term towards disaster. In adjectival or adverbial form, the good and bad senses balance each other, with five instances each of 'happy', which is always positive, and five of 'mishappy / unhappy / unhappily', all negative. In every case, good or bad, the adjectives are stronger than their modern equivalents: not just cheerful or sad (for which Chaucer's words are 'glad' or 'merry' and 'sorrowful'), but favoured or not by fortune or destiny or the gods.

'Aventure' has a different range of meanings again. The word comes into English by way of French from the Latin *advenire*, to happen, but the kinds of adventures that happen are subtly differentiated. As a singular noun, it can be specified as positive ('good aventure'), but it frequently connotes something more threatening. 'In aventure' means 'in jeopardy', and jeopardy implies a bad outcome. Its accompanying adjectives include perilous, 'unsely' and cruel. It often collocates with hap, destiny or Fortune, with all the ill omen so often implied by those. Perhaps the most famous run of synonyms to include it, however, occurs in the 'General Prologue' (*CT* I.844), when the Knight draws the short straw to start the storytelling:

> Were it by aventure, or sort, or cas.[6]

It is a line that protests too much – or in Boethian or Chaucerian terms, where what may appear 'hap' is really a matter of the causes being hidden. Doublets for words of chance may be commonplace, but three is too many. Harry Bailey, we may assume, is fixing the draw.

'Aventure' too has its privative form, or rather two: 'disaventure' and 'misaventure'. Both carry a strong sense of something bad, something forcefully negative. Troilus complains of 'this infortune or this disaventure' (*TC* IV.297), as twinned examples of the world going wrong, and his 'disaventure' is set in apposition to Criseyde's 'untrouthe' (V.1448). 'Misaventure' connotes something much worse than the 'something amiss' meanings found in other 'mis-' words, of something going astray. Six of its ten usages collocate with disease, wretchedness, mischance, sorrow, infortune and mischief, and another with jealousy. Neither privative form appears in

Gower, although he uses 'aventure' abundantly. The adjectival form, 'aventurous', makes only three appearances in Chaucer, but they are likewise not good: once it is a synonym for 'no thing certeyne' (*CT* VII.1667); to Philosophy, 'thise happes aventurous' are opposed to 'the resoun of God' (*Boece* I pr. 6, 91–2) and 'aventurous welefulnesse' is to her a meaningless term (II pr. IV, 15–16). Chaucer never uses an adjectival 'misaventurous', but one gets the impression that it would be nasty.

The plural, 'aventures', is more neutral than the singular: adventures are often just events. In about half Chaucer's usages, however, it carries a more distinctive meaning, as effectively a literary-critical term relating to storytelling in general and romance in particular, just as romances written now or in the Middle Ages may concern the 'adventures' of questing knights. The Host invites the company of pilgrims to tell tales of adventures, and the Clerk to tell 'some murie thing of aventures' (*CT* IV.15); shortly before his tale-telling is cut short, the Squire promises to 'speken of aventures and of batailles' (*CT* V.659), and the Franklin notes how in former times the Bretons 'of diverse aventures maden layes' (*CT* V.710) . Despite this, however, and despite the fact that the range of genres in which Chaucer wrote was unparalleled in Middle English (or perhaps in all English literature), one striking omission from his works is a full chivalric romance. There has been general critical reluctance to commit either *Troilus* or the 'Knight's Tale' to the genre solely of romance, despite their courtliness. *Troilus* avoids adventure, and almost entirely battle too, in favour of love; neither text involves a quest, a knight taking the adventure that shall fall to him; and both Troilus and Arcite finish up dead. The 'Wife of Bath's Tale' comes closer to quest romance, but the quest there is undertaken as punishment, it has something of the folktale about it, and its moral, about the ethics of marital behaviour, is not exactly chivalric – less so indeed than Gower's story of Florent, whom Gower compares to a 'knyhte aventurous' in his one usage of the adjective.[7] The 'Squire's Tale' has the potential for being chivalric romance, but it never quite gets round to demonstrating it. Chaucer's avoidance cannot have been because the genre was too hackneyed: if the *Gawain*-poet could do it, Chaucer could have done so too. The Host enjoins the pilgrims to tell stories 'of aventures that whilom han bifalle' (*CT* I.795), but none of his party follows his guidance in the romance sense associated with 'aventures'. For Chaucer, perhaps, taking the adventure predicted a very different outcome from the happy endings associated with the quest romance.

The uneven distribution of these various words of chance and mischance across Chaucer's works largely accords with the concerns of the different poems, though there are some surprises. They are notably sparse in the more religious of the *Canterbury Tales* and in the *ABC*: God or the Virgin are what is at issue there, not the order of Fortune. The *Parliament of Fowls*, with its subject of the order of Nature under God, likewise contains very few; so too, more surprisingly in view of its concern with the arbitrariness of fame, does the *House of Fame*, even though its presiding goddess is sister to dame Fortune (1547). There are surprisingly few too in the *Legend of Good Women*, perhaps because the women's misfortunes have such an overt cause, in the shape of their unfaithful lovers. The shorter poems such as *Gentilesse* and the *Former Age* are concerned more with ideals than with the uncertainties of the world as it is, and the *Former Age* operates by negating labour and war rather than chance: the corn growing 'unsowe of mannes hond', armour 'unforged' (10, 49). There is however one poem constructed entirely out of the vocabulary of Fortune, and that is *Fortune* itself.

Like the *Consolation of Philosophy*, *Fortune* consists of a dialogue between 'le Pleintif', the equivalent of the Prisoner, and a personification, though in this instance it is Fortune rather than Philosophy. Its Envoy turns it into a begging poem, a plea for patronage, but the Envoy does not appear in four of the early textual witnesses, and without it the work becomes a much more purely Boethian disputation on the nature of Fortune.[8] The Pleintif starts by complaining of 'this wrecched worldes transmutacioun', against which he can offer only a refrain of 'Fynally, Fortune, I thee defye'. Fortune, however, insists on a very Boethian role for herself: no one is wretched who does not believe himself to be so; she shows the difference between true and false friends; she teaches an understanding of the mutability of this world. Her refrain, 'eek thou hast they beste frend alyve' (32, 40, 48), is commonly taken to refer to a patron, perhaps even to the king, and the Envoy makes such a meaning explicit. Up until that point, however, the poem suggests a somewhat different reading. Patronage of any kind falls into the category of uncertain and transient gifts, whereas what Fortune offers is an altogether more reliable guide to living in a world of 'brotelnesse' (63). However counterintuitive the idea may be, without the Envoy the 'beste frend' would most logically be herself. This would fit with the thoroughly Boethian definition she provides for herself as ultimately subject to God:

> Lo, th'execucion of the majestee
> That al purveyeth of his rightwysnesse,
> That same thing 'Fortune' clepen ye...
> The hevene hath propretee of sikernesse,
> This world hath ever resteles travayle.
> Thy laste day is ende of myn intresse. (65–67, 69–71)

If the earlier speeches by the Pleintif and Fortune represent the rival premises of a syllogism, this verse is the conclusion, where they come to agree that Fortune is no more than a limited human perspective on Providence. A proper understanding of the nature of fortune offers the best way to live in this mutable world until death takes him beyond her reach, and so she can indeed claim to be his best friend.

For once, this discussion of fortune is conducted almost entirely without grammatical privatives: the negative words of the poem – errour, ignoraunce, variaunce and so on – are not calqued on positive terms. The one privative comes in the penultimate line of the quotation above, though it is a suffix rather than a prefix: 'resteles'. Mutability is an inevitable condition of this world. The stability of rest is to be found only in heaven, and the analogous movement beyond this world at the end of both the 'Parson's Tale' and *Troilus* confirms that. The Parson closes his treatise with an image of heaven where privatives are used to cancel out both time and death: 'endelees', 'inmortal' (X.1076, 1078). *Troilus* ends with an image of the Trinity 'eterne on lyve' (V.1863), but then adds another telling line:

> Uncircumscript, and al maist circumscrive. (V.1865)

God is the circle without a circumference, the author who cannot himself be written. If the *ABC* and the 'Retractions' mean what they say, Chaucer had a fear of damnation inevitable for the period when he lived. Modern criticism has been notoriously reluctant to accept that Chaucer's intentions (in the medieval sense of *intentio auctoris*, the meaning the author wants his readers to draw from his work)[9] ever actually equate with his own beliefs without any mediating irony, but there is no reason why passages of the kind offered by *Fortune*, begging poem or not, should not express his own internal debate, as they did Boethius's. Such a belief in the dominance of

Providence is however far from easy to put into practice or to make imaginatively real, and the outcome of hap and unhap remains in God's hands, beyond human sight. To restate the one thing that everyone thinks they know about Chaucer, he is not a religious poet; but his secularity is not entirely because of his interest in the surface of life. It is also because of his deep concern with mischance – the things that go wrong, where Providence seems to fail, or simply has nothing to do with what happens. In terms of the emphasis given to the concepts in his poetry, Chaucer is the scribe of Fortune rather than God, and that is one of his great strengths as a poet of this world;[10] but his very consciousness of infortune and all it means perhaps also underlay a yearning for the security offered him by Boethius's Philosophy and that uncircumscript God.

Helen Cooper is Professor Emerita of Medieval and Renaissance English at the University of Cambridge. She is the author of *The Structure of the Canterbury Tales* (Duckworth, 1983) and *Oxford Guides to Chaucer: The Canterbury Tales* (Oxford University Press, 1989, 1996), as well as numerous books and articles on medieval and early modern literature.

Notes

1. John S.P. Tatlock and Arthur G. Kennedy's *A Concordance to the Complete Works of Geoffrey Chaucer* (1927; repr. Gloucester, MA: Peter Smith, 1963) has been invaluable in the compilation of this study; for Gower, I have used *A Concordance to John Gower's Confessio Amantis*, ed. J.D. Pickles and J.L. Dawson (Cambridge: D.S. Brewer, 1987). Information on etymology and dates of first usage comes from the online editions of the *Oxford English Dictionary* and *Middle English Dictionary*.

2. Textual references are to *The Riverside Chaucer*, general ed. Larry D. Benson, 3rd edn (Boston, MA: Houghton Mifflin, 1987; Oxford: Oxford University Press, 1988). Abbreviations are *BD*, *Book of the Duchess*; *CT*, *Canterbury Tales*; *TC*, *Troilus and Criseyde*.

3. A notable exception is the Man of Law's apostrophe to Custance, 'He that is lord of Fortune be thy steere!' (*CT* II.448), where Fortune is explicitly placed under the command of God; Theseus's closing soliloquy has already been mentioned, though that remains within the limits of what a pagan character might think.

4. There are also a generous number of references to Fortune in the translation of the *Roman de la Rose*, the author of whose second part, Jean de Meun, himself translated Boethius into French. Chaucer's thoughts on Fortune may have been influenced by the *Roman*, but as all the citations of the concept in the English

Romaunt occur in the second and third fragments, which were almost certainly translated by someone other than Chaucer, the work is left out of account in this article.

5. *Boethius: The Theological Tractates and the Consolation of Philosophy*, ed. H.F. Stewart (Cambridge, MA: Harvard University Press, 1968), V pr. 1, 7 ff. Chaucer uses 'fall' and 'befall' as verbs in a similar sense.

6. 'Sort' (romance derivation) seems to carry a meaning halfway between destiny and chance – between this being the Knight's lot, and the way a lottery comes out.

7. *John Gower: Confessio Amantis*, ed. Russell A. Peck, 3 vols. (Kalamazoo, MI: TEAMS, 2000–2004), Bk 1.1523.

8. For the textual history and the problems of interpretation, see *The Minor Poems: Geoffrey Chaucer*, ed. George B. Pace and Alfred David, Variorum Chaucer vol. V (Norman, OH: University of Oklahoma Press, 1982), 103–119.

9. For the terminology, see A.J. Minnis, *Medieval Theory of Authorship* (London: Scolar Press, 1984).

10. In terms of quantitative statistics of word usage, God is a clear winner, but a very high proportion of those come in idioms and exclamations (not least from the Wife of Bath). The 'Monk's Tale' contains twenty-nine citations of God to thirty-one of Fortune.

Chapter 3

Chaucer's Tears

Barry Windeatt

Weeping is so prevalent in Chaucer's writings that interpretation of tears is a significant part of reading his works. Chaucer's characters usually weep more than their prototypes, and this greater disposition to weep can be plotted in Chaucer's borrowed and translated narratives where there is a source or close analogue for comparison. Chaucer may not always add new tears to his sources (though he does do that), but he augments the tears he finds, he repeats them, or moves them to more emotionally affecting points. The effect is that Chaucer's characters weep more often and more extendedly, and they do so at more significant moments – but the question why and to what intended effect often remains puzzling.

What were the horizons of expectation for Chaucer's early audiences in interpreting instances of weeping in his poems, given that models for medieval thinking about tears tend to derive largely from religious tradition?[1] It can be helpful to see the abundant tears wept in Chaucer's poems as part of the same aesthetic as the tears in affective devotion, where tears, by being understood to constitute a mode of prayer, become instrumental to a form of discourse. Tears in Chaucer are not merely some emotional by-product subservient to speech. Chaucer's characters do not communicate despite tears but with and through them. Tears formulate a discourse and idiolect of their own kind. This role of weeping as a discourse in Chaucer's poems can be illuminated further by the paradoxes in religious tears. One such paradox includes the relative value placed on inward as against outward weeping. Another is whether weeping is to be valued because it is a gift, spontaneous and involuntary, yet also valued for being an acquired craft that might be learned and practised.[2] Such an *ars lacrimandi*, or art of weeping, can be curiously both passive and active, or possibly a middle voice between the two. If accounts of weeping in medieval texts often appear strangely disproportionate to modern readers, and hence hard to assess, how can this guide us to calibrate our interpretation of tears and also of any gendered dimensions to weeping?

'Some believe that the word for tears (*lacrima*) comes from an injury of the mind (*laceratio mentis*)' was Isidore of Seville's etymology for tears,[3] but any such connection between tears and the mental processes behind them remains tantalizingly undeclared and implicit in many medieval texts, including Chaucer's. A popular encyclopaedia says no more about involuntary tears than the purely physical ailment of watering eyes, but tears were traditionally believed to derive from the brain when it was compressed in response to emotions.[4] The one occasion where Chaucer's writings expressly address the merits of weeping, and the relation between weeping and cause, comes early in 'The Tale of Melibee'. After the attack on his wife and daughter, Melibee weeps and cries like a mad man. His wife Dame Prudence reminds herself of Ovid's advice to allow a grieving mother to weep to the full for a dead child but, bearing in mind that their daughter has survived, Prudence eventually remonstrates about her husband's weeping. Melibee, however, insists on weeping as if over a death, recalling how 'Jesus wept' over Lazarus (John 11:35). Confronted with this disproportion between cause and tears, Prudence responds:

'attempree [moderate] wepyng is no thyng deffended to hym that sorweful is, amonges folk in sorwe, but it is rather graunted hym to wepe [citing Romans 12:15: 'weep with them that weep']. But though attempree wepyng be ygraunted, outrageous [excessive] wepyng certes is deffended'. (VII.988–90)[5]

Prudence's advice is predictably prudent in counselling against disordinate weeping excessively prolonged. But even if 'outrageous' weeping is discouraged, Prudence's stoical advice is still that 'attempree' weeping is allowable. Tears over a loss may indicate that the mourner grieves too much for people and things of this world, but grieving tears do have their moment and their worth. It is unclear whether Chaucer attached particular significance to such a proportionate balance between cause and tears, because 'Melibee' is so closely translated from its source. What *is* clear is that many characters in Chaucer's poems pay scant attention to Dame Prudence's advice on disordinate weeping.

Since so many of Chaucer's characters are so susceptible to tears, and since Mary Magdalene was celebrated for her weeping, one of the fascinating imponderables in Chaucer's approach to weeping is how he might have handled his now-lost version of Pseudo-Origen's *De Maria Magdalena*, listed among Chaucer's early works in the Prologue to the *Legend of Good Women* ('He made also, goon is a gret while, / Origenes upon the Maudeleyne', F 427–28). The Pseudo-Origen text opens with the wish, 'Let us try to understand why she cries ... May her weeping edify us'.[6] The Pseudo-Origen's whole focus is to meditate on the ironies of tears which are sincerely heartfelt – but uncomprehending and misdirected – in the weeping Magdalene's encounter with the angels at the tomb and with the risen Christ, whom she mistakes for a gardener (John 20:11–18). The text identifies warmly with the woman's predicament and with her essential boldness, while wondering for what reason the angels or even Jesus should ask Mary why she is weeping when they already know the answer, and commenting of Christ who had wept over Lazarus: 'For if he had once commended your tears, perhaps he would not have been able to suppress his own'. The text highlights a woman's consciousness – fallible, yet passionately loving and grieving – and explores the relation between understanding and weeping in a way that, even in the absence of Chaucer's version, it is tempting to see as a formative model for Chaucer's sympathetic representations of his heroines' states of mind and feeling, and for his explorations of the implications of weeping more largely throughout his work. If *Origenes upon the Maudeleyne* is indeed a lost early work of Chaucer's, it invites parallels with the interactions in the *Book of the Duchess* between someone bereaved and another who probes why that person is grieving. Chaucer's impetus to intensify the tearfulness of the moment for characters, by-standers and readers is alert to the value placed on tears in prayerful and devotional contexts and the rhetoric that promotes sentiments of sorrow, compunction and compassion.

In the Pseudo-Origen's meditation, tears are both admirable and imitable yet also surpassed by hope in Christ. Twice in the Gospel narrative Mary Magdalene is asked, 'Why do you weep?', and this same question is introduced by Chaucer when creating his version of Dante's account of Ugolino from *Inferno*. Dante's Ugolino proudly insists that he does *not* weep when he hears his prison being sealed up like a tomb, although his children weep and ask what is troubling their father (*Inferno*, 33.49–54). Chaucer deliberately reverses Dante's account in his version for 'The Monk's Tale', so that it is now the father who weeps ('Therwith the teeris fillen from his eyen') and his little son who asks, 'Fader, why do ye wepe?' (VII.2430–32). Why is this question about the purpose of weeping transposed? It is evidently more meaningful for a father to weep rather than his hungry small children, and for his weeping to prompt the child's poignantly innocent question. This very question about the purposes of tears is posed more largely across Chaucer's poems and across their very different cultural and chronological contexts.

Figures from the Old Testament or from Classical sources weep, or weep more, in Chaucer's versions of their stories. Nebuchadnezzar and Samson, who never weep over their fates in the Old Testament, grow tearful in Chaucer's accounts of them. Restored with more wisdom to his former state, Chaucer's Nebuchadnezzar 'thanne with many a teere / He thanked God...' ('The Monk's Tale', VII.2178–79). Samson's tragedy is preceded and concluded by Chaucer's references to the tears he sheds: 'But soone shal he wepe many a teere ... Now maystow wepen with thyne eyen blynde / Sith thou fro wele art falle in wrecchednesse' (VII.2061, 2077–78). In Chaucer's versions of Classical pagan stories there is also a comparable impetus to add tears to his sources. In 'The Physician's Tale', when her father tells Virginia her fate, 'The teeris bruste out of hir eyen two / And seyde, "Goode fader, shal I dye?"' (VI.234–35), although such weeping is no part of the character of Livy's Virginia. Or again, in Chaucer's legend of Philomela, having excluded Ovid's horrifyingly violent conclusion in infanticide, cannibalism and metamorphosis, Chaucer instead ends his narrative with Procne reunited with her raped and mutilated sister, 'Wepynge in the castel, here alone' (*Legend of Good Women*, 2378). Tears and complaint become an eloquent testimony to women's suffering. Chaucer's Old Testament and Classical pagan characters can weep because for Chaucer's readers sorrow at sin and for others is now high virtue after the Gospel's dispensation. The old, non-Christian stoicism and restraint is surpassed, because Christians can admit the depth of all sorrow since they have hope of full renewal – even of earthly love. Since nothing is now hopeless, all sorrow can be released, and Chaucer's pagans participate in this.

That Chaucer may indeed be influenced by the value set upon weeping in Christian prayer and devotion is suggested by the increased incidence of tears in the newly Christianized Northumbria of 'The Man of Law's Tale', where comparison with its Anglo-Norman source in Nicholas Trevet's *Cronicles* reveals Chaucer recurrently adding instances of weeping. In Chaucer's account, when the constable discovers his wife's murdered body he weeps and wrings his hands ('The Man of Law's Tale' II.606), as he does not in Trevet (*SA*, 309).[7] But what is particularly striking is how often Chaucer adds weeping to the reactions of the heroine's husband, the newly Christianized King Alla. When he writes back kindly to instruct that his wife and her supposedly monstrous child be cared for, 'This lettre he seleth, pryvely wepynge' (768), although Trevet's Alla does not weep at this point (*SA*, 313). Chaucer, but not Trevet, reports that Alla 'wepeth and siketh soore' for his wife after learning too late of his mother's treachery (985). In Trevet, when Alla meets Constance again in Rome, he simply exclaims, 'I have found my wife!' (*SA*, 325). Chaucer instead has Alla 'weep that it was routhe for to see' (1052) on first seeing his wife, and then 'He weep, and hym excuseth pitously' (1059). It is only after further and lengthy mutual sobbing that there is a reconciliation. And when eventually after Alla's death Constance returns to be reunited with her father in Rome, she is described as 'wepynge for tendrenesse in herte blithe' (1154), as all her wanderings find tearful closure in her final return to the eternal city. In the even more tearful close to 'The Prioress's Tale', Chaucer highlights tears of devotion as the response to the miracle, which prompts the abbot and his monks to a climax of collective tearfulness, a kind of *tableau pleurant*:

> And whan this abbot hadde this wonder seyn,
> His salte teeris trikled doun as reyn ...
>
> The covent eek lay on the pavement / Wepynge ... (VII.673–78)

Here, a plenitude of tears might be seen to substitute affectively for a prayerful response in words.

According to Margery Kempe's report of their conversation, Julian of Norwich acknowledges the sheer power in such plenitude of tears, citing Romans 8:26:

> Whan God visyteth a creatur wyth terys of contrisyon, devosyon or compassion he may and owyth to levyn that the Holy Gost is in hys sowle. Seynt Powyl seyth that the Holy Gost askyth for us wyth mornynggys and wepyngys unspeakable; that is to seyn: he makyth us to askyn and preyn wyth mornynggys and wepyngys so plentyvowsly that the terys may not be nowmeryd.[8]

In devotional contexts, there was a highly developed tradition for appraising the role and value of tears as signs of spiritual benefit and progress. Margery Kempe herself has a popular understanding of the connections between weeping and praying – she can pray because she can weep:

> But hir thowt it was no savowr ne swetnesse but whan sche myth wepyn, for than sche thowt that sche cowde preyin. (ch. 82)

Tears compel God's attention.[9] With compunction one might weep for one's own sins and for those of others. Compassion for the Passion of Christ might move to tears, just as some wept from longing for heaven. Chaucer too can be seen to pursue these associations of weeping with prayer, petition, complaint and expressions of compassion and pity.

The close identification of weeping with prayer is something that Chaucer can be traced to add to his sources in pagan as well as Christian contexts, sometimes if not always signalling virtue in those who weep and pray. In 'The Man of Law's Tale', Custance converts the Northumbrian pagan Hermengyld to Christianity 'In orisons, with many a bitter teere' (II.537), and Chaucer's Lucretia prays for her absent husband and then weeps (*Legend of Good Women*, 1731–32), while Dorigen's admirer Aurelius also weeps when praying imploringly to Apollo in 'The Franklin's Tale' (V.1078–79).

Another instance of a pagan weeping and praying is created by Chaucer in recasting Boccaccio's *Filostrato* into *Troilus and Criseyde*. When Boccaccio's Troiolo believes the fainted Criseida has died, he simply dries her face, stained with her tears, and tearfully declares she is dead (4.118). But Chaucer's Troilus first lets his tears rain down on Criseyde's breast ('with his teeris salt hire brest byreyned'), and it is then his own tears that he dries from Criseyde's body, before proceeding to pray for her soul: 'He gan tho teeris wypen of ful dreye / And pitously gan for the soule preye' (4.1172–74). It is hence Chaucer who introduces this connection between prayer and weeping in the behaviour of his rather piously prayerful Troilus, concerned about his lover's soul. Chaucer also modifies the tears from his source for 'The Knight's Tale', in this case to imply that the advantage lies with the more tearfully prayerful lover. In both 'The Knight's Tale' and Boccaccio's *Teseida*, Emelye weeps in Diana's temple (1.2327; cf. *Teseida*, 7.84), and Boccaccio describes Arcita's personified prayer as having a tearful face when it travels to the temple of Mars to deliver its message (7.29). But it is Chaucer's decision to make Palamon open his prayer to Venus with the plea 'Have pitee of my bittre teeris smerte' (I.2225) as the first petition in his prayer, and to omit all reference to any tears accompanying Arcite's prayers. This has the effect that in Chaucer's version of the story it is the eventually successful lover who prays tearfully, while the losing lover prays without weeping.

As with prayer, so too with petition, which Chaucer suggests is much more potent when accompanied by tears. Since it was believed that the drawn-up knees helped form the eye sockets of the foetus in the womb, both the knees in kneeling and the eyes in weeping signal a need for mercy, as Isidore of Seville explains in his *Etymologies*, commenting that the knees are 'co-engendered with the eyes as signs of tearfulness and an appeal for mercy' (238). In *On The Properties of Things*, Trevisa also explains this 'to menynge men wepen þe rather ȝif þey knele, for kynde wole þat þe yȝen and þe kneen haue mynde where þey were ifere in þe modir wombe' (267).[10] Indeed, it is some responses to crucial instances of petitionary weeping which shape the structure of 'The Knight's Tale'. When he comes across Palamon and Arcite fighting a private duel in *Teseida*, Boccaccio's Teseo sorts out his own reactions for himself with good sense (5.88–93). It is Chaucer's Theseus who first flies into a dangerous rage, and then has to be influenced by the tears of his kneeling wife and her ladies: 'And eek his herte hadde compassioun / Of wommen, for they wepen evere in oon' (I.1770–71). The subsequent action of the tale flows from this instance of how women's weeping successfully influences a male sovereign. A consequent crisis is also resolved in Chaucer's version, but not Boccaccio's, by the influence of tearful female petition. In the *Teseida*, Mars and Venus agree between themselves how to resolve the problem of their having granted the prayers of both Palamon and Arcite and, in effect, Mars chivalrously gives in to Venus (7.67, 9.2–3). Instead, Chaucer represents Saturn, before the battle, as responding to the tearful imploring of Venus ('Now weep namoore; I shal doon diligence', I.2470). When Palamon is duly defeated in the tournament, Venus weeps again:

> What seith she now? What dooth this queene of love,
> But wepeth so, for wantynge of hir wille,
> Til that hir teeres in the lystes fille?
> She seyde, 'I am ashamed, doutelees.'
> Saturnus seyde, 'Doghter, hoold thy pees!' (I.2664–68)

Once again Venus's tears serve to act upon Saturn and produce the desired confirmation of what she wants, when Saturn contrives Arcite's death. It is intriguing in 'The Knight's Tale' that a narrative that on one level suggests the powerlessness of Emelye can also suggest the potency of female influence through the medium of tears and their power to petition successfully.

Even more common than petitions among Chaucer's characters is the framing of complaints and lamentations, the openings of which are often inseparable from weeping:

> Who shal me yeven teeris to compleyne
> The deeth of gentillesse and of franchise?

asks the Monk (VII.2663–64), and Anelida begins writing her complaint tearfully:

> Upon a day, ful sorowfully wepinge,
> She caste her for to make a compleynynge. (*Anelida*, 207–8)

Both male lovers in 'The Knight's Tale' weep while uttering complaints about their fates, and Palamon weeps such that 'The pure fettres on his shynes grete / Weren of his bittre, salte teeres wete' (I.1279–80). Perhaps Palamon's more conspicuously lachrymose complaining here is another pointer to his eventual reward.

Tears in Chaucer's poems are evidently intrinsic to an impetus to realize the maximum potential for pathos and pitifulness. In the New Testament, St Paul had described himself as tearfully writing his Epistle to the Philippians:

> For many walk of whom I have told you often, and now tell you even weeping, that they are the enemies of the cross of Christ. (3:18)

It is characteristic of a much broader pattern in Chaucer that when citing this apostolic weeping in his sermon, Chaucer's Pardoner doubles the emotional intensity of the apostle's tears, by repeating how pitiful his weeping utterance is:

> The apostel wepyng seith ful pitously,
> 'Ther walken manye of whiche yow toold have I –
> I seye it now wepyng, with pitous voys ...' (VI.529–31)

Chaucer recurrently introduces tears into contexts already full of pathos: in 'The Clerk's Tale' it is Chaucer who adds to his sources the tears of Griselda's old father as he fumbles 'ful sorwefully wepynge' to clothe her with her 'olde cote', now too small for her, after the Marquess sends her away (IV.914; cf. *SA* 127, 161). Chaucer will even substitute piteous weeping for a joyful response he finds in his sources. When Constance is washed up on the Northumbrian coast, Trevet's constable goes down to meet her with great joy (*SA*, 2.305), whereas Chaucer's constable goes with his wife and both weep 'for routhe', having 'so greet pitee' because Constance claims to have lost her memory ('The Man of Law's Tale', II.526–29). Instances are everywhere of this disposition to 'pitous' tears in Chaucer's poems, sometimes in Chaucer's added insistence that tears already present in his sources are 'pitous' or 'for pitee' – which is the case with the tears shed by the executioner in 'The Second Nun's Tale' (VIII.371, 401) – for such pitiful tears will have prompted an observer's response.

Whether tears are public and witnessed, or solitary and private, is an important factor in their impact and significance. But alongside the distinction between public and private tears, there is also a parallel distinction in religious writing between outward material tears and weeping inwardly, which some of Chaucer's writing may be seen to ponder. Julian of Norwich writes succinctly of an inward weeping in spirit, distinct from material tears:

> I sey we never stinten of moning ne of wepyng. This weping meneth not al in poring out of teares by our bodily eye, but also to more gostly understondyng.[11]

In religious contexts Chaucer's works also show themselves alert to the distinction between inward and outward weeping. Friars – who are supposedly wedded 'To wepynge, misericorde and clennesse' ('The Summoner's Tale', III.1910) – may by their preaching prompt tears from those who hear them: 'But precheth nat, as freres doon in

Lente / To make us for oure olde synnes wepe' ('The Clerk's Tale', IV.12–13). Indeed, as reported in the 'General Prologue', the Friar manages to exploit a distinction between inner and outer tears in order to make a profit out of those who cannot weep outwardly as they should:

> For many a man so hard is of his herte
> He may not wepe, althogh hym soore smerte.
> Therfore in stede of wepynge and preyeres
> Men moote yeve silver to the povre freres. ('General Prologue', I.229–32)

Even so, as the Parson comments: 'Wepynge, and nat for to stynte to do synne, may nat avayle' (X.89). The Parson advises tearful confession but allows for an inward weeping:

> thy shrift sholde be ful of teeris, if man may, and if man may nat wepe with his bodily eyen, lat hym wepe in herte (X.993)

although the implication here is that inward weeping is almost a poor substitute for demonstrative outward weeping.

This is also the implication of some striking instances in more secular contexts where the impact of witnessed tears is almost unendurably powerful on the perceiver. At the lovers' last night together in *Filostrato*, the spirit weeps in Criseida's heart to go away from the sight of Troiolo (4.158), whereas for Criseyde 'The pure spirit wepeth in myn herte / To se yow wepen' (*Troilus*, IV.1620–21), such is the impact upon her of watching Troilus weep. Chaucer's Criseyde had earlier promised Pandarus to stop weeping in front of Troilus ('me to restreyne / From wepyng in his sighte...' IV.940–41), whereas Criseida simply promises to compose herself (4.107–8). For his part, Troilus thinks it 'no strokes of a yerde / To heere or seen Criseyde, his lady, wepe' and experiences a deathlike spasm 'For everi tere which that Criseyde asterte' (III.1065–71), while this powerful impact on witnesses of tears *heard* as well as seen – presumably in sobbing – recurs in Chaucer's poems ('And weep that it was pitee for to heere ... Therwith he weep that pitee was to heere', 'The Knight's Tale', I.2345, 2878). *Lenvoy de Chaucer a Bukton* warns against tears' impact on a witness with 'Ne no man him bewayle, though he wepe' (16). Indeed, such is the emotion triggered by witnessing weeping that it may be insupportable to remain within sight. In 'The Clerk's Tale', Griselda's dry-eyed response to the removal of her baby daughter comes from Petrarch ('she neither weep ne syked', IV.545; *SA* 121), as also does her profuse weeping when her children are restored to her (IV.1082–85; *SA* 129), but it is Chaucer who adds here not only how the bystanders are moved to tears by the sight of Griselda's tears but also how they can scarcely bear to remain in the presence of such weeping:

> O many a teere on many a pitous face
> Doun ran of hem that stooden hire bisyde;
> Unnethe abouten hire myghte they abyde. (IV.1104–6)

Something similar occurs when Chaucer adds his Pandarus's sensation of claustrophobia, so compassionately responsive is he to Criseyde's weeping: 'That in the hous he myghte unnethe abyde / As he that pite felt on every syde' (4.823–24).

Once tears are no longer shed alone for whatever reason, they can prompt developments. The character of the Merchant remains a closed book because he prefers not to enlarge on how he has 'wept many a teere / Ful pryvely, syn I have had a wyf' (IV.1544–45). The Man in Black – accustomed to 'wepynge whan I am allone ... Allas, than am I overcome!' (*Book of the Duchess*, 696, 707) – is drawn away from solitary sorrow by his exchange with the dreamer, during which he is not reported to weep. Lovers weep 'prively' during secret affairs (*Anelida*, 138), but Pandarus ridicules Troilus for his secret, solitary tears, which can have no outcome if unwitnessed (1.806–12). More effective to contrive a tear-stained letter – 'Biblotte it with thi teris ek a lite' (II.1027) – as palpably material witness to the lover's weeping. Yet in adding to his source that Troilus inwardly weeps tears of blood at having to part from Criseyde at dawn – 'The blody teris from his herte melte' (III.1445) – Chaucer adds a gravity of inward weeping that aligns Troilus's distress with recollections of the bloody tears wept by the Virgin Mary at the crucifixion.[12]

The religious tradition of careful scrutiny of the nature and value of tears informs the reception of weeping more widely. The tears of Chaucer's characters become more meaningful in the context of the paradox that valid religious tears might – in different contexts – be involuntary or crafted. There is a view that weeping, to be authentic, is uncontrivedly spontaneous. Yet there is also a view that weeping can be an acquired art, a craft learned and practised in devotion. Weeping is understood to come from deep within us yet is expressed outwardly. The emotion behind weeping might be interpreted as passive but is actively expressed. Is there some fusion of active and passive in weeping, which might be seen as a kind of middle voice, neither wholly active nor passive?

Despite all the travails of her life, Margery Kempe never records weeping simply because she feels miserable or sorry for herself. Kempe's tears are not personally expressive in any such direct way; she views them as a gift and vocation with devotional causes and objectives, but the validity of her tears and accompanying cries as a sign of holiness becomes the subject of repeated question. Much of Kempe's narrative is consequently shaped by challenges to the meaning of her tears. In their own way, the interpretation of Chaucer's poems often turns on an understanding of tears as a special mode of communication. Not unlike Kempe, the Man in Black in the *Book of the Duchess* views his tears as a gift, although in his case a baleful one, which he attributes not to the divine but to the influence of planets and elements:

> For there nys planete in firmament,
> Ne in ayr, ne in erthe noon element
> That they ne yive me a yifte echone
> Of wepynge whan I am allone. (*Book of the Duchess*, 693–96)

Pursuit of love in medieval literature is also a devotion and a craft, in which tears are a part of observance: 'The sacred teeris ... That loves servantz in this lyf enduren' figure prominently in the wall paintings in Venus's temple ('The Knight's Tale', I.1921–23). Indeed, outward tears might not be all they appear and might be misleading; such signs and tokens needed careful interpretation. Noting that some of his readers might 'for tendrenesse of kynde bien sone stired to wepyng of teeris', *The Chastising of God's Children* explores how to turn to God's worship 'suche teeris and other goostli comfortis, of whiche he was in doute whether thei camen of tendirnesse of kynde or noon'.[13]

Compassionate responses to weeping assume that tears are an involuntary and unfeigned expression of inward feeling. Yet tears can be induced falsely and insincerely, and Chaucer includes arch exaggeration about volumes of tears and processes of weeping.[14] Faked weeping subverts assumptions of sincerity, and the discovered falsification may come as a shock and affront. In texts like the *Legend of Good Women* or 'The Squire's Tale', it is false and insincere male suitors who – as Phyllis discovers – are able to 'weep by craft':

> 'Wel may I pleyne ...
> And on youre teres falsly out yronge.
> How coude ye wepe so by craft?' quod she,
> 'May there swiche teres feyned be?' (*Legend of Good Women*, 2525–29)

just as the female falcon in 'The Squire's Tale' recalls how she was deceived by false tears ('Til he so longe hadde wopen and compleyned', V.523), and just as Dido is deceived by the tears of Aeneas ('Therwith his false teres out they sterte', *Legend of Good Women*, 1301). In summarizing Damyan's weeping, the narrator of 'The Merchant's Tale' coolly implies that such a male lover's weeping is just so much routine observance ('But there I lete hym wepe ynogh and pleyne', IV.1781).

Not that men have any monopoly on faked and insincere weeping. Women's falsified tears were proverbial, as in the Latin gloss 'Lying and weeping God gave to women', found in many manuscripts alongside the Wife of Bath's declaration that:

'Deceite, wepyng, spynnyng, God hath yive
To wommen kyndely, whil that they may lyve'. (III.401–2)

Proserpina admits that women exploit the impact of tears in fooling men:

'Yit shul we wommen visage it hardily,
And wepe, and swere, and chyde subtilly,
So that ye men shul been as lewed as gees' (IV.2273–75)

and there has already been an example of that in May's tearful manipulation of January:

But first and forward she bigan to wepe
'I have,' quod she, 'a soule for to kepe
As wel as ye ...'. (IV.2187–89)

Tears remain an ambivalent indicator, and the *Chastising of God's Children* acknowledges problems in distinguishing spiritual tears and in developing tears beyond the merely natural:

It is harde to knowe of suche maner teeris whiche bien of kynde and whiche bien above kynde, for because thei bien so liche ... whiche paraventure were first but of natural kynde, withoute merite, mowen be made meritorie and above kynde. (ch. 2)

Just as holy tears could compose forms of prayerful communication, Chaucer's readers might assess his characters' weeping as its own mode of utterance. It is no accident that Chaucer begins and ends, or otherwise accompanies, significant speeches with tears (sometimes altering his sources to do so), because weeping is a significant communication and a kind of statement in its own right, rather than simply an involuntary corporeal symptom of inward emotion. Chaucer's strategic identifications of weeping with discourse include Criseyde's first reaction to the news of Troilus's love, and Hypermnestra's agonized soliloquy in the *Legend*. So when Chaucer's Criseyde is confronted with her uncle's startling news of Troilus's love for her, 'she began to breste a-wepe anoon' (II.408) and presumably is to be understood as weeping through the next eight stanzas in which she gives voice to her shock and bewilderment, since it is only at the end of this that she is noted to stop weeping ('and stynte for to wepe', II.469). There is a similar augmenting of tears in Chaucer's account of Hypermnestra from Ovid's *Heroides* in his *Legend of Good Women*. Ovid's Hypermnestra weeps after lamenting that she must kill her new husband (14.67–68), but Chaucer mentions her weeping both before and after her soliloquy of complaint ('Ful tenderly begynneth she to wepe ... And wep ful tenderly upon his face', 2679, 2706), implying that speech and weeping are concurrent in constituting one discourse. Something similar is seen in the ready tears of Chaucer's Dorigen. Her complaint about the rocks is prayerful ('But thilke God ... As kepe my lord! ... But wolde God ...', V.888–92) and is observed to be concurrent with her weeping: 'Thus wolde she seyn, with many a pitous teere' (894). Her lengthy complaint lamenting the fates of various Classical heroines is implicitly both speech and weeping in one, in that her returning husband finds her still weeping (1461–62). Chaucer's aligning of weeping with such major soliloquies in the cases of these women characters is a pointer to the understanding of weeping more widely in Chaucer's works as functioning much more like a mode of discourse than some incidental emotional symptom.

As Chaucer's most tearful narrative, *Troilus and Criseyde* offers especially significant evidence for attitudes to weeping.[15] Chaucer's engagement, possibly concurrently, with translating Boethius into English and composing *Troilus* – and hence with two texts with such distinct evaluations of weeping as Boethius's *Consolation of Philosophy* and Boccaccio's *Filostrato* – may have negotiated an accommodation between the two assessments which builds the distinctively reflective tearfulness found in Chaucer's poems more largely. In the *Consolation*, Chaucer would know how the Boethius figure begins with his vision obscured by tears – a tearful opening echoed in the opening of *Troilus*. His former companions, the Muses, are prompting Boethius the author to match words to his tearful mood, but Philosophy briskly banishes such lachrymose themes as fit subjects for the work. The *Consolation*'s trajectory is to leave tears and tearful self-absorption behind, discovering that Fortune 'neither heereth ne rekketh of wrecchide wepynges ... sche leygheth and scorneth the wepynges of hem, the whiche sche hath maked wepe with hir free wille' (*Boece*, 2.m.1). Fortune has both a laughing and a weeping eye – 'She ys fals, and ever laughynge / With oon eye, and that other wepynge' (*Book of the Duchess*, 633–34) – and both are insincere, as Alexander the Great, like others, will discover: 'And for thee ne weep she never a teere' ('The Monk's Tale', VII.2662). When Boethius is instructed 'And forthy drye thi teeris, for yit nys nat every fortune al hateful to theward' (2.pr.4), this is very different from the narrative of increasing tearfulness that Chaucer encounters in *Filostrato*.

Chaucer's alertness to the significance of tears is decisively influenced by the emotional intensity of *Filostrato*'s sustained lyrical lachrymosity, which lingers feelingly, almost lovingly, over the lovers' tearfulness, yet which Chaucer actually intervenes to augment with his own emphasis, in ways that further his thematic development of Boccaccio's material. Troilus's weeping has paralysed modern criticism with embarrassment, but the hero's tearfulness forms a major emotional and thematic touchstone in the poem. Troilus's tears betoken a capacity to feel and suffer which is intrinsically admirable, although sometimes comically excessive in context. Correspondingly, Chaucer adds new instances of Criseyde's weeping, as part of a larger impetus to give greater parity to her in the narrative. In Book III, after Criseyde has regretted Troilus's jealousy and offered to subject her faithfulness to trial by ordeal, 'With that a fewe brighte teris newe / Owt of hire eighen fille' (III.1051–52). In a context where tears can be so abundant, especial power resides in these few fresh tears, and their effect on Troilus is so literally stunning that he cannot weep in return ('That from his eyen fil there nought a tere', III.1087), all his vital spirits turn in on themselves, and he promptly falls down in a faint. In Book V, Chaucer also quietly adjusts towards a parity of weeping: going back to Benoît de Sainte-Maure's *Roman de Troie* to restore Criseyde's tears when Diomede is wounded by Troilus (V.1046), but also adding Criseyde's weeping in the soliloquy in which she bids farewell to Troilus ('And with that word she braste anon to wepe', V.1078).

In his fourth book of *Troilus*, Chaucer inherits from *Filostrato*'s fourth part a succession of tearful scenes, yet Chaucer intervenes not simply to make his version more intensely tearful for its own sake, but rather to focus on tears as a uniquely potent mode of communicating mental processes. Criseyde's tears are likened to an April shower ('Therwith the teris from hire eyen two / Down fille as shour in Aperil ful swithe', IV.750–51), and Troilus's tears resemble the distillation in an alembic ('This Troylus in teris gan distille, / As licour out of a lambyc ful faste', IV.519–20), because the overstatement of the English lovers' tears constitutes a form of utterance. The danger of drowning in one's tears is a conceit which has already applied to Troilus's earlier weeping – 'Til neigh that he in salte teres dreynte' (*Troilus*, I.543) – but which Pandarus invokes with wry overstatement that communicates the lovers' feelings: 'What helpeth it to wepen ful a strete, / Or though ye bothe in salte teeris dreynte?' (*Troilus*, IV.929–30). Shedding tears is likened to the tricklings or marmoreal fixity of Ovidian metamorphoses and thereby objectified into potent statements. The lovers' bitter tears are compared with the tears exuded by unhappy Myrra through the bark of the tree into which she has been transformed ('So bittre teeris weep nought, as I fynde, / The woful Mirra thorugh the bark and rynde', IV.1138–39), just as Pandarus warns Troilus to avoid any such fate as 'To walwe and wepe as Nyobe the queene, / Whos teres yet in marble ben yseene' (I.699–700). Overall, there is some glancing irony about profusion of tears, including some play on how tears might be a quantifiable commodity ('Wol he han pleynte or teris er I wende? / I have ynough if he therafter sende', IV.860–61), or whether one may weep through deputies and proxies: 'So tendrely she weep, bothe eve and morwe, / Hire nedede no teris for to borwe!' (V.725–26). When Diomede warns Criseyde 'That ye for any wight that dwelleth there / Sholden spille a quarter of a tere' (V.879–80), his dismissal of tears into fractions underlines how far he is from understanding the idiom of weeping as a statement of both suffering and of love.

Filostrato's culture of tearfulness is absorbed, anglicized and augmented in *Troilus*, but is also implicitly set in conversation with a very different evaluation of weeping in Boethius. Yet although the *Consolation* initially rejects self-pitying tears as theme or mode, it includes at a crucial point in its argument an account of how the weeping song of Orpheus has the power to move the Furies from rage and vengeance towards tears of compassion:

> '[Orpheus] spak and song in wepynge ... And he sang with as mochel as he myghte of wepynge, and with as moche as love that doublide his sorwe myghte yeve hym and teche hym, and he commoevede the helle ... And the thre goddesses, furiis ... wepyn teeris for pite' (3.m.12)

Conventionally, singing is the antithesis of weeping,[16] but here the combinative power of tearful song is a good that enables tearful compassion and even liberty: it is an endorsement of the creative power of tears. The negotiation between the *Consolation* and the *Filostrato* that lies behind *Troilus* produces its own complex accommodation of the role and significance of tears, in a pattern seen more largely across Chaucer's works, whereby indulgent and purposeless tears may be reproved, yet characters continue to weep abundantly, and readers are left to judge or not to judge, according to context.

To consider instances of weeping across Chaucer's works is to discover that tears offer varying signals. Tears imply humanity but were not thought to be something definingly human, since stories about weeping animals were available.[17] Nor had tears yet acquired the gendered and cultural restrictions whereby it is women, children and excitable foreigners who weep – because weeping supposedly betrays a weakness of reason and will – although this still means that most of humankind weeps readily.[18] Unburdened by such later constrictions, the many tears in medieval texts are open to more positive interpretation, betokening empathy, compassion and sensibility in those who weep in sympathy or in distress.[19] By nature, women were believed to be more disposed to weep – 'And for a womman is more mylde than a man sche wepith sooner than a man' – while children 'wepith more for the losse of an appil thanne fore the losse of theire heritage'.[20] Men could weep freely without this necessarily being unmanly behaviour in itself, although other factors might make such weeping reprehensible.[21]

A modern reader's instinctive suspicion that weeping in medieval texts verges on excess (and is meant to be understood comically) needs to account for how Chaucer's poems suggest no reservations about men weeping, when there is good cause. Pandarus becomes impatient less with Troilus's weeping than with the inaction that it betokens (I.806–12). Pandarus himself dissolves into tears when declaring to Criseyde of Troilus 'That yet fele I myn herte for hym wepe' (II.567), or when 'Pandare wep as he to water wolde' (III.115) during the lovers' first meeting. If this is Pandarus's excessive and insincere display of tearfulness, why is the very same wording employed in 'The Squire's Tale' when Canacee 'weep as she to water wolde' (V.496) at the female falcon's sad story? Empathy in the form of ready tears is part of the emotional fabric from which such narratives are shaped and presumes at least some empathy from the reader, which need not preclude critique in context, as perhaps with the Prioress ('She wolde wepe, if that she saugh a mous / Kaught in a trappe', 'General Prologue', I.144–45). Every character, male or female, in 'The Franklin's Tale' weeps over something: Aurelius (V.1078), his brother (1116), the Breton clerk (1182), as well as Dorigen. It is when Arveragus suddenly 'brast anon to wepe' (1480) – between nobly telling Dorigen to keep her promise and threatening to kill her if she ever reveals it – that Chaucer deploys tears as a mode of middle voice between passive and active, addressing what language cannot express.

Indeed, failure to weep may count more negatively than any excess of weeping. Inability to weep is a sign of moral depravity when Nero gazes dry-eyed on the opened-up body of his mother whom he has had murdered ('No teere out of his eyen for that sighte / Ne cam ...', 'The Monk's Tale', VII.2487–88), a moment that recalls the account in Boethius ('ne no teer ne wette his face', 2.m.6). This is a tyrant who has senators killed for the pleasure of witnessing their tears ('To heere how that men wolde wepe and crie', VII.2481), just as Antiochus in his wickedness 'many a man made to wepe and pleyne' (VII.2629). Seen in this context it is notable that Chaucer omits the tears that overwhelm Walter in the sources when he agrees to Griselda's request at least to keep her smock when she is supposedly divorced. Chaucer's Walter can barely speak 'for routhe and for pitee' (IV.893) but he does not weep uncontrollably as in the Latin and French sources (*SA*, 1.124, 161). In an altogether humbler context in 'The Reeve's Tale', Malyne shows her emotional limitations by not quite weeping at the lovers' dawn parting ('And with that word almoost she gan to wepe', I.4248).[22]

Since Chaucer's Troilus is never reported as laughing during his lifetime, it is all the more striking that he laughs as his spirit ascends from Earth after death, and what he laughs at is the tears of those still alive who are mourning his death:

> And in hymself he lough right at the wo
> Of hem that wepten for his deth so faste ...
> (*Troilus and Criseyde*, 5.1821–22)[23]

From beyond this life, the tears of this world – tears of grief for its things and people – may seem laughably misplaced to Chaucer's Troilus, formerly so tearful. For those still in this world, and precluded from such otherworldly detachment, tears inevitably remain more complex and difficult to appraise. Tears may not possess one stable significance across Chaucer's large and diverse oeuvre, but this is because tears present less a single message than a variable mode of self-consciousness, reflection and statement – a discourse in both body and mind, outward and inward, passive and active – in which much can be communicated and read. Margery Kempe found endorsement in the weeping of the beguine Marie d'Oignies, who remarked: 'Thes teeris ... are my refresshynge ... my sustynauns nyghte and daye that dissese not the hede but feden the mynde ...'.[24]

Barry Windeatt is Fellow and Keeper of Rare Books at Emmanuel College, Cambridge. Recent publications include a parallel-text edition of the short and long texts of Julian of Norwich's *Revelations of Divine Love* (Oxford University Press, 2016) and a new translation of both texts (Oxford World's Classics, 2015).

Notes

1. See Pierre Adnès, 'Larmes', *Dictionnaire de Spiritualité*, IX.287–303 (Paris: Beauchesne, 1976); Sandra McEntire, *The Doctrine of Compunction in Medieval England: Holy Tears* (Lewiston, NY: Edwin Mellen, 1990); K.C. Patton and J.S. Hawley, eds., *Holy Tears: Weeping in the Religious Imagination* (Princeton, NJ: Princeton University Press, 2005); and Gary L. Ebersole, 'The Function of Ritual Weeping Revisited: Affective Expression and Moral Discourse', *History of Religions* 39 (2000): 211–46.

2. See R.M. Garrett, 'De Arte Lacrimandi', *Anglia* 32 (1909): 269–94; Piroska Nagy, *Le Don des larmes au Moyen Age: un instrument spirituel en quête d'institution, Ve–XIIIe siècle* (Paris: A. Michel, 2000). The Sarum Missal includes a votive mass for tears, opening with a prayer for tears of compunction.

3. *The Etymologies of Isidore of Seville*, trans. Stephen A. Barney et al. (Cambridge: Cambridge University Press, 2006), XI.i.41, 1367–68.

4. *On the Properties of Things: John Trevisa's Translation of Bartholomaeus Anglicus De Proprietatibus Rerum*, ed. M.C. Seymour (Oxford: Oxford University Press, 1975), 1.362–63. Ancient medicine explained tears as caused by a humoural excess triggered when the matter of the brain is compressed. Expounding this traditional physiology in his *A Treatise of Melancholie* (London, 1586), Timothie Bright describes the 'matter of teares' as 'the excrementitious humiditie of the brayne', declaring that 'teares rise of the braines thinnest & most liquide excrement; wherof (being the moystest part of the whole bodie ...) it hath great plenty' (144–5). Emotional reactions prompt contractions, by which tears are squeezed from the brain through the eyes despite attempts at retention, as Bright explains: 'Nature maketh such contraction of the substance of the braine ... that as one

desirous to hold fast with his hand that which is apt to flowe forth, loseth by his hard handlinge and compression, which otherwise he might retaine, so it expresseth that which by thinnesse is readie to voide, and forcing with spirit, & pressing with contracted substance, signifieth by shower of teares, what storme tosseth the afflicted hart, and overcasteth the cheerfull countenance' (146–7).

5. All references are to *The Riverside Chaucer*, ed. Larry D. Benson (Oxford: Oxford University Press, 1988).

6. Rodney K. Delasanta and Constance M. Rousseau, 'Chaucer's *Orygenes Upon the Maudeleyne*: A Translation', *Chaucer Review* 30 (1996): 319–42.

7. *Sources and Analogues of the Canterbury Tales* (hereafter *SA*), ed. Robert M. Correale and Mary Hamel, 2 vols. (Woodbridge: D.S. Brewer, 2002–5).

8. *The Book of Margery Kempe*, ed. Barry Windeatt (Harlow, 2000; repr. Woodbridge: Boydell and Brewer, 2004), ch. 18.

9. 'No man comez any tyme to God bot wepynge ... Prayer quemez [pleases] God, but the tere constreynez; prayer softez, the tere compellez', *Speculum Christiani*, ed. G. Holmstedt, EETS, o.s. 182 (Oxford: Oxford University Press, 1933), 'De Lacrimis', 214.

10. See further Jacqueline Tasioulas, '"Heaven and Earth in Little Space": The Foetal Existence of Christ in Medieval Literature and Thought', *Medium Aevum* 76 (2007): 24–48, here 32–33.

11. *Julian of Norwich: Revelations of Divine Love*, ed. Barry Windeatt (Oxford: Oxford University Press, 2016), ch. 72.

12. From the cross Christ urges Mary: 'Thu wasse awey tho blodi teren'; see Carleton Brown, ed., *English Lyrics of the XIIIth Century* (Oxford: Oxford University Press, 1932), 89. At Thame in Oxfordshire a wall painting of the Pietà shows Mary weeping tears of blood; see Richard Marks, *Image and Devotion in Late Medieval England* (Stroud: Sutton Publishing, 2004), 137.

13. *The Chastising of God's Children and the Treatise of Perfection of the Sons of God*, ed. Joyce Bazire and Edmund Colledge (Oxford: Blackwell, 1957), ch. 2.

14. 'For thogh I wepe of teres ful a tyne [barrel] ...' (*To Rosemounde*, 9).

15. See Mary Carruthers, 'On Affliction and Reading, Weeping and Argument: Chaucer's Lachrymose Troilus in Context', *Representations* 93 (2006): 1–21.

16. 'Frend, shal I now wepe or synge?' asks Troilus (II.952), and hearing music torments lachrymose lovers (*CT*, I.1368; *Troilus*, V.456–62). '"Musik in wepynge is a noyous thyng": that is to seyn: as muche availleth to speken bifore folk to which his speche anoyeth as it is to synge biforn hym that wepeth' ('Melibee', VII.1045). See also Ecclesiasticus 22:6.

17. Ad Vingerhoets, *Why Only Humans Weep: Unravelling the Mysteries of Tears* (Oxford: Oxford University Press, 2013). See also Jerome Neu, *A Tear is an Intellectual Thing: The Meanings of Emotion* (Oxford: Oxford University Press, 2000) and Tom Lutz, *Crying: The Natural and Cultural History of Tears* (New York: W.W. Norton, 1999). Chaucer allows a droll uncertainty about whether animals weep: 'ther nys tygre, ne noon so crueel beest ... That nolde han wept, *if that he wepe koude*, / For sorwe of hire ...' ('Squire's Tale', V.419–22; my italics).

18. 'Englishmen rarely cry except under the pressure of the acutest grief', Charles Darwin, *The Expression of the Emotions in Man and Animals* (London, 1872), 155.

19. Elina Gertsman, ed., *Crying in the Middle Ages: Tears of History* (New York: Routledge, 2012).

20. *On the Properties of Things*, 1.301–2. After his sexual discomfiture in 'The Miller's Tale', Absolom 'Ful ofte paramours he gan deffie, / And weep as dooth a child that is ybete' (I.3758–59).
21. See Katherine Harvey, 'Episcopal Emotions: Tears in the Life of a Medieval Bishop', *Historical Research* 87 (2014): 591–610.
22. When Mars must leave Venus at dawn 'for his nature was not for to wepe, / In stede of teres, from his eyen tweyne / The firi sparkes brosten out for peyne' (*Complaint of Mars*, 94–96), highlighting the conventional expectation of lovers' tears. On weeping in and at Griselda's story, see Nicole Sidhu, 'Weeping for the virtuous wife: laymen, affective piety and Chaucer's "Clerk's Tale"', in *Medieval Domesticity: Home, Housing and Household in Medieval England*, ed. Maryanne Kowaleski and P. J. P. Goldberg (Cambridge, 2008), 177–208.
23. Boccaccio's Troiolo laughs at the lovers in the temple (1.21), but Troilus limits himself to a smile (I.194).
24. Jennifer N. Brown, ed., *Three Women of Liège: A Critical Edition of and Commentary on the Middle English Lives of Elizabeth of Spalbeek, Christina Mirabilis, and Marie d'Oignies* (Turnhout: Brepols, 2008), 94.

Chapter 4

In Appreciation of Metrical Abnormality
Headless Lines and Initial Inversion in Chaucer

Ad Putter

In Memory of Alan Gaylord

Departures from metrical norms and rules are not usually well liked by people working on metre, for understandable reasons. When you are trying to work out the regularities of a poet's metrical system, exceptions to such regularities are a nuisance, and (to speak from personal experience) it is enormously satisfying to read and to produce research that makes them go away. In the field of Old and Middle English, we are blessed with ways of achieving this goal. For instance, it may be possible to show that exceptions are scribal rather than authorial, or that they have some linguistic peculiarity in common that makes them regular after all. The favourite word in metrical scholarship for exceptions that cannot be explained away by such means is 'licences'. The word grants immunity from prosecution to poets found deviating from the rules, but it is firmly on the side of law and order, and does not attempt to comprehend the purpose of 'irregular' behaviour on its own terms. Critics more accepting of such behaviour often say that poets adopted it 'to avoid monotony',[1] but this does not get us much further. Are we really to believe that, when a poet – say Shakespeare – wrote a line that is metrically atypical, he did so for the sake of introducing variation? As a form of logical reasoning, this explanation is rather limited (Shakespeare did things differently so as not to do the same), and as an explanation of how poets work it is more limited still. If good poets arrange their words in an unusual metrical pattern, they presumably do so because they think the pattern supports what they wish to convey, and not just because they fancy a change.

My aim in this article is to take sides with metrical abnormality and to write more appreciatively than I have seen others do about two 'licences' that Chaucer took, both in his short four-beat verse and in his iambic pentameter. In the short line, Chaucer's normal metrical template was x/x/x/x/(x) (where x stands for an unaccented syllable, / for a beat, and (x) for an optional final offbeat); in the longer line, it was x/x/x/x/x/(x). An anacrusis, that is, an unaccented syllable at line opening, was evidently the norm in Chaucer, but he sometimes opened his line with a beat, either through initial inversion (also known as 'trochaic inversion' of the first foot), yielding /xx/x/(x) in the short line and /xx/x/x/(x) in the long line, or by suppressing the initial offbeat altogether, resulting in a 'headless' line – /x/x/ (x) or /x/x/x/(x) – that is a syllable shorter. I am interested, firstly, in how Chaucer used these patterns, and, secondly, in whether there are any precedents for his usage in earlier English poetry.

That Chaucer permitted himself both variations is now generally accepted.[2] Of the two, initial inversion has been the least contentious (though, as we shall see, it is just as rare in Chaucer's short lines as headless lines are in Chaucer's long lines), possibly because it has been a feature of English iambic poetry throughout its long history. However, the fact that Chaucer wrote headless verses has been disputed, and indeed many English poets through the ages did not countenance them. Alexander Pope, for instance, strictly avoided them,[3] and so did Chaucer's contemporary John Gower. None of the octosyllabic verses in Gower's *Confessio Amantis* is truncated,[4] and I have also found no headless lines in the 375 pentameter lines of Gower's poem 'In Praise of Peace'.[5] Trochaic inversion of the first foot (and the second and third) is vanishingly rare in Gower's octosyllabic line,[6] but more common in his pentameter. Gower was stricter than Chaucer with regard to the syllable count. After the manner of French syllable-counted poetry, he always wrote lines of eight syllables (in his tetrameters) or ten (in his pentameters), not counting optional feminine line endings.[7] It is the existence of this tradition of strict syllable-counted poetry that explains Chaucer's personal apology for headless lines in *The House of Fame*, where he asks Apollo, the God of wisdom, to make his poetry 'agreable / Though som vers fayle in a sillable' (1097–1098).[8]

Admitting that Chaucer took liberties with the anacrusis is one thing; learning to love them is another, and the history of metrical scholarship is one of grudging acceptance rather than enthusiasm. W.W. Skeat, who claims to have been the first person to notice the existence of headless lines,[9] conceded that Chaucer 'allowed himself to accept the principle of dropping the first syllable of the line'.[10] In his editorial practice, however, Skeat set about restoring the anacrusis. In Derek Pearsall's words, 'what Chaucer "allowed himself to accept" is clearly something that Chaucer accepted against his better judgment, or, more properly, against Skeat's better judgment, and the way is clear for the editor to remove as many of these unfortunate evidences of indulgence as he decently can'.[11] Bernhard ten Brink drew a distinction between Chaucer's short line, where 'the anacrusis may ... be suppressed', and the long line, where this should not be allowed:

> Personally, when in reading a Chaucerian poem in heroic metre I come upon a verse without anacrusis, I experience a jarring sensation for which I should be loth to make the poet responsible.[12]

In other words, headless pentameters should be attributed to Chaucer's scribes rather than to the great man himself. That this view is untenable was demonstrated by Markus Freudenberger, who showed that most headless lines in Chaucer have overwhelming manuscript support, but he, too, says nothing in their favour. Headless lines are genuine, he concludes, but 'whether Chaucer let them slip without notice or whether he was conscious of their abnormality is practically impossible to determine'.[13] In view of Chaucer's above-cited comments in *The House of Fame*, Freudenberger assumes that Chaucer knew what he was doing.

Needless to say, I share this assumption, but I do wish that something more positive was said about Chaucer's 'abnormality'. In this chapter, I shall attempt to do so by analysing the kinds of situations in which Chaucer saw fit to begin his line with a stressed syllable.

My study is based on an in-depth analysis of three poems, two in long-line verse, 'The Knight's Tale' and 'The Nun's Priest's Tale', and one, *The Book of the Duchess*, in short-line verse. To indicate that the patterns I observe in these poems are general ones in Chaucer, and that they go back to earlier English poetry, I also discuss some examples from Chaucer's other works and from an older English poem, *Cursor Mundi* (c. 1300).[14] My research suggests that it makes sense to consider initial inversion and headlessness together. Certainly, the two licences differ with regard to the syllable count, and there is good evidence to show that poets were sensitive to this difference, but the effect of both licences is comparable, and, as we shall see, Chaucer used them in the same situations.

Let us begin with some facts and figures. Edgar Shannon usefully provided some hard statistics in his study of Chaucer's octosyllabic verse. Comparing Chaucer's *Book of the Duchess* with *The House of Fame*, he notes that the percentage of headless lines is actually higher in the latter (13.6 per cent) than in the former (10.2 per cent). Since *The House of Fame* is also chronologically later, the headless line cannot be regarded as a sign of immaturity in Chaucer.[15] Trochaic inversion, which metrists have found less objectionable, is actually infrequent in both poems. Shannon found twenty-four examples in *The Book of the Duchess* (1333 lines), which amounts to 1.8 per cent, and only seventeen in *The House of Fame* (2158 lines), which is 0.8 per cent.[16] These are remarkably low figures, and, having examined Shannon's examples of trochaic inversion in *The Book of the Duchess*, I believe the real numbers are lower still. Various instances listed by Shannon are problematic: he posits disyllabic pronunciation for a word ('whether') that is often monosyllabic in Chaucer (whatever the manuscript spelling);[17] he assumes inflectional -e in contexts where this is questionable,[18] while the scansion of lines with disyllabic function words (e.g. prepositions such as 'under' and 'after') in initial position (and not just there) is more complicated than Shannon allows. Readers who are used to parsing iambic verse may have noticed how frequently such disyllables occur in positions where an iambic foot might be expected, both in Chaucer and in other poets. For instance:

> After my yonge childly wyt (*Book of the Duchess*, 1095)
> After the scole of Stratford-atte-Bowe (*CT* I.125)
> She longed so after the king (*Book of the Duchess*, 83)
> And heeld after the newe world the space (*CT* I.176)

> After our sentence plaining comes too late (Shakespeare, *Richard II*,
>   I.iii.471)[19]
> After thy innocent and busy stir (Wordsworth, *Prelude* 4.34)[20]

Of course, when pronounced in isolation such disyllables carry word stress on the first syllable, but what makes them malleable in verse is that in connected sentences both syllables are likely to be unstressed. In normal pronunciation, then, *Book of the Duchess*, 1095 is not stressed as /xx/x/x/, but rather as xxx/x/x/, and I.176 (of *CT*) not as x//xx/x/x/, but as x/xxx/x/x/x. And, given the expectations of the metre, three unstressed syllables can easily be assimilated to an iambic pattern. As Derek Attridge has observed, there are 'times when the indefiniteness of stress in a minor category word allows two possible scansions, and the line hovers between them'.[21] His examples – 'That comes to all, but torture without end' (Milton, *Paradise Lost*, 1.67) and 'Pride, Malice, Folly against Dryden rose' (Pope, *An Essay on Criticism*, 458) – illustrate the flexibility of disyllabic function words: word stress on the stronger syllable can certainly elevate it to a metrical beat, but the fact that function words are typically unstressed in a sentence also makes it possible for that syllable to function metrically as an offbeat.

It is remarkable how unusual trochaic inversion is when compared with headlessness in Chaucer's short-line verse. The contrast with Chaucer's pentameter is striking in this regard. 'The Nun's Priest's Tale' (626 lines) provides some revealing figures. By my reckoning (more conservative than Shannon's), there are forty-three cases of initial inversion in that tale (6.9 per cent),[22] but only eight cases of headless lines (1.3 per cent).[23] It thus appears that in his short line the syllable count mattered less to Chaucer than the regular alternation of stressed and unstressed syllables, while the reverse is true for his long line. This makes good sense. As Attridge has noted, the rhythm of the four-beat line is more insistently dipodic (i.e. alternating between beat and offbeat) than pentameter rhythm,[24] and since headlessness, unlike initial inversion, does not affect dipodic rhythm, Chaucer was naturally less inclined to begin his short line with /xx/ than he was to open it with /x/x. Since, however, Chaucer learned his pentameter lines from Romance models, the French decasyllable and the Italian hendecasyllable,[25] which were syllable-counted, and since long-line verse is less insistently dipodic, the long line is, conversely, more hospitable to initial inversion than to headlessness.

Given the dearth of initial inversions in Chaucer's tetrameter verse and the corresponding dearth of headless lines in Chaucer's pentameter, one can understand the temptation of trying to emend them out of existence. On closer inspection, however, Chaucer's omission of the initial anacrusis in both types of line turns out to be highly regular – not in the sense that it is statistically normal but in the sense that it tends to occur in predictable circumstances.

There is still much to be learned about these circumstances from an old study by Charles Langley Crow who examined Chaucer's prosody in *The House of Fame* in the light of two earlier English poems in the shorter couplet form, *Harrowing of Hell* (extant in the Auchinleck manuscript) and the Northern *Cursor Mundi*.[26] Crow noticed some interesting patterns with regard to headless lines in the two earlier English poems: they regularly occur at the start of a section or at the beginning of speeches, and they mark matters of earnest importance. In *Harrowing of Hell*, for instance, Crow found a clustering of headless lines in emotive speeches, in the dialectical debates of the disputants, and in verses that give orders and exhortations.[27] In *Harrowing of Hell*, the suppression of the anacrusis occurs so often that it is hard to know whether we are dealing with deliberate artistry or not, but in *Cursor Mundi* the percentage of headless lines (10 per cent, according to Crow) is more or less the same as that of Chaucer's *Book of the Duchess*, and the same patterns of usage obtain: in *Cursor Mundi*, too, the anacrusis is often dropped at the beginning of sections and speeches. Crow also observed another pattern in *Cursor Mundi*: headless lines are often found in the context of lists and in emphatic statements.[28] In *The House of Fame*, according to Crow, Chaucer similarly uses headless lines to mention something striking or extraordinary ('Twenty thousand in a route', 2119),[29] in lists ('By abstinence or by seknesse, / '*Prison*-stewe or gret distresse', 25–26; '*Lowd* or pryvee, foul or fair', 767); he uses them in asseverations and imprecations ('*Turne* us every drem to goode!', 58; '*Herke* wel, hyt is not rouned', 1030); and Chaucer, too, uses them at the beginning of sections and speeches (468, 729, 765, 1066, etc.).[30]

How does Crow's research stand up against advances in more recent scholarship? I offer a representative example of modern thinking:

The octosyllabic couplet had been used in English poetry for over a century and Chaucer uses it with great freedom. In actual fact, the octosyllabic couplet is particularly prone to produce a monotonous

> and droning measure. But Chaucer infuses its unvarying note with variety by frequent 'enjambement' and by irregularities in the verse (the first metrical foot often has only one syllable, there are unexpected inversions, etc. ...).[31]

Crow is much more insightful, in my view. First, he provides evidence to show that, in allowing 'irregularities' in his verse (including enjambement, as we shall see), Chaucer was not an innovator but a follower of the art of earlier English poetry; second, he gets beyond the reductive (and empirically unverifiable) argument that Chaucer took metrical liberties in order to avoid monotony. If Crow is right, Chaucer and poets before him had more immediate objectives in mind when they began lines with a beat: they wanted, for instance, to announce the beginning of a speech, to mark the transition to a new section, to flag up items in a list and so on.

I think that Crow's observations are not only on the right track but also have applicability over and beyond the specific metre he studied (octosyllabic) and the specific phenomenon he was interested in (headless lines). In fact, they apply equally to Chaucer's pentameter verse and to his use of initial inversion. A closer look at some of Crow's categories will hopefully bear this out.

A good category to begin with is that of orders and exhortations, to which we should add interrogatives. Instances can easily be found by looking out for line-initial verbs in the imperative, subjunctive or interrogative. Below are some examples from *The Book of the Duchess*:

> *Passe* we over until eft (41)
> *Helpe* me out of thys distresse (110)
> '*Go* we faste!' and gan to ryde (371)
> *Shulde* y now repente me / To love? (1116–1117)

The first of these (*Passe* is subjunctive plural) is probably a rare instance of an octosyllabic line with trochaic inversion. Once we recognize this pattern in Chaucer's short line, it is easy to see that he carried it across into his pentameter, where headless lines and initial inversion again frequently coincide with line-initial imperatives, subjunctives and interrogatives, as in the following examples from 'The Knight's Tale' and 'The Nun's Priest's Tale'.

> Thanked be Fortune and hir false wheel (I.925)
> Love if thee list, for I love and ay shal (I.1183)
> Seyeth youre avys, and holdeth you apayd (I.1868)

> Foyne, if hym list, on foote, himself to were (I.2550)
> Seyde he nat thus, 'Ne no fors of dremes'? (VII.2941)
> Ware the sonne in his ascenscioun (VII.2956)
> Mette he nat that he sat upon a tree / [...?] (VII.3139)
> Redeth Ecclesiaste of flaterye (VII.3329)
> 'Turneth again, ye proude cherles alle!' (VII.3409)
> Taketh the moralite, goode men (VII.3440)

The last of these lines, which I think scans '/x/x/x/x/', is a rare head-less line,[32] as probably is VII.2956.[33]

When the verb is not merely stating something (indicative) but ordering, asking, exhorting (imperative, interrogative, subjunc-tive), Chaucer, like poets before and after him,[34] clearly felt there was something to be gained by pushing that verb into the position normally occupied by a quiet unstressed syllable, whether by initial inversion or initial truncation. The bittiness of isolated examples cannot really bring out Chaucer's design, so it is worth looking at continuous passage. Below is the first stanza from Chaucer's *Com-plaint to Mars*:

> *Gladeth*, ye foules, of the morowe gray;
> Lo, Venus, risen among yon rowes rede.
> And floures fressh, honoureth ye this day,
> For when the sunne uprist then wol ye sprede.
> But ye lovers, that lye in any drede,[35]
> *Fleeth*, lest wicked tonges yow espye.
> Lo, yond the sunne, the candel of jelosye! (*Complaint of Mars*, 1–7)

I have italicized the verbs responsible for the trochaic inversion, and it surely matters that they are imperatives.

The emphasis provided by the abrupt beginning is obviously one of the factors behind the omission of the anacrusis here. This con-sideration is also relevant in cases when metrical marking points up rhetorical devices, as in this example from 'The Knight's Tale':

> How greet a sorwe suffreth now Arcite!
> The deeth he feeleth thurgh his herte smyte.
> He wepeth, wayleth, crieth pitously;
> To sleen himself he waiteth prively.
> He seide, 'Allas that day that I was born!
> *Now* is my prysoun worse than biforn,
> *Now* is me shape eternally to dwelle,
> *Noght* in purgatorie, *but* in helle.' (I.1219–1226)

The last three lines begin with a beat, the final one (a rarer headless line) emphasizing the antithesis ('Noght ... but') and the preceding two reinforcing the anaphora (Now is ...). Chaucer uses a similar ploy in Saturn's speech:

> '*Myn* is the drenchyng in the see so wan;
> *Myn* is the prison in the derke cote;
> *Myn* is the stranglyng and the hangyng by the throte ...' (I.2456–2458)

Here, as in the previous passage, Chaucer achieves striking rhetorical effects by combining anaphora with rhythmical inversion.

In contexts of logical (or pseudo-logical) argument, where Crow noticed the suppression of the initial offbeat in earlier English poetry, the omission of the anacrusis is also a form of rhetorical emphasis. 'The Nun's Priest Tale' provides many delightful examples, because the speakers in the tale are so comically argumentative. Here is Pertelote (a hen!) maintaining that dreams are unreliable:

> Nothyng, God woot, but vanitee in sweven is.
> *Swevenes* engendren of replecciouns ... (VII.2922–2923)

And here is Chauntecleer (a cockerel) adducing the Latin proverb that women cannot be trusted:

> For al so siker as *In principio*,
> *Mulier est hominis confusio* –
> Madame, the sentence of this Latyn is:
> *Womman* is mannes joye and al his blis. (VII.3163–3166)

Although Chauntecleer gives a preposterous translation of the Latin saying, he does try to make the English 'translation' sound as authoritative as the Latin maxim. The metrical inversion in the phrase 'Womman is', paralleling *Mulier est*, produces the sound of table-thumping logic. Chauntecleer adopts the same hectoring tone when he expounds the saying that 'murder will out':

> O blisful God, that art so just and trewe,
> Lo, how that thow biwreyest mordre alway!
> *Mordre* wol out, that se we day by day.
> *Mordre* is so wlatsom and abhomynable
> To God, that is just and resonable,
> That he ne wol not suffre it heled be,
> Though it abiye a yeer, or two, or thre.
> *Mordre* wil out; this my conclusioun. (VII.3050–3057)

This is the prosody of a logician who thinks he has hit the nail on the head. The narrator of 'The Nun's Priest's Tale' suffers from the same addiction to bombast and didacticism, and the metrical device of initial inversion is brilliantly used to expose his plodding scholasticism:

> Wheither that Goddes worthy forwityng
> Streyneth[36] me nedely for to doon a thyng –
> '*Nedely*' clepe I simple necessitee – (VII.3243–3245)

We have strayed from poetry into academic pedantry, and Chaucer's metre knows it.[37]

In the cases of line-initial imperatives, subjunctives and interrogatives, however, we need to consider the possibility that prosody served not only for emphasis but also to guide interpretation by clarifying grammar. In Modern English, punctuation performs this crucial hermeneutic function. The imperative mood of a verb can be indicated with an exclamation mark, the interrogative with a question mark, and so on. In an age when writers did not have our system of punctuation at their disposal (and could not trust any of the punctuation marks they *did* use to be accurately transmitted), metre may have had a clarifying function like that of modern punctuation.

The use of line-initial beats to mark the beginning of new sections, speeches and addresses, a technique that Chaucer must have picked up from earlier English poetry,[38] can similarly be considered both as a form of emphasis and as a form of signposting equivalent to punctuation. In a modern edition, where new sections are typically indented and where speech is marked with inverted commas, the rhetorical effect is perhaps the first thing we notice. Here, for example, is Chaucer's transition from Theseus's philosophical reflections as it appears in the *Riverside Chaucer*:

> [']I rede that we make of sorwes two
> O parfit joye, lastynge everemo.
> And looketh now, wher moost sorwe is herinne,
> Ther wol we first amenden and begynne.
> 	'*Suster*', quod he, 'this is my fulle assent...' (I.3071–3075)

The initial inversion in the address 'Suster' is heard as a break in the iambic metre, which reinforces Theseus's shift from one address (*we*) to another (Emily), and from one rhetorical mode (general advice) to another (personal direction). Were we to read this without the aids of a modern edition, however, we might be more conscious of the fact that the initial inversion has a clarifying function equivalent to that of the modern indent and the inverted comma. The widespread use of initial inversion and initial truncation to alert readers (and listeners) to changes of speakers or direct addresses should probably be understood in this context.

> *sir* ho said befor thi barnage (*Cursor Mundi*, 13162)
> *lorde* ho saide thai are away (*Cursor Mundi*, 13752)
> '*Geffrey*, thou wost ryght wel this' (*House of Fame*, 729)
> '*Sir*', quod I, 'this game is doon' (*Book of the Duchess*, 539)
> '*Sir*', quod I, 'wher is she now?'
> '*Now*', quod he, and stynte anoon (*Book of the Duchess*, 1298–1299)
> '*May*, with alle thy floures and thy grene' (*CT* I.1510)
> '*Lordynges*', quod he, 'now herkneth for the beste' (*CT* I.788)
> '*Nay*', quod the fox, 'but God yeve hym meschaunce' (*CT* VII.3434)
> '*Sir*, your glove.' 'Not mine; my gloves are on' (*Two Kinsmen of Verona*, II.ii.1)
> '*Gentlemen*, importune me no father' (*Taming of the Shrew*, I.i.48)

It has been suggested that Shakespeare learned this trick from Marlowe,[39] but the continuities of metrical practice in English poetry, which in turn draw on continuities in the English language, make it hazardous to claim anyone as an inventor.

The main visual cues that medieval scribes had at their disposal to signal narrative transitions were large capitals and paraphs. In some Chaucer manuscripts (notably Ellesmere and Hengwrt), paraphs and capitals are regularly used to mark new sections. Visual and aural cues frequently coincide:

> ¶ffirst in the temple of Venus / maystow se
> Wroght on the wal / ful pitous to biholde[40]
> The broken slepes / and the sike coldes ...
> (Ellesmere: I.1918–1920; cf. 1975)[41]

The beginning of the description of the Temple of Venus is here doubly marked by the paraph and the break in the metre ('ffirst ...'). Of course, paraphs and line-initial beats do not always go together – see, for example, *CT* I.1914 – but anyone trying to collect examples of lines without anacrusis will gather a good crop by looking for indents (in modern editions) or for paraphs and large capitals (in medieval manuscripts).[42]

We have already mentioned that lines without anacrusis sometimes usher in direct speech. Below is an example from 'The Knight's Tale', where Ellesmere has a large capital instead of a paraph:

> And doune he kneleth / with ful humble chere
> And herte soor / and seyde in this manere
> **F**airest of faire / o lady myn Venus ¶ The preyere of Palamon
> (Ellesmere: I.2219–2221)

In this category we should also include lines without anacrusis which, conversely, mark the resumption of the story after direct speech, as in the example below:

> And euerich of vs / take his auenture
> **G**reet was the strif / and long / bitwix hem tweye
> (Ellesmere: I.1186–1187)

Comparing these passages in different Chaucer manuscripts, it is clear that the use of enlarged capitals and paraphs is very inconsistent.[43] The aural marking of transitions, even when Chaucer may already have marked them visually, should therefore be regarded not as an added flourish but as a much more future-proof method for signposting narrative segmentation.

As noted by Crow, another context in which the stressed line opening frequently occurs is the catalogue. From a poetic perspective catalogues are fascinating, and the metrical problems they pose, both for poets and readers, are akin to the intellectual problems we face when we are exposed to 'lists of various items': is every new item just 'more of the same' or is it different? In other words, how do we sort one item from the other? Discerning rhythmical patterns is a form of 'sorting', and Chaucer's catalogues sometimes set us difficult prosodic challenges. Below is a case in point:

> But how the fyr was maked upon highte,
> Ne eek the names how the trees highte,
> As ook, firre, birch, aspe, alder, holm, popler,
> Wylugh, elm, plane, assh, box, chastein, lynde, laurer,
> *Mapul*, thorn, bech, hasel, ew, whippeltree,
> How they weren feld shal nat be toold for me ... (*CT* I.2919–2924)

One important lesson we learn from this and comparable catalogues (from *Cursor Mundi* to Milton[44]) is that linguistic stress and metrical stress are not the same; rather, metrical stress is abstracted from linguistic stress. In English, each item in a list tends to be stressed (so the linguistic stress pattern of 2921 is $x////x/x/$). However, as W.K. Wimsatt rightly pointed out, metre has a coercive effect and, where an iambic metre has been established, sequences of even syllables (whether unstressed or stressed) will resolve themselves into regular metre.[45] As Wimsatt put it provocatively, line 2921 is 'perfectly regular':

```
x  /  x   /   x  / x   /   x  /
As ook, firre, birch, asp, alder, holm, popler
```

Although I accept Wimsatt's argument, there is, of course, something knowingly irregular about these lines. Making these lines work as iambic pentameter involves us telling our 'oak' (beat) from our 'fir' (offbeat), and the metrical challenges seem to mount as the list continues. In I.2921, etymology can help us to distinguish 'alder' (Germanic, with initial stress) from 'popler' (French-derived, with final stress), but in the next line French-derived 'chestain' and 'laurer' need to be stressed differently, and 'wylugh' (willow) needs to be pronounced without the second written vowel (easier to do for Chaucer and his readers, for whom the monosyllabic pronunciation was normal[46]):

```
  x   /    x   /   x   / x   /  x  /
Wylugh, elm, plane, assh, box, chastein, lynde, laurer,
```

Finally, in the last line of the list, the trick is to slur the final vowel of 'hasel'.[47] The line is headless:

```
 / x   /   x   /  x  / x  /
Mapul, thorn, bech, hasel, ew, whippeltree,
```

The lines may be 'perfectly regular', but there is a lot of sorting out to be done, as might be expected in a list.

Thus, in Chaucer's catalogues (and those of earlier poets, as Crow noticed) we often (though by no means always) find a tension between linguistic stress and metrical stress. The frequent occurrence of initial inversion and headless lines in lists (cf. *Book of the Duchess*, 349, 850, 954, 956, *CT* I.1926–1927, I.1931–1932, I.2012, I.2501, I.2509, I.2511, I.2928, IV.869–871) is symptomatic of that tension, which runs through some of Chaucer's most memorable lines:

And goodly of hire speche in general,
Charitable, estatlich, lusty, fre;
Ne never mo ne lakked hire pite;
Tendre-herted, slydynge of corage ... (*Troilus* V.822–825)

The suppression of the anacrusis (note that *Troilus* V.823 and V.825 are headless lines) is a knowing concession to the linguistic reality that in normal language items in an asyndetic list form a succession

of beats, though Chaucer, in refusing to surrender entirely to linguistic normality (as when demoting some items in a list to off-
beats), acknowledges that making poetry out of normality is an art
that requires the agile processing skills of a poet as well as those of
his readers.

In catalogues, too, however, deviations from normal prosody have
the function of clarifying grammatical relationships. In the passage
above, for instance, the line-initial beats on 'Charitable' and 'Tendre-
herted' could be said to do the work that in a modern edition is
accomplished by the preceding comma and semi-colon: they signal that we are in list-mode. This hermeneutic function is crucial
in cases of enjambement. That Chaucer liked run-on lines is well
known, but I do not think anyone has observed that in Chaucer, and
in earlier English verse, enjambement is often followed immediately
by a line-initial beat. Below are some examples:

> quarfore he saide thus has thou
> *haldin* the gode wine to nowe (*Cursor Mundi*, 13407–13409)
>
> Quen herodes herd that ho wald non
> *Gift* take bot the heued of John (*Cursor Mundi*, 13168–13169)
>
> This es yur sun, thai said, and yee
> *Sai* that blind man born was he. (*Cursor Mundi*, Cotton Vespasian,
> 13601–13602)
>
> Hath wonder that the king ne com
> *Hom*, for it was a longe terme (*Book of the Duchess*, 78–79)
>
> But, goode swete herte, that ye
> *Bury* my body (*Book of the Duchess*, 206–207)
>
> I was ryght glad, and up anoon
> *Took* my hors (*Book of the Duchess*, 356–357)
>
> Right as the humour of malencolie
> *Causeth* ful many a man in sleep to crie (VII.2933–2934)
>
> And atte thridde tyme yet his felawe
> *Cam*, as hym thoughte ... (VII.3013–3014)
>
> Affermeth dremes, and seyth that they ben
> *Warnynge* of thynges that men after seen. (VII.3125–3126)
>
> That, as of light the somer schene
> *Passeth* the sterre ... (*Parliament of Fowles*, 299–300)

Here metre comes to the aid of syntactical comprehension. Sense
units and line units normally coincide, and a new line and a new
sense unit normally begin with an offbeat; but in cases of enjambe-

ment, where this is not the case, the lack of an anacrusis usefully signals that we have not in fact embarked on a new sense unit. Instead of an unstressed syllable to mark a new beginning, what we get is linguistic and metrical stress on a grammatical complement that clamours for our attention because we need it to make sense of the preceding verse. Visual cues to warn readers of enjambement were not unknown to medieval readers and writers,[48] but metrical structures are more stable in manuscript transmission than punctuation marks, and line-initial beats seem to be have been used by Chaucer and earlier poets to make enjambement audible.

Dryden referred to iambic feet that lack the initial offbeat as 'lame feet',[49] and in the lines I have cited this halting effect is palpable: it is almost as if the words in italics have been forced back and prevented from joining the rising rhythm of the verse. When Chaucer uses enjambement to increase speed and velocity, this halting effect is evidently not what he wanted, and it is obvious that in many cases of enjambement the suppression of the anacrusis is neither needed nor desirable.[50] However, when quickening the tempo is not the point of enjambement, Chaucer's use of initial inversion to reunite grammatical partners separated by line breaks needs, I think, to be recognized as a subtle aspect of his poetic art. We only need to open *Troilus and Criseyde* to see how common and how deliberate this technique is:

> Now fel it so that in the town ther was
> *Dwellyng* a lord of gret auctorite (1.64–65)

> And seyde, 'Lat your fadres treson gon
> *Forth* with meschaunce, and ye yourself in joie
> *Dwelleth* with us, whil yow good list, in Troie.' (1.116–118)

> I dar wel seyn, in al, that Troilus
> *Seyde* in his song, loo, every word right thus. (1.396–397)

The use of prosody to assist comprehension in cases of enjambement has a clear analogue in constructions where grammatical connections are severed by parenthetical phrases or clauses:

> Allas, I se a serpent or a theef,
> That many a trewe man hath doon mescheef,
> *Goon* at his large ... (I.1325–1327)

> And yet hath love, maugree hir eyen two,
> *Broght* hem hider ... (I.1796–1797)

> That is to seyn, that wheither he or thou
> May with his hundred, as I spak of now,
> *Sleen* his contrarie ... (I.1857–1859)

> Til that the pale Saturnus the colde,
> That knew so manye of aventures olde,
> *Foond* in his olde experience an art (I.2443–2445)

> Lo, how that Jacob, as thise clerkes rede,
> Be good conseil of his mooder Rebekke
> *Boond* the kydes skyn aboute his nekke (IV.1362–1364)

> As Chauntecleer, among his wives alle,
> *Sat* on his perche ... (VII.2883–2884; my punctuation)

> Criseyde, which that herde hym in this wise,
> *Thoughte*, I shal felen what he meneth, iwis. (*Troilus*, 2.386–387)

In all these examples, the italicized verb is one that has been held over after a parenthetical phrase/clause that separates the verb from its grammatical subject. What the prosody does is to ask us to take note of the verb and to remind us that we have unfinished business with the main clause. This technique, too, goes back to earlier English poetry.[51]

There are some other interesting patterns in Chaucer's use of initial inversion and headless lines that cannot be dealt with in detail here but that should be briefly mentioned. Clauses that begin with a present participle or a past participle – for example, 'With the sharpe swerd over his heed, / *Hangynge* by a soutil twynes threed' (*CT* I.2029–2030) and 'His cote armure was of clooth of Tars / *Couched* with perles white and rounde and grete' (*CT* I.2160–2161) – often lack an anacrusis. Here, too, metre has a clarifying function equivalent to modern punctuation. Grammatical inversion involving adjectives ('Bright was the sonne', *CT* I.1062, 'Blak was his berd', *CT* I.2139) or adverbs ('Stille [quietly] in that feeld he took al nyght his reste', *CT* I.1003, 'Faire in the sond ... / Lith Pertelote', *CT* VII.3267–3268) are naturally accompanied by metrical inversion. The class of adverbs that linguists call affirmative adverbs are more likely than others to be involved in inversion and headless lines ('Certes', *CT* IV.346, VII.2926, VII.3303, 'Soothly', II.495, 'Trewly', *Book of the Duchess*, 981), as is the adverb 'right' in the sense of 'exactly', 'immediately' (*CT* I.2904, VII.2933, VIII.3065). There is much more that could be said, but I want to end this analysis by saying that not all examples are susceptible to grammatical or rhetorical explanations. Sometimes Chaucer simply begins a line with a metrically accented word that does not bear much linguistic stress at all. This class is probably the most offensive to metrical purists, and some have wished it away – 'Probably Mr. Skeat is right in admitting a monosyllabic foot, but it should not be accepted in any particular case, unless the single syllable it contains has a decided stress'[52] – but the class certainly exists:

> Wel koude she carie a morsel and wel kepe
> *That* no drop ne fille upon hire brest. (*CT* I.130–131)

> God for his manace hym so soore smoot
>
> ...
> That in his guttes carf it so and boot
> *That* his peynes weren importable. (*CT* VII.2599–2602)

These headless lines actually begin with xx/ in terms of linguistic stress, and it is only the metrical expectation of alternating stressed and unstressed syllables that realizes *That* as a beat (note that it is an offbeat in *CT* VII.2601).[53] Linguistic rhythms, as we have already observed, are sometimes at variance with metrical ones, but as long as they have not modulated too far away from each other, metrical regularity can be extracted from wayward rhythms.

What can we learn from this analysis of lines without anacrusis? One conclusion to be drawn from it is that Chaucer was not in all formal respects the father of English poetry. He may have pioneered the iambic pentameter, but headless lines, initial inversion and enjambement (phenomena that turn out to be closely related) all occur in earlier English poetry, under the same discursive conditions. Chaucer kept the old art alive in his own verse and passed it on to later poets (as we have seen, some of Shakespeare's headless lines are comparable to Chaucer's). A second conclusion is that the licences he embraced in his short-line verse are also found in his long-line verse, but in inverse proportions. Headless lines, which occur frequently in his short-line verse, are very rare in his long-line verse, and conversely initial inversion, common in Chaucer's pentameter verse, is very rare in his short-line verse. The explanation is probably to be found in the more rigidly dipodic nature of the four-beat line and in the syllable-counted models from which Chaucer developed the pentameter. A third conclusion is that, in both his short-line and his long-line verse, headless lines and initial inversion tend to occur in particular discursive environments – which in turn suggests that Chaucer had particular discursive ends in mind. These obviously include emphasis, as when initial inversion and truncation occur alongside rhetorical devices (anaphora), grammatical inversion and in the context of logical argumentation. However, they also occur in contexts where metre appears to have an analytical function, for example in lists and catalogues, at the beginning of speeches and sections, and in sentences where enjambement or parenthetical clauses and phrases create potential difficulties for readers and listeners. In these contexts, the metrical pointing does not primarily serve rhetorical purposes but clarifies narrative segmentation and grammatical relationships. Of course, the expressive and heuristic functions of metre need not exclude each other, as my discussion of line-initial imperatives, subjunctives and interrogatives will have suggested, but these are complications that cannot detain us any longer. Hopefully, future researchers will prefer such complexities to the simpler view that Chaucer introduced metrical variants to avoid monotony.

Ad Putter is Fellow of the British Academy and teaches at the University of Bristol, where he is Professor of Medieval English Literature. He has written extensively on English and European literature of the Middle Ages, and on metre. His books include *Sir Gawain and the Green Knight and French Arthurian Romance* (Oxford University Press, 1996), *An Introduction to the Gawain Poet* (Longman, 1997) and *Studies in the Metre of Alliterative Verse* (Medium Aevum, 2007). He has also edited, with Elizabeth Archibald, *The Cambridge Companion to the Arthurian Legend* (Cambridge University Press, 2009) and, with Myra Stokes, *The Works of the Gawain Poet* (Penguin 2014).

Notes

1. See, for example, G.L. Brook, who in his edition of the Harley Lyrics explains the substitution of a four-beat line verse by a three-beat line as a 'form of licence to avoid monotony': *Harley Lyrics* (Manchester: Manchester University Press, 1956), 18. It is salutary to read Thomas G. Duncan on this argument: 'And with the phrase "a form of licence to avoid monotony", all further analysis ... is abandoned' ('Two Middle English Penitential Lyrics: Sound and Scansion', in *Late Medieval Religious Texts and Their Transmission: Essays in Honour of A.I. Doyle*, ed. Alastair Minnis [Cambridge: D.S. Brewer, 1994], 55–65, here 56).

2. Good recent descriptions of Chaucer's metrical practice are offed by Donka Minkova, in 'The Forms of Verse', in *A Companion to Medieval English Literature and Culture c.1350–c.1500*, ed. Peter Brown (Oxford: Wiley-Blackwell, 2009),

176–195, and by Martin J. Duffell, *Chaucer's Verse Art in its European Context* (Tempe: Arizona Center for Medieval and Renaissance Studies, 2018). Both Minkova and Duffell accept headless lines and lines with initial inversion as possible variations on Chaucer's normal metrical structure.

3. Derek Attridge, *The Rhythms of English Poetry* (London: Longman, 1982), 211.

4. Martin J. Duffell, *A New History of English Metre* (London: MHRA, 2008), 90–91.

5. G.C. Macaulay, ed., *The English Works of John Gower*, EETS o.s. 39, 56 (London: Oxford University Press, 1900–1901), 2 vols, II, 481–494.

6. Edgar F. Shannon, 'Chaucer's Use of the Octosyllabic Verse in the *Book of the Duchess* and the *House of Fame*', *Journal of English and Germanic Philology* 12 (1913): 277–294.

7. Macaulay, *English Works of John Gower*, I, cxx–cxxi.

8. All Chaucer quotations are taken from *The Riverside Chaucer*, ed. Larry D. Benson et al. (Boston, MA: Houghton Mifflin, 1987). I am not convinced by Paull F. Baum's argument that Chaucer here 'means that some syllable in a line may here and there be not altogether right, metrically', and that he points up this meaning in 'fayle in a sillable' by 'forcing the metrical stress on *a* and on the suffix –*able*': *Chaucer's Verse* (Durham, NC: Duke University Press, 1961), 7. In alternating rhythm, the second of three unstressed syllables will naturally be perceived as accented (so there is no question of 'forcing' it), while a French-derived noun 'often retains its original accent in Chaucer': Bernhard ten Brink, *The Language and Metre of Chaucer*, rev. Friedrich Kluge, trans. M. Bentinck Smith (London: Macmillan, 1901), 199. Cf. the pronunciation of 'sillable' (also with stress on the second syllable) in Gower, *Confessio Amantis* VIII, 2049, in Macaulay, *English Works of John Gower*.

9. But note John Dryden in the 'Dedication and Preface' to his *Fables*: 'It were an easy matter to produce some thousands of his verses which are lame for want of half a foot ... and which no pronunciation can make otherwise': *The Poems of John Dryden*, ed. Paul Hammond and David Hopkins (Harlow: Longman, 1995–2005), 5 vols, V, 33–90, here 70.

10. W.W. Skeat, ed., *The Complete Works of Geoffrey Chaucer* (London: Oxford University Press, 1894), 6 vols, VI, lxxxviii.

11. Derek Pearsall, 'Chaucer's Meter: The Evidence of the Manuscripts', in *Medieval Literature: Texts and Interpretation*, ed. Tim W. Machan (Binghamton, NY: Medieval and Renaissance Texts and Studies, 1991), 41–57, repr. in *The Art of Chaucer's Verse*, ed. Alan T. Gaylord (New York: Routledge, 2001), 131–144, here 132.

12. Ten Brink, *Language and Metre of Chaucer*, 215.

13. Markus Freudenberger, *Über das Fehlen des Auftaks in Chaucers heroischen Verse*, Erlanger Beiträge zur Englischen Philologie IV (Erlangen: Deichert, 1889), 84 (my translation from the German).

14. I examined lines 12527–13961, in the edition by Richard Morris, ed., *Cursor Mundi*, EETS o.s. 57, 59, 62, 66, 68, 99, 101 (London: Oxford University Press, 1874–1913), 7 vols, III. Quotations are from the Fairfax manuscript unless otherwise indicated, and thorns and yoghs have been modernized.

15. Shannon, 'Chaucer's Use of the Octosyllabic Verse', 279–281.

16. Percentages have been rounded up/down to the first decimal place.

17. This affects the scansion of *Book of the Duchess*, 121 and 1134 (1133 in Shannon's numbering). Manuscript spelling cannot be taken as a reliable guide. For

instance, as Friedrich Wild observed (*Die sprachlichen Eigentümlichkeiten der wichtigeren Chaucer-Handschriften und die Sprache Chaucers* [Vienna: Braumüller, 1915], 281), metre demands monosyllabic *wher* ('whether') at *CT* I.1125, even though the manuscripts have a disyllabic spelling. Cf. *Book of the Duchess*, 886. Even if the form *whether* were disyllabic, trochaic inversion cannot be assumed. See my comments about disyllabic function words below.

18. For instance, at *Book of the Duchess*, 110, 'Helpe me out of thys dystresse', we are dealing with an imperative of a verb that was strong and so did not take inflectional -e, as the subsequent line confirms, 'And yeve me grace my lord to se', and at 736, 'Nolde nat love hir, and ryght thus', we are dealing with an auxiliary that might or might not take final -*e* (cf. *CT* III.1842, VII.76).

19. This and all subsequent quotations from Shakespeare are from *Shakespeare: Complete Works*, ed. J.W. Craig (Oxford: Oxford University Press, 1980).

20. William Wordsworth, *Complete Poetical Works* (London: Macmillan, 1888).

21. Attridge, *Rhythms of English Poetry*, 222. Ten Brink called this 'level stress': 'There are altogether three methods conceivable for the reconciliation of accent and rhythm when at variance: either the accent must yield to the exigencies of the verse – accent-shift; or the rhythm must conform to the normal accentuation – inversion of the metrical measure; or finally, in delivery a compromise must be attempted of such a character that the hearer remains conscious both of the natural accentuation and of the claims of the rhythm – level stress – veiled rhythm' (*Language and Metre of Chaucer*, 190). In his examples (224), disyllabic closed-class words are well represented.

22. See 2844, 2881, 2884, 2906, 2923, 2926, 2927, 2933, 2934, 2941, 2969, 2997, 3014, 3052, 3053, 3057, 3065, 3100, 3126, 3130, 3132, 3134, 3139, 3151, 3166, 3185, 3193, 3195, 3199, 3201, 3223, 3228, 3244, 3262, 3267, 3303, 3329, 3332, 3356, 3392, 3409, 3433, 3443.

23. See 2956, 3026, 3235, 3245, 3256, 3257, 3394, 3440.

24. In Attridge's words, 'The five-beat line does not bring with it the sense of a strong underlying rhythm; it observes the heightened regularity of movement created by the alternation of stressed and unstressed syllables, without those rhythmic pulses grouping themselves consistently – and insistently – into twos and fours' (*Rhythms of English Poetry*, 126).

25. On the influence of the Italian model in particular, see Martin J. Duffell, '"The craft so long to lerne": Chaucer's Invention of the Iambic Pentameter', *Chaucer Review* 39 (2000): 269–288.

26. Charles Langley Crow, *Zur Geschichte des kurzen Reimpaars im Mittelenglischen* (Göttingen: Kästner, 1892).

27. Ibid., 13–14.

28. Ibid., 26–27.

29. This usage vindicates the headless pentameter line describing the numerous books owned by the Clerk in the 'General Prologue': 'Twenty bookes, clad in blak or reed' (I.294). The headless line has the support of the best manuscripts (El, Hg, Gg, Cp, Pw, La), though Ps 'corrects' the syllable count with 'Twenty good bookis …' (cited from the edition of Ps by Meredith Clermont-Ferrand, *Jean d'Angoulême's Copy of the Canterbury Tales: An Annotated Edition of Bibliothèque Nationale's Fond Anglais 39* [Lewiston, NY: Mellen, 2008]).

30. Crow, *Zur Geschichte*, 48–50.

31. Wolfgang Clemen, *Chaucer's Early Poetry*, trans. C.A.M. Sym (London: Routledge, 2013), 121.

32. 'Goode' as a plural adjective would normally take pronounced inflectional -e, but in the phrase 'goode men' Middle English poets had the option of treating it as a compound element (cf. VII.3445, 'As seith my lord, so make us alle goode men', and see *Middle English Dictionary* s.v. *god man, god-man*).

33. Cf. Norman Davis: 'Some imperatives of short-stemmed weak verbs are written with -*e*, but meter seldom shows it to have been pronounced' (*Riverside Chaucer*, xxxiii).

34. Cf. *Cursor Mundi*, 13731, 13754, 13785, 13796, etc., and the following examples of headless lines in Shakespeare:

    > Hark, Ventidius / I do not know (*Antony and Cleopatra*, II.ii.16)
    > Say you so? Then I shall pose you quickly (*Measure for Measure*, II.iv.51)
    > Come my Lord. I'll lead you to your tent (*1 Henry IV*, V.iv.9)
    > Know you Don Antonio, your countryman? (*Two Kinsmen of Verona*, II.iv.54)

35. With this line compare *Troilus and Criseyde*, 4.323: 'O ye loveris, that heigh upon the whiel', where the line-initial beat signals, as elsewhere in Chaucer (cf. II.20, VII.2239), a direct address to an audience.

36. For the use of initial inversion in this line, see the discussion of enjambement below.

37. A comparable example of characterization through metre is found in the 'General Prologue'. Chaucer tells us the Summoner is loud (he does not speak but *cries* [I.646]), and Chaucer registers his aggressive assertiveness as he switches from indirect to direct speech: 'For in his purse he sholde ypunnysshed be. / "*Purse* is the erchedekenes helle", seyde he' (I.658–659). In *The Book of the Duchess*, the corrections which the Black Knight offers to his own reasoning and that of the Dreamer's are consistently marked by headlessness (1045, 1075, 1115, 1137).

38. Crow's observations apropos of *Harrowing of Hell* and *Cursor Mundi* are well founded. In my sample from *Cursor Mundi*, the poet's tendency to begin new sections (usually marked with paraphs in the manuscripts) with a line-initial beat is plain to see. For instance:

    > ¶ leue we him a litel quyle (13000)
    > ¶ Lordingis in that ilk cuntree (13360)
    > ¶ Efter that this signe was done (13520)

    Beginnings of speeches are also frequently marked by the absence of anacrusis:

    > lorde thai saide quat is this man (13529)
    > how gat thou thi sight quod thai (13565)
    > ¶ herde ye this lurdan, quod thai (13660)

39. Peter Groves, in an otherwise excellent article, 'Shakespeare's "Short" Pentameters and the Rhythms of Dramatic Verse', in *Stylistics and Shakespeare's Language: Transdisciplinary Approaches*, ed. Mireille Ravassat and Jonathan Culpeper (New York: Continuum, 2011), 119–138.

40. In this parenthetical line, the trochaic inversion, 'Wroght on the wal', also clarifies organization (in this case grammar): see discussion below.

41. Diplomatic transcriptions of 'The Knight's Tale' from the Ellesmere manuscript are based on *A Six-Text Print of Chaucer's Canterbury Tales*, ed. F.J. Furnivall,

Chaucer Society Publications, first series, 1 (London: Trübner, 1869), which I have checked against the online Ellesmere manuscript (San Marino, Huntington Library, MS EL 26 C9): http://hdl.huntington.org/cdm/ref/collection/p15150coll7/id/2838. Otiose final flourishes have been ignored.

42. See, e.g., I.1126, I.1975, I.2483.

43. For instance, MS Gg uses very few paraphs and capitals to mark sections; see Furnivall's *Six-Text Print*.

44. Cf. 'mark, luke, matthew his felawes / bot John was sot[i]list in his sawes (*Cursor Mundi*, 13442–13443), 'Yong, fresh, strong, and hardy as lyoun' (*Troilus*, 5.829), both headless lines, and, with anacrusis, 'With floures white, blewe, yelwe, and rede' (*Parliament of Fowles*, 186), 'Words, vows, fits, tears and love's full sacrifice' (Shakespeare, *Troilus and Cressida* I.ii.440) and 'Rocks, caves, lakes, fens, bogs, dens, and shades of death' (*Paradise Lost*, 2.621).

45. W.K. Wimsatt, 'The Rule and the Norm: Halle and Keyser on Chaucer's Meter', *College English* 31 (1970): 744–788.

46. See Wild, *Sprachlichen Eigentümlichkeiten*, 264, who compares *sorwe, folwe, holwe*, etc.

47. Ten Brink, *Language and Metre of Chaucer*: 'A weak *e* in the final syllable before a single final consonant may be slurred if the following word begins with a vowel' (88). Cf. 'fader of' (I.2469) and 'candel at' (III.334).

48. See Malcolm Parkes, *Pause and Effect: A History of Punctuation in the West* (London: Ashgate, 1992), 96–97; and Derek Pearsall, 'The Wollaton Hall Gower Manuscript (WLC/LM/8) Considered in the Context of Other Manuscripts of the *Confessio Amantis*', in *The Wollaton Medieval Manuscripts*, ed. Ralph Hanna and Thorlac Turville-Petre (Woodbridge: Boydell and Brewer, 2000), 57–67.

49. Dryden, 'Dedication and Preface', 70.

50. A fine example is the breathless sequence of run-on lines in 'The Pardoner's Tale', where the 'riotoures' run to get to the gold under the tree: 'And everich of these riotoures ran / Til he cam to that tree, and ther they founde / Of floryns fine of gold ycoyned rounde / Wel ny an eighte bushels, as hem thoughte' (VI.668–671).

51. Cf. *Cursor Mundi*: 'This forsaide mary magdalayn, / within this castel I of talde, / *mught* ho do all atte he walde' (13995–13997), and 'Simonde, that sir was o that hame, / *Wondred*, and said in his thoght' (14020–14021).

52. A.J. Ellis, *On Early English Pronunciation*, Early English Text Society, e.s. 2, 7, 14, 23, 56 (London: Trübner, 1867–1889), 5 vols, I, 333.

53. See also *CT* IV.1630, *Troilus* I.490, and further examples in Freudenberger, *Über das Fehlen*, 12.

Chapter 5

Blanche, Two Chaucers and the Stanley Family

Rethinking the Reception of *The Book of the Duchess*

Simon Meecham-Jones

After six centuries of sustained critical attention, many elements of Chaucer's working practices remain obscure. In the absence of reliable witnesses, interpretations of Chaucer's texts have routinely become overwritten by extraneous (and often spurious) discourses and the accumulation of post-hoc speculation, wish fulfilment and misreading. None of Chaucer's poems has suffered more grievously from such distracting obscuration than *The Book of the Duchess* (hereafter *BD*), but it is clear, also, that the poem's textual history offers a potentially crucial resource to begin the process of cleaning away the patina of many centuries of error and presumption.[1]

This may seem a surprising contention, given the ragged and apparently disorganized survival of Chaucer's poetry. Derek Pearsall's confidence that 'Chaucer secured the canon of his major works and their attachment to himself with ... care'[2] seems generous to the point of indulgence, when one recalls the absence of Chaucerian

autograph manuscripts, or even of exemplars that can be securely
dated before the poet's death. This absence must be recognized as
a loss – a prodigious loss of crucial evidence about patronage, textual revision and the circulation of texts in a manuscript culture.
Nor is it easy to reconcile the intensely self-aware poetic practices
of a writer so conscious of the unpredictable challenges of posterity
that he felt obliged to write the *retracciouns* to the *Canterbury Tales*,
The House of Fame and the Prologue to *The Legend of Good Women*,
among other recognitions of his authorial responsibilities, with the
(apparent) lack of care shown in the presentation and – by implication – post-mortem preservation of his texts.[3]

As a result of this deficiency, and probably from the moment of
Chaucer's death, if not before, Chaucer's readers have been dependent on the kindness of strangers, a profusion of gentleman editors,
professional scribes and semi-professional critics, from Hoccleve,
Adam Pynkhurst (perhaps), Shirley, Stowe and Thynne to Furnivall,
Brusendorff, Skeat and beyond.[4] It was inevitable that each of these
'editorial' interventions would influence the nature of what survived,
particularly since these intermediaries did not share a common
locus standi to approach the texts, or a shared tradition of what their
function might require or entitle them to achieve. Differing ideas
prevailed as to the reasons why, and the methods how, to recover
texts from prior ages.[5]

But the issue runs deeper than merely which model of 'copying'
the text is to be passed on. Also at stake when faced with textual
variability are difficult questions regarding what material was to be
accepted to be within the perimeters of Chaucer's texts, and what was
to be excluded. Although Chaucer's editors deserve praise for their
tireless, often perceptive and sometimes (almost) selfless efforts,
the difficulties raised by this dilemma mean that the results of their
labours can never fully escape being misleading. Seeing Chaucer's
poems in a grand edition like the *Riverside Chaucer* or, come to that,
earlier collections, such as Speght's edition of 1598, we see the poems
(mostly)[6] in a single fixed text, which implies that Chaucer's writing
practice aspired to create a single 'best text' – an aesthetic expectation that might be regarded as becoming more prevalent and, if not
more necessary, at least more expected, as printing replaced manual
copying. In fact, even the poems that survive in few copies display a
considerable level of textual variation, requiring the editors to 'reg-
ularize' the texts. If some texts or textual variants were lost through

this process of textual selection and standardization, one result of this tradition of incessant and necessary mediation was that, at least to some degree, those of Chaucer's texts chosen to be transcribed became imbued with the critical preoccupations of their editors.

The critical history of the *BD* should be regarded as exemplifying this dilemma with particular clarity, since these processes of mediation do not merely concern interpretation of the text, but also influence our understanding of what comprises the text. In the construction of what has become recognized as the 'critical' (or valorized) text, editors have introduced or reinstated material that cannot be identified with any surviving manuscript witness. There is something unsettling in the realization that we have become familiar with the *BD* in an arrangement that might be some distance from any version Chaucer envisaged or was familiar with. Of course, the fact this text has been edited and perhaps amended by anonymous scribal hands is acknowledged in textual notes, but the disputed provenance of the lines absent from the manuscript sources has not been highlighted, presumably in order not to fracture the unity of the text.

Paradoxically, the survival of the *Canterbury Tales* in the Hengwrt (NLW MS Peniarth 392D) and Ellesmere manuscripts (Huntingdon Library, San Marino MS EL 26 C9) means that this sense of the provisional nature of the surviving text has remained a critical concern for Chaucer's final work. Although these two witnesses offer two versions of the poem, showing some considerable range of variation not merely in lexis but also in design and organization, they have been credited primarily to the same textual hand writing a decade or more after Chaucer's death.[7] The questions raised by the copying of the *Canterbury Tales*, together with Gower's *Confessio Amantis*, have proved a key concern of much of the research associated with, or deriving from, the Medieval Scribes Project, with its concern to identify a non-courtly circle of readers and copyists centred on Guildhall.[8] The widespread presumption that Chaucer 'fell from grace' socially in the 1380s has become fused with this pattern of research,[9] fostering the idea that the style and design of the *Canterbury Tales* was influenced by the different interests of this projected scribal 'circle' – 'class' is too broad a word for what has been projected and 'coterie' too narrow.[10]

Whatever the merits of this approach, in practice it risks becoming another reason for concentrating attention on the textual history of the *Canterbury Tales* at the expense of his previous works. If there was a developing circle of readers in 'non-court' circles, they appear to have shown no interest in *BD*. Some critics have interpreted this as being consistent with the conviction that Chaucer's style and/or choice of subject matter becomes more 'serious' or more 'democratic' in the *Canterbury Tales*, perhaps reflecting differing audience expectations from a class who had no time for courtly fictions of the 'floure and the leafe'.[11] It is surely no accident that the emphasis on this priority conveniently aligns the perceived concerns of fifteenth-century readers with a widespread twenty-first-century critical distaste for many styles of medieval rhetorical display. Such an interpretation of Chaucer's later work, refocusing its concerns in socio-political terms, accommodates the political or ideological objection many critics have espoused towards the idea of 'courtly' poetry, certainly in English. Often, they underestimate the crucial role of the courtly style as a means of accessing the lyrical mode in an unfriendly political and intellectual climate. Even before the imposition of restrictions outlined in the Arundel constitutions, the idea of secular vernacular poetry was not reliably established in England, and there was widespread and influential hostility to many modes of the free expression of ideas germinating elsewhere in Europe.

If recent critical fashion has ascribed to the *Canterbury Tales* an enhanced ethical and political achievement, the idea has been reinforced by the presumption of the 'courtly' nature of Chaucer's prior poetry, which guarantees its diminished claims to an equivalent seriousness. For all the pre-*Canterbury* verse, the danger of such an approach lies in the consequent overlooking of the originality of complex texts without precedent in English, and intriguingly distinct in design and mood from models and possible influences in French and Latin. This tendency has been reinforced for the *BD* since the interpretation of the poem as a courtier's trifle has proved compatible with an older critical tradition which read the poem as evidence of the close and continuing association of Chaucer and John of Gaunt.

In consequence, the poem has enjoyed a fair degree of familiarity, compared for example with such overlooked works as *Anelida and Arcita* or the *Complaint of Mars*, or even the (still) less familiar, if now critically fashionable, *House of Fame*. *BD* has become a not infrequent element in medieval literature courses, benefiting from its brevity but also from its presumed link with recognized historical figures and circumstances. Compared to the ironizing uncertainty which so often distinguishes Chaucer's style, this poem has been characterized as less complex and more knowable, both in content and in date of composition. This sense of familiarity is anchored in a confidence that the poem can be more securely linked to Chaucer's life and material circumstances than any of his other poems, a consensus summarized in three 'verities': that the poem is Chaucer's first completed work; that it was written as an elegy for Blanche of Lancaster; and that it was commissioned by Blanche's husband, John of Gaunt. This final idea, in casting John as an early and loyal patron of the aspiring poet, long before he eventually became his brother in law, has itself proved fruitful.

Yet none of these propositions is to be relied on, and their continual repetition has smothered discussion of the aims and achievements of an ambitious, idiosyncratic and experimental poem. Furthermore, a consideration of the manuscript and publication history of the poem in its first 250 years demonstrates how improbable each of these three claims proves to be when the evidence is considered.

Chaucer appears to refer to the poem twice, as 'the Deeth of Blaunche the Duchesse'[12] and in the *retracciouns* as 'the Book of the Duchesse'. It seems clear that we are encouraged to make a link between the poem's composition and the death of John of Gaunt's consort. However, critics have been tempted to over-interpret this suggested identification of the poem with the death of Blanche, Duchess of Lancaster. There is nothing in Chaucer's brief description to justify subsequent readings which assert that the poem was written as an elegy, commissioned by her grieving family, and presumably written between Blanche's death in 1368 (or 1369)[13] and John of Gaunt's remarriage in 1371.[14] The theory of a close and companionable bond between Chaucer and John of Gaunt, the dominant political magnate of the age, has long pleased critics and historians. It is an association which promises to shed lustre on both sides. So, in the sixteenth century, Speght follows Stowe in the assurance that:

> Friends he had in the Court, of the best sort ... But chiefly Iohn of Gaunt Duke of Lancaster, at whose commandement he made the treatise of the alliance betwixt Mars and Venus: and also the booke of the Duchesse.[15]

The patronage of Chaucer's (precocious) talent forms an important element of Kantor's presentation of John of Gaunt as an embodiment of chivalric values, and he has no doubt that 'Chaucer's *BD* was an

elegy on the recently deceased Blanche, written for the Duke'.[16] For
Deanne Williams, 'The *BD* was written to commemorate Blanche,
Duchess of Lancaster, who died of the plague in 1368 ... Written
early in Chaucer's career, at a time when he was working hard in the
service of the king, the *BD* is likely a bid for attention or patronage
from the court and aristocracy'.[17] But whether or not the impetus
came from an actual commission, Williams considers this to have
been a successful transaction:

> Chaucer's efforts paid off; in 1374, John of Gaunt awarded him a life
> pension of ten pounds.[18]

Much has been made of this grant. Staley reminds us that Chaucer
received grants from John of Gaunt and, in 1395, from his son
Henry, but the accounts do not record for what services the grants
were awarded.[19] If the grant were for the composition of the *BD*,
then 1374 seems a surprisingly late date, suggesting a certain lack of
urgency in John's gratitude. Furthermore, John's marriage, together
with his 'inheritance' of the full estates of the Duchy of Lancaster
following the death in 1362 of Blanche's sister Maud, Countess of
Leicester, gave him access to immense reserves of land and wealth,
far beyond those available to the crown. Plentiful evidence survives
as to how John, and then his son Henry, drew on the Lancaster incomes to sustain the role of bounty-giver as a means of guaranteeing
the loyalty of their adherents:

> The scale of Duchy spending on annuities partly reflects Henry's
> attempt at a political 'balancing act' in the insecure years after 1399,
> as he not only sought to reward the loyalty of his own men, but also
> tried to reconcile both his opponents and the uncommitted through
> wide-ranging use of the patronage at his disposal.[20]

Viewed in the context of such sustained practices of patronage to
purchase an obligation of 'retainership', we do not need the poem
to explain John's willingness to grant cash to a young man of talent,
who might one day prove useful. Certainly, as Goodman notes, there
is no mention of such services in the account book:

> Gaunt retained Chaucer in 1374 with a standard annuity for esquires
> of £10, with no stipulation for war service or provision for *bouche de
> court* (daily fare) and household wages.[21]

If the evidence from John of Gaunt's accounts is of limited value
in supporting the idea of the poem as a commissioned elegy, there

are other strong reasons for doubting the likelihood of the theory. Perhaps the most troubling is the absence of references (either to the commission or to the poem itself) or allusions to the poem by Chaucer's contemporaries. It is surprising that in their commemorative praise of Chaucer, Hoccleve and Lydgate do not mention what might have been considered a singular distinction for him, particularly since Blanche's son had now assumed the throne. It seems remarkable, also, that Chaucer's peers were able to resist the opportunities to curry favour offered by recalling his praise of Blanche. There seem to be two obvious explanations for this failure to engage with the poem – either that the poem was not widely known or available, or that it was disapproved of by the Lancaster family. Why Chaucer's contemporaries might have been unfamiliar with the poem presents an intriguing puzzle. By definition, an elegy would be intended for the public expression of sentiment, but no evidence survives of such circulation. The single exception to this dearth of contemporary allusions is a contested one. Wimsatt has argued that Froissart's *Dit dou Bleu Chevalier* imitates Chaucer's *BD*, where Cartier argued for Chaucer's imitation of Froissart.[22] But, even if accepted, such close interchange between poets offers no evidence of public familiarity, but rather suggests a narrow and presumably personal circulation of the material, which would not preclude the circulation of material Chaucer regarded as being unfinished or in draft form.

At this point, it seems prudent to be somewhat sceptical of the certainty with which the surviving versions of the poem have been dated. It has been accepted that this poem represents Chaucer's first significant work, and Chaucer's references to the death of Blanche seem to support the idea that the initial inspiration for the poem was her death in 1368 (or 1369). It does not however guarantee that the surviving text represents that original *ur*-text, if such a text was indeed written in the months following Blanche's death. It is certainly striking that this poem has many allusions to the characters of *The Legend of Good Women*, which was apparently written nearly twenty years later. The reader of the *BD* is expected to be already familiar with the stories of 'Cupid's martyrs' Dido, Phyllis, Medea and Penelope, as well as other iconic women such as Polyxena and Esther, whose stories are in the *Legend* but are referred to in the *BD* in a series of glancing allusions. Given this extensive overlapping of concerns and material, it seems reasonable to wonder if the text of the *BD*, as it survives, is not that written by the young poet, but actually represents a late(r) version, revised during or after Chaucer's experiences in composing the *Legend*.

The dating of all Chaucer's poetry notoriously raises difficult questions,[23] and will probably never be settled. However, the dating of the *BD* is significant, because it has bolstered the idea of this poem as 'early work',[24] in which critics have not expected to find the complexity and self-consciousness of later work.[25] Similarly, the idea that the poem was commissioned as an elegy has provided several reasons for not reading it as a seriously intended poetic statement, but rather as work expected to fulfil some practical purpose, as a memorial, or even as an exercise in 'therapeutic concerns'[26] for John of Gaunt.[27] In part, the idea that a commissioned work cannot express personal feeling is a holdover from Romantic notions of inspiration – in Wordsworth's terms, a commissioned elegy would risk being incompatible with 'the spontaneous overflow of powerful feelings', nor would its formal register permit the use of 'simple and unelaborated expressions ... arising out of repeated experience and regular feelings'.[28] However, if the *BD* was designed as an elegy, then it must be considered a failure. The poem includes a plethora of unexpected materials that distract attention from the poem's celebration and commemoration of Blanche's virtues, and which threaten to depose her from her (presumed) centrality to the poem. The retelling of Ovid's account of Morpheus's cave introduces a note of unexpected levity to a hymn of mourning. Similarly hard to reconcile with the poem's supposed purpose is the lengthy interpolation of the story of Seys and Alcyone, which seems a wholly inappropriate subject for an elegy for a wife who predeceased her husband. There are many other spots of awkwardness in the texture of the work, which also require explanation. Many of the claims of a commission have started from a presumption of the close acquaintance or friendship of Chaucer and John of Gaunt, influenced in part by the fact they were sleeping with sisters (Chaucer's wife Philippa, and John of Gaunt's mistress Katherine Swynford, who finally became John's third wife in 1396, eleven years after the death of her sister).[29] Posterity has deduced from this circumstance a family closeness, but while this is plausible, no substantive evidence exists in the Life Records. Chaucer presents us with a projection of himself in the poem as a narrator who has no knowledge of Blanche, and who is consequently also unaware of her death. Although the uninformed narrator is a familiar Chaucerian projection, for a commissioned elegy it is inappropriate. Of course, his ignorance within the poem acts as a narratorial feint, which enables the Black Knight to extol at length his dead wife's exemplary qualities, but in doing so, the reliability of her praise is shaded. The Black Knight might well be presenting a justified and accurate account of Blanche's attributes and conduct but, as a bereaved lover, his testimony must be recognized as that of a partial witness, and so its value is compromised. Chaucer even reminds us of the inherent unreliability of the Black Knight's testimony when he explains his lady's pre-eminence through a less than wholly coherent image of her as a mirror:

> For I dar swere wel, yif that she
> Had among ten thousand be,
> She wolde have be, at the leste,
> A chef myrour of al the feste (*BD* 971–74)

Its connotations cause the reader to pause. If Blanche is imaged as a mirror, then what the Black Knight and his putative ten thousand companions will see in Blanche is not her, but themselves.[30] How, then, to explain the poem's curiously distracted focus on the dead Blanche?

Novelty (in English poetic practice) must have made notable what would have been unremarkable in French or Italian, and although Chaucer was drawing heavily on the example of works by Froissart and Machaut, by comparison with these writers, his position may have seemed isolated. While his French peers were writing within an established *milieu* that permitted comment, allusion, rivalry and satire, Chaucer, writing in English, had, so far as we know, no pre-existing peer group (with a record of poetic achievement in English) to act as support, goad and critic to his performance in English.[31] Though the evidence from Grandson, Deschamps and Froissart shows us Chaucer on the fringes, at the very least, of French literary circles,[32] it is unclear how francophone poets would have regarded Chaucer's attempts to adapt themes and forms from French poetry in a different language. If we accept Butterfield's account of Middle English as one strand within the great tapestry of French culture, then perhaps Chaucer's endeavour might not have seemed odd or challenging to his French peers.[33] However it is important to remember that what Butterfield is describing is less a statement of fact than an interpretation of how things were (or are) perceived, which will inevitably have shifted in accordance with the perspective of who is or was asked. It might have seemed plausible to Froissart, a poet from Hainault, who had worked at the English court where the queen was from the same region, that the English language had become 'contained by French', and we might cite his adaptation of Chaucer's work in his own *Dit dou Bleu Chevalier*. It is far less certain that, if John of Gaunt had commissioned the work, his projected audience would have felt the same. First, if there were no social or political advantage to be exploited by writing in English, then one might have expected him to have preferred a poem in the more fashionable medium of French, a language accessible to much of his readership in England. Second, there is no evidence that fourteenth-century English society was prepared to tolerate the addressing of magnates by poets as if they were socially interchangeable.[34] In France, by contrast, the device was well established, showing the influence of *trouvére* practice, such as Bertran de Born's creation in Occitan of secret names and sexually charged figurations of Henry II, Eleanor of Aquitaine and their daughter Matilda.[35]

Cannon notes that 'the narrator of Chaucer's first original composition of any length, the *BD* presumes familiarity with John of Gaunt, Earl of Richmond and Duke of Lancaster, probably the most powerful man in England'.[36] Although the sheer scale of Lancastrian involvement in the creation of literature in late fourteenth- and early fifteenth-century England has become ever-more apparent, there is nothing in this substantial corpus to suggest that John of Gaunt or his family would have welcomed a presumption of such familiarity. Maybe there is a danger that English interpretations of Chaucer are unduly sensitive to what has been perceived as the marginality of his class identity, but certainly there must have been sensitivities in the presentation of a figure so powerful as John of Gaunt, and so conscious of his reputation, by a tyro poet without substantial independent means.

The assumption that the *BD* is evidence of the intimacy of Chaucer and John of Gaunt was elegantly dismissed by John Burrow, who drew attention to the difficulties of decorum in respecting another's mourning, exacerbated in this instance by the difference in social rank between the two men. For Burrow, 'the problem is one of "san et corteisie", of politeness'[37] which Chaucer seeks to address using 'one of the chief strategies of courtesy, that is, indirectness'.[38] This indirectness leads Burrow to conclude that 'these devices place *The BD* at the furthest possible remove from consolations addressed directly by the poet to the bereaved'.[39] Muscatine, in contrast, had seen in the poem's denial of precision a strategy of politeness, which also reaped artistic benefits:

> Chaucer ... uses the device of the dream ... to exclude those reminders of common life, of business, war and politics, that would cling to a realistic representation of his subject and thus smudge the purity of the feeling appropriate to the occasion.[40]

It is debatable how far a more direct representation of the dead Duchess would have smudged the 'purity' of any representation of grief, in what might have been expected to serve for the commemoration of a specific death, rather than as a general meditation on the shortness of human life. Certainly, the blurring of specific detail undermines the poem's claim to fulfil the primary role of the elegy as a public statement of recognition and regret, which could be shared and adopted by the whole community. The poet attempts to avoid this danger by concealing hints of identification in the poem, which become all but insistent in the closing lines:

> A long castel with walles white,
> Be Seynt Johan, on a ryche hil. (*BD* 1318–19)

However the 'veiling' of Blanche and John risks turning a public commemoration into a shadow-play for initiates, which perhaps anticipates some political concerns about the eulogizing of a woman whose dowry had helped to raise John to a level of power and prominence that would not have been predicted at the time of his birth as the king's fourth son. Nonetheless, what we see is more evidently the result of a crisis of status for vernacular poetry in England, where there was no precedent for the writing of such 'personal' literature. England had no recognized class of professional vernacular writers to parallel the medieval Welsh tradition of *barddoniaeth*, which offered the constant presence of writers from whom rulers could commission praise-poetry and elegies (*marwnadau*).[41]

It is clear that Chaucer's use of an English adaptation of the lyrical *dit* form presented challenges in the framing of an elegy, though they need not have proved insoluble. Central to the poem's failure as an elegy is the absence of an authoritative narrator to praise the dead lady. In contrast, in a *Lay* written to commemorate the death of Edward III's queen (and John of Gaunt's mother) Philippa of Hainault in 1369, Froissart provided exactly such a testimony. Wimsatt notes that 'unnaturally for a lyric lay, the 219-line poem offers unmediated factual commemoration',[42] albeit perhaps, in his view, at the expense of the elegance of the poetry. If John of Gaunt had commissioned Chaucer to write an elegy for Blanche, then Froissart's poem is probably far closer to what he might have expected, and required, than Chaucer's hybrid, elusive and beguilingly frustrating work.

Having acknowledged the difficulties that Chaucer would have faced if the poem had been commissioned as an elegy, it remains puzzling why critics remain reluctant to take notice of the many strands of evidence that disprove the theory. To cite one telling example: Blanche of Lancaster's daughter, Philippa of Lancaster, was involved in the literary circles of the age; she was also to be commemorated in poetry, having been depicted by Deschamps in a *ballade* in the debate of the leaf and the flower as a strong supporter of the cult of the flower.[43] Following her marriage in 1387 to King João I of Portugal, Philippa has generally been considered responsible for commissioning the translation into Portuguese of Gower's *Confessio Amantis* in a version that included the highly favourable depiction of Richard II commissioning the poem on a boat on the Thames.[44] Whether Philippa's commissioning (or encouraging of the commission) of the translation reflects her love of literature, or an awareness of the political role literature could play in projecting an image or, most likely, both, it is certainly strange that, if she knew of a poem commemorating her mother, she would not have ordered its translation also – unless she considered it unsuitable for its purpose. If the *BD* was circulating in literary circles in the 1370s, then it would have been inconceivable that Philippa would be unaware of a poem that touched her family's concerns so closely. It therefore seems probable that she was either not comfortable or familiar with the poem.

Philippa's lack of interest in the poem seems to have been more than matched by her father and her brother. The marriage to Blanche, and the accession to the Duchy of Lancaster, provided John not merely with extensive estates and huge incomes, but also a major network of feudal interests and loyalties, which were crucial in entrenching his political prominence during Richard II's minority. Throughout his life, John was careful to respect this connection, organizing annual lavish masses for the benefit of Blanche's soul, and it was the effigy of Blanche that lay alongside that of John, right hands clasped, in Old St Paul's.[45]

Whether we interpret this, as Staley does,[46] as evidence of a deep and genuine affection or, more cynically, as the astute conduct of a man very aware of the value of political theatre (and the two options are scarcely incompatible), it is striking that Chaucer's 'elegy' played no role in the annual celebration of the dead Duchess. The poem's obscurity seems even more striking when we remember that Blanche's son took the throne as Henry IV. Much has been written in recent years about the co-option of English poets, particularly Gower, to write political poetry in support of what was to become the 'Lancastrian' cause.[47] The records do not indicate how far this exploitation of the propaganda power of the written text was encouraged by John of Gaunt or Henry personally, or whether it was conceived and organized by their supporters, but clearly the *BD* was not perceived as being sufficiently sympathetic to their purpose. Whether or not Henry had much personal interest in books and poetry, few men are indifferent to a compliment to their mother. Rather, it seems as if John of Gaunt and his children regarded the *BD* as serving Chaucer's purposes better than those of Blanche's family.

If we accept as likely that the Lancaster dynasty disliked or, at best, failed to identify with the poem, then the poem's apparently surprising manuscript history begins to make sense. The poem is noticeably absent from most of the important collections of fifteenth-century Chaucerian material, such as MS Arch Selden B.24, Cambridge University Library MS Gg.4.27, Cambridge University Library MS Ff 1.6 and MS Longleat 258, each of which contains the *Parlement of Fowles*, a selection of Chaucerian lyrics[48] and selections of poems associated with Chaucer, or wrongly attributed to him.[49]

The most immediately striking conclusion is how slow the *BD* was to establish its place in the canon. If we consider as a contrast *The House of Fame*, it has long been accepted that readers from the fifteenth to the mid-twentieth centuries considered the self-referential aesthetic musings of the *House of Fame* too abstruse for a broad audience, even if we ignore the question of whether the poem reaches a conclusion or merely 'ends' inconclusively. Despite this, the text was printed by Caxton in 1483, for which he wrote a concluding paragraph in case anyone was in any doubt as to the state of the poem. In manuscript, the poem survives in three mid-fifteenth-century witnesses: MS Bodleian Fairfax 16, MS Magdalene College Cambridge Pepys 2006, and MS Bodley 638.

The *BD* may seem more central to Chaucer's expected themes and to the trajectory of his career, but the poem survives only in a very restricted range of sources. Editors have relied on four witnesses for the text – three manuscripts, supplemented by Thynne's printed edition of 1532, which contains readings not found in any manuscript. The three manuscripts are Bodleian Library MS Fairfax 16, Bodleian Library MS Bodley 638 and Bodleian Library MS Tanner 346,[50] which Hammond regarded as a discrete 'group' which she named the 'Oxford Group'.[51] The term 'Oxford Group' is unhelpful in so far as it refers to their current location in the Bodleian Library, but it appears to have encouraged the assumption that the manuscripts were compiled in Oxford, for which there is no evidence. There are significant correspondences between the three manuscript witnesses (including some presumed misreadings), which led Dickerson, Blake and Brusendorff to conclude that the three manuscripts are related, but that Fairfax 16 and Bodley 638 are more closely connected.[52] More contentious is Hammond's presumption that Thynne's edition and Tanner 346 appear to share a common, now lost, ancestor. There are few indications as to the nature (or location) of the connections between these manuscripts. Norton-Smith, developing an idea from Brusendorff, argues that Fairfax 16 is an 'example of a manuscript produced to order by a commercial scriptorium or bookseller, either in Oxford or in London, for a single owner belonging to the landed gentry' and compiled from pre-existing booklets:

> The bookseller who made up Fairfax 16 made it up 'to order', according to choices offered to John Stanley ... Stanley did not choose single works or authors but booklets containing authors or works possibly in already existing saleable copy, or ready to be copied up from resident display booklets.[53]

But, if the *BD* was available among a selection of existing booklets, the reason why the Oxford Group alone preserves this substantial poem becomes more difficult to explain. Curiously, Caxton did not choose to print the poem, a decision which deserves more consideration than it has so far received. Instead, the *BD* was not received into the printed canon of Chaucer's works until Thynne's edition of 1532, and the aura of novelty is still palpable in Speght's editions at the end of the century. Curiously, critical responses to the strikingly similar manuscript histories of the two poems have not been consistent. It has been generally accepted that *The House of Fame* was barely known or circulated until its reappearance in manuscripts in the mid fifteenth century.[54] In contrast, it has been assumed that the *BD* was in circulation from its composition, despite the lack of references by other writers. The non-appearance of the poem in any of the major fifteenth-century manuscript collections could be explained in several ways – by the vagaries of manuscript transmission, by changes in fashion in courtly circles, or by the political connotations that inevitably adhered to a poem about Henry IV's mother – but its non-appearance in any of them should not be disregarded. We cannot conclude with certainty that the poem was disliked by Blanche's family (in particular, by her children) but, even if we link its omission to a scarcity of manuscripts to be copied, that in itself demonstrates the poem's lack of popularity in the fifteenth century which, during the reigns of Blanche's son and grandson, demands to be noticed.

It appears that circulation of the *BD* dates back only to the middle of the fifteenth century, which raises questions about why and how the poem was restored to notice. The reappearance of the poem may owe more to the ebb and flow of dynastic rivalries than to any changing critical appreciation of the poem's literary merits. If we see England in the fifteenth century as dominated by the often hostile contentions of John of Gaunt's descendants with their cousins, then this poem, with its potentially disruptive depiction of John and Blanche alongside Chaucer, could not escape being politically sensitive.

Viewed in this context, Norton-Smith's notion of MS Fairfax 16 having been assembled by a professional scribe from pre-existing samples deserves to be treated with scepticism. Not merely is the model implausible, it is also unnecessary. The manuscript displays clear evidence of its commission, the importance of which has yet to be recognized. On folio f. 14 b appears an illustration, which is personalized by the appearance of heraldic arms in the lavish marginal decoration. The device depicted is 'the arms, quartering Stanley and Hooton ... of John Stanley (died by 1469), Usher of the Chamber to Henry VI from 1450–1455'.[55]

Though John Stanley of Hooton has been largely forgotten by history, he belonged to one of the most important families that rose in this period. The dynastic rivalries of the Wars of the Roses were played out, in large part, through the military and political support of aristocratic and gentry families, such as the Nevilles and the Courtneys, who used the squabbles of princes to consolidate their regional powerbases. The Stanleys were initially landowners in Cheshire and Staffordshire. In the late fourteenth and fifteenth centuries, through political manoeuvring and dynastic marriages, the family extended its influence into Lancashire, the Wirral, North Wales and the Welsh March. These areas were to prove crucial spheres of influence, as Stanley land and priorities increasingly abutted those of the royal estates of Richard II and the vast patrimony of the Duchy of Lancaster.[56] Yet despite their expanding power, the Stanley family has attracted little interest for their role as patrons of medieval and early modern literature. This is the more striking since Sir John Stanley (c. 1340–1409) has been suggested as a model, patron or even composer of *Sir Gawain and the Green Knight*[57] while Stanley involvement has also been suggested for the seventeenth-century *Percy Folio*.[58]

The Stanleys of Hooton were the senior branch of the Stanley family, though their prominence was to be eclipsed when the Stanleys of Lathom were raised to the peerage in 1456. Both branches of the family were descended from advantageous marriages made by the two sons of William Stanley (c. 1337–98). Members of both branches were influential at the court of Henry VI, involved in the many crucial episodes of jockeying for power in the fifteenth century. John Stanley of Hooton held a number of prominent positions as well as serving as a member of parliament. Wedgwood and Holt note that his offices include those of Captain of Caernarvon 1427–60, Serjeant of the Armoury 1431–60, and Usher of the Chamber 1440–55.[59] The dates are important, since they show Stanley achieving notice early in King Henry VI's reign,[60] and maintaining his positions during Richard of York's regency in 1454. During the regency, Henry's household was substantially reduced[61] but Watts notes how Stanley's career demonstrated an ability to weather difficult political waters:

> Note that those appointed to remain in the household included the Beauchamps, John Stanley and other well-known members of the pre-1454 establishment.[62]

The recognition of John Stanley as a popular and influential member of the young king's court is of crucial importance for the consideration of MS Fairfax 16. It seems clear to me that the selection of material for this manuscript reflects the taste of its commissioner, John Stanley, rather than the whim of a scribe or editor. The poetry transcribed here was the poetry favoured and circulated at Henry VI's court, and in Fairfax 16 there are tantalizing hints of political interconnections underlying this literary milieu. The fifth quire includes a set of twenty English *ballades*. Though the first *ballade* is generally attributed to Charles of Orléans,[63] the authorship of the remainder is contested. The most favoured candidate remains William de la Pole, Earl of Suffolk,[64] whose career was initially promoted by Cardinal Henry Beaufort, the second son of John of Gaunt and Katherine Swynford, and who rose to become Henry VI's most valued and powerful courtier until his sudden and precipitous fall in 1450, following his denunciation by parliament. There seems to be no reason to doubt Suffolk's literary interests, which had made him an ideal host for the captured Charles d'Orléans. There is plentiful evidence to link Suffolk with the Stanley family.[65]

The manuscript is dated 1450, and that date proves crucial both for the Stanley family and for the afterlife of the manuscript. Mounting resentment at Suffolk's perceived influence over the king led to him, and leading named supporters (including both Stanleys), being attacked. Suffolk's predicament became more perilous, and it must be significant that, as Henry sought to shield Suffolk from his enemies, 'in January 1450 the duke of Suffolk was committed to the keeping of Stanley, Minors and Staunton'.[66] The choice of Stanley suggests that Henry regarded him as a loyal associate of Suffolk's, who could be trusted to keep the earl safe until the king could return him to favour – though that is not, of course, how events transpired. After Suffolk's death, the cry was forcefully taken up by parliament in November 1450 against the Stanleys.[67]

The date on the manuscript of 1450 represents a sobering reminder of the reversals of court life. Both John Stanley and his influential kinsman Thomas Stanley survived the fall of Suffolk, and subsequently the fall of Henry VI. But if Bodleian MS Fairfax 16 was designed to celebrate Stanley's intimacy with the Suffolk circle, by the time of its completion it was no longer politically advantageous. Instead it became an inconvenient reminder of abandoned loyalties.[68]

If MS Fairfax 16 represents a written reminiscence of the literary association of Suffolk and John Stanley, then the presence in it of *BD* and *The House of Fame* also needs to be reconsidered. It seems clear that neither text was widely available, far less admired, in the period, but Stanley may have enjoyed a privileged access to these texts, which caused him to include them. Suffolk's wife was Alice Chaucer, granddaughter of the poet, and there are reasons to believe she may have played a significant role in the intellectual life at Henry VI's court, which has subsequently been rendered largely invisible since it threatened to undermine the Yorkist projection of Henry VI as an imbecile.

Alice Chaucer has not been lucky in her posthumous fame, having proved less adept than the Stanleys at knowing when to change sides. The most vivid testimony of her character has been offered by her political enemies – from the Pastons[69] to the calls in parliament for her to be brought to justice – which led to a humiliating, if ultimately fruitless trial in 1451. The records show a determined and intelligent woman but offer a frustrating lack of information about her spiritual and intellectual life. In an influential paper on Alice's household manuscripts, Carol Meale asserts both the difficulty and the value of attempting to 'see Alice Chaucer as a figure in her own right',[70] but it is hard to deny that scant evidence leaves her seeming as inscrutable as her alabaster effigy in the church at Ewelme.

If there is no clue as to how she viewed the heritage of her grandfather's art, there are signs that she engaged with contemporary literature. A list of Alice's books from Ewelme includes a copy of Christine de Pizan's *City of Ladies*.[71] She has been identified as the probable commissioner of a poem on the interpretation of the Mass by Lydgate[72] and it may be significant that Suffolk's arms and crest appear on what Meale terms 'the earliest, and best copy of the *Siege of Thebes*' (BL MS Arundel 119).[73] The patronage of Lydgate by Alice's father Thomas Chaucer, as well as by Alice herself and her second and third husbands, suggests both an interest in literature and an awareness of the political implications of composition and patronage. It is very tempting, then, to speculate that the re-emergence of the *BD* and *The House of Fame* (a poem that engages precisely with such issues) resulted from a willingness by Alice to share material from her personal archive. This willingness must have been influenced by her perception of changed political circumstances, not least due to the prominence of Katherine Swynford's Beaufort descendants at court, determining the reading of a poem which seems to show Alice's grandfather associating himself with John of Gaunt. This might have seemed politically advantageous or, at the very least, less objectionable than it might have appeared in the 1370s or the early 1400s, when Henry IV had (perhaps a touch reluctantly) accepted the legitimation of his Beaufort siblings. Maybe, even if only for a moment, the appearance of the *BD* in Fairfax 16, with its depiction of the poet at John's right hand, was perceived as offering prestige for Stanley and for his sponsors at court.

The recovery of the two poems from Chaucer's papers offers a plausible explanation for one of the most puzzling features of the poem – its textual lacunae. Early in the poem, all three manuscripts display a gap of more than sixty lines.[74] The lines – which tell of the narrator taking up a book of 'fables', and then begin the story of Alcyone – seem essential to the logical progression but are absent in MS Bodley 638 and MS Tanner 346. There is no medieval witness of these lines, which caused Blake to question their reliability.[75] In Fairfax 16, the lines are omitted in the fifteenth-century text, but a gap is left, in which the lines were inserted by a seventeenth-century hand, presumably copied from Thynne's printed text. Curiously, the reinstated lines are not found in Stowe's edition of 1561, though he must have seen the gap in Fairfax 16, since the manuscript bears a number of marginal notes in his hand. The lines do appear, though, in Thynne's printed edition of 1532 which, at other points in the text, often seems to follow Tanner 346. If Thynne's edition seems to have drawn heavily on Tanner 346 (or, in Norton-Smith's formulation, an earlier booklet from which Tanner 346 was also copied), then the absence of these lines in the Oxford Group seems odd, if they are indeed genuinely Chaucerian. The leaving of a gap in Fairfax 16 could suggest that it was copied from a damaged exemplar, though that would not have precluded the manuscript, or those of Tanner 346 and Bodley 638, from patching together lines to bridge the awkward and unmotivated transition into the Alcyone story. The idea of a scriptorium repeatedly copying such a patently imperfect booklet stretches credibility (particularly since Bodley 638 and Tanner 346 leave no gap to mark a break in the text), unless a folio was removed as an editorial choice. But if a folio was excised from the manuscript, what might cause an editor or reader to suppress these sixty or so lines?[76] It seems clear that the final twenty-nine lines beginning the story of Alcyone would be unlikely to cause offence, particularly since the remainder of the story is copied. The most likely objection might have been to the lines that 'foe there is phisicien but oon / That may me hele' (39–40), which, with its implied play on images of Christ as healer/redeemer might have seemed ill-advised, or worse, in the climate following the Arundel Constitutions of 1409.[77]

As well as the absence of lines 30–96, there are other limited discrepancies between Thynne's text and that preserved in the Oxford Group manuscripts.[78] Unless Thynne took on an otherwise unparalleled editorial role, and interpolated lines 30–96 himself (presumably from his own imagination), then the disparity between his edition and the surviving manuscripts raises interesting (though unanswerable) issues. Blake notes that

> ... if Thynne had two manuscripts, of which one was apparently better because it contained such good readings as the inclusion of lines 31–96, one would naturally have to provide some compelling reason as to why he apparently used a bad manuscript such as the ancestor of Tanner for much of his text, since he shares so many common errors.[79]

But he disregards the most plausible solution to the problem he has identified. Having accepted that 'the second manuscript, if it existed, would clearly belong to a different textual tradition',[80] he fails to consider the possibility that the two (or more) manuscripts presented different recensions of the work, one perhaps showing revision by Chaucer at a later stage in his career, which Thynne used to darn an imperfect text.

Again, if Alice were the guardian of her grandfather's papers, it must be plausible that she either possessed and allowed to circulate distinct and contrasted drafts of the poem, possibly written some time apart, or alternatively that she held a damaged or unfinished draft, for which she might have commissioned material as part of the launching of a previously unfamiliar text. Considering such possibilities offers new opportunities for the interpretation of the *BD*. We are not obliged to consider the lacunae in the poem as certainly the result of chance and the perils of manuscript circulation. It would be interesting, for example, to speculate whether the more explicit stating of the theme of insomnia – and the assertion that it did not result from love – in lines 30–44 was added later, to make clearer the meaning of the opening lines, or if it was removed by a more mature poet as being superfluous, perhaps diminishing the distress of the opening lines, which also might explain the absence of the lines in the three surviving manuscripts. There are other moments of awkwardness which might also suggest that the poem was subject to tactful revision which, for whatever reasons, Thynne reversed. Perhaps on reflection, it was a mistake to have had the words of the Black Knight, mourning his lost love:

> Ne hele me may no phisicien (*BD* 571)

anticipated by the narrator's account of his distress, 'For ther is phisicien but oon' (*BD* 39).

The appearance of the *BD* in a mid-fifteenth-century manuscript commissioned by a senior figure at court obliges us to consider more seriously the processes of selection and editorial intervention that returned the poem to critical notice. If Alice Chaucer was involved in these processes, whether in making the text available or in more actively promoting familiarity with the poem, we can see an ironic re-enactment of the indirect assertion that is so central to her grandfather's aesthetic. Where Meale has reminded us of the importance of 'the act of recovery and interpretation of evidence – to engage with the broader issue of the silencing of women's voices within both the medieval and the modern periods'[81] in tracing the possibility of Alice's involvement with the recovery of the *BD*, maybe we can recover from the shadows the stratagems of a woman surreptitiously challenging those processes of silencing.

Simon Meecham-Jones has lectured for the English Faculty, University of Cambridge in medieval literature and the history of the English language. From 2008 to 2014 he also held a part-time research fellowship at Swansea University. He has researched and published on Chaucer and Gower, twelfth-century Latin lyrics, medieval language contact (particularly code-switching), and the representation of Wales and the Welsh people in medieval literature. He edited (with Ruth Kennedy) *Writers of the Reign of Henry II* (Palgrave Macmillan, 2006) and *Authority and Subjugation in Writing of Medieval Wales* (Palgrave Macmillan, 2008). He is currently completing a study entitled *Chaucer and Imagination*.

Notes

1. This article has benefited greatly from a meeting with Professor Ralph Griffiths. I am most grateful for his kindness.
2. 'Though he did not supervise a chronologically ordered "collected edition" of his poems as did his French predecessors and contemporaries, Machaut, Froissart and Deschamps, Chaucer secured the canon of his major works and their attachment to himself with a care only less remarkable for being less obtrusive than that of his friend John Gower, who went to the length of adding a Latin colophon at the end of his *Confessio Amantis* in which he listed and described his three major works.' Derek Pearsall, *Life of Geoffrey Chaucer: A Critical Biography* (Oxford: Blackwell, 1992), 1–2.
3. All quotations from Chaucer's works are from *The Riverside Chaucer*, ed. Larry D. Benson (Oxford: Oxford University Press, 1988), except where otherwise stated.

4. The tradition is traced in *Editing Chaucer: The Great Tradition*, ed. Paul Ruggiers (Norman, OK: Pilgrim Books, 1984).

5. The differing priorities and methodologies of eighteenth-century reclamation of medieval material might be demonstrated by comparing the contrasted poles of Percy's blithe amendment of textual cruces, including almost incontrovertible examples of scribal error, to enhance and elucidate the reading of the text, to Ritson's preference for retaining the probable error, as a form of historical evidence. Arthur Johnston, *Enchanted Ground* (London: Athlone Press, 1964), 120–47 (Ritson), 76–85 (Percy).

6. Only for the two Prologues of *The Legend of Good Women* has it become customary to print alternative versions of the poem, rather than 'selecting' a composite 'best version'.

7. J.S.P. Tatlock, 'The Canterbury Tales in 1400', *PMLA* 50 (1926): 100–39, here 128; A.I. Doyle and M.B. Parkes, 'The Production of Copies of the *Canterbury Tales* and the *Confessio Amantis* in the Early Fifteenth Century', in *Medieval Scribes, Manuscripts and Libraries: Essays Presented to N.R. Kerr*, ed. M.B. Parkes and Andrew G. Watson (London: Scolar Press, 1978), 163–210; Christopher de Hamel, 'The Hengwrt Scribe', in *Meetings with Remarkable Manuscripts* (London: Penguin, 2016), 426–65.

8. Linne R. Mooney and Estelle Stubbs, *Scribes and the City: London Guildhall Clerks and the Dissemination of Middle English Literature 1375–1425* (York: York Medieval Texts, 2013); Linne Mooney, 'Chaucer's Scribe', *Speculum* 81 (2006): 97–138; Jane Roberts, 'On Giving Scribe B a Name and a Clutch of London Manuscripts from c. 1400', *Medium Aevum* LXXX.2 (2011): 247–70.

9. E.g. Pearsall, *Life of Geoffrey Chaucer*, 202–9; Lee Patterson, *Chaucer and the Subject of History* (London: Routledge, 1971), 23–26; D.S. Brewer, *Chaucer and His World* (Cambridge: D.S. Brewer, 1992), 156.

10. Evidence about Chaucer's circle has been considered by Strohm and Sobecki: Paul Strohm, *Social Chaucer* (Cambridge, MA: Harvard University Press, 1989); Sebastian Sobecki, '"And gret wel Chaucer when ye mete": Chaucer's Earliest Readers, Addressees and Audiences', *Critical Survey* 29, no. 3 (2017): 7–14.

11. E.g. Lynn Staley, *Languages of Power in the Age of Richard II* (University Park: Pennsylvania State University Press, 2005), 11, 139; Christopher Cannon, 'The Lives of Geoffrey Chaucer', in *The Yale Companion to Chaucer*, ed. Seth Lerer (New Haven, CT: Yale University Press, 2006), 31–54, here 47.

12. Prologue, *Legend of Good Women*, F 418, G 406.

13. 1369 was long the accepted date, but the consensus has now shifted to 1368: J.J.N. Palmer, 'The Historical Context of the *BD*: A Revision', *Chaucer Review* 8 (1974): 253–61.

14. A rare exception is proposed by Edward Condren, who argues that, while the poem does offer a memorial to Blanche of Lancaster, it was written after a period of reflection, towards the end of Edward III's reign. Edward I. Condren, 'Of Death and Duchesses and Scholars Coughing Ink', *Chaucer Review* 10 (1975): 87–95.

15. G. Speght, ed., *The Workes of Our Antient and Learned English Poet, Geffrey Chaucer, Newly Printed* (London: Adam Islip, 1602).

16. Norman F. Kantor, *The Last Knight* (New York: Free Press, 2004), 71.

17. Deanne Williams, 'The Dream Visions', in Lerer, *The Yale Companion to Chaucer*, 147–78, here 150.

18. Ibid., 150.

19. Staley, *Languages of Power*, 183, 186.

20. Helen Castor, *The King, the Crown and the Duchy of Lancaster* (Oxford: Oxford University Press, 2000), 29. These patterns of patronage are also considered by Saul and Given-Wilson: Nigel Saul, *Richard II* (New Haven, CT: Yale University Press, 1997), 265–66, 440; Chris Given-Wilson, 'The King and the Gentry in Fourteenth-Century England', *Transactions of the Royal Historical Society* 5th Series 37 (1987): 87–102, here 99.

21. Anthony Goodman, *John of Gaunt: The Exercise of Princely Power in Fourteenth-Century Europe* (Harlow: Longman, 1992), 362–63.

22. J.I. Wimsatt, 'The *Dit dou Bleu Chevalier*: Froissart's Imitation of Chaucer', *Mediaeval Studies* 34 (1972): 388–400; Normand Cartier, '*Le Bleu Chevalier de Froissart et La livre de la Duchesse* de Chaucer', *Romania* 88 (1967): 232–52; John M. Fyler, 'Irony and the Age of Gold in the Book of the Duchess', *Speculum* 52, no. 2 (1977): 314–28.

23. Kathryn L. Lynch, 'Dating Chaucer', *Chaucer Review* 42 (2007): 1–22.

24. Brewer presumes this as a means of justifying his view of Chaucer's poetic formation as being a pre-Ricardian phenomenon: 'Chaucer therefore was formed in the court of Edward III. ... Chaucer's first datable poem is *The BD*, almost certainly written in October 1368, as an elegy for John of Gaunt's recently deceased wife'. Derek Brewer, 'Chaucer's Anti-Ricardian Poetry', in *The Living Middle Ages: Studies in Mediaeval English Literature and Its Tradition. A Festschrift for Karl Heinz Göller*, ed. Manfred Markus Böker and Rainer Schöwerling (Stuttgart: Belser, 1989), 115–28, here 121.

25. This view is efficiently summarized by Stephen Knight, *Geoffrey Chaucer* (Oxford: Basil Blackwell, 1986), see 15. Of course, there is no reason why an artist's earliest work might not display greater subtlety, originality and technical daring than their later works, before the edge of their talent was blunted by critical neglect and failure, or by success.

26. Louise Fradenburg, '"Voice Memorial": Loss and Reparation in Chaucer's Poetry', *Exemplaria* 2, no. 1 (1990): 169–202, here 177.

27. As an example of the characteristic evaluation of the poem, one might quote Jordan: 'As an elegy the *BD* is both a eulogy of the dead and a consolation for those who remain to grieve'. Robert M. Jordan, 'The Compositional Structure of the *BD*', *Chaucer Review* 9 (1975): 99–117, here 102.

28. William Wordsworth, Preface to *Lyrical Ballads 1802*, in William Wordsworth, *Lyrical Ballads, and Other Poems, 1797–1800*, ed. James Butler and Karen Green (Ithaca, NY: Cornell University Press, 1992), 173.

29. Strohm goes so far as to suggest that the grants to Chaucer were a favour to his wife, rather than the poet himself. See Paul Strohm, *The Poet's Tale: Chaucer and the Year that Made the Canterbury Tales* (New York: Profile Books, 2015), 30–48.

30. Wimsatt interprets the image as part of a sequence adapting imagery associated with the Virgin to reassure the reader of Blanche's reception in Heaven. Nonetheless, the application of Marian imagery to a contemporary woman, however virtuous, must have raised some questions of decorum, in the context of partisan

aristocratic loyalties and, perhaps, more troublingly, in the turbid religious climate of late fourteenth-century England. See J.I. Wimsatt, 'The Apotheosis of
Blanche in the Book of the Duchess', *Journal of English and Germanic Philology*
66, no. 1 (1967): 26–44.

31. Butterfield, commenting on the influence of the *Roman de la Rose* on Chaucer's
practice, notes that 'his subtle reinterpretation of the Rose's double authority
shows Chaucer a vernacular literary history of immense collaborative power of
which, as yet, there is no echo in English'. Ardis Butterfield, *The Familiar Enemy*
(New York: Oxford University Press, 2009), 283.

32. Wimsatt raises the interesting question whether Chaucer and Froissart's paths
might have crossed during Froissart's sojourn in London: 'Beyond the indirect
evidence of their literary borrowings from each other, there is no document
which tells us even that they were acquainted. But ... how could they not have
been well acquainted? The question seems to be not whether they knew each
other, but what the nature of their relationship was'. James I. Wimsatt, *Chaucer
and His French Contemporaries* (Toronto: University of Toronto Press, 1991), 175.

33. 'For writers and readers of both languages (who were likely to know Latin as well)
"English" is not therefore a single concept that works merely in polarity with
French; it contains and is contained by French in a subtle, constantly changing,
and occasionally antagonistic process of accommodation' (Butterfield, *Familiar
Enemy*, 99).

34. See, for example, Butterfield's account of Machaut's creation of a textual relationship between himself and the Duc de Behainge (*Familiar Enemy*, 277).

35. *The Poems of the Troubadour Bertran de Born*, ed. William D. Paden, Tilde Sa-
hovich and Patricia H. Stäblein (Berkeley: University of California Press, 1986).

36. Cannon, 'Lives of Geoffrey Chaucer', 35.

37. John A. Burrow, 'Politeness and Privacy: Chaucer's *BD*', in *Studies in Late Medieval and Early Renaissance Texts in Honour of John Scattergood*, ed. Anne Marie
D'arcy and Alan J. Fletcher (Dublin: Four Courts Press, 2005), 65–75.

38. The idea of indirectness as a means of showing respect is taken up by Rayner,
also, for whom the poem provides a picture of communication between classes
at court: 'The *BD* is a courtly poem, in a courtly setting, and reveals a great deal
of the inner workings of court life; the communication of characters portrayed
shows some of the nuances of relationships between those of differing status,
and the choice of material included in the dream shows how the life of the late
fourteenth century English nobility maintained its perception of itself as a place
of highly mannered, cultured style. ... The social dynamics provide tension within
the poem; Chaucer the poet and the character of the Dreamer are both firmly
lower on the social scale than the Royal duke of Lancaster or the Black Knight
of the poem. How, then, can Chaucer touch on an intimate topic without trans-
gressing those boundaries, a subject that even without such social complexities
would challenge the sympathiser's powers of tact and courtesy?' Samantha J.
Rayner, *Images of Kingship in Chaucer and His Ricardian Contemporaries* (Woodbridge: D.S. Brewer, 2008), 86.

39. Burrow, 'Politeness and Privacy', 74.

40. Charles Muscatine, *Chaucer and the French Tradition* (Berkeley, CA: University of
California Press, 1957), 102.

41. Thomas Parry, *Hanes Llenyddiaeth Cymraeg* (Cardiff: Gwasg Prifysgol Cymru, 1955), 40–53, 99–127; Thomas Parry, *A History of Welsh Literature*, trans. H. Idris Bell (Oxford: Oxford University Press, 1955), 49–63, 127–62.

42. 'Froissart dwells on such matters as the number of Philippa's children and her provision of a tomb for herself' (Wimsatt, *Chaucer and His French Contemporaries*, 179).

43. Eustache Deschamps, ballade 765, in Eustache Deschamps, *Oeuvres Complètes*, ed. le Marquis de Queux de Saint-Hilaire (Paris: SATF, 1878–1903), 4: 259–60. The ballade is reprinted by Coleman with an English translation: Joyce Coleman, 'The Flower, the Leaf, and Philippa of Lancaster', in *'The Legend of Good Women': Context and Reception*, ed. Carolyn P. Collette (Cambridge: Boydell & Brewer, 2006), 57–58.

44. Both aspects of Philippa's literary influence have been examined by Joyce Coleman, 'Philippa of Lancaster, Queen of Portugal – and Patron of the Gower Translations?' in *England and Iberia in the Middle Ages, 12th–15th Century: Cultural, Literary, and Political Exchanges*, ed. Maria Bullón-Fernández (New York: Palgrave Macmillan, 2007), 135–65; Coleman, 'The Flower, the Leaf', 33–58. See also R.F. Yeager, 'Gower's Lancastrian Affinity: The Iberian Connection', *Viator* 35 (2004): 483–515. Philippa's importance has been reassessed in a series of essays in Ana Sáez-Hidalgo and R.F. Yeager, eds., *John Gower in England and Iberia* (Cambridge: D.S. Brewer, 2014).

45. Staley, *Languages of Power*, 220.

46. Ibid., 229.

47. E.g. David R. Carlson, *John Gower, Poetry and Propaganda in Fourteenth-Century England* (Cambridge: D.S. Brewer, 2012). Goodman describes the young Henry as 'developing strong literary interests' (Goodman, *John of Gaunt*, 92).

48. So, for example, the lyric *Truth* appears in Bodley MS Arch Selden B.24, Cambridge University Library MS Gg.4.27, and Magdalene College MS Pepys 2006; the *L'envoy de Scogan* in MS Gg.4.27 and MS Pepys 2006; The *Complaint of Mars* in MS Arch Selden B.24, MS Longleat 258 and twice in MS Pepys 2006.

49. So, Hoccleve's *Book of Cupid* is found in Bodley MS Arch Selden B.24 and Cambridge University Library MS Ff 1.6; the *Temple of Glass* is found in MS Gg.4.27, MS Longleat 258 and MS Pepys 2006.

50. Two of these manuscript witnesses (MS Bodleian Fairfax 16 and MS Bodley 638) also contain *The House of Fame*.

51. Eleanor Prescott Hammond, *Chaucer: A Bibliographical Manual* (New York: Macmillan, 1908), 336–39.

52. Aage Brusendorff, *The Chaucer Tradition* (Oxford: Clarendon Press, 1925), 182 ff.

53. *Bodleian Library MS Fairfax 16*, with introduction by John Norton-Smith (Aldershot: Scolar Press, 1979), vii-iii.

54. The evidence from Lydgate, for example, is ambiguous. Brusendorff notes how, when Lydgate repeated Chaucer's list of works from the Prologue to the *Legend of Good Women* in the Prologue to the *Fall of Princes*, 'he omits one of the items mentioned by Chaucer, *"the bok that highte the hous of fame"'*. He further notes that the otherwise puzzling reference 'He wrot ... Dante in ynglyssh' might refer to the poem; that 'By Skeat the phrase is regarded as a synonym for the one work in Chaucer's lists not mentioned by Lydgate, the *House of Fame'* (Brusendorff,

Chaucer Tradition, 148). John Lydgate, *Lydgate's The Fall of Princes*, vol. I, ed. Henry Bergen (London: EETS e. s. 120, 1924), 9.

55. Julia Boffey and John J. Thompson, 'Anthologies and Miscellanies: Production and Choice of Texts', in *Book Production and Publishing in Britain 1375–1475*, ed. Jeremy Griffiths and Derek Pearsall (Cambridge: Cambridge University Press, 1989), 279–316, here 304.

56. Barry Coward, *The Stanleys, Lord Stanley and Earls of Derby 1385–1672: The Origins, Wealth and Power of a Landowning Family* (Manchester: Chetham Society, 1983); Peter Edmund Stanley, *The House of Stanley: The History of an English Family from the Twelfth Century* (Edinburgh: Pentland Press, 1998).

57. Gervase Mathew, *The Court of Richard II* (New York: William Norton, 1968), 166; Edward Wilson, '*Sir Gawain and the Green Knight* and the Stanley Family of Lathom, Storeton and Hooton', *Review of English Studies* ns. 30, no. 119 (1979): 308–16; Andrew Breeze, 'Sir John Stanley (c. 1350–1414) and the *Gawain* Poet', *Arthuriana* 14, no. 1 (Spring 2000): 15–30.

58. Aisling Byrne and Victoria Flood, 'The Romance of the Stanleys: Regional and National Imagery in the *Percy Folio*', *Viator* 46, no. 1 (2015): 327–51.

59. Josiah C. Wedgwood, DSO MP in collaboration with Anne D. Holt, *History of Parliament: Biographies of the Members of the Commons House 1439–1509* (London: His Majesty's Stationery Office, 1936), 797–98.

60. 'In 1450 the Issue Roll (no. 777) mentions that he had been a King's servant [for] 19 years' (Wedgwood and Holt, *History of Parliament*, 798).

61. Bertram Wolffe, *Henry VI* (London: Eyre Methuen, 1981), 282–83.

62. John Watts, *Henry VI and the Politics of Kingship* (Cambridge: Cambridge University Press, 1996), 311 n. 220.

63. Charles's authorship of poetry in English has been challenged by Calin and Poirion: Daniel Poirion, *Écriture poétique et composition Romanesque*, Medievalia no. 11 (Orléans: Paradigme, 1994); William Calin, 'Will the Real Charles of Orléans, Please Stand! Or, Who Wrote the English Poems in Harley 682?' in *Conjunctures: Medieval Studies in Honor of Douglas Kelly*, ed. Keith Busby and Norris J. Lacey (Amsterdam: Brill, 1994), 69–86.]

64. His authorship was first suggested by MacCracken, and his claims have recently been re-investigated by Jansen, Neilly and Pearsall. H.N. MacCracken, 'An English Friend of Charles d'Orléans', *PMLA* 26 (1911): 155–74; J.P.M. Jansen, 'Charles d'Orléans and the Fairfax Poems', *English Studies* 70 (1989): 206–24; Mariana Neilly, 'William de la Pole's Poetic "Parlement": The Political Lyrics of Bodleian MS. Fairfax 16' in *Authority and Diplomacy from Dante to Shakespeare*, ed. Jason Powell and William T. Rossiter (Farnham, UK: Ashgate, 2013), 57-68; Derek Pearsall, 'The Literary Milieu of Charles of Orléans and the Duke of Suffolk, and the Authorship of the Fairfax Sequence', in *Charles d'Orléans in England*, ed. Mary-Jo Arn (Cambridge: D.S. Brewer, 2000), 145–56.

65. Ralph Griffiths draws attention to the Stanleys' growing influence in North Wales, exercised by Sir Thomas Stanley of Lathom, who shared the duties of justiciar of North Wales and Chester with Suffolk himself. Ralph Griffiths, *The Reign of King Henry VI: The Exercise of Royal Authority 1422–1461* (London: Benn, 1981), 360.

66. Wedgwood and Holt, *History of Parliament*, 797.

67. Griffiths notes that both Stanleys were denounced by parliament: 'The same strength of will is apparent during the parliament which met on 6th November 1450. The petition that twenty named members of the Kings Household and court – including Sir Thomas Stanley and John Stanley should be dismissed and removed from the king's presence by 1 Dec was rejected in all essentials'. Ralph A. Griffiths, *King and Country: England and Wales in the Fifteenth Century* (London: Hambledon Press, 1991), 296. Wedgwood and Holt (*History of Parliament*, 798) note that John Stanley had previously been accused by Jack Cade, but that neither attack had persuaded Henry to dismiss him: 'Stanley was one of the favourites denounced by Jack Cade at Rochester, July 1450; by November they were denouncing him in parliament also but he retained his posts. He received a general pardon in May 1455, two days before the battle of St Albans. He was pardoned again [in] 1458'.

68. 'Three times the family transferred their allegiance to a new dynasty, abandoning the weak and incompetent Richard II, and the feeble-minded Henry VI (who, following a mental breakdown, was at times an imbecile and unfit to rule)' (Stanley, *The House of Stanley*, 6).

69. The *Paston Letters*, ed. J. Gairdner, 4 vols. (Edinburgh: John Grant, 1910). The Pastons' often fraught dealings with the Countess are mentioned, for example, in II, 207–8; III, 482; IV, 106–7, 130.

70. Carol M. Meale, 'Reading Women's Culture in Fifteenth-Century England: The Case of Alice Chaucer', in *Mediævalitas: Reading the Middle Ages* (Cambridge: D.S. Brewer, 1996), 81–102, here 83.

71. Ibid., 87.

72. Brusendorff, *Chaucer Tradition*, 38; Meale, 'Reading Women's Culture', 91–93.

73. Meale, 'Reading Women's Culture', 92.

74. Lines 30–96 in the Riverside edition, from 'But men myght axe' to 'Such sorwe this lady to her tok'. MS Bodley 638 also lacks the six preceding lines.

75. Norman Blake, 'The Textual Tradition of the *BD*', *English Studies* 62 (1981): 237–48, here 248. Blake's conclusions were contested by Helen Phillips, and her reservations then answered by Blake: Helen Phillips, 'The *BD* Lines 31–96: Are They a Forgery?' *English Studies* 67 (1986): 113–121; Norman Blake, 'The *BD* Again', *English Studies* 67 (1986): 122–5.

76. All three manuscripts lack lines 31–96, but Bodley 638 also lacks lines 24–30.

77. All three manuscripts are also missing lines 288 and 886. Both Fairfax and Bodley leave a gap for the missing lines, which, in Fairfax, are written in by a later hand.

78. That is to discount a few minor differences, which seem likely to be the result of chance. Bodley 638 is also missing lines 24–30, and line 97, which, it has been suggested, may result from a missing leaf, and lines 791–92.

79. Blake, 'The *BD* Again', 125.

80. Ibid.

81. Meale, 'Reading Women's Culture', 82.

Chapter 6

'Tu Numeris Elementa Ligas'

The Consolation of Nature's Numbers in *Parlement of Foulys*

C.W.R.D. Moseley

More than once, Chaucer shows he is aware of his poems operating in two not necessarily convergent modes. *Troilus and Criseyde* (*T&C*) often addresses the plural, listening audience presumed in '...Wherever thou art herde, or elles songe...' (V.1797–1798), yet V.270 addresses the single *reader*: 'thow, reder'. *Canterbury Tales* models the acts of oral delivery and reception, yet it is a book where a reader can 'turne over the leef, and chese another tale' (A.3177). Both audiences experience the same words, but *not* the same poem, for a poem lives in the transaction between poet and audience, and change the audience, change the poem.[1] Further, a reader has a readier grasp of total form than most listeners, and aspects like shape and number were part of the hermeneutic toolkit that some scholars would readily deploy in pre-Romantic ages. 'Form is meaning': Cleanth Brooks famously stated this as one of his 'articles of faith', and he was not saying anything to which our medieval forebears could not have assented.[2] A familiar example, extreme in detail but not in essence, of word, form and image on the page converging is Hrabanus Maurus's *De Laude Sanctae Crucis* in Bodley MS Douce 192, where form, words and image constitute a *quartum quid* greater than the sum of the parts.

Some attention has been given to oral recitation or, as I would prefer, performance of medieval poems.[3] (Poems like *Parliament of Fouls* [PF] or *T&C* do perform extremely well.) Many manuscript (MS) illustrations show people performing, reading, to an audience (e.g. the best known, Corpus Christi College Cambridge MS 61, fol. 1[vo]). This highlights just how much we cannot know. For of a performance no simple text can record speed and inflection of delivery, tone of voice, the language of gesture and expression where merely arching an eyebrow can quite alter reception. Indeed, over all interpretation of, say, medieval 'social' poetry (or, for that matter, Jacobethan drama), there is a shadow of unknowability. While we may be confident that in writing a poem the *poet* had an intention, and performed it when delivering to an audience, on subsequent occasions that might have been modified, and when the poem is released to other speakers it may serve quite other agendas.

But the implications of solitary *reading* and reception are also greatly interesting, and equally problematic. We easily assume that to read is to read in our way, but by definition (not only by differences of type face, or MS style, or *mise en page*) medieval readers will read differently, in a different country circling a different sun.[4] Nobody in the first five centuries of its existence read *PF* in a critical text in awareness of a body of scholarship and interpretation behind it. What did – could – our predecessors notice and enjoy that perhaps we do not?

Composing for a plural *audience* certainly implies some awareness of the common denominator in the group: an occasion, a set of shared memories or assumptions. But composing in awareness of single readers is different. Milton, who like many of his predecessors accepted Augustine's dictum that 'that which is discovered with difficulty is remembered with pleasure' (*De Doctrina Christiana*, II. 6.8), was expressly happy with a 'fit audience, though few'[5] for *Paradise Lost* (*PL*). Indeed, *PL* was first an oral poem: Milton composed and then dictated it, and then it was mediated into print. It may well have been – still is! – read aloud, as its rhetorical register seems to demand; but the solitary reader, who can move back and forth at will, sees things no hearer could.[6] Similarly with *PF*: this article will examine features a reader could discover and a listener simply could not. Neither is the whole 'truth' of the poem – indeed, their implications contradict. An alert reader will be aware of how flawed his first reading was, yet it in turn criticizes the second. But both are 'true'. Chaucer is exploring/exploiting that gap between what we might call linear and panoptic reception.

Almost certainly *PF* was written for an occasion now forgotten, but we still read it with a pleasure not limited to historians. Like the squabbling birds, commentators seem able to agree only on disagreement about its issues.[7] Most accept that at the heart lies ambiguity and dubiety, but what that surrounds, be it philosophical, moral, political or literary (or any combination of these) seems to depend as much on what readers project onto the verbal text as on the text itself.[8] This article of course courts exactly this same criticism, and so I must excuse myself for adding another voice to the noise of foules to ben delivered. Attention to the structure, I suggest, reveals a subtext of philosophical concepts of order and harmony that must qualify our inferences from the words. The narrator's perplexity[9] neatly figures the problems at the poem's heart, and his hesitancy about his understanding is a warning that every available analytical tool must be used on the reported 'experience' and on its reporting, if anything like the truth lying behind his (or our) partial apprehension of it is to be grasped. But the formal and mathematical structures he cannot see may convey other important concepts, as well as reflect on the imprecision of human utterance.

Immediately to plunge *in medias res* – literally – would bring us up sharply against a highly patterned block of stanzas listing the birds exactly at the poem's midpoint.[10] (Incidentally, choosing to write in stanzas, by definition, invites attention to form *qua* form.) Working outwards from this centre – as no listener could – reveals balanced, symmetrical structures flanking it. But merely to demonstrate the existence of patterned structure is unhelpful without some understanding of why a poem might have been so built. After all, if the patterns result from planning, as I shall show they do (e.g. note 40 on Chaucer's use of *Teseida*), then it is important to draw on them. So to see what Chaucer was up to demands some glance at the 'olde bokes totorn' and acknowledgement of the tradition he inherited.

A constructionist aesthetic based on elaborate patterning and subdivision of form as a control on apprehended meaning is traceable back at least as far as the Alexandrian School.[11] It was clearly understood by Augustine (*De Vera Religione*, XXX, 55, 56), whose influence, with Boethius and Martianus Capella, on medieval aesthetics is profound. Pattern and number were not just *ad hoc* for a given work, but had an agreed value outside and prior to its creation.[12] It is a theological truism that the Mind of God is seen in His Creation (cf. *Romans* I.20), that everything was disposed by the Great Architect[13] by number, proportion and weight,[14] and that analysing arithmetical, geometrical and musical patterns of the universe will reveal Him. Numbers as tools in reading the Bible were discussed by Augustine in *De Doctrina Christiana*;[15] his own aesthetics are strongly structurally orientated (*Confessions*, X.viii, and cf. *De Musica*). Not only does a Richard of St Victor use all the resources of typology and *figura* and the numerology they exploit on the inspired record of Divine Providence recorded in Scripture by human hand; these resources are also used on secular literature, for example when Bernard the Chancellor deploys them to analyse the *Aeneid*. Alain de Lille's account of the creation of the perfect man in *Anticlaudianus* mirrors in content and form the creating operation of the Word, and interestingly stresses the capacity of number and proportion to clarify meaning:[16]

> Hic pictura loquens scripto clamansque figuris,
> Muta tamen, totam numerandi predicat artem. (III, 229–231)

(Alain is a peculiarly apposite authority in discussing *PF*.[17]) A poet, therefore, with an idea of human art as able to communicate what will be worth the getting is likely to assume his audience's familiarity with these common exegetical tools and write with deliberate allusiveness, pattern and obscurity.[18] His activity is derivative from, analogous – though vastly inferior – to the operation of the Creating Word, so a work of art is amenable to discussion with those same tools that God Himself seems to have used. Pattern and symmetry – *aequalitas* – are poetic mimesis of the Unity and Beauty that are supreme attributes of God. For Aquinas, *proportio sive consonantia* made one of the three things in which Beauty consisted.[19]

Use of these tools does not seem limited to works broadly speaking religious. The *Divina Commedia*'s complex numerological structure and symbolism is well known. Dante's *Letter to Can Grande*

della Scala,[20] clear evidence of the concept of poetic art and practice
by writer and reader held by at least some of Chaucer's immediate
predecessors, emphasizes division of the poem into its individual
parts,[21] exactly Dante's technique in his own commentary on *La Vita
Nuova*. It perfectly fits the implications of his view of poetry in *De
Vulgari Eloquentia* and in the *Convivio*.[22] John Gower uses number
patterns he expected his readers to know.[23] The *Gawain*-poet is a
master of patterned form.[24] Form, pattern, number and proportion
reveal serious meaning,[25] and the signals of the verbal text are modified by what is imposed on them by correspondence, memory and
other extraneous factors. Even today, after exposure to centuries of
prose fiction as a dominant form, we have no difficulty in reading,
say, a sonnet or a villanelle with certain expectations both of subject
and formal meaning.

Concepts of *ars poetica* held, and demonstrably practised,[26] are
helpful. There is the presupposition (which the *trovères* shared) that
appreciating poetry and art is open only to the inner circle, the élite
who know how to read it. The basic structural techniques of medieval art, including poetry, are aggregative, and meaning is often juxta-
positionally conveyed – in other words, pattern is an important part
of meaning.[27] Chaucer was no exception to his age; however nicely
ironic it may be to have Pandarus, hardly the model of the successful
or morally responsible artist, borrow Geoffroi de Vinsauf's analogy
between housebuilding and the writing of a poem (*T&C*, I.1066), it
also shows awareness of common ideas and a readiness to exploit
his audience's knowledge of them. The detailed mathematical structure in *Troilus and Criseyde* has been demonstrated;[28] on a much
smaller scale, *An ABC* shows assured handling (improving considerably on its source) of the common acrostic poem with a strongly
marked chiastic pattern.[29] Indeed, chiastic patterns were exploited in
architecture and music long before and after *PF*,[30] but also, at nearly
the same time, Petrarch uses them brilliantly in the *Trionfi*, a book
whose title self-referentially warns us to watch for them. The very
fact that *PF* is in rime royale, to all intents and purposes Chaucer's
very noticeable import into the armoury of English poetics, suggests
concern with form *qua* form. Even when heard, a poem in those
stanzas never lets you forget it is so written when every seven lines
that double couplet stops the forward movement dead. Seeing any
formal pattern is even easier when it is read in MS or print: the eye
does it for you.

Given this, my next concern is to explore the poem's mathematical and proportional dispositions, and some of the numerological clues.[31] Modern lineation gives the poem 699 lines. Strictly, it consists of 98 seven-line stanzas and a roundel. The MSS are unclear on the number of lines in the roundel:[32] the fullest version is in a fifteenth-century hand later than the rest of the MS in Cambridge University Library MS Gg.4.27. Roundels at this time vary from nine to fourteen lines, and Skeat's thirteen-line reconstruction, based on a pattern used by Machaut, though generally followed, is as arbitrary as would be scribal abbreviation of a song whose repeated lines the tune might imply. (The 'note' in 677 may imply a tune Chaucer's audience knew.[33]) But in a poem of such regularity of form and structure, as this article will demonstrate, a line total of 699 might seem odd, and repeating 682 twice rather than once would be consistent with the roundel form and give a poem of 700 lines. Even so, just as the *Gawain*-poet finesses the expectation of perfect symmetry in the 101, not 100, stanzas and laisses of *Perle* and *Sir Gawain*, so Chaucer may well have decided in this teasing and inconclusive poem to do the same.

But 699 or 700, the middle is at l. 350, with the cock; and if 700 is indeed the length, 351 too, with the sparrow. These birds' usual symbolism seems important:[34] throughout the poem Chaucer emphasizes time passing from morning to evening, and the sparrow, 'Venus sone', is explicitly connected with Love. (It is the only bird in the list linked to a deity, which supports its importance.) These lines are the centre of a four-stanza block in a parisonic and anaphoric style which distinguishes itself syntactically, sonically and visually – each line beginning 'the' – from the poem's normal narrative. We are led into the bird catalogue by a stanza (s. 48, ll. 330–336) in a looser style that distinguishes the hierarchy of the raptors, and out of it (s. 53) by a summarizing statement of the presence of 'every kynde' of bird and their desire to choose mates. These four stanzas connect a whole aviary adjectivally with human experience, problems and concerns. It is impossible not to notice the oddity of this passage even if one misses (as one must, on first encounter) its mathematically central position.

The significance of the number 4 might suggest why the catalogue is in four unusual stanzas. 1, 2, 3, 4 were the basis of all other numbers and harmony. Several medieval philosophers also attached to 4 significations referring to Man and the Cardinal Virtues. These

cohere in connection with life on earth in time and mutability, and
the birds present a moral mirror of men's orders, disorders, virtues
and vices. However, 4 leads further; the sum of the first four numbers, ten, is the 'tetractys', which is both a symbol of totality and
unity and the square root of 100, which also symbolizes totality, a
return to unity and the ultimate perfection.[35] Now, this four-stanza
block is a subdivision at the exact centre of the poem, and of a block
of ten stanzas (ss. 46–55, ll. 316–385) which begins and ends with
closely similar descriptions of Nature – specifically Alain's Nature,
given charge by God over the Created Universe.[36]

This block is clearly marked off and symmetrically constructed:

> S. 46, ll. 316–22: identification of Nature, who bids each take 'his
> owne place';
> > S. 47, ll. 323–329: the classes of birds; their hierarchy; Nature's
> > power over them, beginning with the 'foules of ravyne';
> > > S. 48, ll. 330–336: introduction to catalogue;
> > > > Ss. 49–52, ll. 337–364: **central block**: emphasis on Time
> > > > and Love;
> > > S. 53, ll. 365–371: summary of catalogue;
> > S. 54, ll. 372–77: the noble formel and Nature's delight in her;
> S. 55, ll. 378–385: Nature again described, and her means (number)
> of maintaining her rule over the four elements.

So this ten-stanza block, that number symbolizing unity and creation, straddles the poem's centre in a triumphal pattern as neat
as anything ever used by Petrarch or Milton. But this block is itself enclosed by two other stanzas, 44 and 56 (308ff. and 386ff.),
each opening with 'seynt Valentines day' and the birds' choosing
of mates. This constitutes a block of twelve stanzas. Twelve is one
root of the number of the Blessed in *Revelations*. But St Valentine's
day suggests the repeating cycle of the twelve months (Time again!)
and thus a new beginning.[37] Since the centre of the block is clearly
concerned with Man's moral behaviour and the outer skirts of it
with order and renewal, it may not be fanciful, finally, to see the
factor seven in the total of eighty-four lines as symbolizing Man
himself, a hybrid of three souls in four elements. The choice of
rime royale thus could become an added felicity in the composition
of the poem.[38]

The probability of this clearly designed and proportioned pattern
at the apex of this poem being accidental is remote. It is amenable to
numerological interpretation that harmonizes with what the words

are saying. Such complexity does not come with breezes on the Aeolian harp, and its careful design prompts a look elsewhere for similar patterns.

The polarized opposites that are so notable a feature of *PF* – Nature/Venus, noble birds/common birds, two contradictory inscriptions over the gate and so on – suggest, after Nature's realm, examination of the composite narrative block covering the Garden and the temple of Venus (ss. 27–42, ll. 183–294).[39] The Garden is closely imitated from Boccaccio (though with changes that strongly support my contention about Chaucer's technique[40]) and relies on one of the most familiar *topoi* in all medieval and Renaissance literature. Audience expectations and indeed values are automatically present (though not yet focused) as soon as Chaucer writes 'A garden saw I'. This could become either the allegorical Garden of Love or the Paradisal Garden[41] depending on the emphases employed. How it is structured as well as the semantic content decides the options. The whole passage occupies sixteen stanzas: the number symbolized, in its four-square structure, and in the double octave, Justice and Judgement. Judgement is a major concern in the poem – both formal judgement as in the court of Nature, and judgement about human cognition.[42] Indeed, lines 496/497 virtually sum up the narrator's, the birds' and our perplexity as well as raising the question to which throughout his career Chaucer keeps returning, the nature of knowledge. Here it is applied to Love:

> How shold a juge eyther parti leve
> For ye or nay, withouten any preve?[43]

It is useful, first, to take the block as a whole, since the stanzas describing Venus and her temple form a noticeable climax to the Vision of the Love Garden. The structure could lead the audience to expect the rest of *PF* to develop as a psychomachic allegory of personal love; and despite any unease they might – if alert – feel with the not altogether pleasant associations of the adjectives and references describing Love and Venus, it could be taken at face value. But Chaucer finesses this cleverly. For a start, the centre lines of the block give us the doves of Venus,[44] and Dame Pees; we are not allowed to overlook the connection of Love and the Peace that expresses harmony. And the poem is clearly concerned with the problematic nature of the one and the difficult achievement (in 'comune profit') of the other.

But the block also breaks into two subdivisions, ss. 27–37, ll. 183–259, eleven stanzas, and ss. 38–42, ll. 260–294, five stanzas: total sixteen. The eleven stanzas describe the outside, the Garden, while the five discuss the 'prive corner' where Venus lies. Eleven is usually the number of transgression, of imperfection,[45] and the centre of this sub-block is occupied by three stanzas (ss. 32–34, ll. 211–231) of prosopopoiea of distinctly ambivalent nature – Lust, Craft, Folye ('disfigurat'), Foolhardynesse, Flatterye are hardly delightful. The centre line (221) of the three stanzas is significant:

To don by force a wyght to don folye (cf. note 40)

This recalls a view of human affective love we might find in the moralists, or indeed in Lydgate's *Reason and Sensuality*: a snare to someone seeking moral good. So the Love Garden's internal climax tends to reinforce the negative values of the second of the two contradictory balanced inscriptions over the gate while its surface décor might suggest the first. The stylistic parallel between the middle lines of those two stanzas of inscriptions (ll. 130ff., 137ff.) underlines the contrast between the promised fruitfulness of a normal spring, and barrenness; in the first, the dry trees of the second hide behind adjectives. (With *hindsight*, one is forced to refer this to the mating – fruitful, one supposes – of the common birds and the elegant sterility of the noble at the poem's close.) The Garden description thus cuts both ways rather sharply, but the structural devices provide a firm control on how it can fit into the economy of the poem.

The Venus passage provides the same sort of ambiguity. The picture of Venus is titillating, yet surrounded by oppressive darkness and pictures of familiar tragic lovers. The undeniable force of lust is surrounded by warnings of its consequences. The centre (277) of the five stanzas actually refers us not only to the key figure but also wittily to the way the block itself is structured:

And as I seyde, amyddes lay Cypride.

Moreover, five is important: Venus certainly uses the five senses as the *Roman de la Rose* pointed out, but five is also one of the two marriage numbers. Chaucer thus uses it elsewhere when in *Troilus and Criseyde* V.799ff. he gives the chiastically structured description of Criseyde flanked by Diomed and Troilus, in stylistic, structural and lexical balance, in a five-stanza block. Again, number and structure provide ironic comment on content.

Description of the Garden and of Venus begins immediately after a stock, much imitated, catalogue of trees (s. 26), whose adjectives, like those of the birds, relate them to human life and death. This stanza has emphatic use of *parison* and *anaphora*, and lacks finite verbs – stylistically identical to that of the central catalogue of birds. Like that, it sticks out sonically as well as visually; it signals our having reached a division point in the poem – indeed the stanza marks the transition from the dreamer's perplexed rehearsing of the contradictory possibilities of his dream's origin (and therefore significance) to the description of the Garden. It occurs a quarter of the way through the poem, and another important division is underlined.

The second quarter of the poem, then, leads up to the centre block we have already discussed. In the stanza (s. 75) ending at the three-quarter point (525), Nature intervenes in what was turning into a pointless gaggle to take control of the debate. Sixteen stanzas before this, at s. 59 (l. 406), Nature calls on the royal tercel and lays out the terms of the choice and judgement, thus initiating the debate. This beginning comes two stanzas after the end of the twelve-stanza block at the centre; that centre block is separated from the Venus/ Garden block by two stanzas. These two pairs both refer (one by description, one by Nature's actual speech) to Nature's authority and power. The concluding lines of the two pairs of stanzas, 308 and 406, contain words from the same lexical set, 'dom' and 'choys'. There is thus an exact symmetry.

The sixteen stanzas after Nature tells the tercel 'the choys is to the falle' (407) again emphasize judgement, and they are delicious in their logical as well as their mock-heroic comedy. Can we really believe that birds, let alone men, really mean what the hyperboles of Love say they mean? That it is possible to hold the view of one's total unworthiness at the same time as to plead one's deserts?[46] But the speeches' real keynote is the idea of proof in love – the very thing that is impossible and, even if it were, would be irrelevant. The birds are pleading judgement on merits when merits are beside the point. The third eagle – a rather low fellow, one feels – comes nearest to recognizing this when he says:

> ... as possible is to me to deye today
> For wo as he that hath ben languysshyng
> This twenty wynter... (471ff.)

Yet even he slips back immediately into misunderstanding, as all three do, the absolute prerogative of grace. But there is a serious problem in the comedy too, for though it is impossible to deserve grace, it is not impossible to commit grievous faults that would deserve punishment. A man (or bird) may indeed 'don folye'; the note sounded in the central position of the Garden passage recurs in the central points of the speeches of the first two birds:

> And if that I to hyre be founde untrewe,
> Disobeysaunt, or wilful necligent... (428/429)
> ... if she me fynde fals,
> Unkynde, janglere, of rebel any wyse (456/457)

This recognition is important to any moral life. But the third eagle has no such knowledge of frailty; this avian Diomed is very sure of his merits. His style too Chaucer distinguishes from that of the other two; it is brusque, rhythmically emphatic, the sentences are shorter, lacking the subordinate clauses that create a sense of polished urbanity in the other eagles. All his terms are comparative, to his advantage against the others. And so the three speeches together subtly present us with a basis for serious discussion of folly, judgement, fault and desert, and grace. And, of course, Love.

For Love is the immediate issue. The noble birds have argued in a world bounded by their own sensibility and moeurs. Yet within the ambit of their judgement, because of their hierarchical importance, comes the interest of the rest of the commonwealth. The other component in these stanzas is how the lower birds react. Polished language blows away in an explosion of animal noise; from them, whence we might least expect it, comes the important assertion that proof is necessary to judgement, and that here there is none (496/497). Quite properly, when nobles forget, the commons can recall them to a sense of 'comune spede' (507). This perspective *must* be included in judgement, and the echo of the emphasis on 'comune profit' in the summary of the *Somnium Scipionis* in the first quarter of the poem is a powerful control on our understanding of the parameters of this debate.

When this block is set against its balance, the Garden/Venus passage, the thematic links are clear. The mating activity (or inclination thereto) of the waterfowl takes up the icon of Priapus; the eagles' high courtoisie (or, strictly, attempt at it) reflects and is valued against the allegorical personages, and they are valued by the struc-

ture into which Chaucer put them. The position of Venus as monarch to be supplicated (278/279) is occupied by the formel. The list of
unhappy lovers suggests where these eagles might find themselves
in time. Must noble Love always be destructive and sterile? Is it only
mating that matters? Clearly not, for just as the successful pairing
of the lower birds values the lack of satisfaction of the noble, so the
nobility of the eagles, however comic, is attractive enough to show
how inadequate a view of Love the other birds have. For despite its
ambiguous adjectives, the Garden of Love is set in a *topos* alluding to
harmony and perfection. The semantic and conceptual similarities
between the two passages are underpinned by their linking in the
structural pattern.

The existence of this complex pattern at the centre prompts comparison of the first and last quarters of the poem. Three quarters
of the way through, Nature, who 'alwey hadde an ere / to murmur
of the lewednesse behynde' (519–520), reassumes control over the
squabbling by setting up formal debate. This pattern recalls not only
the procedures of Court and Parliament but also the *quaestio* with
its balanced statements of opposing positions. Sixteen stanzas take
us from the moment of the birds' assent to her ruling (526) to her
conclusion (637). Appropriately, the judgement number reappears.
The passage subdivides into the bird-speakers and Nature's summing up. The alternating arguments (and ranks) of the speakers are
immediately noticeable, and almost as obvious is the juxtaposition in
two significant beaks of the two possible views of Love at the centre
of this parade.

The triumphal position is held jointly by the dove – perhaps one
of those flying round the temple? – who advocates loving unselfishly
and permanently in total commitment,[47] and the duck, 'stroyere of
his owne kynde' (360), who pours contempt on this, recommend-
ing loving solely for advantage. These views are mutually exclusive,
and both have considerations in their favour. In the perpetual moral
perplexity that constitutes life on earth, the right course is rarely
clear. But that there *is* a right course in all occasions (even if beyond
human discernment) is a certainty that Chaucer has built into the
poem by his summary of the *Somnium Scipionis* (see below). The
poem seems to posit an idea of social or political 'love', which, like
Gower's in Prologue to *Confessio Amantis*, is a subset of the total
idea of Love just as much as is sexual love. (And, as in Gower, what
are in fact subsets *seem* exclusive of each other.) This ideal is stated

in general terms in the first quarter of the poem, where 'comune profit' is first mentioned;[48] in the last quarter its specific application (as the 'comune spede' of the bird commonwealth) is at issue in the problem of choice. The bird debate, then, with its double central emphasis, balances the *Somnium* passage. The closely related concerns of the two refer to each other across the poem's central structure.

The conclusion of this block is Nature's summing up (ss. 89–91, ll. 616–637). Here she accepts the unknowable nature of Love and the impossibility of proof. She recalls what the eagles said they accepted but clearly forgot: the formel's choice is absolute. Grace is inscrutable and would not be grace if it were determined by desert. It is this idea that Chaucer put into the central line of the speech as climax to the idea of choice first raised at 621:

... Shal han right hym on whom hire herte is set. (627)

The whole sixteen-stanza block emphasizes, like the *Somnium* passage, the necessity of moral choice, the inevitability of judgement, and the bases on which judgement may be made. But where in the *Somnium* passage Affrycan emphasizes the need for Works (74–76), this passage underlines the complete freedom of the formel to bestow her grace where she wishes. Her grace and freedom make all the previous discussion a waste of time; yet Grace, as we are reminded by St Paul, is the source of Works.

The last block I analyse is the summary of the *Somnium Scipionis*. Old books can be made, we might say, to bring forth new corn, and Chaucer has shifted the concerns of Cicero's text away from – but not *right* away from[49] – the best form of government and the best type of citizen, which the *Somnium* as epilogue to *De Re Publica* implies, to 'comune profite' and the reward of bliss after death. The summary is angled to emphasize moral choice and moral action, an emphasis reinforced by the artifice of the structure.

Like the central four stanzas, the block stands out stylistically. Its rhetoric resembles that of another of Chaucer's strategic literary summaries, the *Aeneid* in *The House of Fame*. The summary proper occupies 7 seven-line stanzas (ss. 6–12), one (l. 32) supposedly for each chapter.[50] (Its structuring in seven stanzas is important, for in addition to commonly signifying Man, seven can also refer to Wisdom – a major concern here.) Every verse but the last begins with the same adverb + verb + pronoun structure, the centre five all beginning 'Thanne'. The style is more indecorate and paratactic than elsewhere in the poem and clearly, like the central four stanzas, would sound different. By doing so it can warn the audience that they are in a secondary structure complete in itself yet crucial to the background from which it is distinguished. (This emphasizes that the book is within the illusion of the poem, yet, existing as it does outside it as well, is parallel to, commenting on, and thus a clue to the illusion the poem handles.) The regularity of the syntactic pattern makes the structural organization remarkably clear. Our attention even on first reading or hearing is drawn to the repetition of 'blisful place' twice (48, 76/77), 'comune profit' twice (47, 75) and to the opening and closing of the section.

To summarize:

S. 6, ll. 36–42. Affrycan appears to Scipio in a dream.
  S. 7, ll. 43ff. Affrycan shows Carthage; concern for 'comune profit'; bliss after death.
    S. 8, ll. 50ff. Life on earth; its relation to death.
      S. 9, ll. 57ff.(**centre**) Earth in respect of the Heavens; Heavenly Harmony.
    S. 10, ll. 64ff. Life on earth. Time.
  S. 11, ll. 71ff. Concern for 'comune profit', resultant heavenly bliss.
S. 12, ll. 77ff. Affrycan's closing lines; punishment and eventual forgiveness.

Once again, a symmetrical, chiastic structure. Particularly noticeable is the verbal parallel between the last three lines of the second stanza (47–49) and those of the sixth (75–78). But what is most important, as usual, is placed in the central stanza, stressing the relation of this 'litel spot of erthe' to the Heavens, the harmony of the nine spheres, and the connection between the harmony of perfection and the highest art in this our world. Music is thus the clue to the connection between moral life and the order of the universe.

Two other details support this idea of music. In that central stanza, nine is twice emphasized: the totality of the universe, including the sphere of the fixed stars and of the Primum Mobile, is thus stressed. And this is in the ninth stanza of the poem. Furthermore, the stanza's central line (and thus the block's) is 'And after that the melodye herde he' – the melody is the exact centre, the hearing of it vouchsafed to a human being. But this line also syntactically links to l. 62, 'That welle is of musik and melodye', the twenty-seventh line of the block. Now 27, as Milton knew in the Hymn in the *Ode on the*

Morning of Christ's Nativity,[51] and as Henryson also knew in *Orpheus and Euridice*, symbolizes the World-Soul or Entelechy – indeed, the Logos. Thus, the operation of the Creating Word is deftly indicated as the source of that which can be analysed and quantified, and that analysis and description is the ultimate basis for man's moral knowledge of himself and his world. The Divine Mind is visible in Creation[52] – indeed, it is in Creation alone that our little limited intellects can glimpse the ineffable.[53] But music, the highest art and the one that grasps most, is beyond words. The poem thus marks out its own limitation and supercession.

The *Somnium* summary is a variation on the venerable 'Books I have been reading' *topos*, and, as usual, it closes certain options and open others about the poem. Chaucer had already shown how skilfully he could handle this in the delicious yet ultimately seriously affecting mess the narrator makes of the story of Seys and Alcyone in *The Boke of the Duchess*. Here the *topos* is tightly integrated into the thematic structure of the whole poem and its own internal structure provides not only a gloss on itself but an anchor point for the entire subsequent discussion. I noted above the link between issues of 'comune profit' here and 'comune spede' in the debate; we should also note that the harmony at the centre here is echoed in the decorative birds in the Garden, parodied in the 'noise of foules to ben delivered', and last heard at the end of the poem in the patterned, circular roundel the birds sing. (Yet the birds have not changed their song.) This structuring of an authority summarized many times before adds a philosophical and cosmological context for moral discussion and action, and therefore for the concerns of the whole poem.

Those concerns are adumbrated in the poem's masterly first stanza. It is not at all uncommon for Chaucer to tease his audience by shifting their expectations[54] and suggesting false scents. This stanza certainly does. The *sententia* of line 1 suggests a topic different from that at the syntactic climax in line 4, and our expectations are upended; yet the irony is that the shortness of life and the difficulty of the art of knowledge *are* integral to the poem's key concerns. The Parliament happens against a background of the seasonal cycle implied in the return of spring; the difficulty of knowledge underlies not only the whole attempt at judgement in the birds' council but also the narrator's detached position and utterance. Moreover, the stanza's construction provides not only hints about the matter of the poem but also clues about how that matter will be structured. In fact, it is a miniature model of the whole poem.

The *anaphora* and *parison* of lines 1–3 and their lack of a main verb create a suspense that is only resolved in line 4, on the word 'Love'. 'Love' is in the central rhythmical unit of the stanza. It is not the concept that we would immediately expect to be qualified by the *sententia* from Hippocrates, via Horace; nor is it what we automatically expect from the bitter images of military struggle and fleeting time in ll. 2–3 – though afterwards, of course, they do not surprise, for we recognize the 'Love/battle' image complex. But the syntactic link is emphatic, and it is reinforced by the rhetorical and rhythmical structure. The first line is built as a *contentio*, and consists (to use an anachronistic term) of five iambic feet with a strong caesura after the second foot to separate the contrasting halves of the thought. The second line keeps to an identical rhythmic pattern, but the *contentio* hardens up into a chiasmus (noun/adjective: adjective/noun take the voice ictus). The pattern and contrast is thus sharpened. The third line is again the same rhythmical pattern, but here the contrasting second half of the first two lines has been replaced by a relative clause emphasizing ephemerality, and the first half has tightened up the rhetorical contrasts of the first two lines into an oxymoron, 'dredful joye'. The regularity of the rhythmical balance in these three lines throws equal weight onto contradictory elements, to the point where we do not know which is the final answer – and, of course, there isn't one, for the oxymoron links opposing ideas in an indissoluble syntactic unit. But now comes a massive pause before the main clause in line 4 – we hold our breaths before plunging down onto the reversed rhythmical pattern of the line. Line 4 starts with a heavy stress on the first syllable and puts the caesura not four but six syllables from the beginning of the line. Instead of a pattern we can call iambic, the first four syllables form a trochaic one; the voice ictus falls on 'Al' – that is, all the contradictions and seesaw confusions of ll. 1–3, which the poem will explore; on 'mene', which emphasizes at once the narrator's desire to say something and his hesitation in saying it; and finally on 'Love'. This word is in the key rhythmical, syllabic, spatial, numerical and conceptual position in the stanza. The enormous emphasis thrown onto it must be a clear signal that this is the subject discussed at the heart of the poem, however hedged about by ambiguity it may turn out to be.

After this rhetorical climax, the rhythm becomes much less assured. There is semantic emphasis on the narrator's problematic
perception ('felynge', 'Astonyeth', 'wonderful', 'thynke', 'Nat wot
I wel'), and the fluttering rhythm of l. 5 and the double caesura of
l. 6 emphasize this. The stanza closes with a return to the *contentio*
figure of line 1, whose contrast ('flete'/'synke') is syntactically dependent on the narrator's confusion.

The artistry of this stanza eludes adequate discussion. It is clearly
designed to highlight the word 'Love'. An audience familiar from
elsewhere with the techniques of symbolic and metaphorical structuring of works of art and literature could not have helped noticing
this and would, I feel sure, have accepted it as a clue to the *dispositio*
of the poem. (Perhaps we tend to forget that audiences for poetry
as well as for music can be highly skilled; in fact, experience of medieval and Renaissance poetry shows that the reading or receiving of
poetry is as much a serious art for 'understanders' as the writing of
it.[55]) The high register and style of the first lines makes it obvious the
stanza is important. With knowledge of the whole poem, however,
it would work differently. Then it can be seen to act like an overture
or contents list, where the themes are briefly opened. The pattern of
the stanza can thus correct the emphases of a first reading or hearing when we reconsider the poem. The central concept, Love, is the
major surface concern of the poem. Because of the normal limited
usage of the term, we tend to apply it to affective or emotional love.
But the centre of the whole poem is occupied by the central block,
which deals not only with the birds and their mating but also the
ordo[56] in which they have their being. This block is dominated by
Nature, God's vicegerent, who holds contradictory and warring elements from chaos by her 'evene nombres of acord', her harmonious
rule (379–381). Those contradictory elements appear not as absolutes but as details in the *contentiones* of the first three lines of the
stanza. The stanza's mathematical structure thus figures Nature's
control. The first line stresses the shortness of life and the need to
learn, just as the first major block, the *Somnium* passage, does. The
military images of the second line adumbrate those of the second
inscription over the gate and point us to the ambiguous delights of
the Love Garden. The third line's 'dredful joye' is fully explored in
Venus's temple. The fifth, sixth and seventh lines stress confusion,
the impossibility of certain knowledge or judgement, exactly as does
the council of birds. The stanza closes, like the poem, with the nar-

rator's confusion about his knowledge. I suggest this stanza is not only a model to help us read the poem, but also that demonstration of this stanza's rhetorical organization supports my analysis of the whole poem's design.

The narrator's uneasiness about his perception[57] is of a piece with the difficulty of knowledge (and, so, of utterance), which is a major interest in all Chaucer's work. Here the question is raised by the narrator's ignorance, detachment, inexperience and uncertainty; it is also integral to the discussion of judgement in the birds' council. This brings us to the last thing I want to look at, the gap between language and perceived reality. (It is hinted at in the semantics of stanza 1.) For example, there is an obvious contradiction between what the noble birds say and what we know of bird behaviour outside the poem.[58] This impossibility of communicating perception is mooted openly twice. Stanza 30, ll. 204ff., an addition to the Boccaccian original, describes the Paradisal Garden. Its emphasis falls on its permanence, and the inability of language to describe it:

Yit was there joye more than a thousandfold
Than man can tell; ne nevere wolde it nyghte,
But ay cler day to any manes syghte.

The other place is s. 70, ll. 484ff. Here the *persona* sums up the pleas of the noble birds: such gentility had never been heard before and had never been described. Both these *occupationes* thus contain ideas of perfection and its communication and contrast ideas of time and no-time. Now, between these stanzas, respectively the thirtieth and the seventieth, from the end of the first to the end of the second, are forty stanzas. Forty, the 'modified tetractys' (4×10), signifies trial or test – like the forty days of Christ's temptation. Important ideas in the debate and in the *Somnium* passage, as we have seen, are trial and judgement. But the stanzas warn of the unreliability of linguistic formulation; the birds' speeches are comically off-target, and no basis for judgement. So we are left with the certainty of trial and judgement, but also with an apprehension of the limited approximation of language to truth and knowledge.

The contrast in these stanzas between an eternal world and one where the sun sets veils allusion to Man's life in time as a preparation for the eternal life of which this World-in-Time is the *umbra*. The *Somnium* passage had emphasized this point (ll. 53ff., 64ff., 73ff.), and also refers us to the Great Year (ll. 67–68) when time shall have a stop. The context of human choice and judgement and thus of moral life *in* Time is ultimately a world *beyond* Time. But this ultimate reality, beyond words, can only be glimpsed in music (ll. 57ff.). Therefore, in a poem composed of words, Chaucer undercuts his own medium by reminding us of the higher art whose basis was mathematical. The point of contact between the music the blessed hear and the impermanence of words is in mathematical structure. In this alone can the other human arts aspire to the condition of music. Music is both fulfilment and supercession of poetry, and poetry, indeed, is to be seen as part of *musica* rather than quite separate from it.

It is appropriate, then, to close with the birds' song. In the roundel, the poem's oppositional patterns have their last mention, contrasting winter and summer, light and dark. But the opposition is harmonized in words plus music in a form that carries with it important overtones; for as George Puttenham said later, a roundel is the poetic counterpart to the circle 'resembl[ing] the world or universe, and for his indefinitenesse having no speciall place of beginning nor end, beareth a similitude with God and eternitie'.[59] The poem's virtually last note, then, reassures us that opposites *can* be held together in the perfection of eternity; the first note, in that remarkable first stanza, had been the statement, in a form almost as highly patterned as the roundel, of opposites and contradictions subsumed in the central idea of Love. The roundel form reminds us of the ultimate Author and Judge; and the squabbling birds are drawn into a harmonious *ordo*. Only the narrator, still locked in his temporal consciousness, like us, is left when they fly away. The last assertion of the poem is that reading must be diligent and there is in it the possibility of 'faring the bet'. The end of reading and study is virtuous action.

The statistical probability of these patterns being merely accidental is small. Some find it difficult to believe that techniques such as seem to be used in *PF* could be received and appreciated by early audiences, who either heard the poem performed or read it in MSS with unnumbered lines. But our own intake of poetry is so overwhelmingly via the eye that we probably have no idea of the sophistication of response possible for an *audience*, for which most literary experience was aural. However, in the early days of sound broadcasting, an extraordinary sensitivity to the heard word, in for example spoken

drama, was rapidly developed, and where some traces of an oral tradition of literature survive, as in Crete or the Balkans, scholars have
demonstrated the complexity of construction and reception of long
poems.[60] A similar sophistication is seen in the way a trained musical ear is able to separate and appreciate simultaneously the strands
in, say, polyphonic writing *and* remain conscious of the design into
which the composer is weaving them. Perception of verbal echoes
and even symmetry I do not think beyond the listening audience,
and even the importance of the central block (though not, obviously,
its mathematical centrality) might well be grasped by people hearing
it for the first time from the shifts in rhetorical organization and
sonic pattern. I was once reading *PF* with a pupil who had been principal oboist in a major orchestra, and remarked on how puzzled I
was about how the patterns might have been heard, and she replied,
'Oh, if you are a musician, it's perfectly easy: you see them coming,
it's what you expect'. Certainly, Renaissance dramatists do not seem
to have fought shy of symmetrical and balanced compositions, and
there is no reason to suppose their ancestors had a less versatile audience than they did. But we do not live in the same world: we piece
half-understanding together from the shards of what once might
have been second nature, like improvising a fugue in four voices
on an organ.

The niceties of numerology and the detailed exegesis of the
poem that depends on examining the actual text are another matter.
Even allowing for the power of memory to reflect and re-examine,
these areas cannot have been open in any full sense to a listening
audience. But this is precisely the point; the poem did not simply
exist as sound, it also existed as *texts*. Examples of private reading
abound. Rogier van der Weyden's Magdalene reads sitting on the
floor. Pandarus sits reading an old romance; *Troilus and Criseyde* is
a written text to be read by a single reader *as well as* heard (V.270,
1765ff., 1776, 1786–1789; and cf. 1058–1060). The Egerton and
Cotton translators of *Mandeville's Travels* imply the same.[61] The
application of immensely detailed analysis to texts in this period
needs no emphasis. This is despite their lack of numbered lines:
even the Bible was only divided into chapters in the time of Stephen
Langton in the 1220s, and into verses not until the 1500s. Analytical
commentary used every exegetical tool on the written word. A poem
exists as pattern on a page to which the mind can return and employ
the tools of number, measure and logic to pierce the veil draped

over the truth.[62] Medieval and Renaissance people said they read like this, and, one must presume, wrote like this, and we have to accept this even if direct theoretical evidence for this being applied to secular writing in Chaucer's period is to be found more easily on the continent than it is in England – in Dante, Petrarch and Boccaccio, sources of so many later generally accepted critical ideas.[63] Dante's criticism presupposes as normal exactly the techniques I have used in reading *PF*. Chaucer, indeed, may well be alluding, fleetingly and jokingly, to the knowledge communicated by number in *The Boke of the Duchess* ll. 435–440. Such techniques may be rarely mentioned because they are taken for granted: what everyone knows, nobody bothers to record.

The difficulty of analysing a MS, when compared with our ease in analysing a text with numbered lines, is more apparent than real. Well-written MSS have a regularity of appearance not much inferior to the printed page; numbers of lines per page are regular, and the mind can easily learn to analyse them. Stanzaic form makes it even easier. In any given poem, then, we are concerned not with one but with two audiences – the social/oral and the private/visual.[64] The patterns of rhetorical structures and numerological clues are as integral to the poem's semantic economy as sound or syntax.[65] The poem heard conveys part of its meaning; the poem read qualifies, expands, develops that first experience. With *PF*, the second analytical reading substantially modifies our linear understanding of the verbal text. Our first reading of the poem demands revision by the second; yet both are 'true' even if contradictory. Yet that ambiguity is balanced by a clarity of statement in the form, asserting that behind everything lies Order and harmony. This is of course one more contradiction in the poem – form against language – but an entirely necessary one, for the paradox it figures is nearer the truth than either glib assertion of order or an equally facile rejection of the possibility of discerning would ever be.

The consolation of form is a serious one. For the limitedness of apprehension and language does not deny the poet's capability to make a model that will relate, however shadowily, to the nature of the universe. As Augustine remarked, our minds suffer the mutability of error, and so there must be 'above' us, in the Mind of God, a standard by which we perceive beauty as harmony (*convenientia*) – a harmony that is expressed by balance or equality through the symmetrical placing of equal parts or the ordered pattern of unequal parts (*De Vera Religione*, XXX, 55, 56). The great attraction of the art of spatial and numerical composition is that someone seriously exploring the flawed nature of human perception and language can invoke a system of meaning which *ex hypothesi* is a closed, logical and neutral medium, free of personally superadded and therefore unquantifiable values. It is also a system that – as was believed – best describes the nature of the world we live in and the Mind of God who created it. Mathematics is the ultimate image of that *ordo* towards which the whole creation groaneth in travail.

The poem's pattern constitutes in its exact balance, its chiastic structures, its numerical ordering and its circularity an image of the ultimate harmony of the realm ruled by Nature – the one in which we dwell, clothed in this muddy vesture of decay. But that harmony is visible only from the outside, as it were, just as we need to see the whole poem (as the narrator never could) to see its pattern. (The *persona* entering the Garden hears birds singing in heavenly harmony, but they are in fact quarrelling – quarrelling that resolves itself at the end, as he moves away, into the harmony of the roundel: all are true, none is the only truth.) In life, we, like the birds, are on the inside, squabbling and perplexed and comic in our self-importance. Questions do have to be decided that relate to our bodily, mental and spiritual needs; we are involved in political struggles in the fallen world[66] where neither side is all right or all wrong. The only certainties we have are Time, Change and Death; and that we have to make choices.

C.W.R.D. Moseley teaches in the Faculty of English at the University of Cambridge, and has been Director of Studies in English for several colleges of the university as well as Programme Director of the university's International Summer Schools in English Literature and Shakespeare.

Notes

1. Cf. Jill Mann's remark: 'Meaning is something that resides in the interaction between text and reader, endlessly remaking itself' ('Chaucer and Atheism', *Studies in the Age of Chaucer* 17 [1995]: 5–19, see 9, 19).
2. 'The Formalist Critics', *The Kenyon Review* XIII, no. 1 (Winter 1951): 75.

3. Ruth Crosby, 'Oral Delivery in the Middle Ages', *Speculum* 11 (January 1936): 88–110; Crosby, 'Chaucer and the Custom of Oral Delivery', *Speculum* 13/14 (October 1938): 413–432; D.H. Green, 'Orality and Reading: The State of Research in Medieval Studies', *Speculum* 65, no. 2 (April 1990): 267–280; Evelyn Birge Vitz, Nancy Freeman Regalado and Marilyn Lawrence, eds., *Performing Medieval Narrative* (Ipswich: D.S. Brewer, 2005), esp. chapters by Busby, Lawrence and Azéma; Joyce Coleman, *Public Reading and the Reading Public in Late Medieval England and France* (Cambridge: Cambridge University Press, 2010).

4. Cf. Arthur Bahr, *Fragments and Assemblages: Forming Compilations of Medieval London* (Chicago: University of Chicago Press, 2013) on the construction of MSS as implying literary criticism and response.

5. *Paradise Lost*, VII, 31.

6. Cf. my note, 'A Note on Possible Acrostics in *Paradise Lost*', *Notes and Queries* 233 (June 1988): 162–163.

7. M.R. Kelley, 'Antithesis as a Principle of Design in Parlement of Foulys', *Chaucer Review* (1979/1980): 61–73 summarizes these changing views. The enigmatic quality of the poem is illustrated. I am much indebted to the edition by D.S. Brewer (*The Parlement of Foulys*, 2nd edn [Manchester: Manchester University Press, 1972]) and J.A.W. Bennet's *The Parlement of Foules* (Oxford: Oxford University Press, 1957). Cf. also L.M. Sklute, 'The Inconclusive Form of PF', *Chaucer Review* (1980/1981): 119–128; B.K. Cowgill, '*PF* and the Body Politic', *Journal of English and Germanic Philology* (1975): 315–335; and the interesting discussion by P. Boitani, *English Mediaeval Narrative in the Thirteenth and Fourteenth Centuries*, English trans. (Cambridge: Cambridge University Press, 1986), 168ff.

8. Cf. D. Aers, '*PF*: Authority, the Knower and the Known', *Chaucer Review* (1981/1982): 1–18. It will be seen that I do not altogether follow Aers' argument. Cf. J. Mann, 'The Authority of the Audience in Chaucer', in *Poetics: Theory and Practice in Medieval English Literature*, ed. P. Boitani and Anna Torti (Ipswich: D.S. Brewer, 1991), 1–12. See also the subtle discussion in William A. Quinn, 'Chaucer's *Parliament of Fowls* and the Pre-Text of Narration', in *Narrative Development from Chaucer to Defoe*, ed. G. Bayer and E. Klitgård (New York: Routledge, 2010), pp.79–96.

9. Cf. Aers, '*PF*: Authority', 14. The narrator is less guide than Gulliver, a figure whose reaction pre-empts our own first thoughts and forces second ones.

10. R.M. Jordan, *Chaucer and the Shape of Creation: The Aesthetic Possibilities of Inorganic Structure* (Cambridge, MA: Harvard University Press, 1967), stressed the inorganic system of medieval aesthetics, grounded in Pythagorean number theory and Platonic ideas of rational order, and carried into the Middle Ages by Augustine, Boethius and Macrobius. See also his 'The Question of Unity and the *Parlement of Foules*', *English Studies in Canada* 3 (1977): 373–385.

11. See A. Hurst, *Apollonios de Rhodes: Manière et Cohérence: Contribution à l'étude de l'esthétique alexandrine* (Bibliotheca Helvetica Romana, VIII), (Institut Suisse de Rome, 1967). In Antiquity, the formal patterning may well have functioned as a sort of *aide mémoire*. Cf. R.T. Eriksen, 'Mnemonics and Giordano Bruno's Magical Art of Composition', *Cahiers Elisabéthains* (1981): 3–10, esp. 4; and also the discussion by F. Yates in *The Art of Memory* (Chicago, IL: University of Chicago Press, 1966). E.R. Curtius, *European Literature and the Latin Middle Ages*

(London: Routledge and Kegan Paul, 1953), Excursus 10, also notices the habit of numerically ordered compositional techniques.

12. Victoria Rothschild, '*The Parliament of Fowls*: Chaucer's Mirror up to Nature?', *Review of English Studies* 35 (1984): 164–184, explores numerological significance and astrological allegory in *PF*. Pandarus's quoting of Geoffroi de Vinsauf's analogy between constructing a poem and housebuilding suggests Chaucer's audience's awareness of an aesthetic like Alberti's in *De Re Aedificatoria* (1443–1452), which assumes the use of numerology. To take a later example: when we find George Herbert writing a 'round' or 'circle' poem, we cannot exclude the common extraneous symbolism of the form itself from the reading of the poem. That common symbolism is not only clearly marked out in emblems but is also explicitly discussed by, for example, George Puttenham, *Art of English Poesie* (London, 1589), 56ff.; cf. A. Henkel and A. Schone, *Emblemata Handbuch zur Sinnbildkunst des XVI und XVII Jahrhunderts* (Stuttgart: Metzler, 1967), cols. 5, 6, 7.

13. Suger of St Denis speaks of God as Artifex – a craftsman – (importantly) exactly the same concept as the Europe-wide idea of the poet or artist as 'maker' or (in Dante's crucial case) *fabbro*.

14. *Wisdom of Solomon*, XI, 21. There is also Boethius, *De Consolatione Philosophiae* III met. IX: 'tu numeris elementa ligas' – with which one might compare *PF* 381. Cf. Marvell's witty echo of *Wisdom* in 'On Paradise Lost'.

15. Cf. Jacob Bazak, 'Numerical Devices in Biblical Poetry', *Vetus Testamentum* 38, fasc. 3 (July 1988): 333–337. M.-S. Røstvig (*Fair Forms* [Cambridge: Cambridge University Press, 1975], 54n3), remarks that Renaissance reading of the Bible (at least) continued this ancient practice of extracting meaning via many levels. The reader who expects so to extract may also be the poet who caters for that extraction.

16. There are, naturally, several levels of allegorical meaning. Alain puns elsewhere on *numerus* as 'military formation' as well as 'number'; it can also mean 'line of poetry', as it did for Pope.

17. Also cf. Sarah Powrie, 'Alain of Lille's *Anticlaudianus* as Intertext in Chaucer's *House of Fame*', *Chaucer Review* 44, no. 3 (2010): 246–267.

18. These are key attributes of the *trobar clus* style, admired by Dante and profoundly influential on thirteenth-century French and Italian vernacular poetry.

19. *Summa Theologiae*, I, q. 39, a. 8c.

20. Even if spurious, as some suggest, it could be plausibly held to indicate what people were convinced Dante thought about the creation of the greatest poem of the Middle Ages.

21. This is common ground in the Renaissance: cf. Landino's remark that the world was God's poem (*Dante con l'espositione de Cristoforo Landino* [Venice, 1564], sig.**3v; 1st edn Florence 1481); and cf. Can Grande's self-proclaimed descendant, Julius Caesar Scaliger, *Poetices Libri Septem* (Lyons, 1561), 3. But the thought also underlies many of the self-referential remarks in the *Divina Commedia*, and Boccaccio (*De Genealogia Deorum*, XIV, caps. 7 and 8; cf. XV, 6 and *Vita di Dante*) sees poets as the first theologians and the inspiration of the Muses as the operation of the Holy Spirit in another form. Cf. M.C. Nahm, *The Artist as Creator* (Baltimore, MD: Johns Hopkins, 1956).

22. The analytical descriptive method in the *Letter* and the synthetic construction of the poem correspond to the systems of the Scholastics and encyclopaedists. On the importance of *forma tractandi* in medieval theories of literary criticism, see A.J. Minnis, *The Mediaeval Theory of Authorship* (London: University of Pennsylvania Press, 1984).

23. Robert F. Yeager, *John Gower's Poetic: The Search for a New Arion*, Publications of the John Gower Society II (Woodbridge: D.S. Brewer, 1990), 216.

24. T.A. Shippey, 'Chaucer's Arithmetical Mentality and the *Book of the Duchess*', *Chaucer Review* 31, no. 2 (1996): 184–200, esp. 192. Edward I. Condren, *The Numerical Universe of the 'Gawain-Pearl' Poet: Beyond 'Phi'* (Gainesville, FL: University of Florida Press, 2002), grounds some central arguments in analysis of mathematical structures. Numerological patterning in *Perle* is accepted even by the urbanely sceptical D.S. Brewer (*Parlament of Foules*, 189). See also Chapter 3 of Edward I. Condren, *Chaucer from Prentice to Poet: The Metaphor of Love in Dream Visions and 'Troilus and Criseyde'* (Gainesville, FL: University of Florida Press, 2008). For his use of number patterns elsewhere, see H. Kasmann, 'Numerical Structure in Fitt III of *SGGK*', in *Chaucer and Middle English Studies in Honour of Rossell Hope Robbins*, ed. B. Rowland (London: Allen and Unwin, 1974), 131–9. Cf. Eugenie R. Freed, 'Quy the Pentangel Apendes ...': The Pentangle in "Sir Gawain and the Green Knight"', *Theoria: A Journal of Social and Political Theory* 77 (May 1991): 125–141.

25. This ignores the important idea of poetic inspiration by some higher power. Dante and Milton are clearly aware of this, but its clearest statement is in Boccaccio and Petrarch: *De Genealogia*, XIV, caps. 6ff., and Petrarch, *Invective against a Physician*, I, 3.

26. Understanding the mathematical ratios of musical harmony is key to Orpheus's knowledge of the universe and recognition of his own nature as intellectual soul in Henryson's *Orpheus and Eurydice*. See J. MacQueen, 'Neoplatonism and Orphism in XVth Century Scotland: The Evidence of Henryson's New Orpheus', *Scottish Studies* 20 (1976), 69–89. Much said above about Renaissance aesthetic ideas also applies to earlier centuries. Cf. S.K. Heninger, *Touches of Sweet Harmony: Pythagorean Cosmology and Renaissance Poetics* (Huntingdon Library, San Marino, CA, 1974); M.S. Røstvig et al., *The Hidden Sense and Other Essays*, Norwegian Studies in English 9 (Oslo: Norwegian Universities Press, 1963); Alastair Fowler, *Triumphal Forms* (Cambridge: Cambridge University Press, 1970); E. Wind, *Pagan Mysteries in the Renaissance* (New York: W.W. Norton, 1968)

27. Jordan, *Chaucer and the Shape of Creation*, and E. Mâle, *The Gothic Image* (repr., London: Dent, 1961). See also Helen Phillips, 'Structure and Consolation in *The Book of the Duchess*', *Chaucer Review* 16 (1980/1981): 107–115. It is worth noting the charming grace-note Chaucer builds into *The Book of the Duchess*, which celebrates the dead Blanche. She died aged twenty-nine, and the poem has critical divisions at the lines whose numbers are divisible by that number. See also E. Panofsky, *Gothic Architecture and Scholasticism* (New York: Meridian, 1957), esp. 38–39; and W. Ryding, *Structure in Mediaeval Narrative* (The Hague: Mouton, 1971), 116 on the inclusive diversity of medieval art.

28. See T.E. Hart, 'Mediaeval Structuralism: "Dulcarnoun" and the Five-Book Design of Chaucer's *Troilus*', *Chaucer Review* 16 (1980/1981): 129–170.

29. Comparing with De Guileville's poem, of which it is *translatio*, shows that the modifications are purposive. Chaucer knew (as did Dunbar, later) the formal demands of a type of religious poem whose ancestry goes back at least to the 'prudent Sedulius' and 'sedulous Prudentius' Giles Fletcher admired. The form of Psalm 119 may partly account for the enduring popularity of the acrostic in religious verse.

30. Cf., for example, Hurst, *Apollonios de Rhodes*; Eriksen, 'Mnemonics'; and Eriksen, *The Building in the Text: Alberti to Shakespeare and Milton* (University Park, PA: Penn State Press, 2010); see also M.S. Røstvig, 'Structure as Prophecy', in *Silent Poetry*, ed. A. Fowler (London: Routledge and Kegan Paul 1970), 57–72. Røstvig demonstrates that Spenser, Milton and Chaucer all use these devices, e.g. placing a symbolic action, object or idea at a numerical centre.

31. In what follows I rely heavily (without further citation) on: John MacQueen, *Numerology: Theory and Outline History of a Literary Mode* (Edinburgh: Edinburgh University Press, 1985); V. Hopper, *Mediaeval Number Symbolism: Sources, Meaning, and Influence on Thought and Expression* (New York: Courier Corporation, 1938); Fowler, *Triumphal Forms*; Honorius of Autun, *De Imagine* and *Speculum Ecclesiae* (in Migne, *Patrologia Latina*, 172); Boethius, *De Arithmetica*; Rabanus Maurus, *De Numero*; Hugh of St Victor, *Exegetica* (Migne, *Patrologia Latina*, 175); Isidore of Seville, *Liber numerorum*; Pietro Bongo, *Numerorum Mysteria* (Bergamo, 1591). See bibliography by Michael J. Batts, 'Numerical Structure in Medieval Literature', in *Formal Aspects of Medieval German Poetry: A Symposium*, ed. Stanley N. Werbow (Austin, TX: University of Texas Press, 1969), 93–121.

32. See Larry D. Benson, *The Riverside Chaucer*, 3rd edn (Oxford: Oxford University Press, 2008), 1150, n. to 680–692, and 1001–1002, n. to 675.

33. See note to 677, p. 1002. This might suggest that copyists (at least) seem to have known (or thought they knew) to what Chaucer referred. Skeat's point, which F.N. Robinson cites (*The Works of Geoffrey Chaucer* [London: Oxford University Press, 1957], 796), about the difficulty of fitting a four-stress musical line to a decasyllabic poem holds good, of course, if the song was sung rhythmically; not if it was sung isochronously. It will be seen that I disagree with Brewer, *Parlement of Foulys*, 127.

34. The cock recalls Man's sin, and the rising sun striking the steeple's weathercock recalls Peter's denial.

35. As clearly the *Gawain*-poet is aware, in his avoidance of the expected total of perfection numbers in *Sir Gawain and the Green Knight* and *Perle*. The *Divina Commedia*, that most Trinitarian of poems, returns to Unity in the 100th canto.

36. The reference to 'evene nombres of acord' gives the audience enough to go on. Nature, as commonly in fourteenth- and fifteenth-century poetry, is the personified operation of the Creating Word. The reference to Alain is an absolute anchor for the poem, avoiding any possible misapprehension about her. It is not improbable that the audience would be expected at least to know of Alain's work. Did Chaucer intend his audience to remember that in Alain's poem Nature's rule was flouted by sinful man in thrall to appetition? Alain (in Migne, *Patrologia Latina*, 210, col. 435) calls his list *animalium concilium* (*De Planctu Naturae*, Prose 1) – a Parliament, in fact. But there is one huge difference between his description and Chaucer's: in *De Planctu* the birds are embroidered on Nature's dress, and even though, as Alain says, they seem to 'live' there in a literal sense, their existence

is figurative. (He is casting more than a glance in the direction of Boethius's *Philosophia*.) Chaucer is clearly using them figuratively too, but has externalized them from Nature to emphasize her as ruler. (The attributes of the birds are frequently similar; this is to be expected in view of the *topos*'s descent from Pliny and the Bestiaries.) There is a similar use of anaphoric pattern.

37. In the Renaissance at least, 84 (7 x 12) was connected with the New Year. See Fowler, *Triumphal Forms*, 147ff.

38. Henryson certainly seems so to use it, structuring the majority of the stanzas in the *Fabillis* and *The Testament of Cresseid* as four lines of state plus three of action or thought.

39. What Kelley ('Antithesis as a Principle of Design') called the 'antithetical principle of design' is undeniably important, and rhetorically *contentio, antimetabole, antithesis* and *chiasmus* are extraordinarily abundant.

40. The imitation has been noted before of *Teseida*, VII, 51–56. Comparison, however, reveals not only verbal closeness but also striking differences. For example, Chaucer's modifications of detail are all towards greater specificity (cf. Brewer, *Parlement of Foulys*, 44–45); occasionally (as in ll. 211ff., cf. s. 54) he moves away from the flat allegorical thought of Boccaccio. Whereas Boccaccio's Ozia and Memoria simply temper Cupid's arrows (witty enough in itself), in Chaucer Will *files* them and we are told of their various effects. Further, where Boccaccio's ss. 52 and 53 have birds singing and instruments playing, there is only the weak comparison '*quasi in ogni canto / di spiritei*' to suggest anything out of this world. But Chaucer adds important ideas of angelic harmony and the music God hears – that is, the music of the spheres (cf. below). Examples of such detailed alterations could be multiplied. Moreover, Chaucer clearly did not simply lift the passage and slot it in his own, but rearranged it, creating a structure with different force. The stanza beginning l. 211 is inserted into the Boccaccian sequence; it has no parallel, and again, like the music, reminds us of Paradise. This addition allows positioning at the exact centre of his description (see below) of eleven – a number of imperfection! – stanzas of Boccaccio's lines:

'c'hanno potestate
Di fare altrui a forza far folia',

not so positioned in Boccaccio. Really striking change comes with the five-stanza description of Venus. The stanzas beginning 260, 267, 274, 281 and 288 respectively correspond to Boccaccio's stanzas 64, 65, 66, 61 and 62. Again, verbal links are close; but despite the closeness of detail there is no 'Cypride' lying 'amyddes' in Boccaccio, and Chaucer's list of lovers is much more sinister. The closeness of the imitation, plus the clear and significant alteration *in order* proves Chaucer's structure in *PF* to be deliberate. Gerald Morgan, 'Chaucer's Adaptation of Boccaccio's temple of Venus in *the Parliament of Fowls*', *The Review of English Studies*, New Series, 56, no. 223 (February 2005): 1–36 is beautifully and thoughtfully detailed, but does not make the point with my emphasis about the reordering into the chiastic structure.

41. The *topos* can allude to both – the one does not exclude the other, as Milton knew.

42. Cf. Aers, '*PF*: Authority', 13. Verbs of knowing or understanding (or not doing so) are common when the narrator talks of his experiences; in the Parliament, words belonging to the lexical set connected with judgement are particularly

common: chese, 388; ordinaunce, 390; eleccioun, 409; chese, 417; jugement, 431; (ideas of judging and penalty in ll. 428ff. and 456ff.); dom, 484; pletynge, 495; juge, 496; preve, 497; juge, 524; verdit, 525; diffyne, 529; termine, 530; preve, 534; replicacioun, 536; argumentes, 568; juges dom, 546; etc.

43. Cf. especially *Prologue to Legend of Good Women* F, 27ff., and the difficulty of interpreting phenomena that is so important in *Nonne Preestes Tale*.

44. A neat anticipation (like the mention of the 'armonye' of the birds, l. 191) of the talking birds in Nature's train. Yet ironically what is first heard as harmony is later seen to be quarrelling – then resolves itself into song! But did the *birdsong* ever change?

45. Since it goes beyond ten.

46. And with only one formel and three tercels, two tercels must live celibate for the rest of their lives, if they mean what they say. But of course they do not; this Valentine's Day assembly is by definition an *annual* thing.

47. Dr Jennifer Fellowes noted in a private communication that in Bestiaries two kinds of dove were recognized – those seen as a type of lechery, and those signifying faithful love. In this case, the doves round Venus's temple could be the former. Here again is an idea capable of antithetical understanding being suggested by a single inclusive word.

48. Hence the importance of the echo of Dante, *Inferno*, III.1ff. in the double inscriptions over the gate. Chaucer links by verbal echo the emphasis on 'blisful place' as virtuous reward in the *Somnium* passage with the 'blisful place' the Garden figures. Cf. Rothschild, '*The Parliament of Fowls*', note 5.

49. Cicero's concern for the relation of the individual to the state is not lacking in *PF*. After all, men, like birds, are organized hierarchically into a state. 'Comune spede' is both personal moral issue and political concern. Cf. Aers, '*PF*: Authority', 14f.

50. Macrobius's book is not usually divided into seven chapters. Chaucer's decision to say it was is either explained by assuming his copy really was or – more likely, I think – that he deliberately included the number seven as significant.

51. See Røstvig et al., *The Hidden Sense*, 54ff. The Hymn's twenty-seven stanzas not only allude to the inaudible music of the divine numbers used in the work of Creation (60); they are also the cube of 3, symbol of the Trinity, and half the sum of the numbers in what is called the 'Lambda Stemma':

        1
      2   3
      4   9   (squares)
      8   27   (cubes).

The sum of 1, 2, 3, 4, 8, 9 equals the cube of 3.

According to the Pythagoreans, all numbers derive from this, and the Lambda comes to symbolize the Entelechy. The multiples of 27 are frequently used to signify this. (Cf. Plato, *Timaeus*). The Lambda Stemma is used by traditional commentaries on the Mosaic account of Creation and on *Job* 38.4–8 (Røstvig, *Fair Forms*, 56).

52. Psalm 19; *Romans* I.20; cf. Henryson, *Fabillis*, 1650ff.

53. Noticing the line positions in the blocks can yield fruitful results. For example, here the words 'comune profit' occur in lines 12 and 40 of the block (ll. 47 and 75). Twelve is one of the Blessed numbers, and forty the number of Trial

(see below). The first mention concerns the blessedness of those who love 'comune profit'; the second, by its conjunction with those who do not (and are therefore punished), is concerned with judgement.

54. Sklute, 'The Inconclusive Form of PF', 121.

55. And was so regarded, not least in the Renaissance. Chaucer's own frequent use, however ironic, of the *diminutio* figure would be senseless if the idea of a skilled audience was untenable. In 1633, Miles Flesher addressed his printing of Donne's *Poems* to 'the understanders'; and cf. Dekker's contemptuous punning dismissal of 'Readers' against 'Understanders' in *A Strange Horse Race* (London, 1613, STC6528), sig. A3ro.

56. Cf. *Boece* ii.m.8. I use the Augustinian term because of his linking of it with virtue and 'cosmic' love.

57. Cf. Michael R. Near, 'Chaucer's Parliament of Fowls: Reading as an Act of Will', *Pacific Coast Philology* 20, no. 1/2 (November 1985): 18–24: 'The narrator ... does not present us with his understanding but with his struggle to understand, a struggle which terminates in dissatisfaction and irresolution ... the object of the quest is not as important as the fact of the quest itself' (19).

58. That Chaucer intends us to make this (and later the turtle-dove's) guarded commitment to the allegorical birds is proved, I think, by the formel's blushing; forget that birds in real life cannot blush and it is not at all funny. Yet it is clearly meant to be deliciously so.

59. *Arte of English Poesie* (London, 1589), 98–99.

60. Milman Parry, 'Studies in the Epic Technique of Oral Verse-Making. I: Homer and Homeric Style', *Harvard Studies in Classical Philology* 41 (1930): 73–143; Parry, 'Studies in the Epic Technique of Oral Verse-Making. II: The Homeric Language as the Language of an Oral Poetry', *Harvard Studies in Classical Philology* 43 (1932): 1–50; Francis P. Magoun, Jr, 'Oral-Formulaic Character of Anglo-Saxon Narrative Poetry', *Speculum* 28 (1953): 446–467. See also G.S. Kirk, *The Songs of Homer* (Cambridge: Cambridge University Press, 1962), 55–101.

61. See my edition of *Mandeville's Travels*, 2nd edn (Harmondsworth: Penguin, 2010), 189. Chaucer is clearly worried about the accuracy of future copyists, aware that his book is open to the same problems of transmission, interpretation and comprehension that affect earlier writers by whom alone *any* knowledge of Troy is possible (*T&C*, V.1786ff.). A nice point, for it subtly questions the authority of poetry while asserting its importance, and makes us see *T&C* as provisional in its interpretation of an unknowable past. Chaucer has here a remarkable imaginative glimpse into a future from which he will be as remote as Dares and Dictys are from him.

62. Dante, *Convivio*, II.i, and Boccaccio, *De Genealogia*, XIV, 12.

63. Dunbar, Henryson, Douglas, Holland and Lydgate all seem to use figured form; Henryson's *Orpheus and Euridice* hints at it theoretically, and Henryson offers a paradigmatic use of the technique in the crucial fable of 'The Cok and the Iasp'.

64. Obviously, the audience that would read rather than hear would be more restricted. But there seems no doubt that such an audience existed – the proliferation of MSS in English at this very period argues for a demand-led industry. See also J.W. Thompson, *The Literacy of the Laity in the Middle Ages* (New York: Burt Franklin, 1960), *passim*.

65. Thus, Sklute's assertion ('The Inconclusive Form of PF', 119) of structural confusion in *PF* is unlikely: Chaucer knew his job.

66. It is worth noticing that the noble birds are of 'ravyne', and several common ones are thieves or rogues. Augustine had said (*De Civitate Dei*, IV, 4) that all earthly states are basically bands of robbers: that idea could be implied here. (Chaucer alludes to it, linking it with how semantics can alter 'truth' in *Manciple's Tale*, IX (II), 220ff.) (cf. Aers, '*PF*: Authority', 84). But Augustine also recognizes the need for the imperfect State and the respect the Christian owed it, for it has been instituted by God *in remedium peccatorum*.

Chapter 7

Troilus and Criseyde and the 'Parfit Blisse of Love'

Simone Fryer-Bovair

Troilus and Criseyde can be called a love story on many counts. Its story celebrates the development of Troilus and Criseyde's romantic love for one another and then laments the dissolution of their relationship. The conclusion of the poem is a celebration of divine love, and an injunction to its audience to forgo the empty, temporary, goods of the world for the stability of God's love. The poem has been read by some as contrasting divine love and earthly love – true love and false love – in which the latter is ultimately renounced.[1] It is, indeed, a poem of many dichotomies: true and false felicity; 'wo' and 'wele'; hope and fear; desire and reason; transcendence and stagnation; the poem's narrative progression and its ending. However, unifying these disparate aspects of the poem is the transcendent goodness of virtuous love. In this article, I argue that Chaucer perceives a tension in Boethius's *Consolation of Philosophy* about the value of romantic love (on which Boethius is noticeably, and perhaps inevitably, silent)[2] and seeks, in *Troilus and Criseyde,* to dignify romantic love and establish its place in the chain of love.[3] Whereas

Notes for this section begin on page 152.

Boethius asks his readers to detach themselves from the world and to seek self-sufficiency, Chaucer believed that it is *through* virtuous worldly engagement that one can access divine love and true felicity.

Boethius was clearly relevant to Chaucer's thinking around romantic love, and it is interesting that both in *Troilus* and elsewhere he uses Boethius's image of Fortune's wheel to represent the experience of his lovers (*Canterbury Tales*: 'The Knight's Tale', I.1235–43; 'The Merchant's Tale', IV.2057). In *Troilus*, Chaucer's use of Boethius is more profound. Chaucer inherits from Boethius the image of a love that binds the 'erthe and se' with 'hevene' (III.1744, 1745). As I will discuss below, Chaucer extends this vision of the chain of love to include romantic love – 'a thing so vertuous in kynde' (I.254) – and couples who live in 'vertu' (III.1749). This expansion of Boethius's vision enables Chaucer to reveal how Troilus is morally improved through his love of Criseyde (I.1079–85; II.848–54; III.1804–6). It is through love that he cultivates the virtues of truth and *gentilesse* – virtues that remain after his loss of Criseyde. Ultimately, it is his moral goodness that makes the poem's ending, and Troilus's ascent to the eighth sphere, fitting. Creating a sharp division between romantic and divine love, as some critics have, especially by reading the poem in light of its ending and with the benefit of hindsight, is reductive.[4] Doing so leads the reader to conclude that the 'ultimate meaning' or 'moral' of the story is that 'human love, and by a sorry corollary everything human, is unstable and illusory'.[5] Instead, the poem needs to be read as Chaucer intended it to be read – sequentially and with an acceptance of the linear progression of its narrative. This dimension of narrative is what brings it closest to life – both must be 'lived forwards but understood backwards'.[6] The supremacy of God's love will be revealed later, but, when it is, the value of virtuous romantic love is not negated but rather made subservient to a higher end. At the poem's conclusion, the reader should be able to see both the potentially morally elevating virtue of romantic love and the ultimate supremacy of God's love.

C.S. Lewis, in his personal meditation on love, reaches a conclusion that resonates strongly with the philosophy of *Troilus and Criseyde*. In the *Four Loves*, Lewis wrangles with the Augustinian warning that one must not give one's heart to anyone, or anything, other than God; 'all natural loves', Lewis writes, 'can be inordinate', but:

> *Inordinate* does not mean 'insufficiently cautious'. Nor does it mean 'too big'. It is not a quantitative term. It is probably impossible to love

any human being simply 'too much'. We may love him too much *in proportion* to our love for God; but it is the smallness of our love for God, not the greatness of our love for the man, that constitutes the inordinacy.[7]

As a pagan, Troilus cannot know that his love for Criseyde is 'too much *in proportion*' to his love for an unknown God – his love for God is as small as it comes, but that is not his fault but a matter of history. Troilus's paganism enables Chaucer to explore a world in which romantic love is able to be 'the highest of man's spiritual aspirations'[8] before he then assimilates this world with a Christian vision of the love of God.[9] In doing this, Chaucer demonstrates that he is part of an intellectual tradition that assimilates Neo-Platonic thinking with Christianity. It was for love that God created the universe and it is love that links that universe to God. In *Troilus and Criseyde*, Chaucer engages in this philosophical discussion not, as Boethius ostensibly does, by renouncing the role of poetry (*Consolation*, 1P1), but by demonstrating the power of poetry (and narrative) in philosophical thinking.

Romantic Love in *Troilus* and the *Consolation*

Boethius is conspicuously silent on the issue of romantic love. In the first three books of the *Consolation of Philosophy*, he outlines the nature of false goods and paves the way for his argument that they should be rejected, in favour of what he reveals to be true goodness. The false goods are 'rychesses, honours, power, glorie, and delitz' (*Boece*, 3P2: 76–78); these are ties to the 'prysone of the erthe' from which the soul is freed in death (*Boece*, 2P7: 154).[10] Boethius briefly alludes to marital love when he discusses the 'delyces of body' (*Boece*, 3P7: 1), but he only mentions that the 'honest' 'gladnesse' (*Boece*, 3P7: 18, 17) of having a wife is offset by the anguish that children can bring (*Boece*, 3P7: 18–26). There is no explicit condemnation of romantic love, and it is only implicitly associated with the denounced delights of the body. In places, Boethius (in the voice of Philosophy) even speaks fondly of love and lovers: Boethius's wife is described by Philosophy as 'atempre of wyt and passynge othere wommen in clennesse of chastete' (*Boece*, 2P4: 33–35), and Orpheus's loss of his wife is tenderly lamented in the poetic conclusion to what ought to be a metrum renouncing the false loves of this world (*Boece*, 3M12: 52–59).[11] More problematic than these narratorial demonstrations

of sympathy are the philosophical tension between the place of romantic love in the chain of love, as presented by Boethius in 2M8,
and the rejection of romantic love implicit in the *contemptus mundi*
tradition, which Boethius articulates in the previous prose section,
2P7, and throughout his work.

The concept of the chain of love runs through the *Consolation*,[12]
and is articulated at length in 2M8. Following a prose section on the
nature of Fortune, 2M8 articulates a vision of the universe that has
its roots in Plato. In his *Timaeus*, Plato states that there is a guiding
principle that binds the universe together in harmony; he calls this
philia – love.[13] Boethius's poem echoes this principle directly:

> Hanc rerum seriem ligat
> Terras ac pelagus regens
> Et caelo imperitans amor. (2M8: 13–15)[14]

> Al this accordaunce [and] ordenaunce of thynges is bounde
> with love, that governeth erthe and see. (*Boece*, 2M8: 14–17)

It is love that holds the natural and human worlds together. It keeps
the 'fluctus avidum mare' ('the see, gredy to flowen', *Boece*, 2M8:
8–9) contained, and the lands stable (2M8: 9, 11–12). This Platonic
vision unites all elements of the created world, through love. Plato's
chain of love emphasized the unity between the created world and
its creator who, envying nothing, wished to create a world in his
image (see *Timaeus* 29–30).[15] Love has an analogous role in Christian
philosophy where it links God with the created world:

> For Truthe telleth that love is triacle of hevene:
> May no synne be on hym seene that that spice useth.
> And alle his werkes he wroughte with love as hym liste,
> And lered it Moyses for the leveste thyng and moost lik to hevene,
> And also the plante of pees, moost precious of vertues:
> For hevene myghte nat holden it, so was it hevy of hymselve,
> Til it hadde of the erthe eten his fille. (*Piers Plowman*, I.148–54)[16]

In this powerful image, William Langland imagines the love of God
being so heavy that it comes down to earth through the Incarnation
(John 1:14). In both the Platonic and the Christian philosophies, it
is love that links the created world with the creator.

However, while the Incarnation establishes the union between
God and man, it also exposes the potential separation between the
two. In the ultimate gesture of love, God 'leet his sone dye / Mekely
for oure mysdedes, to amenden us alle' (*Piers Plowman* I.167–68): it

was for our sins that Christ, sinless himself, died. The existence of sin in the universe increases the separation between man and God and is the basis on which the *contemptus mundi* topos is predicated:

> Love not the world, nor the things which are in the world. If any man love the world, the charity of the Father is not in him. For all that is in the world, is the concupiscence of the flesh, and the concupiscence of the eyes, and the pride of life, which is not of the Father, but is of the world. And the world passeth away, and the concupiscence thereof: but he that doth the will of God, abideth for ever. (1 John 2:15–17)

Boethius's *Consolation*, which essentially implores readers to detach themselves from the world, is the 'most famous literary expression'[17] of the *contemptus mundi* topos.

Romantic love impinges both on the concept of the chain of love (in which it is an aspect of divine love) and on the concept of the *contemptus mundi* (where it is a perversion of divine love). Even though Boethius is non-committal about the status of romantic love as a false good, he does state that a marital, familial version of love has a place in the chain of love:

> Hic et coniugii sacrum
> Castis nectit amoribus,
> Hic fidis etiam sua
> Dictat iura sodalibus. (2M8: 24–27)

> This love halt togidres peples joyned with an holy boond, and knytteth sacrement or mariages of chaste loves; and love enditeth lawes to trewe felawes. (*Boece*, 2M8: 21–25)

When Chaucer recasts this metrum as Troilus's hymn in Book III (III.1744–71), an original inclusion in his poem, he replaces Boethius's familial love with romantic love (III.1749) and, in doing so, draws romantic love into the discussion of the chain of love. In fact, Chaucer's treatment of this metrum (2M8) is indicative of his broader response to Boethius's text and is worth attention.

Although Boethius's influence can be observed throughout *Troilus*, 2M8 is one of the few passages from the *Consolation* that Chaucer transplants, largely intact, into his poem.[18] The changes Chaucer does make are notable and significant. Chaucer, firstly, makes the predominant theme of Boethius's metrum – unifying Love – immediately apparent. In Boethius's poem, Love is revealed as the metrum's topic, significantly, in its central line (l.15) but Chaucer places it as the opening word of the first three lines of

Troilus's hymn; Chaucer takes the issue that is, literally, at the heart of Boethius's poem and asserts its significance in the opening lines of his own. The second structural change that Chaucer makes is to bring forward and prioritize Boethius's section on fraternal and marital love (Chaucer's lines 3–6 to Boethius's lines 22–27). Moreover, as we have seen, he replaces Boethius's married lovers with more secular lovers: 'Love, that knetteth lawe of compaignie, / And couples doth in vertu for to dwelle' (III.1748–49).[19] This alteration is, of course, appropriate to Troilus's situation – he and Criseyde are bound by history to be unmarried[20] – but it also emphasizes an overriding concern of the *Troilus*: to dignify the romantic love of 'hem that ben trewe' (III.1771). This line is taken from the final stanza of Troilus's hymn, original to Chaucer. In this final stanza, Troilus implores 'God, that auctour is of kynde' (III.1765) to 'cerclen hertes alle and faste *bynde*' (III.1767; my italics).[21] His cosmic song concludes with a stanza on the human heart and its experience of love. However, Chaucer does not seek to dignify every kind of romantic love. Although he asks God to 'rewe' on 'hertes colde' and 'sore' (III.1769, 1768, 1771), it is specifically *virtuous*, romantic love that he emphasizes a place for in the chain of love.[22]

While Troilus's hymn concludes with an invocation to God to protect virtuous lovers,[23] Boethius's metrum concludes with a different vision:

> O felix hominum genus,
> Si vestros animos amor
> Quo caelum regitur regat. (2M8: 28–30)

> O weleful were mankynde, yif thilke love that governeth hevene
> governede yowr corages. (*Boece*, 2M8: 25–27)

Significantly, it is Boethius's closing lines, which emphasize the *potential* division between man and God, that Chaucer omits when he re-appropriates 2M8 as Troilus's hymn. Chaucer's omission of Boethius's concluding lines removes the longing for a cosmic love that rules the human heart – 'O weleful were mankynde, yif thilke love that governeth hevene governede yowr corages' (*Boece*, 2M8: 25–27) – 'presumably', as Barry Windeatt argues, 'because in Troilus' view it *does*'.[24] By removing Boethius's concluding lines, Chaucer closes the gap between cosmic and human love and envisions and articulates a *version* of romantic love that has a natural place in the chain of love.

Chaucer's vision of a chain of love is articulated at the height of Troilus's experience of passionate, romantic love; he and Criseyde have consummated their love and their relationship is evolving. This context has caused some to argue that the hymn is an ironic exposition of Troilus's earth-bound, lust-driven ignorance; that he is foolishly confusing divine love with human love. Robertson, for instance, claims that Troilus 'makes of his own feeling a cosmic force' substituting Boethius's divine love for 'his idolatrous lust'.[25] Frankis, who perceives a similar deficiency in Troilus, states that his paganism makes his vision 'faulty' and prevents him from gaining 'an apprehension of the eternal God of Christianity'.[26] In Morgan's argument, the juxtaposition between human and divine love in the hymn fixes 'the auditor's imagination upon the insufficiency and im-perfection of earthly loves in comparison with the completeness of the love of God'.[27] To make this argument work, Morgan (like Rob-ertson and Frankis before him) retrospectively makes the 'Christian truth that is made explicit for us in the conclusion of the poem'[28] the framework for the central narrative of the poem. This is a dangerous method: we cannot assume that the postmortem perspective from which Troilus views the world at the end of the poem is the one adopted here.

Troilus's hymn is sung at the height of his love and is the most profound experience of love in the poem *so far*. It is true that Troilus's hymn expresses 'the maximum of good and beauty to be found out-side of Christian belief and the dispensations of faith',[29] but we can be bolder and relinquish the restraints of the 'dispensations of faith' at this point. As Dunning states, Troilus's hymn is a product of his own experience and, in it, 'he has reached a very high philosophical conception of love, even if only in general terms'.[30] Of course, al-though Troilus does not know a Christian God, God is in the minds of the audience; but this is Troilus's narrative and this is an articu-lation of the divine nature of romantic love when experienced in its perfection. It is certainly true that Troilus's joy in love passes.[31] But, as David and Windeatt also argue, the later revelations of the poem do not cancel out this vision of love.[32] Neither does the transience of this relationship diminish the true virtue that Troilus's experience of romantic love generates. In fact, Chaucer is at pains, as we shall see, to distinguish virtuous, romantic love from its antithesis – 'blynde lust' (V.1824) – and to emphasize the link between love experienced in this world and an over-arching divine love.

Interestingly, Chaucer uses Boethian terms elsewhere in *Troilus* to dignify the moral value of love. Boethius's *Consolation* concludes with advice to the reader: 'eschue thou vices; worschipe and love thou vertues' (*Boece*, 5P6: 302–3). Chaucer imports this language and imagery into his discussion of romantic love. Love encourages its subjects to 'flemen alle manere vice and synne' and 'to vertu for t'entende' (II.852, 853); Venus's servants 'dreden shame, and vices they resynge' (III.25); those who do not love are classified as 'hem that they ben in the vice' (III.1392); and because of 'Love – yheried be his grace! ... Pride, Envye, Ire and Avarice / He gan to fle, and everich other vice' (III.1804–6). In its ideal manifestation, romantic love is clearly moralized and discussed in terms of binding:[33]

> Now sith it may nat goodly ben withstonde,
> And is a thyng so vertuous in kynde,
> Refuseth nat to Love for to *ben bonde*. (I.253–55; my italics)

It is Chaucer's aim to dignify romantic love and to assert its place in the chain of love and he does this by conflating the image of the chain of love with the morally improving qualities of romantic love:

> That Love is he that alle thing may *bynde*,
> For may no man fordon the lawe of kynde.
> ...
> And worthi folk maad worthier of name,
> And causeth moost to dreden vice and shame. (I.237–38, 51–52; my italics)

This passage is delivered early in the poem, just before Troilus sees Criseyde for the first time. The passage is a defence of love against those, like Troilus, who 'scornen Love' (I.234). In the narrative to follow, the reader sees the claims of the passage realized – Troilus is transformed from a 'proude knyght' (I.225) to the 'gentileste' (V.1056).

Dignifying Romantic Love

'O what a wonderful thing is love, which makes a man shine with so many virtues and teaches everyone, no matter who he is, so many good traits of character!'

—Andreas Capellanus, *The Art of Courtly Love*

The attitude that Chaucer formed in his response to Boethius – that there is a dignified place for romantic love in the chain of love – also pervades the narrative elements of *Troilus* that are not explicitly influenced by the *Consolation*. Chaucer portrays a romantic love that is morally improving and through which Troilus, through the acquisition of virtuous traits, ascends to a divine love. There is, however, an aspect of romantic love that is not concordant with this honourable vision of love. There is a danger, as Antigone states following her song in Book II, of confusing love with lust:

> But wene ye that every wrecche woot
> The parfit blisse of love? Why, nay, iwys!
> They wenen all be love, if oon be hoot. (II.890–92)

Some, according to Antigone, do not experience true love but the hotness of lust instead, which is antithetical to virtuous love. Today, the word 'lust' carries heavily, almost exclusively, sexualized connotations but although these connotations were also available in the Middle Ages, in Middle English the word usually meant 'desire' (from the verb 'list').[34] When Chaucer uses the word to mean 'lust' in the modern sense, he often qualifies the word with an appropriate adjective, as in 'foule lust of luxurie' ('Man of Law's Tale', II.925), 'horrible lust' ('Wife of Bath's Prologue', III.736), 'likerous lust' ('Clerk's Tale', IV.214), 'blynde lust' (*Troilus*, V.1824) and, interestingly, 'erthely lust' ('Second Nun's Prologue', VIII.74).

Since in Middle English the meaning of 'lust' was more wide-ranging (it included the sense of 'ardour' or a 'lust for life'),[35] 'lust' could be a desirable trait in a lover. As such, 'lust' is included in Criseyde's list of Troilus's positive qualities where it is noted alongside his 'worthynesse', 'his dedes wise' and his 'gentilesse' (III.1550–51). Similarly, the ideal lover in Antigone's song is also described as being both 'Of vertu roote' and 'of lust fynder and hed' (II.844). Of course, Troilus and Criseyde's relationship contains lust in the modern sense (I.442–45; III.1690), but it is nuanced; in the moments before their first physical union it is made explicit that Troilus 'mente / Nothing but wel' (III.1185–86).[36] While the desires associated with romantic love are represented as natural, and even decorous, at the end of the poem it is clear that there is no place for 'blynde lust, the which that may nat laste' (V.1824) in the perfect vision of love. It is significant that, in one of the glosses Chaucer added to his translation to Boethius's 4M7, he notes 'that is to seyn, that when erthly lust is overcomyn, a man is makid worthy to the hevene' (*Boece*, 4M7: 70–72).

The gloss just cited (with its terms 'overcomyn' and 'makid') makes it clear that being made 'worthy to the hevene' is an active process. And it is through a process of moral transformation that Chaucer presents Troilus's narrative. Troilus is young and inexperienced in love (two useful precepts for exploring experience)[37] and, owing to these two things, he is also proud; he has a lot to learn. The cultivation of virtue begins with the banishing of vices; and pride, the root of all vices, is antithetical to love.[38] Pride signals an attachment to the world that opposes the love of God and is denounced in the *contemptus mundi* tradition (1 John 2:16). Chaucer makes the contrast between pride and love explicit in his poem and he enhances his source, Boccaccio's *Il Filostrato*, to emphasize Troilus's initial pride.[39] The pride that Chaucer takes pains to assert in his early presentation of Troilus (his pride is mentioned five times in I.211–31) is explicitly diminished through Troilus's experience of love: 'That he that now was moost in pride above, / Wax sodeynly moost subgit unto love' (I.230–31). In this receptive state, Troilus's character is open to change and when Troilus has seen but not yet met Criseyde, his character is already altered by love:

> For he bicom the frendlieste wight,
> The gentilest, and ek the mooste fre,
> The thriftiest, and oon the beste knyght
> That in his tyme was or myghte be;
> Dede were his japes and his cruelte,
> His heighe port and his manere estraunge,
> And ecch of tho gan for a vertue chaunge. (I.1079–85)[40]

Troilus undergoes an 'encrees of hardynesse and myght / Com hym of love' (III.1776–77), but the change is not just social or military but moral.[41] Troilus himself recognizes that the life of love is the 'right lif' (II.851), which encourages him:

> To flemen alle manere vice and synne:
> This dooth me so to vertu for t'entende,
> That day by day I in my wille amende. (II.852–54)

The change in Troilus is conscious, positive and, as we saw above, in keeping with the final Boethian invocation to 'eschue thou vices; worschipe and love thou vertues' (*Boece*, 5P6: 302–3). The change in Troilus is also recognized and celebrated by others (III.1723–29) and is presented in subtler moments as well as these grand declarations of moral improvement.[42] His *experience* of love is a process through which he learns and changes. This is reflected in the language of the poem: each vice '*gan* for a vertu chaunge' (I.1085; my italics); 'In suffisaunce, in blisse, and in singynges, / This Troilus *gan* al his lif to lede' (III.1716–17; my italics); 'He nought forgat his goode governaunce, / But in hymself with manhood *gan* restreyne' (III.427–28; my italics).[43]

Pandarus, although with his own agenda, first describes Troilus to Criseyde as one:

> In whom that alle vertu list habounde,
> As alle trouthe and alle gentilesse,
> Wisdom, honour, fredom, and worthinesse. (II.159–61)[44]

And when Criseyde recalls the reasons she first fell in love with Troilus, she states that it was not for his 'estat roial' (IV.1667) or 'worthiness / Of yow in werre' (IV.1668–69) but for his 'moral vertu, grounded upon trouthe' (IV.1672) and 'gentil herte' (IV.1674). In this recollection, poignantly delivered during their final encounter before Criseyde is sent to the Greek camp, Criseyde repeats the two virtuous qualities that are most notable in Troilus.

'Trouthe' is a key word not only in *Troilus*, but throughout Chaucer's writings. 'Trouthe' is Troilus's pre-eminent virtue and even Donaldson, who is otherwise critical of the human experience in the poem, states that truth is 'the one human value the poem leaves entirely unquestioned'.[45] Truth is a virtue that links this world to the next; at the close of *Troilus*, Christ is described as he that 'nyl falsen no wight' (V.1845) and the biblical refrain of Chaucer's short poem 'Truth' expresses the relationship he perceives between the cultivation of truth and the acquisition of 'hevenlich mede' (27): 'trouthe thee shal delivere, it is no drede' (based on John 8:32). Troilus also believes that truth is integral to the fate of his soul; he perceives that, if he is untrue to Criseyde, he will go 'down with Proserpyne' (IV.473) and 'wone in pyne' (IV.474). Truth, as we see in Chaucer's *Franklin's Tale*, is a virtue, not unproblematic, that is developed and tested in relationships and between people. It is only through friendship and, more acutely, love that truth can be formed and proven. Elsewhere, in fact, 'Chaucer' protests he has written *Troilus*:

> To forthren trouthe in love and yt cheryce,
> And to ben war fro falsnesse and fro vice
> By swich ensample; this was my menynge.
> (*Legend of Good Women*, F.472–74)

In *Troilus and Criseyde*, Troilus promises Criseyde that he will 'in trouthe alwey hym holde' (II.1084), a promise that he will repeat

(III.133, 141; IV.445–56), and keep.[46] It is through his relationship with Criseyde that Troilus develops truth and constancy (III.1472–91; IV.447; V.435–518); that the object of his constancy and truth is fallible is only relevant later in the poem with the revelation of the truth of God.

It is also through his experience of romantic love that Troilus cultivates true *gentilesse*; through love 'he bicom the frendlieste wight, / The gentilest, and ek the mooste fre' (I.1079–80).[47] The term *gentilesse* refers to both social and moral nobility; while one could be 'gentil' by circumstance of birth (as Troilus, as a royal prince, is), true *gentilesse* had to be demonstrated in action and comes from God alone.[48] As the wyf of the 'Wife of Bath's Tale' says: 'Thanne am I gentil, whan that I bigynne / To lyven vertuously and weyve synne' (III.1175–76); this sentiment is also present in Chaucer's ballade 'Gentilesse':

> What man that desireth gentil for to be
> Must follow his trace, and alle his wittes dresse
> Vertu to love, and vyces for to flee. (2–5)

These lines, which echo the conclusion of Boethius's *Consolation of Philosophy*, 5p6, conflate *gentilesse* with the cultivation of virtue and avoidance of vice, the latter of which, as we have seen, is repeatedly articulated in relation to romantic love in *Troilus* (I.254; II.850–54; III.25, 1392, 1804–6). The cultivation of virtue through love accords with the vision of courtly love described by Larry Benson: '[courtly] love is not only virtuous in itself but is the very source and cause of all the other virtues, that indeed one cannot be virtuous unless he is a lover'.[49] While qualifying him as a lover, Troilus's virtue and *gentilesse* also play a part in his loss of Criseyde.

When Troilus is told that Criseyde is to be exchanged for Antenor, he lets his lover determine their fate (IV.173), much like the knight of the 'Wife of Bath's Tale'. Rather than 'ravysshe' her (IV.637) as Pandarus suggests, Troilus, in a demonstration of *gentilesse*, gives Criseyde sovereignty and, subsequently, loses her to Diomede. Significantly, the reader is told that Troilus would only run away with Criseyde 'if hireself it wolde' (IV.637). It is Troilus's 'gentil herte' that encourages him to protect Criseyde at all costs, even at the cost of losing her. He values virtuous love, truth and *gentilesse*, over wrongful possession of Criseyde.[50] Both Troilus and the knight of the 'Wife of Bath's Tale' are rewarded for handing sovereignty to their lovers; however, unlike the knight, Troilus's reward is not immediate, nor is it tangible. When his reward does come, it comes not in the form of the love of his lady, but as the ultimate reward: divine love.

The fundamental challenge of the poem is the transition it makes at the end between a pre-Christian world, in which 'human love may appear the highest of man's spiritual aspirations',[51] and a Christian framework in which the 'wrecched world' (V.1817) is denounced. The poem challenges us to consider how we might reconcile its two parts.[52] As noted by Barry Windeatt, critics tend to subscribe to one of three views: there are those who state that the ending of the poem negates its story; those who argue that the story negates the poem's ending; and those who argue that the poem and the story are ultimately united, the category into which this study falls.[53] The poem's employment of the *contemptus mundi* topos in its final lines has led to the claim that the moral of the poem is 'that human love, and by a sorry corollary everything human, is unstable and illusory'.[54] However, there is an alternative reading of the poem's conclusion in which love unifies both human experience and divine love. At the poem's end the reader does not have to renounce everything that stems from the world; instead he or she must distinguish the meaningful from the meaningless and simultaneously hold in mind both the potentially morally elevating virtue of romantic love and the ultimate supremacy of the love of God.

The division between the two parts of the poem is initiated by Troilus's death on the battlefield, after which he 'blisfully' (V.1808) ascends to the 'eighthe spere' (V.1809).[55] Troilus looks down onto the 'litel spot of erthe' (V.1815), laughs at those who weep for his death and condemns 'blynde lust' (V.1824). The narrator then advises the audience of 'yonge, fresshe folkes' (V.1835):

> Repeyreth hom fro worldly vanyte,
> And of youre herte up casteth the visage
> To thilke God that after his ymage
> Yow made ... (V.1837–40)

The narrator presents Christ as he who, 'for love', died 'Upon a crois, oure soules for to beye' (V.1843–44), and asks, 'syn he best to love is, and most meke, / What nedeth feynede loves for to seke?' (V.1847–48). The poem clearly states the supremacy of God's love. However, it is not the case that all worldly experience ought to be dismissed. The question posed to the audience – 'What nedeth feynede loves for to seke?' – requires them to determine what they perceive to be true and false love. It is clear that the meaning that the reader gives to romantic love in the poem is critical in how he or she reads its closing message. Ann Astell argues that, 'Ultimately man "nedeth feynede loves for to seke" – including the "feynede loves" of fictive romance – in order to come to know the meaning of divine love with an affective knowledge'.[56] It is important to qualify this argument by insisting, with Chaucer, that, as we have seen, not all love in 'fictive romance' is 'feynede'. The 'blynde lust' that Troilus has just condemned is not synonymous with all romantic love.

While Troilus's death can be seen to divide the poem, it also unifies it. Troilus dies 'for love' (V.1828), just as it was 'for love' (V.1843) that Christ died on the cross.[57] It hardly needs saying that Troilus is distinguished from Christ; however, while their differences are apparent, they are unified by love. The reader is encouraged to consider the relationship between the two, especially as these lines just cited are placed at the opening of two stanzas in close proximity and of identical rhetorical structure:

> Swich fyn hath, lo, this Troilus *for love*!
> Swich fyn hath al his grete worthynesse!
> Swich fyn hath his estat real *above*!
> Swich fyn his lust, swich fyn hath his noblesse!
> Swich fyn hath false worldes brotelnesse!
> And thus bigan his lovyng of Criseyde,
> As I have told, and in this wise he deyde. (V.1828–34; my italics)

> And loveth hym the which that right *for love*
> Upon a crois, oure soules for to beye,
> First staf, and roos, and sit in hevene *above*.
> For he nyl falsen no wight, dar I seye,
> That wol his herte al holly on hym leye.
> And syn he best to love is, and most meke,
> What nedeth feyned loves for to seke? (V.1842–44; my italics)

At the point of death, the meaningful is distinguished from the meaningless; Troilus's worldly identity, possessions, vices and social graces all meet the same end but Troilus's ultimate fate – to 'blisfully' (V.1808) ascend to the eighth sphere – is determined by love.[58] The vision of a salvific love was modelled in the poem's opening lines:

> And preieth for hem that ben in the cas
> Of Troilus, as ye may after here,
> That Love hem brynge in hevene to solas. (I.29–30)

In Troilus's death this vision is realized. As David has observed, the vision of a chain of love that Troilus articulated in his hymn (III.1744–71) returns to the poem, 'this time no longer bound to the unstable condition of earthly happiness'.[59]

As I hope to have shown, Troilus travels a trajectory where his experience of romantic love is related to his ultimate experience of a unifying, divine love. In stark contrast, Criseyde does not ascend, like Troilus, but rather stagnates in a state of earth-bound fear. We are reminded that 'perfect love casteth out fear' (1 John 4:18ff.). Criseyde loves Troilus, but she is so wedded to, and aware of, her precarious social and political circumstances that she is ruled and restricted by fear. She is introduced to us in a state of fear (I.95–98); it is for fear that she initially resists a relationship with Troilus (II.302–3, 449–50, 768–73); and she lives in constant fear for her reputation and safety (II.785–88; IV.1569–70; V.701–7, 1603). She is, indeed, 'the ferfulleste wight / That myghte be' (II.450–510). Chaucer enhanced this aspect of her characterization and, in doing so, created a byword (and an image) for her attachment to worldly concerns.[60] Attachment to the world, as discussed above, was opposed in 1 John and seen as a barrier to God's love; shortly following the passage in which he advocates eschewing the world, John declares that 'fear is not in charity' (1 John 4:18). In a small, but significant, enactment of this sentiment, it seems fitting that Troilus, who ultimately chooses truth and *gentilesse* over Criseyde, is able to ascend to God's love, while Criseyde, who cannot release herself (or be released from) mundane fears, is denied such a fate. Troilus is an idealist who lives and dies by his *trouthe*; Criseyde in contrast declares that she must 'make virtue of necessity' (IV.1584). In her hands, grand moral concepts are reduced to pragmatism.[61] The virtue of prudence, one of whose three eyes Criseyde explicitly states that she lacks (V.744), becomes a pragmatic response to circumstance.

1 John concludes: 'this commandment we have from God, that he, who loveth God, love also his brother' (1 John 4:21). In *Troilus* too, the world is not to be renounced in its entirety; we are shown that through virtuous worldly engagement, one can participate in the love of God. In the poem, divine love subsumes virtuous romantic love, not unlike the way C.S. Lewis articulates it in his personal meditation on love: 'the Divine Love does not substitute itself for the natural ... The natural loves are summoned to become modes of Charity while also remaining the natural loves they were'.[62] It is

through love that God and the earth are linked, after all; God created the universe, in both the Platonic and Christian visions, out of love not necessity; this motivation 'is essential' according to Lewis.[63] As Windeatt has observed, the ending of the poem 'suggests not so much a renunciation and rejection as a transference and redirection of that longing and striving for love instilled in the human heart ... Only through the love for God – truth and reality itself, beyond time and change – can the aspirations of the human power to love be fulfilled'.[64] At the poem's conclusion, the reader must therefore hold in mind both the potentially morally elevating virtue of romantic love *and* the ultimate supremacy of the love of God, not as competing forces but as harmonious aspects of the chain of love.

The Experience of Poetry

To conclude, let us briefly consider the significance of Chaucer's decision to handle these philosophical issues in poetic form and suggest that Chaucer's approach to the role of poetry may well be another element of his complex response to Boethius.

Human experience is central to the poem's narrative and meaning. It is significant that this poem is addressed to 'ye loveres' (I.22) and that the poem reminds us of its immediate audience at its conclusion (V.1835–36). The imagined audience is not made up of ascetic or eremetical men or women, who would denounce all worldly things and thus long for a different application of the *contemptus mundi* topos; it is made up of courtly folk (the kinds of people depicted in the frontispiece to the Corpus Christi College, Cambridge, MS 61) who are embedded in the courtly culture that the poem explores. The imagined audience have experienced, and crucially *are currently experiencing*, romantic love – if only through fiction. Their status identifies them as those who ought to be reminded of the supremacy of God's love (V.1837–39), but also enables Chaucer to capitalize on their experience, which is essential to philosophical understanding, not counter to it. As Jessica Rosenfeld states in her discussion of Aristotelian glosses on Boethius, 'we come to knowledge, even knowledge of concepts and greater truths, through our sensory contact with earthly things'.[65] This is shown to be true for Troilus, whose improvement is driven by love and is philosophical as well as moral.[66] Learning to love is an active process, as demonstrated through Troilus. Its value is immense: the ultimate reward of virtuous love is salvation. With this in mind, Chaucer's contemporary, William Langland, concluded his poem *Piers Plowman* with the following advice:

> 'Counseilleth me, Kynde,' quod I, 'what craft be best *to* lerne?'
> 'Lerne to love,' quod Kynde, 'and leef alle other.' (XX.207–8)

Without love, man may not prosper:

> God loveth, and to love wol nought werne,
> And in this world no lyves creature
> Withouten love is worth, or may endure. (III.12–14)

Again, Lewis can help us access this way of thinking;[67] the necessity of practising virtue on earth, he suggests, 'first sets us, forces us, upon the attempts to turn – more strictly, to let God turn – our love into Charity'.[68] This complex but fundamental relationship between the worldly and the heavenly is not explicitly present in the *Consolation of Philosophy*. Boethius's work instead advocates that man detach himself from the world in its entirety. In contrast, Chaucer envisions a universe where *through* virtuous worldly engagement and human experience one can access divine love and true felicity. He shapes and explores this universe through narrative poetry.

Here, perhaps, Chaucer is addressing another tension he perceives in Boethius – the tension between the value of poetry and the value of philosophy. Boethius's *Consolation of Philosophy* begins with the arrival of Lady Philosophy who banishes the muses of poetry from Boethius's chamber as they 'accustom a man's mind to his ills, not rid him of them' (1P1).[69] In contrast, it is through poetry that Chaucer seeks to dignify virtuous romantic love. In *Troilus*, Chaucer claims that his intention has been to represent 'the forme of olde clerkis speche / In poetrie' (V.1854–55). Chaucer takes his poetry seriously; not only does he invoke the muse of history (II.8) alongside the muse of epic poetry (III.45), his claims for the integrity of his poetry are also reflected in the literary afterlife he envisages for it. At the poem's conclusion, he sends his 'litel bok' (V.1786) to 'kis the steppes where as thow seest pace / Virgile, Ovide, Omer, Lucan, and Stace' (V.1791–92). Chaucer celebrates and reveres the great poets who have gone before him, but at the same time he places himself among their company. He then commends it to 'moral Gower' and Philosophical Strode' (V.1856–57). Chaucer's ambition to create philosophical poetry can be seen in his initial decision to fuse Boccaccio's poem of courtly love with Boethius's *Consolation*, and also in his decision to attempt to assimilate Neo-Platonic thinking with Christianity.

With human *experience* at the poem's narrative and philosophical heart, we can appreciate Chaucer's choice of narrative poetry as the medium through which to explore issues of philosophy, theology and ethics. Narrative poetry is a medium in which, as in real life, the experience of time is fundamental. The philosopher Bernard Williams has asked: 'can the reality of complex moral situations be represented by means other than those of imaginative literature?'[70] Chaucer's decision to explore concepts of morality, divine love and salvation in poetry may come in part from being 'acutely aware that ... Philosophy cannot tell us the whole story'.[71] His approach to *Troilus* then might best be seen as a response to his belief in the limitations of philosophy and his conviction in the potential of poetry to sustain philosophical matters.

Despite first appearances, Chaucer may not be at odds with Boethius here. Although Lady Philosophy banishes the muses of poetry from Boethius's side, it is through poetry that some of the more nuanced and sophisticated arguments of the *Consolation* are presented and clarified. As Marenbon has recently argued, Boethius uses poetry 'as a way of adumbrating truths [Philosophy] cannot capture through straightforward philosophical reasoning'.[72] The *Consolation*, he argues, 'is not a work that rejects philosophy ... but is one that ... explores its limitations'.[73] Chaucer, a sensitive reader of Boethius, may well be responding to these fundamental tensions and, just as he sought to create a dignified place for virtuous romantic love in *Troilus and Criseyde*, he also sought to dignify poetry as an appropriate medium for the discussion of the relationship between virtuous romantic love and divine love – a philosophical topic that has human experience at its core.

Simone Fryer-Bovair completed her PhD, 'Handling Virtue: Chaucer's Narrative Art', at the University of Bristol. She is currently raising her young children when not reading and thinking about Chaucer.

Notes

1. D.W. Robertson's reading of the tale is the quintessential example of such an interpretation; see *A Preface to Chaucer: Studies in Medieval Perspectives* (Princeton, NJ: Princeton University Press, 1963), 24–31.

2. Boethius may have been familiar with Plato's concept of *eros*, but romantic love, as we have come to understand and formulate the term through centuries of discussion, is a concept with which Boethius could not have engaged in the same way we do.

3. There have been some significant recent developments in the study of Boethius's text, and also in the study of Chaucer's response to Boethius. John Marenbon's work on Boethius has revealed the complex, and occasionally inconsistent, nature of the *Consolation* and its arguments: see *Boethius*, Great Medieval Thinkers (Oxford: Oxford University Press, 2003). Marenbon's work demonstrates the need for a more nuanced understanding of Boethius's arguments and for Chaucer's response to Boethius. Marenbon argues that Chaucer was 'more sensitive' than other poets 'to the tensions and uncertainties in Boethius's text' (182). Marenbon's work opens up the way for Chaucerian scholars to respond to these complexities. Among scholars who have done so are John Hill, 'The Countervailing Aesthetic of Joy in *Troilus and Criseyde*', *The Chaucer Review* 39 (2005): 280–97; Jessica Rosenfeld, 'The Doubled Joys of *Troilus and Criseyde*', in *The Erotics of Consolation: Desire and Distance in the Late Middle Ages*, ed. Catherine E. Léglu and Stephen J. Milner (New York: Palgrave Macmillan, 2008), 39–59; and Megan Murton 'Praying with Boethius in *Troilus and Criseyde*', *The Chaucer Review* 49 no. 3 (2015): 294–319.

4. Barry Windeatt cautions against reading the poem through this 'backward panoramic vista' in '*Troilus and Criseyde*: Love in a Manner of Speaking', in *Writings on Love in the English Middle Ages*, ed. Helen Cooney (Basingstoke: Palgrave, 2006), 81–97, here 82.

5. E. Talbot Donaldson, 'The Ending of *Troilus*', in *Speaking of Chaucer* (London: Athlone Press, 1970), 84–101, here 92.

6. This notion is the popularized version of Kierkegaard's notion that 'philosophy is perfectly right in saying that life must be understood backwards. But then one forgets the other clause – that it must be lived forwards'; see *Søren Kierkegaard's Journals and Papers*, 4 vols. (Bloomington: Indiana University Press, 1967–75), I (1967): 450. Here, I am inspired by Ad Putter's application of this philosophy to medieval literature; see Putter's 'Story Line and Story Shape in *Sir Percyvell of Gales* and Chrétien de Troyes's *Conte du Graal*', in *Pulp Fictions of Medieval England: Essays in Popular Romance*, ed. Nicola McDonald (Manchester: Manchester University Press, 2004), 171–96, esp. 193.

7. C.S. Lewis, *The Four Loves* (London: Harper Collins, 1960), 148. Lewis's emphasis.

8. Alfred David, 'The Hero of the *Troilus*', *Speculum* 37, no. 4 (1962): 566–81, here 568.

9. Troilus's limitations, as a pagan, are an extreme manifestation of the limitations of all mankind. Boethius, for one, argues that although humans have reason (something not possessed by animals), while on earth, they lack the intelligence that is unique to the divine (*Consolation*, 5P5). The limitations that have been imposed on Troilus by some critics – that he does not fully understand the Boethian dimension of his narrative, or that he is limited because he does not realize that

his love is inferior to the love of God – are, in comparison, inappropriate and anachronistic to his situation. See, for example, D.W. Robertson, 'Chaucerian Tragedy', *English Literary History* 19, no. 1 (1952): 1–37; T.P. Dunning, 'God and Man in *Troilus and Criseyde*', in *English and Medieval Studies, Presented to J.R.R. Tolkien on the Occasion of His Seventieth Birthday*, ed. Norman Davis and C.L. Wrenn (London: Allen & Unwin, 1962), 164–82; Gerald Morgan, 'The Significance of the Aubades in *Troilus and Criseyde*', *The Yearbook of English Studies* 9 (1979): 221–35; and A.J. Minnis, *Chaucer and Pagan Antiquity*, Chaucer Studies VIII (Cambridge: Brewer, 1982), 93–107.

10. Citations from Chaucer's *Boece*, and all quotations from Chaucer, are taken from *The Riverside Chaucer*, ed. Larry D. Benson, 3rd ed. (Oxford: Oxford University Press, 2008).

11. As Winthrop Wetherbee has observed, 3M12 has an 'undertone of suppressed feeling which is at odds with its ostensibly exemplary purpose'; as a result it gives 'eloquent expression to the very impulse it intended to curb, the attachment to earthly things'; see *Platonism and Poetry in the Twelfth Century: The Literary Influence of the School of Chartres* (Princeton, NJ: Princeton University Press, 1972), 78–79. On the significance of the Orpheus narrative, see also Ann W. Astell, 'Orpheus, Eurydice, and the "Double Sorwe" of Chaucer's *Troilus*', *The Chaucer Review* 23, no. 4 (1989): 283–99; and Phillipa Hardman's 'Narrative Typology: Chaucer's Use of the Story of Orpheus', *The Modern Language Review* 85, no. 3 (1990): 545–54.

12. See also 4P6, 4M6, 3M9, 3P10.

13. Plato, *Timaeus*, 31b–c, 32c, trans. R.G. Bury, Loeb Classical Library (Cambridge, MA: Harvard University Press, 1966), IX, 56–59; 32–33. I use this edition throughout.

14. Anicius Manlius Severinus Boethius, *The Theological Tractates*, ed. Edward Kennard Rand and H.F. Stewart, trans. S.J. Tester, Loeb Classical Library (Cambridge, MA: Harvard University Press, 1973), 226; 'What binds all things to order, / Governing earth and sea and sky, / Is love' (227). I use this edition throughout.

15. For a discussion of this concept, see Arthur O. Lovejoy, *The Great Chain of Being: A Study of the History of an Idea* (Cambridge, MA: Harvard University Press, 1970), 47–49. The Neo-Platonist Plotinus provided the explanation that when 'anything reaches its own perfection, we see that it cannot endure to remain in itself, but generates and produces some other thing', in *Enneads*, V.2.1, cited in Lovejoy, *The Great Chain of Being*, 62.

16. William Langland, *The Vision of Piers Plowman*, The Everyman Library, 2nd ed. (London: Everyman, 1995), 21–22. I use this edition throughout.

17. John V. Fleming, 'The Best Line in Ovid and the Worst', in *New Readings of Chaucer's Poetry*, ed. Robert G. Benson and Susan J. Ridyard, Chaucer Studies, 31 (Cambridge: D.S. Brewer, 2003), 51–74, here 56.

18. On Boethius's influence on Chaucer, see Barry Windeatt, *Troilus and Criseyde*, Oxford Guides to Chaucer (Oxford: Clarendon Press, 1995), 96–109; Bernard Levi Jefferson, *Chaucer and the Consolation of Philosophy of Boethius* (Princeton, NJ: Princeton University Press, 1917); Theodore A. Stroud, 'Boethius' Influence on Chaucer's *Troilus*', *Modern Philology* 49, no. 1 (1951): 1–9; and Frank Grady, 'The Boethian Reader of *Troilus and Criseyde*', *The Chaucer Review* 33, no. 3 (1999): 230–51.

19. To diminish its significance, Gerald Morgan argues that this alteration is 'more likely to appeal to a scholar than to an auditor of the poem', in 'The Significance of the Aubades', 234.

20. As A.J. Minnis states, the 'failure of the lovers to get married ... is an historical fact which must be accepted as such'. Minnis argues that Chaucer, by 'stressing the element of heterosexual love', is adhering to the poem's pagan setting; *Chaucer and Pagan Antiquity*, 101–2. It has been argued that the lovers' exchange of rings and words spoken constitute a marriage. Cathy Hume's recent study, however, argues that the 'form of words used by Criseyde and Troilus to one another when swearing their love does not constitute a marriage vow'; see *Chaucer and the Cultures of Love and Marriage* (Cambridge: Cambridge University Press, 2013), 143.

21. Both Robert O'Payne and John Hill agree that the final stanza of Troilus's hymn depicts sexual love in accordance with cosmic love; see Robert O'Payne, *The Key of Remembrance, a Study of Chaucer's Poetics* (New Haven, CT: Yale University Press, 1963), 295; and Hill, 'The Countervailing Aesthetic of Joy', 289.

22. Among other critics who view Troilus's love for Criseyde sympathetically are David, 'The Hero of the *Troilus*'; Peter Dronke, 'The Conclusion of *Troilus and Criseyde*', *Medium Aevum* 33 (1964): 47–52; Astell, 'Orpheus, Eurydice, and the "Double Sorwe"'; and Robert P. apRoberts, 'The Central Episode in Chaucer's Troilus', PMLA 77, no. 4 (1962): 373–85.

23. On the significance of prayer in Troilus and the Consolation, see Murton 'Praying with Boethius'.

24. Windeatt's emphasis, Troilus and Criseyde, 105.

25. Robertson, 'Chaucerian Tragedy', 28.

26. John Frankis, 'Paganism and Pagan Love in Troilus and Criseyde', in Essays on 'Troilus and Criseyde', ed. Mary Salu, Chaucer Studies (Cambridge: D.S. Brewer, 1979), III: 57–72, here 63.

27. Morgan, 'The Significance of the Aubades', 227.

28. Ibid.

29. Hill, 'The Countervailing Aesthetic of Joy', 284. Howard Patch concedes that, although the hymn is made ironic by its setting, 'the beauty of the lines' is genuine, even though they are spoken by a young man 'engaged in a temporary affair'; The Tradition of Boethius; a Study of His Importance in Medieval Culture (New York: Oxford University Press, 1935), 70.

30. Dunning, 'God and Man in *Troilus and Criseyde*', 175. Dunning goes on to acknowledge, that 'this good, but not exceptionally intelligent, pagan' will never on earth reach 'the matter which is most hardly found out is made clear in Book IV', however, 'his experience of love has led him to the heart of the mystery' (175–76). For a discussion of virtuous pagans, see Minnis, *Chaucer and Pagan Antiquity*.

31. Robertson argues that this gives evidence in the rejection of the human love celebrated in Troilus's hymn; see 'Chaucerian Tragedy', 29.

32. David argues that 'the heartbreaking lesson of the last book [Book V] does not altogether cancel out the vision of Book III'; 'The Hero of the Troilus', 580. To Windeatt, the poem presents an 'extended sequence of experience in which each love successively fills the picture'; Troilus and Criseyde, 304.

33. For a discussion of the various images of bondage in the poem, see Stephen A. Barney, 'Troilus Bound', Speculum 47, no. 3 (1972): 445–58.

34. MED, 'lust', (n. 1[a]) desire, wish, will; a desire, a wish; (n. 1[c]) physical desire, bodily appetite; (n. 1[d]) sexual desire, passion.

35. MED, 'lust', (4[a]) vigor, energy, life; fertility. This positive connotation endures in the adjective 'lusty'.

36. As Helen Phillips observes, in her chapter on 'Love', in III.1184–274, Chaucer 'runs through almost all the species of love deity available to his culture – except any of the potentially negative personifications of passion and physical sex, such as the goddess Venus ..., Priapus, Cupid/Amor, Nature or Luxuria ("lechery")'; *A Companion to Chaucer*, ed. Peter Brown (Oxford: Blackwell, 2000), 281–95, here 285. Troilus's lust is differentiated from his 'delit'; Criseyde later tells Troilus how she admired that 'youre resoun bridlede youre delit' (V.1678).

37. On the significance of Troilus's youth, see D.S. Brewer, 'Troilus's "Gentil" Manhood', in *Masculinities in Chaucer*, ed. Peter G. Beidler, Chaucer Studies, 25 (Cambridge: D.S. Brewer, 1998), 237–52, here 239–41.

38. The image of pride as the root of the vices was commonplace and can be seen in a range of theological and penitential texts, such as Thomas Aquinas's *Summa Theologica*, Raymond Pennaforte's *Summa Casuum* and Vincent of Beauvais' *Speculum Naturale*; see Morton W. Bloomfield, *The Seven Deadly Sins; an Introduction to the History of a Religious Concept, with Special Reference to Medieval English Literature* (East Lansing: Michigan State College Press, 1952), 87, 124, 126. Chaucer uses this image in his own *Parson's Tale*: 'Of the roote of thise sevene synnes, thanne, is Pride the general roote of alle harmes. For of this roote spryngen certein braunches, as Ire, Envye, Accidie or Slewthe, Avarice or Coveitise' (X.388). Following 1 Corinthians 13.13, pride was conceived in opposition to love (*caritas*), root of the virtues and God himself: 'How great the evil of pride is, that it deserves to have as its adversary not an angel or other virtues contrary to it but rather God himself!'; Book XII, Chapter 7 of John Cassian's *Institutes*, trans. Boniface Ramsey (New York: Newman Press, 2000). See also James 4.6; Psalms 17.28; and Proverbs 29.23.

39. For a parallel edition, see *Troilus and Criseyde: A New Edition of the Book of Troilus*, ed. B.A. Windeatt (London: Longman, 1984).

40. For a similar moment in which vices are replaced by virtues, see III.1804–6.

41. Interestingly, unlike the increase in military prowess common to a lover in the 'courtly love' tradition, Troilus's military prowess is most significantly increased after his loss of Criseyde (V.1751–62).

42. See, for example, Troilus's self-governance in III.427–28 and his adherence to the promise he made to Pandarus to be 'diligent and trewe' (I.957) to Criseyde and to 'kep hire out of blame, / ... and save alwey hire name' (III.265–94) in IV.152–59.

43. The verb 'gan' is the thirty-fifth most common word in the poem and, although it is occasionally used pleonastically, its frequency highlights a sense of change, renewal and growth in Troilus; see *A Complete Concordance to the Works of Geoffrey Chaucer*, ed. Akio Oizumi, 10 vols. (Hildesheim: Olms-Weidmann, 1991), VII: 1049.

44. Virtue plays a significant role in the formation of Troilus and Criseyde's impressions of one another, largely through Pandarus's presentation of the two to one another; see II.159–61, 173, 184, 316–17, 331, 339; III.131–33, 257.

45. *Chaucer's Poetry: An Anthology for the Modern Reader*, ed. E.T. Donaldson (New York: Ronald Press, 1958), 974; although he later adds that Troilus's truth is

'hopelessly limited' (976). The word *trouthe* has a complex set of meanings; see Richard Firth Green's study, *A Crisis of Truth: Literature and Law in Ricardian England*, Middle Ages Series (Philadelphia, PA: University of Pennsylvania Press, 1999). Green sets out the four major categories under which truth can be examined (legal, ethical, theological and intellectual). In this article, the word is primarily considered in its ethical context.

46. Troilus's truth is sharply contrasted with Criseyde's infidelity. It is only when Troilus receives 'ocular proof' of Criseyde's infidelity that he realizes she lacks the virtue and true love that he possesses: '"Where is youre love? Where is youre trouthe?" he seyde' (V.1676). Troilus and Criseyde both acknowledge that her moral failing is her lack of trouthe (V.1054–55, 1686–87).

47. Again it is an elevated form of love that is linked with the virtue of *gentilesse*. When Troilus and Criseyde are united in bed for the first time, the narrative voice assumes that 'every wyght, I gesse, / That loveth *wel*, meneth but gentilesse' (III.1147–48; my italics).

48. This is a concept that Chaucer drew from Dante's *Convivio*: 'And this gift [of nobleness] can be given by none save God alone' (Tractate IV, Chapter XX); Dante Alighieri, *The Convivio of Dante Alighieri*, trans. Philip H. Wicksteed, The Temple Classics (London: J.M. Dent, 1903), 326. For a further discussion of *gentilesse* in the poem, see Alan T. Gaylord, '*Gentilesse* in Chaucer's *Troilus*', *Studies in Philology* 61, no. 1 (1964): 19–34; and Brewer 'Troilus's "Gentil" Manhood'.

49. This is a synopsis of Ovid's argument in *Amores*, I.IX.15; see Larry D. Benson, 'Courtly Love and Chivalry in the Later Middle Ages', in *Fifteenth-Century Studies: Recent Essays*, ed. Robert F. Yeager (Hamden, CT: Archon Books, 1984), 237–57, here 240.

50. Those critics who challenge Troilus's virility and masculine power miss the poem's central concern, which is for Troilus's moral, rather than military, power. John P. McCall casts Troilus as 'helpless' and a lecher in 'The Five-Book Structure of Chaucer's Troilus', *Modern Language Quarterly* 23 (1962): 297–308; David Aers discusses the aggressive masculinity of the cultures of the poem in *Chaucer, Langland and the Creative Imagination* (London: Routledge & Kegan Paul, 1980), 117–52; both Stephanie Dietrich and Maud Burnett McInerney consider Troilus to be 'feminised' (as in made effeminate) in their respective chapters in Beidler, *Masculinities in Chaucer*; as does Diane Vanner Steinberg, '"We Do Usen Here No Wommen for to Selle": Embodiment of Social Practices in "Troilus and Criseyde"', *The Chaucer Review* 29, no. 3 (1995): 259–73. In contrast, Jill Mann defends the 'feminine' qualities that Chaucer enhances in his presentation of Troilus: 'unreserved surrender to the force of love is for Chaucer not a sign of weakness but of a generous nobility'; she clearly states that 'feminised' is not to be equated with 'effeminate'; see *Geoffrey Chaucer*, Feminist Readings (Hemel Hempstead: Harvester Wheatsheaf, 1991), 166; Brewer, in 'Troilus's "Gentil" Manhood', also argues that Troilus's *gentilesse* is not antithetical to his manhood.

51. David, 'The Hero of the *Troilus*', 568. An alternative view is that the common good is the highest earthly virtue, for example see *Somnium Scipionis*, Book VI in Cicero's *De Re Publica*: 'a path to heaven ... is open to those who have served their country well' (VI.XXIV). Marcus Tullius Cicero, *De Re Publica, De Legibus*, ed. E.H. Warmington, trans. Clinton Walker Keyes, Loeb Classical Library (Cambridge, MA: Harvard University Press, 1970), 256–83, here 278–79.

52. For a useful discussion of the ending of *Troilus and Criseyde*, and its critical reception, see Chapter 5, 'Narrative Closure: The End of *Troilus and Criseyde*' in A.C. Spearing, *Readings in Medieval Poetry* (Cambridge: Cambridge University Press, 1987), 107–33.

53. Windeatt, *Troilus and Criseyde*, 301.

54. Donaldson, 'The Ending of *Troilus*', 92.

55. There has been much written about the meaning and significance of Troilus's ascension to the eighth sphere, with much debate about the nature of an afterlife available to the pagan Troilus. Chauncey Wood suggests that Troilus only has access to Purgatory; see *Chaucer and the Country of the Stars: Poetic Uses of Astrological Imagery* (Princeton, NJ: Princeton University Press, 1970), 189. Morton Bloomfield focuses on the pagan vision of an afterlife, in 'The Eighth Sphere: A Note on Chaucer's *Troilus and Criseyde*, V.1809', *The Modern Language Review* 53, no. 3 (1958): 408–10; while John W. Conlee considers the complimentary traditions of pagan and Christian visions of the afterlife in 'The Meaning of Troilus' Ascension to the Eighth Sphere', *The Chaucer Review* 7, no. 1 (1972): 27–36. Peter Dronke sees Troilus's ascension in Christian terms as a 'heavenly reward'. The eighth sphere, Dronke argues, is the 'highest heaven open to human beings'; see 'The Conclusion of *Troilus and Criseyde*', 49. Donaldson states that it is 'a heaven that is physically pagan but theologically Christian'. He adds that 'it is not the first time in medieval literature that *trouthe* allows a non-Christian to enter into a Christian heaven, for according to both Langland and Dante the same quality had raised to heaven the Emperor Trajan'; *Chaucer's Poetry*, 979. Helen Cooper states that, in general, Chaucer 'refuses to invent for the characters of his own poetry an ultimate fate beyond death'. This probably reflects, she argues, his 'committed belief that he cannot and should not arrogate God's judgements to himself'; see 'The Four Last Things in Dante and Chaucer: Ugolino in the House of Rumour', *New Medieval Literatures* 3 (1999): 45. Minnis is in accordance with this view. Chaucer, he states, is 'non-committal about what happened to Troilus after death'. Minnis adds that Chaucer is 'more interested in his virtuous behaviour and philosophical vision in life'; *Chaucer and Pagan Antiquity*, 107. I agree with both Cooper and Minnis; it is, however, significant that the reader is told that Troilus ascended 'blisfully' (V.1808), which at least rules out any sense of damnation.

56. Astell, 'Orpheus, Eurydice, and the "Double Sorwe"', 298.

57. Just as it was for 'love', that was so heavy that 'hevene myghte nat holden it' (*Piers Plowman*, I.153), that Christ came to earth 'for oure mysdedes, to amenden us alle' (*Piers Plowman*, I.168).

58. This stanza is not, as Donaldson has claimed, a condemnation of 'not only what merely *seems* good, but also what really *is* good'. Donaldson, writing on the 'swych fyn' passage, states that the 'movement is curious'. He resolves his sense of unease about the stanza (which denounces both concepts of perceived and actual value) to the narrator: it is 'as if the narrator, while forced by the evidence to condemn everything his poem has stood for, cannot really quite believe that it has come to nothing'; 'The Ending of *Troilus*', 97–98.

59. David, 'The Hero of the *Troilus*', 574.

60. On Criseyde's image see Barry Windeatt, 'Gesture in Chaucer', *Medievalia et Humanistica* 9 (1979): 143–61.

61. In English, the first recorded use of the proverb 'to make virtue of necessity' is in Chaucer; see v.43 in B.J. Whiting, *Proverbs, Sentences, and Proverbial Phrases from English Writings Mainly before 1500* (Cambridge, MA: Harvard University Press, 1968). The phrase is in common usage in Middle French before this; see v.79 in James Woodrow Hassell's *Middle French Proverbs, Sentences, and Proverbial Phrases* (Toronto: Pontifical Institute of Mediaeval Studies, 1982). See also Vincent J. DiMarco's explanatory notes to ll. 3041–42 of 'The Knight's Tale' in *The Riverside Chaucer*, 841.

62. Lewis, *The Four Loves*, 161–62. Despite his argument that 'the poet's final statement cancels all the human values which his own loving treatment made real', Donaldson concedes in his 1958 study of the poem that 'in the last lines of the poem Chaucer gathers up all the flickering emotions, the flickering loves with which he has been dealing and unites them into the great harmony of the only true and perfect love. All the conflicting realities and illusions of the old story are subsumed under the one supreme reality'; *Chaucer's Poetry*, 980.

63. Lewis, *The Four Loves*, 153.

64. Windeatt, *Troilus and Criseyde*, 303–4. David also states that 'no man may have his heaven on earth, but that is not to say he may not enjoy a glimpse of heaven. Troilus' celestial laughter recognizes at the same time the absurdity *and* the sublimity of human endeavor'; 'The Hero of the *Troilus*', 580.

65. Rosenfeld, 'The Doubled Joys', 44.

66. As argued by Hill, 'The Countervailing Aesthetic of Joy', 290; and Dunning, 'God and Man in *Troilus and Criseyde*', 175.

67. Unlike elsewhere (see *They Asked for a Paper* [London: Geoffrey Bles, 1962], 24), Lewis makes no claims in his *Four Loves* to have a special ability (as a practising Christian) to access a medieval viewpoint. See, in response, Jill Mann, 'Chaucer and Atheism, Presidential Address', *Studies in the Age of Chaucer* 17 (1995): 5–19.

68. Lewis, *The Four Loves*, 164.

69. For a discussion of the relationship between poetry and philosophy in the commentary history of Boethius's *Consolation* (to which Chaucer had access), see A.J. Minnis, 'Chaucer's Commentators: Nicholas Trevet and the *Boece*', in *Chaucer's Boece and the Medieval Tradition of Boethius*, ed. Minnis (Cambridge: D.S. Brewer, 1993), 83–166; and Astell, 'Orpheus, Eurydice, and the "Double Sorwe"', 296–97.

70. Bernard Arthur Owen Williams, *Morality: An Introduction to Ethics* (Cambridge: Cambridge University Press, 1976), 11. See also Martha C. Nussbaum's *Love's Knowledge: Essays on Philosophy and Literature* (Oxford: Oxford University Press, 1990).

71. Martin Camargo, 'The Consolation of Pandarus', *The Chaucer Review* 25, no. 3 (1991): 214–28, here 226.

72. Marenbon, *Boethius*, 162.

73. In *Boethius*, Marenbon reads the *Consolation* as Menippean satire, a genre in which pretences to wisdom are challenged.

Chapter 8

Hateful Contraries in 'The Merchant's Tale'

John M. Fyler

Twice at least in the *Canterbury Tales* Chaucer translates a single source in two quite different contexts. In the first instance, St Bernard's rhapsodic prayer to the Virgin at the opening of *Paradiso* 33 provides the language for both the Prioress and the Second Nun as they prepare to tell their tales. (Chaucer translates from this prayer a third time in Troilus's hymn to 'Benigne Love', the dispenser of grace in the religion of Cupid [*Troilus* 3.1261–67].) By subtle choices in phrasing, Chaucer differentiates the humble Virgin Mother of the Prioress's prologue, who becomes assimilated with the mother of the *litel clergeon*, from the *mulier fortis* of the Second Nun's, the heavenly intercessor who models the sanctity of the strong woman St Cecilia. These different aspects of the Virgin serve to distinguish two very different versions of the female religious life. Like the Nun's Priest, who also serves the Prioress, the Second Nun outshines her superior; she is the better storyteller and the better nun.

The other doubled quotation appears in 'The Merchant's Tale' and Chaucer's 'Tale of Melibee'. Albertanus of Brescia wrote three didactic treatises in the early thirteenth century, one for each of his sons; in 'The Merchant's Tale' Chaucer quotes from two of them, the *Liber de amore et dilectione Dei* [*Book Concerning Love and Delight in God*] and the *Liber consolationis et consilii* [*Book of Consolation and Counsel*]. 'Melibee' in turn derives directly from Renaud de Louens' French translation of the *Book of Consolation and Counsel*; one particular passage, listing biblical examples of the good counsel that wives like Rebecca, Judith, Abigail and Esther give their husbands, appears also in the marriage encomium at the opening of 'The Merchant's Tale', where we come to realize that every sentiment of praise is to be turned inside out as deadly irony. Although Chaucer is not a punster, at least not in the way Shakespeare certainly is, these doublings of identical passages for very different effects have some of the qualities of the pun as Geoffrey Hartman defines it: 'as two meanings competing for the same phonemic space or as one sound bringing forth semantic twins, but, however you look at it, it's a crowded situation. Either there is too much sound for the sense or too much sense for the sound. This aspect we have named the redundancy principle, and it makes poetry radically oblique in terms of sign function'.[1] Hartman's characterization of poetry as 'radically oblique' accords very well with a more recognizably medieval view of fallen language as inherently equivocal, a view that I outlined at some length in the first chapter of my book, *Language and the Declining World*: 'equivocation may imply contradiction, may create ambiguity, may in fact become antiphrasis, which Isidore defines as "an expression [*sermo*] to be understood by its contrary". It may become sophistry and even prevarication. Equivocation may become, or verge on, all the sins of the tongue'.[2]

Both these instances raise questions of ordering and of manuscript authority. In the Hengwrt manuscript, 'The Second Nun's Tale' comes earlier, situated roughly halfway between 'The Man of Law's Tale' and 'The Prioress'. Since it has many points of contact with the story of Custance, including verbal echoings, this placement makes some sense: if from a rather large distance within the text of the *Canterbury Tales*, the story of St Cecilia looks backward to one tale and forward to another. But Hengwrt does not contain 'The Canon's Yeoman's Tale', which in the Ellesmere manuscript directly follows the 'Second Nun's' in the concluding sequence of tales and is closely allied to it by imagery, theme and diction; this Ellesmere ordering is at least as suggestive, placing the Second Nun not too

long after the Prioress and immediately following the Nun's Priest –
appropriately, the two characters who are defined as subordinates to
the Prioress by their very names, but who comment directly on their
nominal superior's literary performance. Since 'The Second Nun's
Tale' is probably a minimally revised version of an earlier translation
by Chaucer, mentioned in the Prologue to the *Legend of Good Women*
(F 426; G 416), one might assume that its adaptation of Dante was
also the earlier, and Robert Pratt in fact argues that Chaucer adapts
the Prioress's prayer from the Second Nun's, 'without recourse to
the text of the *Paradiso*'.[3] Howard Schless thinks instead that these
'are two separate borrowings from *Paradiso* 33, one affected by the
precedence of the other'.[4] Either way, the Nun's emphasis, stated
and implicit, on good works – summed up by the words 'benygnytee'
and 'magnificence' (lines 54 and 50), taken directly from Dante's
'benignità' and 'magnificenza' (*Paradiso* 33.16 and 20) – suggests a
subtle difference from the ethos and vision of her superior, a difference that appears even in their translations of Dante. The Prioress's
Virgin intercedes to get the light necessary to lead us to her 'Sone'
(480); the Second Nun's Virgin, the 'doghter' of her 'Sone' (36), is
herself the 'sonne of excellence' (52), who as our salvific physician
offers medicine to the 'unworthy sone of Eve' (62) who tells the tale.
There is a subtle but significant difference, I think, between the
Virgin as the beseecher of light, the pathway to her Son, and the
Virgin as soul's doctor, our 'lyves leche' (56), a difference between
sympathetic mediating and active fructifying.[5]

In the Ellesmere order of the tales, 'The Tale of Melibee' appears
later than 'The Merchant's Tale', the uninflected, straight adaptation
of Albertanus after its ironic double, in a striking example of *hysteron
proteron*. For this reason, Emerson Brown suggested that a reversed
order makes more sense: we would after all expect the innocent text
to come first, preparing the ground for its ironic variant – just as
happens when 'The Nun's Priest's Tale' (3164–66, 3256–57) turns
'Melibee' (1102–7) inside out on the question of women's good
counsel.[6] But if the Ellesmere order is literally preposterous, to
use a word that Patricia Parker has revivified,[7] it underlines even
more emphatically the complexities of this double adaptation. In
either ordering, the identical examples and nearly identical phrasing
mean that irony can only be made manifest according to Isidore of
Seville's definition, which understands the term as a type of allegory:
'*Allegory* is *other-speech* [*alieniloquium*]. Namely, one thing sounds,

and another is understood'. Irony is one of the 'species' of this trope: '*Irony* is sense having the opposite meaning by its delivery [its "pronunciation"]'. Unlike *antiphrasis*, which understands a word by its contrary, embedded in the word's etymological origin, irony must rely on tone of voice alone.[8]

The 125-line encomium of wives and marriage in 'The Merchant's Tale' presents an example of irony as *alieniloquium* that is unparalleled elsewhere in Chaucer's poetry. It follows a brief introduction of January the *senex amans*, who wants to find a wife and voices his naïve praise of marriage as a terrestrial paradise: 'Thus seyde this olde knyght, that was so wys' (1266). Whom should we take to be the speaker of this encomium, on whose oral delivery we evidently depend for its meaning? The possibilities are January, who hasn't spoken previously in the tale; the Merchant narrator, a man with an unknown name ('General Prologue', 284), like the unnamed 'man of gret auctorite' at the end of the *House of Fame* (2158); a fusion of the two, one foolishly innocent, the other mordantly sardonic; or perhaps Chaucer himself (if the last, then Chaucer is directly contradicting what he says in his own voice in 'Melibee').[9] Whose is the voice that quotes the calumnies of the *Golden Book on Marriage* for eleven lines, but says 'Deffie Theofraste, and herke me' (1310), and then proceeds with the self-proclaimed authority of 'I speke', 'I gesse' and 'I seye' ten times in the next eighty lines? How are we cued to read the bland complacency of this encomium ironically, as the remainder of the tale insists that we must?

The framing context offers a hint. The Merchant's Prologue, which appears in only some of the manuscripts, promises a tale about the 'art' of being a husband, but a tale that will not discuss the Merchant's own marital misery (1241–43). The Prologue speaker's lament for lost liberty – 'Were I unbounden, also moot I thee, / I wolde nevere eft comen in the snare' (1226–27) – is conspicuously at odds with the encomiast's praise of the 'blisful and ordinaat' life within the bondage of marriage (1284–85), 'that hooly boond / With which that first God man and womman bond' (1261–62). January is, we must infer, as foolish as the Merchant himself once was, just two months previously.[10] Even if this Prologue is discounted as an afterthought at best, adding an unexpected surprise to the Merchant's skimpy biography, the speaking voice in this tale is distinct from the voices in other tales, isolated by its bitter disenchantment; and we may as well describe that voice, certainly not Chaucer's own, as the Merchant's.[11] But the dividing line in the encomium between the naïve January and the no longer naïve narrator can only be marked, as in Isidore of Seville's definition, by 'pronuntiatio', by tone of voice; and there are no pointers for delivery beyond a few caustic hints, as in the claim that January wants to marry, 'Were it for hoolynesse or for dotage' (1253), doddering senility being the only real possibility; or in the suspiciously Pollyannaish evocation of the Griseldan ideal:

Al that hire housbonde lust, hire liketh weel;
She seith nat ones 'nay', whan he seith 'ye'.
'Do this', seith he; 'Al redy, sire', seith she. (1344–46)

If the encomiast's rejection of Theophrastus's authority is meant to show a modern fool refusing to listen to ancient wisdom, the encomiast (1317–18, 1360, 1377–88) and Theophrastus (1296–1306) nonetheless share a fondness for the familiar second-person pronoun, used by both of them to buttonhole us with their sage pronouncements. January's fatuous claim later in the tale that 'A man may do no synne with his wyf, / Ne hurte hymselven with his owene knyf' (1839–40) will be overturned at the end of the *Canterbury Tales* by the countering authority of the *Somme le Roi* and the Parson: 'that opinion is fals' ('The Parson's Tale', 858–59). Likewise, undermining irony makes the major source of the encomium seem fatuous. The two adjoining leaves devoted to the encomium in the Ellesmere manuscript bristle with marginal Latin quotations from Albertanus. Whether or not these annotations are Chaucer's own – an impossible question to answer – they enter into a dialogue of sorts with the text. We are not offered a contrast like the one in the margin of the Wife of Bath's Prologue, which quotes the passages in St Jerome and St Paul that the Wife openly contradicts,[12] even if two of the Latin glosses do counter the translated maxims of Albertanus with a sharper-edged original that the encomium has partly suppressed. 'Ther nys no thing in gree superlatyf, / As seith Senek, above an humble wyf' (1375–76) directly translates Albertanus's Latin – although 'gree superlatyf' threatens to up-end 'humble wyf'. But the encomiast omits Albertanus's immediate proviso, also quoted in the margin, that 'Seneca says … nothing is more savage than an aggressive woman'; a similar omission occurs two lines later when the marginal note adds the qualifier 'if she is worthy' to the injunction that a husband should suffer his wife's tongue (1377).[13] These two glosses, however, are the only ones that do anything to disturb the exact mirroring of the Latin margin and the English text. The other glosses quote Albertanus without attribution, as he uses Jesus, son of Sirach, on a wife as God's gift (glossing 'The Merchant's Tale', 1311); Genesis 2:18, as quoted in the *Liber de amore Dei* (glossing 1325–29); stories of virtuous biblical women, from the *Liber consolationis* (glossing 1362–74); the statement in the *Liber de amore Dei* that 'a good wife is a good and faithful keeper of the household' (glossing 1380); and a selection in the same work of several quotations from Paul's epistle to the Ephesians (glossing 1384–88). Although Albertanus is not named in any of these glosses, their being in Latin gives them the elevated status to back up the encomiast's claim for his own authority.

The problem, of course, is that the narrator of 'The Merchant's Tale' means for Albertanus to seem as absurdly naïve as the speaker whose platitudes quote him directly. The irony is particularly heavy at the point when, with a barrage of examples of women's 'good conseil' or 'wys conseil' (the phrase is repeated in lines 1363, 1367, 1369 and 1372), we are told to 'werken as the wyse' and 'Do alwey so as wommen wol thee rede' (1360–61). In the context of 'The Merchant's Tale', we can hardly forget that all the biblical women cited for their good counsel – Rebecca, Judith, Abigail and Esther (Rebecca and Esther mentioned again later in the setting of the marriage service) – may be seen instead as examples of womanly deceit.[14] But they are all of them examples taken from Albertanus's *Liber consolationis*, and they appear in exactly the same order in 'The Tale of Melibee', where Prudence's admiration for their 'good conseil' certainly has the force of straightforward authority:

> But al be it so that ful many a womman is badde and hir conseil vile and noght worth, yet han men founde ful many a good womman, and ful discret and wis in conseillynge. / Loo, Jacob by good conseil of his mooder Rebekka wan the benysoun of Ysaak his fader and the lordshipe over alle his bretheren. / Judith by hire good conseil delivered the citee of Bethulie, in which she dwelled, out of the handes of Olofernus, that hadde it biseged and wolde have al destroyed it. / Abygail delivered Nabal hir housbonde fro David the kyng, that wolde have slayn hym, and apaysed the ire of the kyng by hir wit and by hir good conseillyng. / Hester by hir good conseil enhaunced greetly the peple of God in the regne of Assuerus the kyng. / And the same bountee in good conseillyng of many a good womman may men telle.
> ('Melibee', 1097–102)

How, then, can identical phrasings have opposite significances, and the mere repetition (or word-for-word anticipation) of an authoritative utterance signify its subversion? In both 'The Merchant's Tale' and 'Melibee', to be sure, a larger context seeps into these utterances and partly undermines them. Prudence's words answer and are framed by misogynist commonplaces within the tale (see 'Melibee', 1084–88 and 1103–6), conspicuously close in their phrasing to the words of the Wife of Bath and Chauntecleer. And as other readers of 'The Merchant's Tale' have pointed out, its repeated references to the ideal of marriage offer 'the assertion of familiar positive values' to counter 'the impression of negation and amorality'.[15] Even so, we seem to be squarely within the fallen world as Jerome describes it, where single utterances, starting with the name 'Eve', can have two diametrically opposed meanings. Aristotle had argued in his *Categories* 5.4a.22 that the same utterance can seem to be both true and false;[16] the evidently true statement that someone is sitting will become false once that person stands up. The contradictory significances of the exemplary biblical wives, on the other hand, reveal the paradoxes within the very same medieval exempla of woman: in Mary Martin McLaughlin's summary, 'the double image of woman, polarized in the familiar antithesis of Mary and Eve, as pristinely good and radically evil, sublime and contemptible, nurturing and destructive, seems to have dwelt quite comfortably in the imaginations of learned writers who could turn their pens readily from fulsome praise of the one to scurrilous denigration of the other. Satire and encomium are, after all, two sides of the same coin, as is eminently clear in the writings of St Jerome, in whose extraordinary combination of affectionate concern for a few women with calumniation of their sex the dual image of femininity was most influentially projected'.[17]

This startling instance of irony is of a piece with the overarching theme of corrupted language in 'The Merchant's Tale'. This tale is certainly the darkest of the four tales in Fragments IV and V – in fact, the most malign of all the *Canterbury Tales*. The two-fragment sequence of which it is part begins with the Clerk's enforced retreat to plain style and ends with the Franklin's dispelling of rhetorical illusion in favour of plain speech. In between, shaping the whole as a chiastic structure, the Merchant and the Squire present versions of the high style. But where the Squire's style exemplifies romantic excess, the Merchant's alternates between the extremes of overwrought rhetoric and an unpleasant disillusionment with the realities such rhetorical language describes and, in his view, falsely prettifies. The sarcasm with which the narrator vilifies January is so corrosive that in the end it reveals the sordid wellsprings of his own character. His irony, his *alieniloquium*, marks a horrifying distance from his own motives, and from any understanding on his part of their dark malignity.[18] His rhetoric, especially his use of euphemism, knowingly covers up the muck underneath, but it also contains the elements of an unknowing self-revelation. Chaucer explores here some of the more extreme implications of Jean de Meun's *Roman de la Rose*, in which Amant is also a notable lover of euphemism, which serves to hide clarity and purity of motive.[19]

In effect, the Merchant reverses and goes farther than Chauntecleer: for him, 'Womman is mannes joye and al his blis' actually does mean *Mulier est hominis confusio*; and he directly contradicts Prudence's claim on this very point, as she concludes her speech on women's good counsel:

> And mooreover, whan oure Lord hadde creat Adam, oure forme fader, he seyde in this wise: / 'It is nat good to been a man alloone; make we to hym an helpe semblable to hymself.' / Heere may ye se that if that wommen were nat goode, and hir conseils goode and profitable, / oure Lord God of hevene wolde nevere han wroght hem, ne called hem help of man, but rather confusioun of man. ('Melibee', 1103–6)

In the Merchant's vulgar rendition of this Genesis text, God decided 'of his grete goodnesse', having seen Adam 'al allone, bely-naked'[20]: '"Lat us now make an helpe unto this man / Lyk to hymself"; and thanne he made him Eve' (1326–29), a 'paradys terrestre' (1332) for Adam just as, the encomiast says, wives have been ever since for their husbands.[21] Although May will indeed turn out to be January's similitude in her self-regard, the narrator evidently means to corrode the authority not only of Albertanus, along with other earthly authorities from Martianus Capella (1732) to the 'cursed monk' Constantinus (1810), but of the Bible itself.[22] He explicitly does so later, when January sings the 'olde lewed wordes' (2149) of the Song of Songs.[23] The encomium itself silently subverts Genesis 2.24: 'O flessh they been, and o fleesh, as I gesse, / Hath but oon herte, in wele and in distresse' (1335–36).[24]

The Merchant narrator thus flouts divine authority as well as human; and his thoroughgoing jaundice makes a bleak backdrop for January's silly optimism. January is a parodic version of Walter in 'The Clerk's Tale',[25] like him a Lombard, like him someone who decides to ignore the rigidity of rank when he chooses a wife. But unlike Walter, he does worry about needing an heir, his 'heritage' (1439); and unlike Walter, he begins by asking his friends to find a wife for him (1412–14), though he decides in the end that 'He wolde abregge hir labour, alle and some' (1614). His decision, when he 'chees hire of his owene auctoritee' (1597), thus comes across as a reckless lack of prudence, a foolish reliance on his narcissistic nightly imaginings of the perfect, pliable young wife, 'As whoso tooke a mirour, polisshed bryght, / And sette it in a commune market-place' (1582–83).[26] Like Walter, he does not care that his chosen wife is 'of smal degree', but he does not include an inborn Griseldan gentility among her desired qualities: 'Suffiseth hym hir yowthe and hir beautee' (1625–26).

Although January decides in the end that he does not need any advice, he gets it nonetheless, opening up the controversy that had been suppressed in the encomium. As happens elsewhere in the *Canterbury Tales*, diversity of opinion signals a futile debate (1469–77)[27] between January's brothers Justinus and Placebo, his good and bad angels, and also as happens elsewhere, their 'altercacioun' is given the verbal trappings of scholastic 'disputisoun' (1473–74).[28] The question of whether or not to marry sums up 'an entire history of academic disputation' as a rhetorical 'favorite in the classroom for two millennia'. Minor changes of phrasing can turn *pro* to *con* or vice-versa.[29] Real argument, with a potential search for a mean between two extremes, is invariably lost to the rhetorical delights of sophistry;[30] dialectic joins rhetoric as a sterile intellectual exercise. January rejects all the valid reasons for marriage – procreation, the avoidance of lechery, the amicable help each spouse can provide the other, the idea that one might 'lyve in chastitee ful holily' (1455) – with the resounding 'But sires, by youre leve, that am nat I' (1456). This line almost exactly duplicates the Wife's answer to what Christ said to 'hem that wolde lyve parfitly; / And lordynges, by youre leve, that am nat I' (Wife of Bath's Prologue, 111–12). January appears to be of the Wife of Bath's 'secte' ('The Clerk's Tale', 1171) without knowing it.

For the Merchant narrator, only one view of marriage has any validity, and it is not the one January espouses when he cuts off Justinus: 'Straw for thy Senek, and for thy proverbes! / I counte nat a panyer ful of herbes / Of scole-termes' (1567–69). The dotard in his foolishness agrees with Placebo, but for the disenchanted Merchant the true authority is Justinus, his own stand-in as disabused husband (as in line 1545). The debaters' names predetermine their arguments,[31] in a pallid version of Eustache Deschamps' *Miroir de Mariage*, where Franc Vouloir is deciding whether to marry, with advice coming from Désir, Folie, Servitude and Faintise on one side, and Répertoire de Science on the other. According to Placebo's 'conseil', a word that he repeats five times in forty lines, January is wisely following Solomon's injunction to 'Wirk alle thyng by conseil' (1485) but in fact needs no counsel since his 'owene conseil is the beste' (1490). He defers to January's wisdom, since as he says, he never contradicts lords of high estate (1497–500). Nature's comments in her *Complaint* about such flattery mark its position as a species of false rhetoric and fallen language:

> What, then, is the ointment of flattery but cheating for gifts? ... For since speech is wont to be the faithful interpreter of thought [*fidelis intellectus interpres*], words the faithful pictures of the soul, the countenance an indication of the will, the tongue the spokesman of the mind, flatterers separate, by a wide distance and divergence, the countenance from the will, the words from the soul, the tongue from the mind, the speech from the thought.[32]

As a courtly echo chamber, Placebo sounds like the misogynist's ideal wife, whose 'counsel' should be to agree in every instance with her wise husband. Justinus, on the other hand, as the voice of the wised-up husband, counters Placebo, though halfway through his speech he abruptly begins speaking to January (1554) – appropriately enough, since Placebo is merely January's double. His 'hard-headed and cheaply cynical counsel'[33] pretends to be judicious, but its commonplace praise of virtuous moderation in married sexuality (1678–80) disguises the standard misogynist claims about the sexual voracity of women (1562–63). By contrast, the Parson's tone is much more truly moderate, and much less reflexively misogynistic, when he comments on the conjugal debt: 'she hath merite of chastitee that yeldeth to hire housbonde the dette of hir body, ye, though it be agayn hir likynge and the lust of hire herte' ('The Parson's Tale', 941). Justinus names the Wife of Bath, the voice of experience, as the great authority on marriage (1685–87). Susan Schibanoff points out that the Wife destroys the book of wicked wives only to have Justinus restore it, in 'an attack on matrimony which makes use of the same antifeminist *exempla* Alysoun had consigned to the flames'.[34] When the tale uses a fictional character as an authoritative source within its own fiction, it implicitly questions the veracity of any authority.

This is a tale, then, in which authorities are exposed as empty wind; and in this tale more than any other, style – especially high style – reveals itself to be empty rhetoric.[35] Time and again, we find a sour contrast between rhetorical flourish and the reality it describes, a contrast that Chaucer uses comically elsewhere. 'The Merchant's Tale' repeatedly displays a severe impatience with amplification, even in 'This fresshe May, that I spak of so yoore' (2116), where 'so long ago' turns out to be only about fifty lines:[36] the fresh innocent bride suddenly falls into the cold light of day as a deceitful wife. This impatience is particularly conspicuous whenever any sentimental or ennobling affirmation appears, as when the wedding ceremony requires a priest to go through the tawdry motions of the sacrament:

> And seyde his orisons, as is usage,
> And croucheth hem, and bad God sholde hem blesse,
> And made al siker ynogh with hoolynesse.[37] (1706–8)

Biblical authority is merely 'olde lewed wordes' (2149), the aged bridegroom's wedding rhapsody no more than the 'jargon' of a magpie (1848). His cough awakens him from a nap for some afternoon sex (1957), while May endows her own cough (2208) with significant meaning: 'And with hir fynger signes made she / That Damyan sholde clymbe upon a tree' (2209–10). This impatience with language is epitomized in the allegorical proper names, which flatten reductively the characters they describe: January, May, Placebo and Justinus. It is one thing to call a *fabliau* heroine Alisoun, or a monk Daun John; or to say that Emelye 'fairer was to sene / Than is the lylie upon his stalke grene, / And fressher than the May with floures newe' ('The Knight's Tale', 1035–37). In 'The Merchant's Tale' personification allegory turns into what Donaldson calls an 'arid double pun' in the abbreviated *effictio* for May:[38]

> I may yow nat devyse al hir beautee.
> But thus muche of hire beautee telle I may,
> That she was lyk the brighte morwe of May,
> Fulfild of alle beautee and plesaunce. (1746–49)

Just as the *fabliau* reality of the tale works against its romance pretensions, or the literal surface of 'The Clerk's Tale' undermines its supposed allegorical significance, so the abstract names of personification allegory deflate rhetoric by emptying its meaning.

Names in 'The Merchant's Tale' become mere caricatures because
they allow little more in the way of complexity than what they de-
note. They universalize this particular marriage into all such marriages between an old man and a young woman, or for that matter,
all marriages *tout court*. But things, as it turns out, will not allow
themselves to be constrained within the limits of abstract names.
May reveals herself to be more than simply a woman 'lyk the brighte
morwe of May' (1748), or 'As fressh as is the brighte someres day'
(1896). She escapes from the mirror image of January's narcissistic
self-reflection.[39] But so too – and the narrator's voice is not aware of
this – the tale as a whole is more complicated than his restraints on
it, and it tells us more about his own voice than he supposes. January
misuses language in one way, the Merchant in another; but the two
aberrances have similar results, as we come to see their unintended,
similarly bleak revelations of character.

The Merchant's rhetorical flourishes are as obtrusive as the Nun's
Priest's, but instead of a comic incongruity between Chauntecleer
and his heroic analogues, this tale describes a sinister incompati-
bility between sentimental aspirations and the realities of human
motive and behaviour. The narrator's apostrophes, like the Nun's
Priest's, conspicuously interrupt the progress of the story, most ob-
trusively when he makes a clumsy overture to addressing Damian:
'Therfore I speke to hym in this manere: / I seye, "O sely Damyan,
allas!"' (1868–69). On five occasions, including this one, the notation
Auctor appears in the margin of the Ellesmere manuscript (1783,
1869, 2057, 2107 and 2125).[40] But these apostrophes – to the 'servant
traytour' Damian and to January, to 'sely Damyan', to 'Fortune unstable', to January again, and to 'noble Ovyde' – all subvert the normal effect of such invocations.[41] The rhetorical figure Apostrophe
asserts connection, with the familiarity implied by its characteristic
use of the informal 'thou' and 'thy'; at the same time, the figure's
self-consciously grand rhetoric of address suggests formal distance.
In 'The Nun's Priest's Tale', this paradox is good-spirited, indeed
richly comic, when the Nun's Priest invokes the fox, Venus, and
Geoffrey of Vinsauf; Ganelon and Judas Iscariot are in almost all
respects unlikely men to be recalled to the author's presence so that
they may claim the fox as one of their number. In 'The Merchant's
Tale', on the other hand, such paradoxes are always more dyspeptic.
'Hoolde thou thy pees, thou poete Marcian' (1732), because 'To
smal is bothe thy penne, and eek thy tonge, / For to descryven of

this mariage' (1736–37). This apostrophe is characteristic of the Merchant's practice: familiarity becomes condescension, jarring against the pretences of dignity in an elevated style. Because these apostrophes have 'no slighting asides or attacks to show us where he stands',[42] they mimic the tonal complexity of the earlier marriage encomium; and they constitute poetic bad taste.

Such lapses of decorum and taste in fact characterize every stylistic flourish in the tale;[43] high style is repeatedly subverted, shown to be incongruous with the sordid narrative it embellishes. When the Merchant speculates on the reasons for May's amorous submission to Damian, in a long series of hypotheses – 'Were it by destynee or by aventure', influence, nature, or constellation (1967–74) – the figure itself is not so different from a similar remark concerning Troilus's good fortune with Criseyde (2.680–86). But cynicism undercuts the figure by making apparent its irrelevance: celestial signs and the mysterious workings of fate are unnecessary to explain May's motives for taking a lover; indeed, the narrator suggests that Damian would have succeeded just as well with 'any womman' (1973). Similarly, as January's long wedding day draws to its inevitable close – 'Parfourned hath the sonne his ark diurne' (1795) – and ushers in an even longer darkness, when 'Night with his mantel, that is derk and rude, / Gan oversprede the hemysperie aboute' (1798–99), the phrasing proclaims its own grandiose absurdity.

In the preceding 'Clerk's Tale', Griselda's hair lay 'untressed / Ful rudely' (379–80) before her makeover, because she was born and raised 'in rudenesse' (397); in particular, the cloth of her old coat is 'rude' and barely sufficient to clothe her (916, 1012, 1116). In 'The Merchant's Tale', Night's 'rude' mantle (1798), which barely covers the intimacies of the wedding night to follow, even more aptly fits its describer, who apologizes to the 'ladyes' in his audience that 'I kan nat glose, I am a rude man' (2350–51) before his blunt description of Damian's brief foreplay. (Much more mildly, the Franklin apologizes in his Prologue for his 'rude speche' [718].) January, in a parody of a standard *aubade* trope, implies that he is like Jupiter himself, as the god appeared dazzlingly to Semele and then during a supernaturally extended night to Alcmena: 'But God forbede that I dide al my myght! / Now wolde God that it were woxen nyght, / And that the nyght wolde lasten everemo' (1761–63).[44] And the elegantly marked astrological sign and setting (2218–24) introducing Pluto and Proserpina soon deflate into bathos: mythic power, with the reminder of Claudian's high eloquence (2232), degenerates into a marital squabble between this archetypal old husband and young wife.[45]

This subversion of high style points to a more extensive disenchantment. 'The Manciple's Tale' will argue for a decorum of moral truth, but only in one, debunking direction: since 'The word moot nede accorde with the dede' (208), and 'moot cosyn be to the werkyng' (210), a 'lady' or 'wyf that is of heigh degree' is no different from a 'wenche' or 'lemman', 'If it so be they werke bothe amys' (216). January short-circuits such decorum by jamming an honorific title, 'lady', into the context of starker adjectives and a less elevated second-person pronoun: 'O stronge lady stoore, what dostow?' (2367): if, as Emerson Brown argues, 'stronge' translates the Latin adjective in *mulier fortis* (Proverbs 31:10), the different stylistic registers of 'mulier' and 'lady' compound the jarring effect of 'stoore' (*strong*, but also *brazen*, especially since it comes as an intensifier for 'stronge').[46] The Merchant provides his tale with a genteel overlay of romance; but although his characters have class pretensions, they act in the crass mode of the *fabliaux*, making their lapse from social and rhetorical high style all the more devastating.

The drop from one to the other is, again and again, remarkably swift, as the terms of social distinction proclaim themselves to be unpersuasive glosses on sordid actualities. When January promises to visit the bedridden Damian, 'a gentil squier, by my trouthe!' (1907) and 'a gentil man' (1924), he is praised by his entourage for his 'gentillesse' (1917), because to make such a visit would be 'a gentil dede' (1919). In this bath of sentiment, one might almost forget that January takes a nap instead, sending May alone with her attendants. May is the one who, ingeniously copying January's merciful willingness to ignore degree, offers to love Damian best despite his social inferiority: 'Lo, pitee renneth soone in gentil herte!' (1986), a notably jaundiced rendering of Chaucer's favourite line (and noble sentiment). In 'The Clerk's Tale', the pretension of a *gentillesse* unaffected by class distinctions comes up against the reassertion of exactly those distinctions, as Walter prepares to marry his second, aristocratic wife. 'The Merchant's Tale' parodies 'The Clerk's Tale' from something like the Manciple's viewpoint: both the ideal of *gentillesse* and the noble pretensions of class are subjected to the same irony. Because 'love is blynd alday, and may nat see' (1598), January contemplates what he thinks to be May's 'wise governaunce, hir gentillesse, / Hir wommanly berynge, and hire sadnesse' (1603–4); but a love supposedly blind to class barriers (1625) is in fact a love deceived about these noble 'gentil' qualities, which are in any case irrelevant to his real concerns.

The sordid actualities belie January's expression of noble sentiment: 'thenk how I thee chees, / Noght for no coveitise, doutelees, / But oonly for the love I had to thee' (2165–67). Likewise May, who displays the 'excellent franchise' of women (1987), who does not want to be a homicide, responsible for poor Damian's death, 'This gentil May, fulfilled of pitee, / Right of hire hand a lettre made she' (1995–96) to save his life. She too has learned the lesson of class-free *gentillesse*, when she decides to love Damian 'best of any creature, / Though he namoore hadde than his sherte' (1984–85), having already responded otherwise to January, 'up sittynge in his sherte' (1852), crowing about his wedding-night prowess.[47] The repeated stripping of Griselda, which sets her clothing, ragged or rich, against the ground of her mysterious and unchanging self, becomes in this tale nothing more than sex in the afternoon, after January's cough has awakened him:

> Anon he preyde hire strepen hire al naked;
> He wolde of hire, he seyde, han som plesaunce;
> He seyde hir clothes dide hym encombraunce,
> And she obeyeth, be hire lief or looth. (1958–61)

May in turn avers that she has to keep her soul and honour, 'And of my wyfhod thilke tendre flour' (2190), and asks that if she ever be false:

> Do strepe me and put me in a sak,
> And in the nexte ryver do me drenche.
> I am a gentil womman and no wenche. (2200–2)

Men are in fact the ones who are untrue, she adds, just at the moment she signals to Damian. If January worries that old widows are too crafty, 'For sondry scoles maken sotile clerkis' (1427), May proves that a 'yong thyng' (1429) can herself quickly learn to work 'sotilly' (2003). This progressive, comic degradation of *gentillesse* reaches its boisterous conclusion in the Host's response to the tale:

> But doutelees, as trewe as any steel
> I have a wyf, though that she povre be,
> But of hir tonge, a labbyng shrewe is she,
> And yet she hath an heep of vices mo. (2426–29)

The Host, like Walter and January, has chosen *gentilly* to stoop in station, picking a 'povre' wife: his grammatical conjunctions set up apparent oppositions, but in reality simply add poverty to the list of his wife's abuses.

Tone in 'The Merchant's Tale' always ends up as disenchanted but goes through some violent shifts in its movement downwards. The Merchant begins by showing January to be a fool, describes him on his wedding night from the horrified perspective of May, but then asks us to pity him as the poor deceived husband, who married his wife for love, not 'coveitise', and can sing 'Yow love I best, and shal, and oother noon' (2323), at the very moment she is about to climb on his back up into the tree to deceive him. Damian the 'gentil' squire, as obsequiously docile as 'a dogge for the bowe' (2014), busily goes about deceiving his lord and doing him a 'vileynye' (1791). And May, at the beginning of the tale a silent cipher, for whom we must feel sympathy in this marriage of horror,[48] turns into everywoman, her deceits – for the Merchant as for Pluto – simply what one must expect from any wife. 'A plague on everyone's house' becomes the operative theme of the tale.

May has in fact learned some lessons all too well from January's example; even her name, Mayus, may imply a latent power of masculine agency, of a piece with her status as a newly trained *mulier fortis*.[49] If January can talk about his taste for 'Oold fissh and yong flessh' (1418), May can feel the 'thikke brustles of his berd unsofte, / Lyk to the skyn of houndfyssh, sharp as brere' (1825), see the 'slakke skyn' on his neck (1849), and decide that she too would prefer young flesh and her own pleasure. For the word 'plesaunce' is nearly as weighted here as it is in 'The Clerk's Tale', where Walter's pleasure of arbitrary will is all-important (658): January worries that an old wife would give him no pleasure and drive him to adultery (1434–35), he bathes in the 'plesaunce' of marriage (1650, 1788) with a wife who is like a bright May morning with all its 'plesaunce' (1749), and he demands that May strip for his 'plesaunce' (1959). Justinus, however, warns that pleasure is not entirely the husband's prerogative: 'Ye shul nat plesen hire fully yeres thre – / This is to seyn, to doon hire ful plesaunce' (1562–63). May too can be a devotee of *fine amour*, responding to the example of Damian, who does all the observances of love, including the noble poetic forms 'of a compleynt or a lay' (1881). As courtly lady, she is a dispenser of 'verray grace' (1997):

> That loveth Damyan so benyngnely
> That she moot outher dyen sodeynly
> Or elles she moot han hym as hir leste. (2093–95)

Dying for love – as Palamon, Arcite and even Nicholas ('The Miller's Tale', 3278–81) remind us – is normally the male lover's malady; May's case suggests that the real cause of such benign love and mortal suffering is for her, as it is for Nicholas, urgent sexual desire.

If the tale ends by attacking a corrupt May, its central focus is on the folly of January. His overriding error is one that is most succinctly described in Augustine's *De doctrina christiana*; and whether or not Chaucer has this work specifically in mind, it illuminates his meaning in 'The Merchant's Tale'. In Augustine's words:

> All teaching is teaching of either things or signs, but things are learnt through signs. What I now call things in the strict sense are things such as logs, stones, sheep, and so on, which are not employed to signify something; but I do not include the log which we read that Moses threw into the bitter waters to make them lose their bitter taste, or the stone which Jacob placed under his head, or the sheep which Abraham sacrificed in place of his son. These are things, but they are at the same time signs of other things. There are other signs whose whole function consists in signifying. Words, for example: nobody uses words except in order to signify something. From this it may be understood what I mean by signs: those things which are employed to signify something. So every sign is also a thing, since what is not a thing does not exist. But it is not true that every thing is also a sign.[50]

January notably turns signs into literal versions of the things they signify; but to hypostasize falsely in this way, to confuse spirit with letter, to construct his own paradisal garden, is to commit a form of idolatry.[51] As Proserpina says of Solomon, 'So made he eek a temple of false goddis. / How myghte he do a thyng that moore forbode is?' (2295–96).[52] January, in turn, wonderfully makes an idolatrous temple of Solomon's Song. In Augustinian/Pauline terms, he chooses the killing letter instead of the spirit that gives life, he enjoys the things of the world rather than uses them: 'when something meant figuratively is interpreted as if it were meant literally, it is understood in a carnal way. No "death of the soul" is more aptly given that name than the situation in which the intelligence, which is what raises the soul above the level of animals, is subjected to the flesh by following the letter. ... It is, then, a miserable kind of spiritual slavery to interpret signs as things, and to be incapable of raising the mind's eye above the physical creation so as to absorb the eternal light'.[53]

'The Merchant's Tale' shows, in a brilliant progression, the macabre comedy of January's foolishness. The beginning of the tale asserts, with a number of variations, January's notion that marriage is a form of paradise (1265), a 'hevene in erthe' (1647).[54] During the marriage encomium, the narrator chimes in to tell us that a wife is 'mannes helpe and his confort, / His paradys terrestre, and his disport' (1331–32);[55] and that on his wedding night, 'Januarie hath faste in armes take / His fresshe May, his paradys, his make' (1821–22).[56] May's response to January's lovemaking is, to be sure, somewhat different: 'How that he wroghte, I dar nat to yow telle; / Or wheither hire thoughte it paradys or helle' (1963–64). January's first error is to take literally what is meant allegorically as a sign of higher things. For Chaucer clearly shows his awareness of the well-known fact that *paradise* means, etymologically, an enclosed garden, a *hortus conclusus*.[57] January quotes at length from the Song of Songs, which proclaims that the Bridegroom's beloved is 'an enclosed garden', but ignores its spiritual meaning.[58] The garden January describes in 'The garden is enclosed al aboute' (2143) is no longer a figure, but a literal garden; he has, with remarkable vulgarity, created a real *hortus conclusus* whose only purpose is carnal: 'thynges whiche that were nat doon abedde, / He in the gardyn parfourned hem and spedde' (2051–52).[59] In his carnality January recalls God's punishment of Adam and Eve, as Augustine describes it: 'the condemnation was of such a kind that man who would have become spiritual even in his flesh, by observing the command, became carnal even in his mind'.[60] May learns from her husband how to be literal-minded. January wants a widowed May to live sole 'as the turtle that lost hath hire make' (2080); in the context that he then quotes from the Song of Songs, 'The turtles voys is herd, my dowve sweete' (2139), January claims to be the improbable 'turtles voys' to May's dove. Instead, she hears another Solomonic exhortation (5.1; AV 4.16): 'Veniat dilectus meus in hortum suum, / Et comedat fructum pomorum suorum' [Let my beloved come into his garden, and eat the fruit of his appletrees] becomes her desire for a particular fruit, Damian's pears, in January's garden.

This garden inevitably has some venerable associations, with Eden and with the garden in the Song of Songs,[61] and it reduces these biblical gardens of plenitude to a single debased purpose.

January had earlier described his evergreen sexual powers (in which he differs from another old man, the Reeve, who compares himself to a white-topped, green-tailed leek [Reeve's Prologue, 3878–79]):

Though I be hoor, I fare as dooth a tree
That blosmeth er that fruyt ywoxen bee;
And blosmy tree nys neither drye ne deed.
I feele me nowhere hoor but on myn heed;
Myn herte and alle my lymes been as grene
As laurer thurgh the yeer is for to sene. (1461–66)[62]

To the contrary, the lover grown old is a microcosm of the world grown old: January's claim of perpetual youth is as ridiculous as his belief that he can create and inhabit his own Paradise. Both are efforts to return from a fallen world to an unfallen one; and they fail literally, morally and linguistically. Instead, the garden January builds 'becomes the scene for a burlesque reenactment of the Fall'.[63]

Indeed, Chaucer takes his frequent joke – that sexual activity in the fallen world, like all else, is a form of labour[64] – and makes it sinister. First January, in order to be an ideal 'werkman', promises to attend to the labour of sex all night: 'This wol be doon at leyser parfitly' (1832–34). And so he does – 'Thus laboureth he til that the day gan dawe' (1842) – just as later, the narrator says 'heere I lete hem werken in hir wyse' (1965). But even after her labouring husband finally rises, May must remain sequestered until the fourth day:

For every labour somtyme moot han reste,
Or elles longe may he nat endure;
This is to seyn, no lyves creature,
Be it of fyssh, or bryd, or beest, or man. (1862–65)

These lines are a startling inversion of the rhapsodic proem to Book 3 of the *Troilus*, where 'man, brid, best, fissh, herbe, and grene tree' all feel the effects of Love, 'And in this world no lyves creature / Withouten love is worth, or may endure' (3.10, 13–14). They are noticeably more crabbed even than the description, set against the springtime freshness and innocence of Canacee, of the weary Tartar court where 'muchel drynke and labour wolde han reste' ('The Squire's Tale', 349). Love's labour here is also far from the idealizing romance world where Arveragus must undertake 'many a labour, many a greet emprise' before he can win Dorigen ('The Franklin's Tale', 732). These lines describe instead a much-needed Sabbath for overworked young brides. January 'wolde paye his wyf hir dette / In somer seson' (2048–49) in his false paradise, the contract work of the conjugal debt itself weighted with the implications of sexuality in the fallen world.[65] Augustine's account of prelapsarian sexuality in the true Paradise reveals a world of difference: 'Between man and wife there was a faithful partnership based on love and mutual respect; there was a harmony and a liveliness of mind and body, and an effortless observance [*sine labore custodia*] of the commandment [of generation]. Man was at leisure, and tiredness never wearied him, and sleep never weighed him down against his will'.[66]

January's description of himself as 'blosmy tree' and laurel makes clearest of all the way in which he is misusing signs.[67] Many readers have noticed the jokes, often bawdy ones, attached to this garden. January asks for a young wife, whom he can mould as one does wax (1429–30). He holds the only key to the garden,[68] but May becomes the gatekeeper and the wax-moulder, when she makes a wax impression in order to give Damian a copy of the key, the 'clyket', so that he can open the 'wyket' (2117–18) – two words, several times repeated, that almost certainly have a bawdy double meaning.[69] By making the wax metaphor literal and preparing for the union of 'clyket' and 'wyket', she effectively counters January's literal actualization of the metaphors by which he describes himself and his paradisal marriage.[70] In 'The beautee of the gardyn and the welle / That stood under a laurer alwey grene' (2036–37),[71] we hardly need Freud to explain what the laurel tree and the well stand for in this tale of corrupted signs.[72] In the end, having falsely given reality to signs, January cannot see what is real; as the Merchant says, reversing with startling effect the expected rhetorical sequence: 'For as good is blynd deceyved be / As to be deceyved whan a man may se' (2109–10).[73]

'The Clerk's Tale' also turns on the tension between literal and figurative, the unresolved question of whether we should read Griselda allegorically as the besieged human soul or literally as the model wife. In 'The Merchant's Tale' the figurative improperly becomes literal. The abuse of language, January's central error, also pertains to the most vexed issues of 'The Merchant's Tale' as a whole: its relation to its putative teller, and the narrator's tone and meaning. The narrative voice of this tale, however we choose to name it, is revealingly bleak and cynical,[74] and it obsessively returns again and again to the nature of irony, of *alieniloquium*, of saying one thing and meaning another, and more generally, the relation of irony to lying, or to hypocrisy and bad faith.

The Merchant narrator, who thinks he is simply attacking a fool who does not know what he himself has learned the hard way, reveals despite himself a continuing blindness and spiritual slavery within his own knowing stance. Chaucer evidently has in mind the commentaries on Genesis, which describe the moment when Adam and Eve's eyes "'are opened" to sinfulness and shame. In the *Merchant's Tale*, May's shamelessness is, if anything, increased after she has enjoyed her "fruit"'.[75] January remains blind, but so does the narrator, despite his self-presentation. In all, he shares the duplicity he ascribes to the scorpion Fortune – he too is someone who, by hypocritically observing verbal decorum, 'subtilly' can 'peynte / ... under hewe of stidefastnesse' (2062–63). But despite his best efforts to suggest that corruption taints everything, the pristine associations of signs cannot be entirely corrupted by even the most abusive treatment and intentions.

From the Merchant narrator's knowing perspective, innocence is merely foolish naïveté (January) or dormant malice (May), and his rhetorical surfeit proposes to lay bare these realities. His expressed concern with euphemism and plain speech is in some respects analogous to the opposition between plain style and high style in 'The Clerk's Tale'. Even closer is 'The Manciple's Tale', in which blurring and erasure of degree, in social class and in style, serve the purpose of plain speech – indeed, as the Manciple confesses, too much speech and too plainly spoken. For the Merchant narrator is not in any real sense a plain speaker, despite his claim 'I kan nat glose, I am a rude man' (2351), as he is about to describe May and Damian copulating in the tree. His abusive deflation of style and levels of diction coexists with a prurient euphemism; and the clash between styles signals his hypocrisy. By telling a churl's tale, in which even more malevolence obtrudes than in 'The Reeve's Tale', the narrator – whatever the genteel overlay of his tale or his own self-presentation as reluctant muckraker – becomes worse than the churls. The Miller's bawdiness is open and open-handed; this narrator's smirking prudery, by contrast, has a baleful effect:[76] 'But lest that precious folk be with me wrooth, / How that he wroghte, I dar nat to yow telle' (1962–63). The squabble between the Friar and the Summoner, which otherwise seems to digress from the sequence of tales concerned with sexual sovereignty, reminds us forcefully that if someone with *gentil* pretensions tells a churlish story, he is in great danger of losing the privileges of his gentility (much as the rapist knight in 'The Wife of Bath's Tale' does by his churlish deeds) and being tarred with his own brush.[77] The Merchant's tale, even more than the Friar's, has this result, as the narrator's scorn for January backfires.

Chaucer takes the joke in the *Roman de la Rose* and the *fabliaux* about falsely delicate language – the joke by which the prudery of the Lover or the fainting maiden is shown to be hypocritical or disingenuous – and pushes it into a more thorough delineation of a flawed psyche. The closest analogue to his accomplishment here, I think, is in the characteristic move of Swift's satire. In 'Cassinus and Peter', the suicidal sophomore is brought to confess his misery, not because the beloved Caelia is dead, unfaithful or marred by the pox, but because he has suddenly learned to his horror that '*Caelia, Caelia, Caelia,* shits'.[78] In 'Strephon and Chloe', the hovering Cupids of a papier-maché pastoral fly away forever on the couple's wedding night, when both of the newlyweds use the chamber pot and let fly rouzers in the other's face, filling the air with noisome stenches.[79] In these poems the satire depends on an excluded middle (in this they are analogous to the *Sic et Non* treatment of authority early in 'The Merchant's Tale') – something between the romantic, foolish naïveté of bodilessness, of Cupids and roses in the air, and the morbid conclusion that all is body, that ideals and sentiment are nothing but deceiving glosses over an excremental essence. The Middle English lyric 'Erthe tok of erthe, erthe with woh' has some similarities to this satiric manoeuvre, but also a crucial difference: the reduction of all earthly things to the earth of which they consist is meant to remind us of the spiritual alternative, of rising above the body. In 'The Merchant's Tale', on the other hand, we are much closer to Swift's 'after': once all ideals have been debunked, nothing but the body remains.[80] May must 'strepen hire al naked', free herself from the 'encombraunce' of her clothes, to put herself at the service of January's desire when his cough has awakened him; whether in paradise or hell, she must 'work' with him until evensong signals the time for them to arise (1955–66).

Swift's satire implies a middle ground, where body and soul, real and ideal, experience and innocence can meet, in a version of Crazy Jane's paradoxical insight that 'Love has pitched his mansion in / The place of excrement'.[81] Rather than offering to build more stately mansions, 'The Merchant's Tale' offers a perverse version of the mordant aphorism – usually attributed to St Augustine – on the inescapable earthboundness of human life: 'We are born between feces and urine'.[82] Yet beneath the narrator's cynicism, and countering it, Chaucer implies a healthier integration of the spiritual and the bodily.[83] He implies as well that there is a linguistic middle ground – a language resigned to its fallen imperfection and making the best of it, not one that, when foiled in its efforts to regain paradisal purity, lapses into prurience and cynicism.

When May reads Damian's love letter, she seeks privacy in the privy, the place 'ther as ye woot that every wight moot neede' (1951) (a phrase that casts an anticipatory excremental pall over Damian in love, going 'about his nede' [2019]). This euphemism is immediately followed by May's reading the letter and tearing it into pieces: 'And in the pryvee softely it caste' (1954). Donaldson points out the exquisite awfulness of the word 'softely' here, which manages to submerge the delicate in the excremental.[84] Elsewhere in the tale the narrator makes a series of nasty puns: the 'sweete venym queynte' (2061) of Fortune's stinging, poisonous tail,[85] and by inference of May's tail as well; the connotations of the pears May so eagerly desires;[86] and the possible double meanings of 'knyf' (1840) and 'twiste' (2349),[87] as well as of 'wyket' and 'clyket' (2117–18). The narrative proffers a hypocritical ambiguity, which sets out with one hand what it genteelly denies with the other. January looks up into the tree,

> And saugh that Damyan his wyf had dressed
> In swich manere it may nat been expressed,
> But if I wolde speke uncurteisly. (2361–63)

The uncourteous voice that the narrator disclaims for himself he then gives to January:

> 'Strugle?' quod he, 'Ye, algate in it wente!
> God yeve yow bothe on shames deth to dyen!
> He swyved thee; I saugh it with myne yen,
> And elles be I hanged by the hals!' (2376–79)

The tale ends with January's ghastly return home, stroking May's belly as he goes (2414).[88]

This is a tale where nothing is as it innocently appears, least of all the paradisal garden, which January 'in honest wyse' has constructed 'honestly' 'Amonges othere of his honeste thynges' (2024–28). This garden was so beautiful 'That he that wroot the Romance of the

Rose / Ne koude of it the beautee wel devyse', nor could Priapus, the god of gardens (2032–36). As John Fleming points out, there are many rich ironies here, pre-eminent among them that Old Age, on the garden wall in the *Roman*, is now inside the garden pretending to be Priapus.[89] January implicitly compares himself not only to Adam but to Jupiter, feeling 'pitee' at the amorous offence his 'corage' must inflict on May as his Semele (1755–60); instead, he is merely the Pluto to her Proserpina.

The culminating scene in the garden, with Pluto and Proserpina themselves presiding, promises to bring on the eternal night that January asked for on his wedding day (1763).[90] It raises the action of the story to a mythic perspective, or at least to the universalizing significance of aetiology, a just-so story to explain how all women since May have been able to profit by Proserpina's gift, to talk their way out of difficulties. But this myth too, which in Claudian's *De raptu Proserpinae* constitutes 'the creation of civilization out of Nature' by Jupiter, who supplants Saturnian, Golden Age plenitude with the need for virtuous human labour,[91] is deflated in 'The Merchant's Tale', with virtuous labour reduced to sexual labouring, and Pluto and Proserpina reduced to another bickering couple, another old husband and young wife. Pluto unsurprisingly feels sympathy for his kindred *senex amans*, 'this olde, blynde, worthy knyght' (2259), another rapist constrained to the role of aggrieved husband. And Proserpina, who sounds very much like the Wife of Bath, and who makes some reasonable enough interpretations of Solomon's meaning and objections to his authority, succeeds not in winning the argument but in subduing Pluto to silence by her threat otherwise to keep on talking.[92] For Robert Edwards, Pluto and Proserpina 'demonstrate the possibility of mature, companionable resolution in a fallen world', a contrast to January and May in their demonstration of the 'practical reasoning' necessary for deciding 'the questions of power, domination, and sovereignty in marriage'.[93] I cannot be quite so optimistic about the implications of their mutual accommodation, of Pluto's 'I yeve it up!' (2312) and Proserpina's 'I wol no lenger yow contrarie' (2319); their countering promises, of blindness restored and insight blinded once again – promises that once made cannot be unmade – suggest instead a perpetual stalemate in the battle between the sexes.[94] It may be that the alienating categories of gender reproduce the divisions of language and rhetoric in the tale, and that the narrator, despite himself, leads us to recognize 'the competing truths of a fallen world', 'rejecting the reductions of misogyny and unexamined orthodoxy alike'.[95] But whatever truths these may be are themselves blasted by his own corrosive vision.

John M. Fyler is Professor of English at Tufts University, and Lecturer at the Bread Loaf School of English. His books include *Language and the Declining World in Chaucer, Dante, and Jean de Meun* (Cambridge University Press, 2007) and *Chaucer and Ovid* (Yale University Press, 1979), and he edited the *House of Fame* for the *Riverside Chaucer*.

Notes

1. Geoffrey Hartman, 'The Voice of the Shuttle: Language from the Point of View of Literature', in *Beyond Formalism: Literary Essays 1958–1970* (New Haven, CT: Yale University Press, 1970), 347. Cf. my essay 'Doubling and the Thopas-Melibee Link', in *Essays on Aesthetics and Medieval Literature in Honor of Howell Chickering*, ed. John M. Hill, Bonnie Wheeler and R.F. Yeager (Toronto: Pontifical Institute of Mediaeval Studies, 2014), 129–41.

2. John M. Fyler, *Language and the Declining World in Chaucer, Dante, and Jean de Meun* (Cambridge: Cambridge University Press, 2007), 57, quoting Isidore of Seville, *Etymologiae, sive Origines*, ed. W.M. Lindsay (Oxford: Clarendon Press, 1911), 1.37.24. Susan Schibanoff notes a marginal gloss, 'antiphrasis', in 'The Manciple's Tale': 'Alle thise ensamples speke I by thise men / That been untrewe, and nothyng by wommen' (187–88): 'The New Reader and Female Textuality in Two Early Commentaries on Chaucer', *Studies in the Age of Chaucer* 10 (1988): 105–6. All quotations from Chaucer are from *The Riverside Chaucer*, ed. Larry D. Benson (Boston, MA: Houghton Mifflin, 1987).

3. Robert A. Pratt, 'Chaucer Borrowing from Himself', *Modern Language Quarterly* 7 (1946): 259–64. In a session at the Medieval Association of the Pacific in March 2007 (at UCLA), H.A. Kelly made the entirely plausible suggestion to me that Chaucer added this Invocation to his earlier translation of St Cecilia's legend, in order to characterize the Second Nun as the storyteller within the new context of the *Canterbury Tales*.

4. Howard H. Schless, *Chaucer and Dante: A Revaluation* (Norman, OK: Pilgrim Press, 1984), 207.

5. Cf. C. David Benson, *Chaucer's Drama of Style: Poetic Variety and Contrast in the Canterbury Tales* (Chapel Hill, NC: University of North Carolina Press, 1985), 133–35. N.S. Thompson, *Chaucer, Boccaccio, and the Debate of Love: A Comparative Study of 'The Decameron' and 'The Canterbury Tales'* (Oxford: Clarendon Press, 1996), 302, notes the use of key words from these hymns, especially 'bountee' and 'benygnytee', to describe Griselda in 'The Clerk's Tale'.

6. Emerson Brown, 'Biblical Women in the Merchant's Tale: Feminism, Anti-feminism, and Beyond', *Viator* 5 (1974): 390, argues for the 'Bradshaw shift', by which 'Melibee' precedes the 'Marriage Group', so that 'The Merchant's Tale' is responding vituperatively to 'Melibee' as well as to the tales of the Wife and Clerk. W. Arthur Turner explains the oddity of the Ellesmere order by arguing that since the 'Melibee' was merely Chaucer's 'translation, not his composition', he decided to leave it unrevised: 'Biblical Women in *The Merchant's Tale* and *The Tale of Melibee*', *English Language Notes* 3 (1965): 95.

7. Patricia Parker, *Literary Fat Ladies: Rhetoric, Gender, Property* (London: Methuen, 1987), 67–68.

8. Isidore of Seville, *Etymologiae*, 1.37.22–25.

9. Donald R. Benson summarizes these possibilities in 'The Marriage "Encomium" in the *Merchant's Tale*: A Chaucerian Crux', *Chaucer Review* 14 (1979): 48–51. For Robert Edwards, 'Chaucer achieves in this speech not indeterminacy but a kind of irreducibility': 'Some Pious Talk about Marriage: Two Speeches from the *Canterbury Tales*', in *Matrons and Marginal Women in Medieval Society*, ed. Robert R. Edwards and Vickie Ziegler (Woodbridge, Suffolk: Boydell Press, 1995), 114. J.D. Burnley argues that this encomium consists of 'imperfectly assimilated material', which cannot be attributed to either January or the narrator: 'The Morality of *The Merchant's Tale*', *Yearbook of English Studies* 6 (1976): 18. Jill Mann, *Feminizing Chaucer* (Cambridge: D.S. Brewer, 2002), 50, points to 'the ironic mode of the passage – a mode specifically designed to allow us to hear two voices speaking at the same time', that is, 'as simultaneously representing the Merchant and January. ... The Merchant's experience speaks through January's innocence'.

10. As Talbot Donaldson says, 'This strife of before and after is a constant tension in the poem and accounts for its extraordinary ironical passages in which the narrator heaps praise on the attitudes he has come to detest': *Chaucer's Poetry: An Anthology for the Modern Reader*, 2nd ed. (New York: John Wiley & Sons, 1975), 1084.

11. Cf. A.C. Spearing, *Textual Subjectivity: The Encoding of Subjectivity in Medieval Narratives and Lyrics* (Oxford: Oxford University Press, 2005), which expands on earlier efforts to detach Chaucer's narratives from their putative narrators. On this tale specifically, see Benson, *Chaucer's Drama of Style*, esp. 14–16 and 127–30; David Lawton, *Chaucer's Narrators* (Cambridge: D.S. Brewer, 1985), 4 and 103; and Robert M. Jordan, 'The Non-Dramatic Disunity of the *Merchant's Tale*', *PMLA* 78 (1963): 293–99.

12. K.P. Clarke has pointed out that some of the marginal glosses have adjusted their source texts to reflect the Wife's phrasing, thus making herself the vernacular authority for their Latin authority: *Chaucer and Italian Textuality* (Oxford: Oxford University Press, 2011), 143–47.

13. Richard Hazelton, 'Chaucer and Cato', *Speculum* 35 (1960): 376, notes 'this artful abridgment' of Cato's *Distichs*, which 'transforms Albertano's sterile and pedantic marshalling of authorities into its comic antithesis'. The next two lines offer the suspiciously cheerful, 'She shal comande, and thou shalt suffren it, / And yet she wole obeye of curteisye' (1378–79).

14. See J.S.P. Tatlock, 'Chaucer's *Merchant's Tale*', *Modern Philology* 33 (1936): 376; M. Teresa Tavormina's Riverside note to lines 1362–74; Brown, 'Biblical Women', 390–91; Edmund Reiss, 'Biblical Parody: Chaucer's "Distortions" of

Scripture', in *Chaucer and Scriptural Tradition*, ed. David Jeffrey (Ottawa: University of Ottawa Press, 1984), 55–56; and Helen Cooper, *Oxford Guides to Chaucer: The Canterbury Tales* (Oxford: Clarendon Press, 1989), 208.

15. Burnley, 'Morality', 25. Also see Michael D. Cherniss, 'The *Clerk's Tale* and *Envoy*, the Wife of Bath's Purgatory, and the *Merchant's Tale*', *Chaucer Review* 6 (1972): 248; and Robert R. Edwards, 'Narration and Doctrine in the Merchant's Tale', *Speculum* 66 (1991): 351n33. Mann, *Feminizing Chaucer*, 49, argues that these biblical examples 'can be ironically interpreted only by the most violent kind of exegetical strait-jacketing', since Prudence offers them in earnest.

16. Marie-Dominique Chenu, O.P., *La théologie au douzième siècle* (Paris: J. Vrin, 1957), 98, notes the philosophical significance of this statement in its widely current medieval form: 'Eadem oratio vera et falsa esse videtur' [The same language seems to be true and false].

17. Mary Martin McLaughlin, 'Peter Abelard and the Dignity of Women: Twelfth-Century Feminism in Theory and Practice', in *Pierre Abélard, Pierre le Vénérable: Les courants philosophiques, littéraires et artistiques en Occident au milieu du XIIe siècle* (Paris: Éditions du centre national de la recherche scientifique, 1975), 309.

18. See E.T. Donaldson, 'The Effect of the Merchant's Tale', in *Speaking of Chaucer* (London: University of London, Athlone Press, 1970), 30–45; and Mary (Carruthers) Schroeder, 'Fantasy in the "Merchant's Tale"', *Criticism* 12 (1970): 175: 'just as January builds his garden in order to enclose and so bring into being all his fantasies, the Merchant creates a world in his tale which responds only to his projected image of what he thinks to be his former self'.

19. See Fyler, *Language and the Declining World*, Chapter Two.

20. According to Martin Stevens, '"And Venus laugheth": An Interpretation of the *Merchant's Tale*', *Chaucer Review* 7 (1972): 128–29, the word 'bely-naked' does not necessarily have the 'profane connotations' that Donaldson finds ('The Effect of the Merchant's Tale', 39). But in fact, as Donaldson says, Chaucer invariably uses the word 'bely' in crass or vulgar contexts: 'The Summoner's Tale', 2267 and 'The Pardoner's Tale', 534.

21. Cf. Geoffrey le Baker's comment, in his shorter chronicle: after Adam was made by God, he was transported into a 'paradise of pleasure' where Eve was created as his consort, 'because without a companion there is no pleasing occupation': *Chronicon Galfridi le Baker de Swynbroke*, ed. Edward Maunde Thompson (Oxford: Clarendon Press, 1889), 157.

22. See Eric Jager, *The Tempter's Voice: Language and the Fall in Medieval Literature* (Ithaca, NY and London: Cornell University Press, 1993), 253–54, on this 'carnal reading', the 'narrator's attempt to taint with sin, or signs of sin, an otherwise innocent state'.

23. A.S.G. Edwards, 'The Merchant's Tale and Moral Chaucer', *Modern Language Quarterly* 51 (1990): 419, notes the 'tonal integrity of the passage, with its intimations of unforced, appropriate emotion', undermined by the narrator.

24. The Ellesmere manuscript lacks a marginal gloss here, but as Edwards, 'Narration and Doctrine', 355, notes, the Hengwrt gloss to these lines underlines their 'Biblical overtones'.

25. See Jerome Mandel, 'The Unity of Fragment IV (Group E): The *Clerk's Tale* and the *Merchant's Tale*', *Hebrew University Studies in Literature and the Arts* 16 (1988): 30–31.

26. George D. Economou argues that this image of the mirror owes at least as much to the *Roman de la Rose* as it does to Boethius (*Boece* 5.m4.26–27): 'Januarie's Sin against Nature: The *Merchant's Tale* and the *Roman de la Rose*', *Comparative Literature* 17 (1965): 251–57. Also see the Riverside note to 1577–87.

27. See 'The Man of Law's Tale', 211 and 'The Squire's Tale', 202. For the proverb 'Quot homines, tot sententiae' [As many opinions as men], see the Riverside note to 'The Reeve's Prologue', 3857.

28. Dorigen complains of the clerical 'argumentz' to explain the rocks on the Breton coast, and dismisses them as irrelevant to her anxious concern: 'To clerkes lete I al disputison' ('The Franklin's Tale', 887, 890). The Nun's Priest refers to the never-ending debate on free will and predestination: 'any parfit clerk' knows 'That in scole is greet altercacioun / In this mateere, and greet disputisoun' ('The Nun's Priest's Tale', 3236–38).

29. Thomas O. Sloane, *On the Contrary: The Protocol of Traditional Rhetoric* (Washington, DC: Catholic University of America Press, 1997), 314–16. Sloane notes that Quintilian and Cicero both describe the use of 'An ducenda sit uxor?' as an exercise in rhetorical argument, Cicero (in the *Orator* 14.16) 'tracing its use back to Aristotle'.

30. See especially Donaldson, 'The Effect of the Merchant's Tale', 38, which describes the marriage encomium as 'a kind of double distortion of reality: a rebuttal of antifeminism erected on the same bases as antifeminism'.

31. See Douglas A. Burger, 'Deluding Words in the *Merchant's Tale*', *Chaucer Review* 12 (1977): 105: this long mock debate, coming after the mock encomium, means that 'a full third of the tale has been consumed by fatuous speech'.

32. Alain of Lille, *De planctu Naturae* 14.129–34, ed. Nikolaus M. Häring, *Studi Mediaevali*, 3rd ser., 19 (1978), trans. James Sheridan, in Medieval Sources in Translation 26 (Toronto: Pontifical Institute of Mediaeval Studies, 1980), 192–93.

33. Donaldson, *Chaucer's Poetry*, 1084.

34. Susan Schibanoff, 'Taking the Gold out of Egypt: The Art of Reading as a Woman', in *Gender and Reading: Essays on Readers, Texts, and Contexts*, ed. Elizabeth A. Flynn and Patrocinio P. Schweickart (Baltimore, MD: Johns Hopkins University Press, 1986), 87.

35. Donald R. Howard, *The Idea of the Canterbury Tales* (Berkeley, Los Angeles and London: University of California Press, 1976), 264, compares the tales of the Merchant and Clerk, which 'complement each other – both are accomplished displays of rhetoric which set realities against ideals. But the Clerk has a feeling for the old ideals and takes an ironic view of present realities; the Merchant heaps contempt on the ideals and takes a bitter view of realities'.

36. Cf. a similar passage in 'The Squire's Tale': 'The knotte why that every tale is toold, / If it be taried til that lust be coold / Of hem that han it after herkned yoore, / The savour passeth ever lenger the moore, / For fulsomnesse of his prolixitee (401–5). See John M. Fyler, 'Domesticating the Exotic in the *Squire's Tale*', *English Literary History* 55 (1988): 10: 'the fear of tedium interrupts this fresh beginning before it has time to wear out its welcome. In a split second fresh morning becomes dusty afternoon'. Cooper, *Oxford Guide*, 211, notes that Chaucer's 'standard epithet for her [May], "fresshe", becomes staler with each recurrence'.

37. On the irony in this final phrase, see, e.g., John S.P. Tatlock, 'The Marriage Service in Chaucer's *Merchant's Tale*', *Modern Language Notes* 32 (1917): 373–74.

38. Donaldson, 'The Effect of the Merchant's Tale', 52.

39. When May judges January's lovemaking to be not worth 'a bene' (1854), she echoes January's dismissive characterization of the unmarried life (1263), as Elaine Tuttle Hansen, *Chaucer and the Fictions of Gender* (Berkeley, Los Angeles: University of California Press, 1992), 260, points out: 'May, like the Wife of Bath, quite literally borrows her husband's idiom as she enters into selfhood'.

40. Edwards, 'Narration and Doctrine', 350, argues: 'The context makes it clear that the performative voice of the tale, not the poet himself, is speaking' in these apostrophes. Earlier on, Placebo and Justinus are named in the margin as the speakers of their opposing arguments.

41. In Derek Pearsall's formulation, this 'is the high style of *Troilus*, but meretriciously applied, like a coat of gloss on a damp and decaying wall': *The Canterbury Tales* (London: George Allen & Unwin, 1985), 205.

42. Schroeder, 'Fantasy', 176. Also see Edwards, 'Merchant's Tale and Moral Chaucer', 420, on the lack of 'any clear or normative moral perspectives. Utterance remains isolated from context or from action, or action isolated from action'.

43. Tavormina's Riverside note (885) outlines 'the tale's apparent failure of decorum, its mixing of genres, styles, voices, and tones, of pagan and Christian elements, even of narrative levels'.

44. See Robert E. Kaske, 'January's "Aube"', *Modern Language Notes* 75 (1960): 1–4, on the aubade parody in the tale. As he points out, January's exhaustion after his wedding night – 'Now day is come, I may no lenger wake' (1856) – exactly reverses what the youthful Aleyn says in 'The Reeve's Tale': 'The day is come; I may no lenger byde' (4237).

45. In the analogues of 'The Merchant's Tale', Christ and St Peter are almost always the observers who restore the husband's sight (W.F. Bryan and Germaine Dempster, eds., *Sources and Analogues of Chaucer's Canterbury Tales* [1941; repr. New York: Humanities Press, 1958], 341–50). Cooper, *Oxford Guide*, 211, notes that Proserpina, 'for all her gathering of flowers when she was ravished (2230–1), is not here a harbinger of new life or of romance-style resurrection'.

46. Brown, 'Biblical Women', 406.

47. Burnley, 'Morality', 17, aptly comments on how 'Chaucer deliberately manipulates our attitudes to May', from being 'the passive object of defilement, the innocent victim of a rapacious old lecher', to an equal in 'the contest of rapacity with duplicity'.

48. See, e.g., Jay Schleusener, 'The Conduct of the *Merchant's Tale*', *Chaucer Review* 14 (1980): 241, on our sympathy with May's predicament.

49. On the implications of the name 'Mayus', see Emerson Brown, 'The *Merchant's Tale*: Why is May Called "Mayus"?', *Chaucer Review* 2 (1968): 273–77.

50. Augustine, *De doctrina christiana* 1.2, 13–15, ed. and trans. R.P.H. Green, Oxford Early Christian Texts (Oxford: Clarendon Press, 1995).

51. Mary Carruthers comments (Schroeder, 'Fantasy', 170): 'All of January's actions in the tale are directed towards turning the world into a material correlative to what he sees in the mirror of his mind'. In the *Filocolo*, Chaucer's source for 'The Franklin's Tale', the beseeching lover is asked, in a subtle *malizia*, to create a May

garden in January. The Merchant's January does exactly that for his May: 'Ris up, my wyf, my love, my lady fre!' (2138).

52. Gertrude White wittily points out that these lines reveal the gods' 'comic blindness to themselves'. 'The speaker of those lines had, no more than January, the power to see herself as others see her!' ('"Holynesse or Dotage": The Merchant's January', *Philological Quarterly* 44 [1965]: 403). At a similar moment, James Simpson notes, Pluto reveals himself to be 'the most spectacular example of a poor male reader in the *Canterbury Tales*'. He 'declares that he has one million stories at the ready to prove the inconstancy of women, a statement made only a few lines after we have been referred to another story, that of the rapist Pluto' (*Reform and Cultural Revolution* [Oxford: Oxford University Press, 2002], 309n126). See especially Mann, *Feminizing Chaucer*, 53–54, on the ironies in this treatment of 'a henpecked rapist'.

53. *De doctrina christiana* 3.5, 141. See White, '"Hoolynesse or Dotage"', 400, on January's self-delusion: 'It is not simply that he is a materialist who substitutes the love of earthly things for that of heavenly things, but that he deceives himself into mistaking the one for the other'. When January quotes the Song of Songs, his 'words are not conscious blasphemy', but an instance of this confusion (401–2). The Merchant despises January, White argues, 'not because he is a sensualist but because he is a sensualist who has intimations, imperfect as they are, of another world' (403).

54. Kenneth A. Bleeth, 'The Image of Paradise in the *Merchant's Tale*', in *The Learned and the Lewed: Studies in Chaucer and Medieval Literature*, ed. Larry D. Benson, Harvard English Studies 5 (Cambridge, MA: Harvard University Press, 1974), 46–47, notes that this 'clerkly ideal of marriage as a paradise on earth' is proposed seriously in *Cleanness* and *Piers Plowman*.

55. January himself rhymes 'disport' and 'confort' at the end of his rhapsody from the Song of Songs (2147–48), as Bleeth, 'Image of Paradise', 47, notes; and Pluto, Proserpina, along with 'al hire fayerye, / Disporten hem and maken melodye / Aboute that welle, and daunced' (2039–41).

56. Cf. Eustache Deschamps, *Le Miroir de Mariage*, which describes not 'repos' [peace] and 'paradis', but 'droiz enfers' [true hell] (816–17). *Œuvres Complètes*, ed. le marquis de Queux de Saint-Hilaire and Gaston Raynaud, Société des Anciens Textes Français (Paris: Firmin Didot, 1878–1903), vol. 9.

57. To pick one reference among many, see Rabanus Maurus, *De universo* 12.3 (*Patrologia Latina* 111:334), the first part of which is taken word for word from Isidore, *Etymologiae* 14.3.2: 'Paradise is a place established in Eastern parts, whose name is translated from Greek to Latin as *garden*. Further, it is called Eden in Hebrew, which is understood in our language as *delights*; which combined makes *garden of delights* ... Paradise is the Church: thus is found in the Song of Songs concerning it: *A garden enclosed is my sister, my spouse*'. For Jerome, *Adversus Jovinianum* (*PL* 23:254), the 'hortus conclusus' is a 'figure of the perpetual virginity of the Blessed Virgin' (Alfred L. Kellogg, 'Susannah and the *Merchant's Tale*', *Speculum* 35 [1960]: 278n1).

58. The Prologue to the Wycliffite Bible describes the interpretive dangers in the Song of Songs: 'this book is so sotil to vndirstonde, that Jewis ordeyneden, that no man schulde stodie it, no but he were of xxx. ʒeer, and hadde able wit to vndirstonde the goostly preuytees of this book; for sum of the book seemith to

fleschly men to sounne vnclene loue of leccherie, where it tellith hi3 goostly loue, and greet preuytees of Crist and of his chirche': *The Holy Bible ... Made from the Latin Vulgate by John Wycliffe and His Followers*, ed. Rev. Josiah Forshall and Sir Frederic Madden (Oxford: Oxford University Press, 1850), 1: 41.

59. See Bleeth, 'Image of Paradise'; Robert E. Kaske, 'Chaucer's Marriage Group', in *Chaucer the Love Poet*, ed. William Provost and Jerome Mitchell (Athens: University of Georgia Press, 1973), 55–56; and in particular Schroeder, 'Fantasy', 170.

60. Augustine, *City of God* 14.15, trans. Henry Bettenson (Harmondsworth: Penguin Books, 1972).

61. See D.W. Robertson, Jr., 'The Doctrine of Charity in Medieval Gardens: A Topical Approach through Symbolism and Allegory', *Speculum* 26 (1951): 24–49; and cf. Richard Neuse, 'Marriage and the Question of Allegory in the *Merchant's Tale*', *Chaucer Review* 24 (1989): 123.

62. Cf. the more edifying version of a Dry Tree (409) alluded to in 'The Squire's Tale'. See Vincent J. DiMarco's Riverside note, and the discussion in Fyler, 'Domesticating the Exotic', 7–8.

63. Bleeth, 'Image of Paradise', 50. Also see Jager, *Tempter's Voice*, 269.

64. Cf. 'The Parson's Tale', 681–84, which outlines the different kinds of labour – as remedies for Accidia – appropriate to the states of innocence, of sinful men and of grace.

65. Pierre Payer, *The Bridling of Desire: Views of Sex in the Later Middle Ages* (Toronto: University of Toronto Press, 1993), 89–97, discusses the precise implications for human behaviour of the *debitum coniugale*.

66. Augustine, *City of God* 14.26, trans. Bettenson, 590 (*PL* 41:434), aptly cited by Wolfgang E.H. Rudat, 'Chaucer's Spring of Comedy: The *Merchant's Tale* and Other "Games" with Augustinian Theology', *Annuale Mediaevale* 21 (1981): 112.

67. See Stewart Justman, 'Medieval Monism and Abuse of Authority in Chaucer', *Chaucer Review* 11 (1975): 205; R.A. Shoaf, *Dante, Chaucer, and the Currency of the Word* (Norman, OK: Pilgrim Books, 1983), 185–209, on 'The Merchant and the Parody of Creation', esp. 202–3; and Jager, *Tempter's Voice*, 251: 'the Merchant debases not only marriage and women but also signs, reducing practically everything to its face value in his own cash economy'.

68. Bleeth, 'Image of Paradise', 56n24, notes that in the *Fasti*, 'Janus is a gatekeeper and is described as carrying a key'; Emerson Brown, Jr., 'Chaucer and a Proper Name: January in *The Merchant's Tale*', *Names* 31 (1983): 82, argues that January wants to be St Peter/Janus as well as the Adam in this paradise.

69. See Tavormina's Riverside note to 2045–46, citing John Bugge, 'Damyan's Wanton *Clyket* and an Ironic New *Twiste* to the *Merchant's Tale*', *Annuale Mediaevale* 14 (1973): 53–62. For the ironies of wax-moulding, see Germaine Dempster, *Dramatic Irony in Chaucer* (Stanford, CA: Stanford University Press, 1932), 51 and 56. Also see Marie Borroff, 'Silent Retribution in Chaucer: The *Merchant's Tale*, the *Reeve's Tale*, and the *Pardoner's Tale*', in *Traditions and Renewals: Chaucer, the Gawain-Poet, and Beyond* (New Haven, CT: Yale University Press, 2003), 57: 'The gate and the pleasure garden, then, are natural symbols of May's external and internal sexual anatomy, respectively'.

70. Burger, 'Deluding Words', 108, expands usefully on Tatlock's comments concerning 'forward allusions' in the tale (Tatlock, 'Chaucer's *Merchant's Tale*', 375–76; also see Charles A. Owen, Jr., 'The Crucial Passages in Five of the

Canterbury Tales: A Study in Irony and Symbol', *Journal of English and Germanic Philology* 52 (1953): 299–300), 'where words materialize ironically into things and people': 'they have a significant effect in corroborating and intensifying the general movement of the tale from deluding words to disillusioned actuality'. Lee Patterson, *Chaucer and the Subject of History* (Madison, WI: University of Wisconsin Press, 1991), 339, focuses on the words *wax, laurer, fruyt, fayerye, May* and *paradys*, to point out that the tale 'is on several levels *about* "fantasye" and self-enclosure, a theme expressed in the various acts of ironic literalization that mark the narrative'.

71. Kellogg, 'Susannah', 276–77, notes parallels to these landscape features in the story of Susannah and the elders (Daniel 13:20), and the laurel in the Middle English poem *Susannah*.

72. See Schroeder, 'Fantasy', 172: 'The garden is the literal expression of his view that marriage is a terrestrial paradise – he builds it for that reason and stocks it with actualizations of his own metaphors for his virility'. The well has often been identified with Guillame de Lorris' fountain of Narcissus: see Bleeth, 'Image of Paradise', 51, who adds, 'The evergreen laurel, emblematic of January's desire for eternal youth, is a carnal analogue of the *lignum vitae*, standing, as does the Tree of Life, beside a spring or fountain' (52).

73. Cf. a similar reversal in the marriage encomium (1385) – 'If thou lovest thyself, thou lovest thy wyf' – on which see Burnley, 'Morality', 21: the Wyclif Bible says instead that 'He that loveth his wijf, loveth hymsilf'. Benson, 'The Marriage "Encomium"', 57, argues that in this reversal *'caritas* has become *cupiditas'*.

74. See, e.g., Edwards, 'Narration and Doctrine', 345: 'The link is not between the portrait in the General Prologue and the rhetorical presentation of the tale; it is between the narrative and the voice that speaks it'.

75. Bleeth, 'Image of Paradise', 54.

76. Norman T. Harrington, 'Chaucer's *Merchant's Tale*: Another Swing of the Pendulum', *PMLA* 86 (1971): 29, describes the narrator's 'morbid preoccupation' with sex.

77. See H. Marshall Leicester, Jr., '"No Vileyns Word": Social Context and Performance in Chaucer's *Friar's Tale*', *Chaucer Review* 17 (1982): 23–24.

78. Jonathan Swift, *Poetical Works*, ed. Herbert Davis (London: Oxford University Press, 1967), 531.

79. Ibid., 519–27.

80. Cooper, *Oxford Guide*, 211, notes that in this tale 'ideals can have no reality', in contrast with 'The Franklin's Tale', 'in which "things" are unstable: the illusions, the beauty of the garden, the rocks. The absolutes of the tale are moral qualities: patience, *fredom* or generosity, *gentillesse, trouthe*' (Cooper, *Oxford Guide*, 245).

81. 'Crazy Jane Talks with the Bishop', in *The Collected Poems of W.B. Yeats* (1956; repr. New York: Macmillan, 1974), 255. A.C. Spearing, *The Medieval Poet as Voyeur: Looking and Listening in Medieval Love-Narratives* (Cambridge: Cambridge University Press, 1993), 173, also thinks of Crazy Jane here, for a slightly different purpose: to describe 'a physiological truth that must be repressed in order to make erotic idealization possible'.

82. Jager, *Tempter's Voice*, 266, notes that 'Chaucer elsewhere suggests that verbal signs, like humans themselves, are born *inter urinas et faeces* [he quotes *Parliament of Fowls*, 597 and 'The Pardoner's Tale', 535–36]. In January's privy, how-

ever, the process is reversed, as words – here, written ones – die and return to the ground and to silence. Thus are signs reduced to mere things, a fate already foretold by their abuse in the carnal letter'.

83. As often turns out to be the case, I find that I am paraphrasing Donaldson's analysis here: *Chaucer's Poetry*, 1086.

84. Donaldson, 'The Effect of the Merchant's Tale', 36–37. Elimination, like sexuality, is a bodily function that would have been very different in Paradise, as in Aquinas's speculation on the consumption of food and its excretion there: *Summa Theologiae* 1a.97, 3 (New York: McGraw-Hill, 1964–76). Spearing, *Medieval Poet as Voyeur*, 174, notes that 'unsofte', describing January's rough beard (1824–25), is an 'unusual and telling word', which appears only one other time in Chaucer's poetry (*House of Fame*, 36) and nowhere else in fourteenth-century texts (296n32).

85. See Janette Richardson, *'Blameth Nat Me': A Study of Imagery in Chaucer's Fabliaux* (The Hague: Mouton, 1970), 145–46, on *queynte* as ambiguously an adjective or noun in this construction; also George B. Pace, 'The Scorpion of Chaucer's *Merchant's Tale*', *Modern Language Quarterly* 26 (1965): 373, which notes a variant manuscript reading 'o sweete venymous queynte'.

86. See Paul A. Olson, 'Chaucer's Merchant and January's "Hevene in Erthe Heere"', *English Literary History* 28 (1961): 207n5, and Bleeth, 'Image of Paradise', 53, for instances elsewhere of bawdy double entendres on *pirum* and *poire*; also see Bruce A. Rosenberg, 'The "Cherry-Tree" Carol and the *Merchant's Tale*', *Chaucer Review* 5 (1971): 268.

87. See Malcolm Andrew, 'January's Knife: Sexual Morality and Proverbial Wisdom in the Merchant's Tale', *English Language Notes* 16 (1979): 273–77; and Bugge, 'Damyan's Wanton *Clyket*'.

88. Kenneth A. Bleeth, 'Joseph's Doubting of Mary and the Conclusion of the *Merchant's Tale*', *Chaucer Review* 21 (1986): 58–66, finds here a likely reminiscence of the Joseph and Mary narrative. He also notes ('Image of Paradise', 55–56) the ironic relevance of the 'Marian exegesis of Canticles', and of 'the exegetical tradition connecting the *hortus conclusus* with Mary's inviolate virginity'.

89. John V. Fleming, *The Roman de la Rose: A Study in Allegory and Iconography* (Princeton, NJ: Princeton University Press, 1969), 32.

90. On the function of Pluto and Proserpina in the tale, see Mortimer J. Donovan, 'The Image of Pluto and Proserpine in the "Merchant's Tale"', *Philological Quarterly* 36 (1957): 49–60; and Karl P. Wentersdorf, 'Theme and Structure in the *Merchant's Tale*: The Function of the Pluto Episode', *PMLA* 80 (1965): 522–27.

91. So argues Edwards, 'Narration and Doctrine', though I am sceptical about his conclusion that for Chaucer as well as Claudian, 'the story of Pluto and Proserpine involves a serious meditation on culture, mutual responsibility, and governance' (362). To be sure, 'The Merchant's Tale' explicitly directs us to 'the stories' of Claudian (2232) and may promise an elevated allegorical meaning by the astronomical placing of this scene around 8 June (2133), in Gemini, 'the Zodiacal sign for May in medieval calendars' (Riverside note to line 2222), just before the summer solstice and the beginning of Cancer, 'Jovis exaltacion' (2222–24).

92. Neuse, 'Marriage and the Question of Allegory', 125, notes the association of women with fairies, here as in 'The Wife of Bath's Tale', for example in the narrator's exclamation about May as bride: 'Hire to biholde it semed fayerye' (1743). Indeed, as Hansen, *Chaucer and the Fictions of Gender*, 255, notes, 'Damyan is

essentially just like January, only younger; both are "ravysshed" by May (cf. 1750, 1774)'. And Pluto and January are both 'ravished raptors' (Edwards, 'Narration and Doctrine', 363). The tales of the Squire and Franklin pick up and develop the emphasis here on appearance and illusion. Mary Carruthers observes that 'every character in the tale is related to January as one projected aspect or another of his fantasy'. Damian 'represents to him both the way in which the old knight would like to conceive of his powers and the fear of being cuckolded which becomes explicit in the later part of the tale' (Schroeder, 'Fantasy', 170). In this respect, the tale differs interestingly from the Reeve's, in which the old, impotent narrator has young surrogates to accomplish the violence, sexual and otherwise, that he wishes to do but can no longer bring off.

93. Edwards, 'Narration and Doctrine', 365.

94. The Riverside note to lines 2225–319 summarizes the range of readings on Pluto and Proserpina and their squabble.

95. Edwards, 'Narration and Doctrine', 366–67. Cf. Patterson, *Chaucer and the Subject of History*, 343–44.

Chapter 9

String Theory and 'The Man of Law's Tale'
Where Is Constancy?

William A. Quinn

> ...incerto tempore ferme
> incertisque locis spatio depellere paulum
> [at random times and places they shift a bit]
> —Lucretius, *De Rerum Natura* (II, 218–219)

Chaucer's 'The Man of Law's Tale' is strange. In the *Riverside* edition, Larry D. Benson introduces it as a rhetorically elaborate, hagiographic romance intended to incite both wonder and compassion.[1] Others, however, have read Chaucer's characterization of the Man of Law himself as a parody of pompous piety. These antithetical responses to the narrative proper, especially when seen within its framing elements, exemplify in miniature the challenge confronting readers of the *Canterbury Tales* as a whole – that is, the difficulty of achieving interpretive certainty in response to an unstable construct. The resulting thematic uncertainty of 'The Man of Law's Tale' can be turned to good; Helen Cooper, for example, suggests that 'what Chaucer seems to be doing in this poem is similar to what he does over the whole *Canterbury Tales*: to set up generically incompatible views of the world and let a pattern of relativity, and therefore of fullness of vision, emerge from the juxtaposition'.[2] There are several voids in the seemingly steady-state universe of the edited *Canterbury Tales*; these lacunae, easily attributable to Chaucer's failure to finish his project before dying ('the atelier theory'), are normally abhorred as vacuums of interpretation. The critical challenge then becomes to deduce what Chaucer might have intended to do (though Chaucer himself may have never settled on one fixed plan). The complexities of interpreting the text, whether addressed in terms of the 'hermeneutic circle' or 'deconstruction', are compounded by the received state of 'The Man of Law's Tale' as a collaborative construct (of author, but also of scribes and editors as intermediary readers). At various stages of the tale's transmission, several wormholes seem to have been opened, gateways to a plethora of mutually valid interpretive universes that now coexist as autonomous yet interconnected options for reader responses. This article explores some of these points of fracture where Chaucer's fictional cosmos might slide for different readers into alternative realities.

The order in which Chaucer introduces his pilgrim-narrators in the 'General Prologue' provides no help at all for placing 'The Man of Law's Tale' in the framing tale-telling context. Nor does the portrait of the Sergeant of Law himself (I, 309–330) clearly determine how his voice is to be heard. Chaucer does emphasize the sergeant's professional prestige and high social status – significant details that the Host fails to perceive because of the Man of Law's 'hoomly' appearance (I, 328).[3] On the other hand, the Ellesmere illustration does not show the attire of the Man of Law to be especially modest. More curiously, two of Chaucer's own comments undercut the lawyer's projected self-importance (I, 313, 321–322).[4] This parallax produced by the General Prologue's ambiguous portrayal of the Man of Law heralds the more radical tonal and thematic indeterminacy of Fragment II.

The sequence of ten 'Fragments' in the Ellesmere MS now informs the 'definitive' position of 'The Man of Law's Tale' within the *Tales*.[5] Although (by definition) there exists no explicit linking statement between Fragments I and II, there is far less doubt about which tales precede 'The Man of Law's Tale' than about what follows it. Even deployment of the Bradshaw shift, which rearranges the tales into 'Groups' – as in W.W. Skeat's editions (1st edn, 1894; 2nd edn, 1900) – does not dislocate 'The Man of Law's Tale' as the fifth component of the *Tales*. Still, there is no imperative to read 'The Man of Law's Tale' immediately after 'The Cook's Tale', though it may be thematically gratifying to read the portrayal of Custance in opposition to the brief mention of the wife of Perkyn Revelour's compeer. The reader's freedom to bridge gaps in the frame of the *Tales* as a whole is paralleled by numerous options of interpretation within Fragment II.

Reading Fragment II, one frequently encounters (especially when participating in a collaborative reading) certain cruces that split critical responses in two: between didactic sincerity and parodic irony – between matter and anti-matter, as it were. Hypothetically, each reader can oscillate between antithetical responses, but more typically interpretation becomes trapped in the black hole of self-consistency which requires some *fil conducteur*, or 'clewe' (*The Legend of Good Women*, 2148), to escape what otherwise seems a maze of endlessly tangled interpretations. Nevertheless, the reader should resist the gravitational attraction of any 'one true explication', even as the Man of Law himself insists upon the fated fixity of his plot.

The *Riverside* edition heads Fragment II with an 'Introduction to the Man of Law's Tale' because the manuscript introduces the tale proper with 'the wordes of the Hoost to the compaignye'. No paratextual prompts in the manuscripts need to be thought of as authorial, nor can they certainly be denied as such. Since each such authorial/scribal/editorial prompt both guides and restricts the reader's choices of tonal and thematic interpretation, the significance attached to each should be held in a state of suspension – neither compelling nor negligible.

In a highly artificial calculation of the 'artificial day' (II, 2), Herry Bailley determines it is 10:00 a.m. on 18 April. Here, Herry is actually reading shadows (II, 7, 10) even though the *artificial* (as distinguished from *natural*) hours are measured by the clock (II, 14) rather than by a sun-dial. Some readers, who question a detail of perhaps un-attempted verisimilitude, find it implausible that it is only 10:00 a.m. on the first day after all of Fragment I has been performed from horseback. Others can contend that the Knight and Miller and Reeve and Cook had plenty of time, given that the pilgrims would have started out at sunrise on an April day. But Herry's overwrought point may simply be that *tempus fugit*; so the pilgrims should avoid idleness (II, 32), though he himself has persuaded the fellowship to indulge in the pastime (or idle distraction) of a tale-telling contest while on pilgrimage. Herry would impose mechanical precision on natural variation. Herry's seemingly impromptu calculations of the hour, which 'could only have been made with astronomical instruments', apparently prove wrong.[6] The day itself, 18 April (II, 5–6), which many readers presume would be the second day of the pilgrimage, seems meteorologically significant, predictive of May's weather. And this impulse to attain the power of prediction (analogous to every reader's desire to anticipate the plot) informs a far more controversial conviction – the Man of Law's apparent belief in judicial astrology:

> Paraventure in thilke large book
> Which that men clepe the hevene ywriten was
> With sterres, whan that he his birthe took,
> That he for love sholde han his deeth, allas!
> For in the sterres, clerer than is glas,
> Is writen, God woot, whoso koude it rede,
> The deeth of every man, withouten drede. (II, 190–196)

However lucidly the Book of Nature may be written, human perception of its significance remains myopic. The Man of Law concludes this entirely pessimistic, so distorted, rendition of a passage from the *Megacosmos* of Bernardus Silvester with scepticism: 'but mennes wittes ben so dulle / That no wight kan wel rede it atte fulle' (II, 202–203). Patricia J. Eberle notes that 'Chaucer's conclusion ... is a marked change from Bernardus's conclusion' – indeed, the Man of Law's darkly fatalistic affirmation of human ignorance is antithetical to his authority's intent.[7]

Inviting the Man of Law to comply to his 'beheste', the Host parrots legal language (II, 34–38) – jargon that the reader may hear as either pretentious (mocking the Host) or sarcastic (mocking the Man of Law). In either event, a legal lexicon seems to delimit – that is, both inform and restrict – the Man of Law's consciousness.[8] And then, Chaucer subjects his career as a man of letters to this lawyer's literary judgements (II, 45–89). The purpose of the Man of Law's somewhat inaccurate inventory of Chaucer's writings provides yet another opportunity to wonder what tonal world we've entered. Does Chaucer, having learned his lesson in the *House of Fame*, mean to mock his supposed celebrity by having the Man of Law fail to recognize his fellow pilgrim as the author under review? Is Chaucer indirectly apologizing for his own, often 'lecherous' early career (X, 1086)? Is Chaucer rebuking John Gower for inclusion of the story of Canacee in *The Confessio Amantis* (only to have the Squire begin this scandalous tale)?[9] Is the Man of Law's and/or Chaucer's confusion of the (loser magpies) Pierides with the winner Muses (who were also called Pierides) ironic or just a gaffe? Is the Man of Law being mocked as a literary critic whose supposedly prodigious memory produces both omissions and false attributions? Or is Chaucer deflating himself with a typical gesture of ironic humility? Or is the point of this entire passage all simply indeterminable because under revision? These substantial tonal uncertainties are punctuated by what seems a merely formal accident when the Man of Law promises to speak in prose, but the following text does not.[10]

Thematically, the most problematic moment of Fragment II occurs in the following rhyme-royal 'Prologe' (II, 99–133). Though its first sixteen lines offer a condensation of Pope Innocent III's *De miseria condicionis humanae*, its concluding celebration of financial *winning* (II, 127) posits a completely contradictory *moralitas*. The Mercers of London might buy into this anticipation of 'prosperity theology' at face value. The questions remain: what voice enframed in the *Tales* would make this declaration, and how sincerely? The Man of Law (as an admirable or as a ridiculous character)? Perhaps some merchant from whom the Man of Law received this tale (II, 132), the plot of which is initiated by Syrian 'chapmen riche' (II, 135)? Perhaps the spectral voice of the pilgrim Merchant (for whom the tale may have been originally intended)?[11] Or perhaps – far more disturbingly – Chaucer himself (in one of his rehearsing avatars as author/persona/compiler)?

Several manuscripts, including Ellesmere 26 C 9 (now Huntington Library) and Hengwrt (Peniarth 392), provide readers of 'The Man of Law's Tale' with *marginal* assistance – that is, glosses of questionable use that indicate correspondences between Chaucer's lines and his sources. At first glance, these annotations seem to invest the Man of Law's pronouncements with authority; on second thought, this summoning of testimony can undermine the Man of Law's claim to authority.[12] Furthermore, if scribal impositions, these glosses may represent an effort to achieve masculine containment of the feminine text, as Carolyn Dinshaw argues.[13] Omitted from modern editions, these scribal addenda may also represent a total failure to do so.

All the conventional interpretive questions regarding Chaucer's narrative 'I' orbit the actual tale of Custance. Having provided a trenchant critique of its numerous narrative-voice readings,

A.C. Spearing proposes that 'what we find in the *Man of Law's Tale*, as in most Chaucerian narratives, is not a fixed deictic centre but one that is liberated from fixity and enables us to imagine narrative events in a whole variety of different spatio-temporal and emotional perspectives'.[14] The tale's recurrent references to 'you' also pose a particularly puzzling tonal feature of the tale because of the Man of Law's excessive use of apostrophe, addressed variously to abstractions, to the tale's characters, to the pilgrim's fictional audience and to the author's readers. It is difficult to assess both how Chaucer intended and how his contemporaries perceived such a conspicuous feature of the Man of Law's oratory: does his (heightened, outmoded, bombastic and/or impassioned) use of the rhetorical device alienate or engage 'us'?[15]

Despite being so derivative, the Man of Law repeatedly reminds us that his version of the tale of Custance is one of his own *devising* (II, 154, 349, 419, 613), often objecting to variants or omissions in his sources. In Middle English, 'to devise' can mean simply 'to tell', but the verb has a strong connotation of relating information that may prove difficult to comprehend.[16] Declaring his own unqualified praise of Custance, the Man of Law invokes the 'commune voys of every man' (II, 155), affirming (with what many consider a very un-Chaucerian opinion) the absolute integrity of the *vox populi*: 'And al this voys was sooth, as God is trewe. / But now to purpos lat us turne agayn' (II, 169–170). However, many feminist critics (including perhaps Alison of Bath) have questioned whether Custance (like Griselda) should be thought a patient saint, a heroic victim or merely a feeble enabler.[17]

Not unlike the Canterbury fellowship's differing responses to the Miller's performance (I, 3857), marriage negotiations between Rome and Syria cause a controversy that seems to resolve itself only as a fatigued compliance with necessity:

> Diverse men diverse thynges seyden;
> They argumenten, casten up and doun;
> Many a subtil resoun forth they leyden;
> They speken of magyk and abusioun.
> But finally, as in conclusioun,
> They kan nat seen in that noon avantage,
> Ne in noon oother wey, save mariage. (II, 211–217)

Hereafter, it proves hard to think of Custance as a protagonist conventionally conceived since she is so passive. Chaucer even denies

Custance the preaching role she had in Nicholas Trevet's chronicle.[18] Rather, Custance serves as a pawn for many tales told within 'The Man of Law's Tale'; Custance becomes thereby an imagined focal point for several fictive universes, for observing all of which the Man of Law is merely the reader's most proximate deviser.[19] Politically, Custance initially functions as a prop in an imperial fantasy of Europe (II, 161) to reconvert Islamdom (II, 236). Romantically, she provides an unseen object of desire for the Sultan's imagination. Her own conduct, however, is always compelled by necessity; she 'moot' each and every plot turn.

Though George Lyman Kittredge did not include 'The Man of Law's Tale' in his original conception of a 'marriage group', Custance does anticipate Alison's declaration of the inevitable woe in marriage (II, 261). Bowing to her parents' sovereignty (subordinate only to Christ's), she nevertheless is allowed briefly to complain: 'I, wrecche womman, no fors though I spille! / Women are born to thraldom and penance, / And to been under mannes governance' (II, 285–287). One might presume that a Man of Law would affirm patriarchy if not contracted marriage as well. Instead, the Man of Law bemoans the revolution of the *Primum Mobile* (in a 'highly untraditional'[20] fashion) and the Emperor's lack of astrologically informed prudence (II, 295–315). Woeful Custance (II, 316) is shipped to Syria and pains herself to maintain a good albeit false appearance (II, 320). However, any empathy for womankind that Custance's situation should invite is overruled by the lawyer's misogynist outburst against the Sultana:

> O Sathan, envious syn thilke day
> That thou were chaced from oure heritage,
> Wel knowestow to wommen the olde way!
> Thou madest Eva brynge us in servage;
> Thou wolt fordoon this Cristen mariage.
> Thyn instrument so – weylawey the while! –
> Makestow of wommen, whan thou wolt bigile. (II, 365–371)

The Brownian motion of the narrator's emotions is especially hard to predict. He can assimilate the paraphrased sarcasm of Custance's persecutors: 'And in a ship al steerelees, God woot, / They han hir set, and bidde hire lerne saille' (II, 439–440), and then, in an instant, directly address Custance with parental pity: 'O my Custance, ful of benignytee, / O Emperoures yonge doghter deere, / He that is lord of Fortune be thy steere!' (II, 446–448). Subsequently, the Man of Law has Custance take an equivalent tonal leap from compassion to misogyny when she blames Eve while praying to Mary: 'Sooth is that thurgh wommanes eggement / Mankynde was lorn, and damned ay to dye' (II, 842–843). Such random fluctuations of feeling might reduce true pathos to banality – or they might not.

The essentially duplicated plotting of 'The Man of Law's Tale' at once increases its predictability while reducing its plausibility. Clearly, the simple escape of Custance from the contingent universe of her arranged marriage might seem utterly unlikely – very much like Hamlet's surprise rescue by pirates. Well-disposed (or inattentive) readers might overlook the implausibility of this plot twist except for the fact that the Man of Law draws unnecessary attention to its unlikelihood:

> Men myghten asken why she was nat slayn
> Eek at the feeste? Who myghte hir body save?
> And I answere to that demande agayn,
> ... God... (II, 470–476)

The Man of Law's apology (for want of a better plot device) appeals to his audience's awareness that their ignorance precludes presumption:

> By certeine meenes ofte, as knowen clerkis,
> Dooth thyng for certein ende that ful derk is
> To mannes wit, that for oure ignorance
> Ne konne noght knowe his prudent purveiance. (II, 480–483)

This fundamental (perhaps simplistic) denial of mere man's ability to comprehend the divine plan is reinforced by some odd side-notes regarding language.[21] For example, Custance's travels pose a post-Babel complication of the viability of the story's dialogue: 'A maner Latyn corrupt was hir speche, / But algates therby was she understonde' (II, 519–520). Furthermore, though a lie may try to supplant the truth, suspicion can call into question spoken testimony: 'This gentil kyng hath caught a greet motyf / Of this witnesse, and thoghte he wolde enquere / Depper in this, a trouthe for to lere' (II, 628–630). The knight's speech has fabricated an alter-Custance. But in the Man of Law's over-writing cosmos, the written (Christian) Truth both readily and miraculously dispels the spoken (pagan) fiction:

> 'Now hastily do fecche a book,' quod he,
> 'And if this knyght wol sweren how that she
> This womman slow, yet wol we us avyse
> Whom that we wole that shal been oure justise.'

A Britoun book, written with Evaungiles,
Was fet, and on this book he swoor anoon
She gilty was, and in the meene whiles
An hand hym smoot upon the nekke-boon,
That doun he fil atones as a stoon,
And bothe his eyen broste out of his face
In sighte of every body in that place. (II, 662–672)

As if this miraculous power of the Gospel as a totem of testimony were not sufficiently intimidating, this admonitory punishment of perjury is explicated by the Divine Voice: 'A voys was herd in general audience, / And seyde, "Thou hast desclaundred, giltelees, / The doghter of hooly chirche in heigh presence"' (II, 673–675). Slandering Custance does not precipitate divine justice: 'Thus hastou doon, and yet holde I my pees!' (II, 676). A textual sacrilege does. The witnesses are amazed and ashamed, and the king's justice is swift: 'This false knyght was slayn for his untrouthe / By juggement of Alla hastifly' (II, 687–688), though Custance herself does not concur with his sentence: 'And yet Custance hadde of his deeth greet routh' (II, 689). Countering if not contradicting masculine justice with feminine mercy, Custance's pity truly imitates that of Christ, but for the narrator then to claim that Jesus Himself 'made' Alla marry Custance (II, 690; cf. II, 693) may seem at once pious and presumptuous.

The Man of Law echoes John the Baptist's warning that all chaff shall be discarded to justify – in a rather prolonged fashion – his abbreviation of any detailed description of the actual wedding ceremony.[22] Indeed, his one-line synopsis of the feast is quite jejune, but his preliminary defence of such brevity sounds rather bloated:

Me list nat of the chaf, ne of the stree,
Maken so long a tale as of the corn.
What sholde I tellen of the roialtee
At mariage, or which cours goth biforn;
Who bloweth in a trumpe or in an horn?
The fruyt of every tale is for to seye:
They ete, and drynke, and daunce, and synge, and pleye. (II, 701–707)

The five iambs and polysyndeton of this last line trot through the festivities. But the Man of Law sounds haltingly prissy when it comes to the marriage's devoutly-to-be-wished consummation:

They goon to bedde, as it was skile and right;
For thogh that wyves be ful hooly thynges,
They moste take in pacience at nyght

> Swiche manere necessaries as been plesynges
> To folk that han ywedded hem with rynges,
> And leye a lite hir hoolynesse aside. (II, 708–713)

Perhaps this prudish understatement suits the compulsory copulation that a contracted marriage requires. Nevertheless, Custance's second royal marriage falsely promises an archetypally comic resolution to all her trials.

The Man of Law's stifled account of Custance's momentary happiness contrasts sharply with the intensity of his prolonged outrage when she is slandered a second time and thereby cast into the alternative reality of being identified as an adulteress. This time the tale's quantum plot shift is achieved by false writing rather than by false speech – that is, by a forged text rather than by a fraudulent oath: a substitute letter 'countrefeted was ful subtilly' by Alla's mother 'wroght ful synfully' (II, 746–747). The Man of Law's tirade against the drunken messenger is as vehement as his reviling of the Sultana because the veracity of the written word has now proven every bit as vulnerable to distortion as the spoken.[23]

Ironically (perhaps), Chaucer has the Man of Law, champion of truth, confess that he cannot compose an adequate account of Donegild's deceit; the only adequate author would be Satan:

> O Donegild, I ne have noon Englissh digne
> Unto thy malice and thy tirannye!
> And therfore to the feend I thee resigne;
> Lat hym enditen of thy traitorie! (II, 778–781)

But the Man of Law can devise an expression of intense sympathy for Custance and her son that conflates the grief of the 'Stabat Mater' (II, 848), the outrage of the Slaughter of Innocents (II, 855) and the heartbreak of the Sacrifice of Isaac (II, 857). Here is an instant of compassion difficult to ironize despite all the other indicators.

Strangely, Custance then thinks of a plausible escape plan for Maurice, which she immediately rejects as implausible:

> 'O mercy, deere constable," quod she,
> 'As lat my litel child dwelle heer with thee;
> And if thou darst nat saven hym, for blame,
> So kys hym ones in his fadres name!' (II, 858–861)

At moments like this, the reader is entitled to feel lost in space as the plot orbits again before returning to the tale's gravitational centre – Rome.[24] Many such narrative moments play in alternative schemes of interpretations. The Man of Law, for example, eschews redundancy as he again condemns duplicity: 'And pleynly al the manere he hym tolde / As ye han herd – I kan telle it no bettre –' (II, 880–881). The messenger is tortured until by such 'wit and sotil enquerynge' (II, 888) a likely suspect is determined.

The Man of Law professes almost simultaneously that the fraud of the substitute letter that launched Custance into the unknown is both transparent and inexplicable. On the one hand, Donegild's penmanship is obvious: 'The hand was knowe that the lettre wroot, / And al the venym of this cursed dede' (II, 890–891). On the other hand, the method of determining her guilt is certainly uncertain to the Man of Law except as a matter of the textual record of his source:

> But in what wise, certeinly, I noot.
> Th' effect is this, that Alla, out of drede,
> His mooder slow – that may men pleynly rede –
> For that she traitour was to hire ligeance. (II, 892–895)

This matricide is a mirror image of part one's filicide. That Alla feels no Orestes-like guilt is utterly ignored though other trivial omissions of detail do seem to require the narrator's note as, for example, when Custance arrives at 'an hethen castel, atte laste, / Of which the name in my text noght I fynde' (II, 904–905). Again, Custance faces sexual assault. And again, the unlikelihood of her escape is addressed: 'But blisful Marie heelp hire right anon; / For with hir struglyng wel and myghtily / The theef fil over bord al sodeynly' (II, 920–922). The narrator's apostrophe invokes Marian intervention, but Custance's physical efforts testify more to the efficacy of jujitsu. Although the would-be-rapist's demise is finally described as an accidental fall, Chaucer has the Man of Law explicitly emphasize the miraculous wonder (or ludicrous implausibility) of Custance's self-defence: 'How may this wayke womman han this strengthe / Hire to defende agayn this renegat?' (II, 932–933). As if she were part of some epic poem's divine machinery, Mary is venerated as the patroness who is about to ordain Custance's happy enough resolution: 'Til Cristes mooder – blessed be she ay! – / Hath shapen, thurgh hir endelees goodnesse, / To make an ende of al hir hevynesse' (II, 950–952).

Meanwhile, the Roman Emperor has sent a senator to lead a quasi-crusade 'On Surryens to taken heigh vengeance' (II, 963). The violent campaign itself supposedly lasted 'many a day', but its narrative account is presented most 'shortly – this is th'ende' (II, 965). Narrative destiny is then fulfilled by a mere coincidence: this returning senator just happens to encounter Custance's ship as it wanders aimlessly about the entire Mediterranean Sea. The absurd odds against this occurrence do not disturb the narrator in the least: 'Thus kan Oure Lady bryngen out of wo' (II, 977). Some long time (II, 979) then passes while Custance lives a prayerful life with the senator's wife (who happens to be her aunt). But regarding this extended time span, the narrator 'wol no lenger tarien' (II, 983). And then Alla, both fortuitously and blessedly, undertakes a penitential pilgrimage to Rome. It could be that the tale thus affirms the salvific legitimacy of both crusade and pilgrimage; it could be that Chaucer subverts the sincerity of any such supposition.[25]

The predestined happy ending of 'The Merchant's Tale' as a whole occurs at yet another archetypally (and minimally) comic feast: 'This senatour is to kyng Alla go / To feste, and shortly, if I shal nat lye, / Custances sone wente in his compaignye' (II, 1006–1008). The lawyer's concern about lying here is both significant and trivial; his worry is whether Custance herself had any agency in the plot's resolution:

> Som men wolde seyn at requeste of Custance
> This senatour hath lad this child to feeste;
> I may nat tellen every circumstance –
> Be as be may, ther was he at the leeste.
> But sooth is this, that at his moodres heeste
> Biforn Alla, durynge the metes space,
> The child stood, lookynge in the kynges face. (II, 1009–1015)

The Man of Law thus simultaneously introduces and dismisses a controversy. He admits doubt while he asserts that it was Custance's idea to have Maurice face Alla at the feast. Be as be may, Alla is thus confronted by an alternative reality to his false story: '"Parfay," thoghte he, "fantome is in myn heed! / I oghte deme, of skilful juggement, / That in the salte see my wyf is deed"' (II, 1037–1039). Of course, divine intervention again readily explains such a contradiction of logic:

> And afterward he made his argument:
> 'What woot I if that Crist have hyder ysent
> My wyf by see, as wel as he hire sente
> To my contree fro thennes that she wente?' (II, 1040–1043)

The marital reunion of Alla and Custance achieves a second comic though hardly happy ending: 'And hastifly he sente after Custaunce. / But trusteth weel, hire liste nat to daunce' (II, 1047–1048).[26]

Having started at 10:00 a.m., the Man of Law seems now to have exhausted almost an entire day: 'I pray yow alle my labour to relesse; / I may nat telle hir wo until to-morwe, / I am so wery for to speke of sorwe' (II, 1069–1071). He will rush the rest: 'But of my tale make an ende I shal; / The day goth faste, I wol no lenger lette' (II, 1116–1117) – that is, he will minimize the edifying impact of his exemplary tale. He will, instead, stumble over alternative versions of the plot's resolution:

> Som men wolde seyn how that the child Maurice
> Dooth this message unto this Emperour;
> But, as I gesse, Alla was nat so nyce
> To hym that was of so sovereyn honour
> As he that is of Cristen folk the flour,
> Sente any child, but it is bet to deeme
> He wente hymself, and so it may wel seeme. (II, 1086–1092)

Such concern with diplomatic protocol is both picayune and the cause of many wars. Husband and wife return to 'Engelond' (II, 1130), but Alla dies after just one year; so widowed, Custance closes the circuit of her elliptical life by returning to Rome. Reunited with her father, Custance gives alms and 'never asonder wende' (II, 1156–1157) to purchase salvation and end this 'thrifty tale' (II, 1165). The tale-proper's closing prayer is that Jesus 'kepe us alle that been in this place' (II, 1162). There may be a certain irony to this note of poor yet spiritually profitable stasis at the tale's conclusion – or not.

At this point, every reader of the *Tales* crosses the text's event horizon into the singularity of the 'Epilogue' to 'The Man of Law's Tale' – 'the greatest textual dilemma posed by the whole work'.[27] This so-called epilogue (II, 1163–1190) appears in only thirty-five of the *Canterbury Tales'* extant witnesses; the otherwise authoritative Ellesmere MS does not include this epilogue, nor does the Hengwrt MS. Twenty-eight extant manuscripts invite the Squire to speak next; six indicate the Summoner; only one specifies the Shipman whom, nevertheless, 'most editors have taken as the most probable' although all proposals 'are most likely scribal inventions'.[28] Oxford MS New College 314 follows the Cook's fragment with the Man of Law, then additional tales for the Squire and Merchant, then the Wife. Lansdowne and Sloane follow the Cook with the spurious 'Tale of Gamelyn', then the Man of Law, then additional tales for Squire and Merchant, then the Wife. Harley 7334 follows the Cook with 'The Tale of Gamelyn', then the Man of Law, then the Wife. On the one hand, this is a mess; on the other, there is a strong tendency to have the Wife of Bath follow (and perhaps 'quit') the Man of Law.

So, the *Riverside* edition introduces the Shipman (II, 1179), whose fabliau, now in Fragment VII (Group B2), may have originally been intended for the 'joly body' of the Wife of Bath, whose name may have been erased and replaced in the 'Epilogue'.[29] The earliest print records of the *Canterbury Tales* reflect both this history of chirographic instability and the editorial impulse to eradicate it: 'William Caxton famously relates how he used a different and better ("very trewe") manuscript to prepare his second edition of *The Canterbury Tales*; and fifty years later William Thynne took pains to find "trewe copies or exemplaries" for his 1532 edition'.[10] In Caxton's first edition of the *Tales* (1476), Fragment I is followed by the Man of Law, then the Squire, then the Wife of Bath. But in the proem to his second edition (1483), Caxton specifically apologizes for the imperfections of his first edition's sequence, promising to publish:

> the conditions and the array of each of them as properly as possible is to be said. and after their tales which be of nobleness, wisdom, gentleness, mirth and also of very holiness and virtue, wherein he finisheth this said book, which book I have diligently overseen and duly examined, to that end it be made according unto his own making.

This revised effort to retrieve Chaucer's intended plan still has 'The Man of Law's Tale' follow Fragment I, but then proceeds to the tales of the Merchant, then Franklin, then the Wife of Bath. What is so thematically disorienting about this sequence of the whole is that the Franklin's tale (normally considered the resolution of the 'Marriage Group') precedes Allison's initiation of the debate.

Chaucer's manuscripts do provide a relatively stable bracketing of the rest of the *Tales* between Fragments I and X. More specifically, the General Prologue and the Parson's Prologue establish *ab quo* and *ad quem* thematic *termini*. But in between (as between London and Canterbury, or between birth and death, or between the Big Bang and the Big Crunch), all remains in flux. Much like recognizing that the Earth is not the centre of the universe, the reader of a definitive edition of the *Canterbury Tales* must be aware that placing 'The Man of Law's Tale' in Fragment II has little gravitational hold on how to interpret Chaucer's composition. Ultimately, readers must decide – perhaps at the whim of Douglas Adams' Improbability Drive – whether Fragment II of the *Canterbury Tales* is attractive as an artistic mass or not.

As the currently un-confirmable 'String Theory' questions whether there is only one 'universe' (though 'singular integrity' is what the first morpheme of the word 'universe' signifies), so too both pre-print and post-print navigation of the *Canterbury Tales* underlines that there may be no such textual entity as THE *Canterbury Tales*. The printed edition in hand should be played as an interactive game of motile scripts rather than as an immutable board game. In the current state of a post-print (as well as post-Newtonian) indeterminacy, this prospect of innumerable viable contexts of interpretation both terrifies and exhilarates.

William A. Quinn is Distinguished Professor of English and former Director of the Medieval and Renaissance Studies Program at the J. William Fulbright College of Arts and Sciences of the University of Arkansas.

Notes

1. Larry D. Benson, gen. ed., *The Riverside Chaucer*, 3rd edn (Boston, MA: Houghton Mifflin, 1987), 9–10. All citations of *The Canterbury Tales* are from this *Riverside* edition, which has long provided the authoritative model of the *Tales*, indeed ever since F.N. Robinson's first Cambridge edition appeared in 1933. A.S.G. Edwards provides a survey of varying, often conflicting readings in 'Critical Approaches to the "Man of Law's Tale"', in *Chaucer's Religious Tales*, ed. C. David Benson and Elizabeth Robertson (Cambridge: D.S. Brewer, 1990), 85–94. For multiple perspectives on 'The Man of Law's Tale' as a saint's life, see Sarah Salih, ed., *A Companion to Middle English Hagiography* (Rochester, NY: D.S. Brewer, 2006).
2. Helen Cooper, *Oxford Guides to Chaucer, The Canterbury Tales* (Oxford: Oxford University Press, 1989), 132.
3. *Riverside*, 855 n33.
4. Richard Firth Green ('Chaucer's Man of Law and Collusive Recovery', *Notes and Queries* 238 [1993]: 303–305) observes that Chaucer's reference to 'fee simple' (I, 19) is also a highly critical remark.
5. Only the Man of Law (II) and Manciple (IX) and Parson (X) have sole occupancy of 'fragments'. Reconstituted as a member of Group B, the Man of Law precedes *seriatim* the Shipman, the Prioress, Chaucer the pilgrim, the Monk and the Nun's Priest. The very notion of 'fragment' (as differentiated from 'groups') has been called into question by Robert Lee-Meyers, who prefers 'blocks' in 'Abandon the Fragments', *Studies in the Age of Chaucer* 35 (2013): 47–83. Carleton Brown also used the concept of 'blocks' but in pursuit of a 'standard text', in 'Author's Revision in the Canterbury Tales', *PMLA* 57 (1942): 29–50. Norman Blake dismisses the possibility of establishing a single manuscript stemma, in 'The Links in the Canterbury Tales', in *New Perspectives on Middle English Texts: A Festschrift for*

R.A. Waldron, ed. Susan Powell and Jeremy J. Smith (Cambridge: D.S. Brewer, 2000), 107–118.

6. *Riverside*, 854. As J.C. Eade contends in '"We Ben to Lewed or to Slowe": Chaucer's Astronomy and Audience Participation', *Studies in the Age of Chaucer* 4 (1982): 53–85, Chaucer's contemporaries would have been much quicker to evaluate such calculations. See also Chauncey Wood, *Chaucer and the Country of the Stars* (Princeton, NJ: Princeton University Press, 1970).

7. Similarly, Chaucer 'changes the emphasis' of his source for lines 190–203 'so that only evil fates are foretold' and 'changes those references he does adopt from a positive to a negative emphasis' (*Riverside*, 858 nn190–203).

8. Rodney Delasanta sees the Man of Law as a pharisaical exhibitionist, in 'And of Great Reverence: Chaucer's Man of Law', *Chaucer Review* 5 (1971): 288–310, and Maura Nolan addresses Chaucer's anxiety in this confrontation of legal and poetic language, in 'Acquiteth Yow Now: Textual Contradiction and Legal Discourse in the Man of Law's Introduction', in *The Letter of the Law: Legal Practice and Literary Production in Medieval England*, ed. Emily Steiner and Candace Barrington (New York: Cornell University Press, 2002), 136–153.

9. Elizabeth Allen recognizes the Man of Law as a mis-reader of the *Confessio*, in 'Chaucer Answers Gower: Constance and the Trouble with Reading', *ELH* 64 (1997): 627–655.

10. A.S.G. Edwards notes the possibility that 'speak in prose' may simply mean 'change the subject', in '"I Speke in Prose": Man of Law's Tale, 96', *Neuphilologische Mitteilungen* 92 (1991): 469–470.

11. For this problematic (and perhaps satirical) fusion (or confusion) of proto-capitalist perspectives, see Roger A. Ladd, 'The Mercantile (Mis)Reader in *The Canterbury Tales*', *Studies in Philology* 99 (2002): 17–32; and Kathryn L. Lynch, '"Diversitee bitwene hir bothe lawes": Chaucer's Unlikely Alliance of a Lawyer and a Merchant', *Chaucer Review* 46 (2011): 74–92.

12. Graham D. Caie considers the glosses authorial in origin but intended to indicate discrepancies, in 'Innocent III's *De Miseria* as a Gloss on The Man of Law's Prologue and Tale', *Neuphilologische Mitteilungen* 100 (1999): 175–185 and '"This Was a Thrifty Tale for the Nones": Chaucer's Man of Law', in *Chaucer in Perspective: Middle English Essays in Honour of Norman Blake*, ed. Geoffrey Lester (Sheffield: Sheffield Academic Press, 1999), 47–60.

13. Carolyn Dinshaw, *Chaucer's Sexual Poetics* (Madison, WI: University of Wisconsin Press, 1989).

14. A.C. Spearing, *Textual Subjectivity* (Oxford: Oxford University Press, 2005), 101–136, here 128. See also A.C. Spearing, 'Narrative Voice: The Case of Chaucer's "Man of Law's Tale"', *New Literary History* 32 (2001): 715–746.

15. Walter Scheps finds the Man of Law rhetorically excessive and sententiously tedious, in 'Chaucer's Man of Law and the Tale of Constance', *PMLA* 89 (1974): 285–295. Ann W. Astell finds him long-winded and fatalistic, in 'Apostrophe, Prayer, and the Structure of Satire in The Man of Law's Tale', *Studies in the Age of Chaucer* 13 (1991): 81–97.

16. See *Middle English Dictionary* s.v. 'devisen' def. 7.

17. This question remains one of the most contested critical issues regarding 'The Man of Law's Tale', pitting Chaucer's 'medieval' sensibility against his 'modern' world-view. Stephen Manning admires Custance's self-sufficient heroism, in

'Chaucer's Constance: Pale and Passive', in *Chaucerian Problems and Perspectives: Essays Presented to Paul E. Beichner*, ed. Edward Vasta and Zacharias P. Thundy (Notre Dame, IN: University of Notre Dame Press, 1979), 13–23. Sheila Delany argues that Custance suffers as 'Everywoman' enduring passively the universal human experience, in 'Womanliness in the "Man of Law's Tale"', *Chaucer Review* 9 (1974): 63–72 and in Sheila Delany, *Writing Woman: Women Writers and Women in Literature Medieval to Modern* (New York: Schocken Books, 1983), 36–46. Eugene Clasby refutes Delany's critique of Custance's degradation, in 'Chaucer's Constance: Womanly Virtue and the Heroic Life', *Chaucer Review* 13 (1979): 221–233. In *Impolitic Bodies* (Oxford: Oxford University Press, 1988), Delany defends her modern critique of Chaucer's characterization of 'the repulsive masochistic qualities' of Custance's saintly submission as medieval propaganda (190–191). Cathy Hume reads the tale as proposing an exceptional level of wifely compliance, in *Chaucer and the Cultures of Love and Marriage* (Rochester, NY: Brewer, 2012).

18. Alastair Minnis, *Fallible Authors* (Philadelphia, PA: University of Pennsylvania Press, 2008), 333.

19. This conflux of multiple voices is emphasized by David Weisberg in 'Telling Stories about Constance: Framing and Narrative Strategy in the *Canterbury Tales*', *Chaucer Review* 27 (1992): 45–64.

20. *Riverside*, 859 nn295–301.

21. Christine F. Cooper attributes a more active role to Custance because of her 'xenoglossia', in '"But algates therby was she understonde": Translating Custance in Chaucer's Man of Law's Tale', *Yearbook of English Studies* 36 (2006): 27–38.

22. In Matthew 3:12, John the Baptist's metaphor refers to Jesus's separation of the blessed and sinners, and to God's anticipated separation of the saved and damned, not to the selection of plot essentials and omission of digressions.

23. For Richard Firth Green, this interception of the true message exemplifies the inherent danger of letters because 'of their semantic profligacy … letters often miscarry in medieval romance', in *A Crisis of Truth* (Philadelphia, PA: University of Pennsylvania Press, 1999), 278. See also Brendan O'Connell, 'Chaucer's Counterfeit "Exempla"', in *Chaucer's Poetry: Words, Authority and Ethics*, ed. Clíodhna Carney and Frances McCormack (Dublin: Four Courts Press, 2013), 134–157.

24. William F. Woods interprets Custance's return to Rome as equivalent to the collapse of narrative space, in *Chaucerian Spaces* (Albany, NY: SUNY Press, 2008). Sarah Stanbury emphasizes the spiritual and commercial centrality of Rome, in 'The Man of Law's Tale and Rome', *Exemplaria* 22 (2010): 119–137. Joerg O. Fichte gives particular attention to the symbolic role of Rome as centre of Christendom, in 'Rome and Its Anti-pole in the Man of Law's and the Second Nun's Tale: Christendom and Hethenesse', *Anglia* 122 (2004): 225–249.

25. Siobhain Bly Calkin argues that Chaucer, while not advocating crusading, affirms the privation of those who take up the cross, in '"The Man of Law's Tale" and "Crusade"', in *Medieval Latin and Middle English Literature: Essays in Honour of Jill Mann*, ed. Christopher Cannon and Maura Nolan (Cambridge: Brewer, 2011), 1–24.

26. Helen Cooper finds the tale's romantic ending 'oddly muted, not least by comparison with *La Manekine* … There is no equivalent to the joyful sexuality of

Manekine and her husband', in *The English Romance in Time* (Oxford: Oxford University Press, 2004), 128.

27. Helen Cooper, *The Structure of the Canterbury Tales* (Athens, GA: University of Georgia Press, 1984), 123.

28. *Riverside*, 863 n1179.

29. Ibid., 862.

30. Margaret Connolly, 'Compiling the Book', in *The Production of Books in England 1350–1500*, ed. Alexandra Gillespie and Daniel Wakelin (Cambridge: Cambridge University Press, 2011), 129–149, here 130.

Chapter 10

The Pardoner's Passing and How It Matters

Gender, Relics and Speech Acts

Alex da Costa

> thise cookes, how they stampe, and streyne, and grynde,
> and turnen substaunce into accident...
> —'Pardoner's Prologue and Tale', ll. 538–539

The question of what is 'accident' and what is 'substaunce' whispers through the 'Pardoner's Prologue and Tale'. Anxieties about the capacity for outward appearance or declaration to depart from underlying reality cluster around the figure of the Pardoner, relics and oaths. 'Chaucer', the narrator, invites the reader to suspect that the Pardoner's clothes conceal an anomalous body in the General Prologue; the Pardoner teases his pilgrim audience with the thought that his (and others') gaudily displayed relics are mere animal bones; and greed makes a mockery of the idea that the three rioters' fraternal oaths create a lasting bond between them. Chaucer's audience is repeatedly put in a position where they must doubt what is presented or promised, even as others continue gaily to trust. The

Notes for this section begin on page 229.

narrator questions the Pardoner's gender as an aside to the audience
rather than voicing his doubt to his supposed fellow pilgrims. The
audience listens as the Pardoner shares the tricks of his trade with
his companions, who nevertheless travel onward, obstinately oblivious to the implications for their own pilgrimage. *Both* audiences
(within and outside the poem) enjoy the privileged knowledge of the
rioters' treacherous manoeuvring even as each continues to believe
that, despite their oath breaking, they are protected by the others'
word. The suppression of doubt by the narrator, the pilgrims and
the rioters is thus as much at the heart of this text as the anxiety
about what is real.

It is ironic then that critics have been ignoring the particular
doubt the narrator raises over the figure of the Pardoner when he
says 'I trowe he were a geldyng or a mare' (l. 691). Even as the Pardoner has been embraced as 'a complicated sort of gay "ancestor"'
by first gay and lesbian studies and later by queer theorists, just one
critic has been prepared to doubt his essential masculinity, though
several have accepted his masculinity as neutered or castrated.[1] 'Over
the years, he has been identified variously as "feminoid", as a literal
or metaphorical eunuch, as a hermaphrodite, as "homosexual" or
"gay", as a "normal" (i.e. "heterosexual") man, etc.'[2] The question
of whether the Pardoner is a 'mare', a woman passing as a man,[3]
was thus ignored, despite being the most straightforward gloss, until
Jeffrey Rayner Myers ventured to suggest in 2000 that 'this sexually
ambiguous character might be a woman'.[4] In this article, I want to
add further support to Myers' assertion and to suggest that understanding it in these terms allows a parallel to emerge between the
figure of the Pardoner, relics and oaths, bringing out a narrative
interest across General Prologue, Prologue and Tale in accident and
substance, doubt and complicity.

The primary, and now overly familiar, reason for the Pardoner
being claimed as that 'complicated sort of gay "ancestor"' lies in the
description of the Pardoner in the General Prologue:

> A voys he hadde as smal as hath a goot.
> No berd hadde he, ne nevere sholde have,
> As smothe it was as it were late shave.
> I trowe he were a geldyng or a mare. (ll. 688–691)

It was Walter Curry in 1919 who suggested that 'gelding' should be
taken as meaning 'eunuch', and Robert Miller built on this in 1955

by suggesting that eunuchry was associated with sin in the Middle Ages, symbolizing a man 'sterile in good works, impotent to produce spiritual fruit'.[5] Monica McAlpine then suggested that 'mare' should be understood as meaning 'effeminate male' and, by association, 'a homosexual'.[6] This meaning then became fossilized in the *Riverside Chaucer*'s gloss of l. 691, 'a eunuch or a homosexual', and has led to 'growing critical interest in the Pardoner as queer'.[7]

Putting aside the problematic assumptions about homosexuals and the anachronistic mapping of modern concepts of sexuality onto the medieval period that underlie the readings of the Pardoner as gay – which have been dealt with comprehensively by others – even a moment of close reading reveals the jarring slips that occurred during this accretive interpretative process.[8] One word, *gelding*, was interpreted as a straightforward simile to mean either a congenital eunuch or a castrated man; the other word, *mare*, was interpreted in a convoluted fashion to mean a man who desires other men. Yet, while there are many instances in the *Middle English Dictionary* of *gelding* being used literally to mean 'a gelded horse' and euphemistically 'a castrated man', the only recorded uses of *mare* are concerned with horses and female promiscuity.[9] As Myers puts it, this is 'one of the oddest misinterpretations ... the term for a female horse, has, with no compelling justification, been interpreted for the last fifty years as meaning the Pardoner might be a homosexual instead of the more obvious implication that "he" might be a "she"'.[10] In other words, the narrator suggests that the Pardoner might be a eunuch or a woman passing as a man, successfully enough but not faultlessly enough to allay entirely the narrator's suspicion of the high voice and lack of beard.

Yet the narrator's assertion that the Pardoner 'were a geldyng or a mare' has only been read in terms of effeminate or impaired masculinity, and once rather confusingly as a 'testicular pseudo-hermaphrodite of the feminine type'.[11] This has provoked readings, such as Carolyn Dinshaw's 'eunuch hermeneutics', that have emphasized lack.[12] As she put it, 'constituted by *absence*, he [the Pardoner] sets his listeners to thinking about Presence, about radical Being in which there is no lack and in which all difference and division are obviated'.[13] Following a similar vein, Robert Sturges argues that '*neither* clearly male *nor* clearly female, indeterminate in gender and erotic practice as well as anatomical makeup, his fragmented gender identity and possibly dismembered body are without authority'.[14] While these critical readings offer much, they only speak to one part of the 'gelding or a mare' line, the part that implies a neutered masculinity.

This critical lacuna is all the more puzzling given that when Chaucer was writing there were several texts in which writers presented women passing as men. The widely circulated *Gilte Legende* included two saints' lives in which a female dresses, lives and passes as male, without suspicion, until her death. Gower included the legend of Iphis and Achilles' successful disguise as a maid in the *Confessio Amantis*. There were also Old French texts with similar episodes, such as *Yde et Olive* and the *Roman de Silence*, while Boccaccio included the tale of Pope Joan in *De mulieribus claris*, as well as the stories of a female disguised as an abbot and a steward in the *Decameron* (Day II, Tales III and IX).[15] Myers alludes to 'a tradition of cross-dressing women' in his article as part of Chaucer's cultural milieu, but the term 'cross-dressing' obscures the extent to which these texts illustrate a medieval understanding that gender could be performed and that someone could 'pass' for a different gender. To cross-dress means to wear the clothes of the 'opposite' gender without necessarily attempting or having the ability to pass, and can imply just the opposite. For instance, when Sir Lancelot dresses as a maid to joust with Sir Dinadan in the *Morte Darthur*, the ruse is immediately apparent: as soon as Sir Dinadan sees 'a maner of a damesell, he dradde perellys lest hit sholde be Sir Launcelot disgysed'.[16] As Judith Butler puts it in a discussion of drag:

> If one thinks that one sees a man dressed as a woman or a woman dressed as a man, then one takes the first term of each of those perceptions as the 'reality' of gender: the gender that is introduced through the simile lacks 'reality', and is taken to constitute an illusory appearance ... we think we know what the reality is, and take the secondary appearance of gender to be mere artifice, play, falsehood, and illusion.[17]

In contrast, when someone passes, 'it is no longer possible to derive a judgement about stable anatomy from the clothes that cover and articulate the body'.[18] Although 'passing' is a modern term, these examples suggest that the underlying notion that someone might be accepted as another gender was familiar to Chaucer's contemporaries and, in particular, the idea that a woman might successfully pass as a man. In such texts, the only people who see through the gender presentation of the figure concerned are the narrator and the reader, who 'know' the anatomy beneath the clothing.

For instance, in Book IV of the *Confessio Amantis*, Gower retells the Ovidian tale of Iphis and Ianthe.[19] The reader is told that King Ligdus had promised to kill any girls his wife bore, and that when she 'hadde a dowhter' (l. 456) she said instead that 'it were a Sone' and 'the fader was mad so to wene' (ll. 459–461). This Iphis is accordingly 'clothed and arrayed so / Riht as a kings sone scholde' (ll. 464–465) and manages to pass so successfully as male that she is married to Ianthe, 'a Duckes dowhter' (l. 469). Although Gower's efficient tale leaves much unsaid, the implication is that beyond the queen's intimate circle, Iphis passes as male in both the king's and the duke's households. In Book V, Gower gives us a similar story in the form of the tale of Achilles and Deidamia, but here it is a son who passes as female and the idea of passing is unpacked further. The reader is told that his mother, Thetis, brings him up as a girl in order to protect him. It is not simply clothing that makes Achilles 'seme a pure maid' (l. 3009), but his 'sobre and goodli contenance' (l. 2964), his 'vois' and his 'pas' (l. 3151), which he has been 'tawht' with 'gret diligence' (ll. 3003–3004). Gower describes Thetis teaching him how 'He scholde his wommanhiede avance' (l. 3006) and so suggests that Achilles' femininity is as much 'his' as any claim to masculinity, and that it might be developed.

More relevant to our purpose, the popular *Gilte Legende* acquainted many devout, late medieval readers with the lives of St Marina and St Theodora, both of whom were supposed to have lived for a substantial period as monks, only being discovered to have female bodies at their deaths. 'The Liff of Seint Maurine' tells the story of a 'noble virgine' who enters a monastery with her father after the death of her mother, the father changing her clothing 'so that men wende that she hadde be his sone'.[20] The reader is told that after many years the father died, but not before swearing Maurine to continued secrecy about her sex and so she 'contynued her lyff as an holy monke vnknouynge to alle creatures that she was a woman' (p. 371). Although the text emphasizes only that Maurine dressed as a monk, the performance of masculinity is so convincing that the abbot believes a local woman's claim that 'the monke Maryn ... hadde gote her withe childe' (p. 372) and is only disabused of this notion after Maurine dies and the monks tasked with washing the body 'perceyued that she was a woman' (p. 372). The 'Liff of Seint Theodore' is very similar in many respects. In this life, there is a prelude in which Theodore commits adultery before repenting so much that 'she toke the clothinge of a man and wente to a chirche of monkes ... and required that she might be receyued withe the monkes' (p. 458). In this Life, it is only supernatural beings that can see through the outward display of masculinity and the 'fend' in particular who sees her as a 'wicked woman ... and avouterere' (p. 458). Even her abandoned husband, who passes near her in town and whom she greets, does not recognize her as female until an angel informs him 'that ... was thi wiff' (p. 458).

While St Maurine and Theodore are portrayed as interacting with relatively few people, and then only on monastic business, enclosed within their monasteries and immediate surrounds, Boccaccio offers the tale of 'de Iohanna anglica papa' or Pope Joan in *De mulieribus claris* in which a woman passes as a male ecclesiast within a much wider world. He begins by saying that 'from her name John [she] would seem to be a man, but in reality she was a woman' and outlines how, after falling in love, she fled her father's house, changed her name and dressed as a young man, following him to England where she was 'universally taken for a cleric' ('clericus ex[is]timatus ab omnibus').[21] He goes on to tell how she discovered a love of learning after her lover died, and progressed through the clerical ranks until she became pope. She was only discovered when – having taken another lover after a long period of virtue – she gave birth in the street during a procession for the Rogation Days, celebrated on 25 April. Boccaccio emphasizes throughout the short tale that Joan 'was believed by everyone to be a man' ('homo ab omnibus creditus', p. 439) and that it was only through childbirth that she revealed 'how long she had deceived everyone except her lover' ('enixa publice patuit qua fraude tam diu, preter amasium, ceteros decepisset homines', p. 441). Moreover, he stresses that she was famous both before and after the deception was revealed. While she was thought to be a man, through her 'outstanding virtue and holiness' ('singulari honestate ac sanctitate', p. 439) she 'became widely known' ('ideo notus a multis', p. 439), and since her discovery, all popes 'condemn her foul actions and perpetuate her infamy' ('detestandam spurcitiem et nominis continuandam memoriam', p. 441). In 'de Iohanna anglica papa', Chaucer would have found all the inspiration he needed for the Pardoner in the form of an English woman passing not just as a man, but as the highest male ecclesiast of them all on a religious procession in April.

All these medieval tales of passing share an interest in uncovering what lies beneath the clothes of their protagonists, as if the imagined

physical body offers a point of stable truth if only the gait, manner-
isms and voice of gender expression can be put aside by stripping
and stilling the body, either in bed or in death. Gower dwells on the
image of Iphis and Ianthe 'liggende abedde upon a nyht ... so that
thei use / Thing which to hem was al unknowe' (ll. 475–479), the last
phrase suggesting both virginal exploration and the use of genitals –
like the Wife of Bath's 'thynges smale' (l. 121). The *Gilte Legende*
displays Maurine's body first to the brethren who 'perceyued that
she was a woman' (p. 372) and then to the abbot, who 'seigh that she
was a woman' (p. 373), and Theodore is similarly seen first by the
abbot who 'vncovered her and fonde her a woman' (p. 460) and then
by the brethren who 'toke aweye the clothe and sayen that she was
a woman' (p. 461). Even more graphically, Boccaccio has Pope Joan
give birth in public. Such moments of revealing work to reassure the
reader that no matter how successful these women's performance of
masculinity is, they remain female bodied.

Diane Watt argues that the reason why Gower doesn't condemn
Iphis for living as a king's son is that, because 'women were perceived to be inferior to men, such a transformation from female
to male could only be seen as an improvement, a change from an
imperfect state to a perfect one; it could bestow on woman a potency
she would otherwise lack'.[22] We could equally apply this to Saints
Maurine and Theodore, but this does not seem to explain the need
to emphasize these figures' naked bodies. Rather, there seems to
be a parallel here with the way in which the subversive potential of
men performing femininity is contained by ultimately emphasizing
the performers' masculinity. For example, in the *Confessio Amantis*,
Thetis takes the decision to disguise her son, not Achilles himself;
he is referred to throughout by male pronouns; he uses his disguise
to gain sexual advantage with a woman; and his male, heroic future
is never in doubt. In another example, the *Morte Darthur*, Lancelot
disguises himself as a maiden only so that he can sneak up on the
unsuspecting Sir Dinadan and strike him off his horse in a show of
martial ability. As Ad Putter puts it, writers partly defuse these episodes' 'subversive potential ... because of the *a priori* assurance that
all its active participants are male anyway'.[23] Such episodes suggest
that Achilles' and Lancelot's performances of femininity are only
transient and that masculinity has only been temporarily surren-
dered, containing any sense of profound upheaval. This is mirrored
in the final emphasis on female bodies in the lives of Maurine,

Theodore and Joan and in the tale of Iphis before Cupid's transformation, as if it assuages an anxiety about the ability of women to lay
claim to masculinity by marking its limitations. Perhaps the emphasis on the underlying feminine body is made all the more necessary
because these tales are primarily about women gaining control over
their lives: by passing as a king's son, Iphis not only escapes death,
but becomes heir to her father and husband to a duke's daughter;
by passing as a boy, Maurine avoids being left an orphan by her
mother's death and father's vocation, as well as gaining a monastic
home and a community; Theodore moves from being an adulterous
wife to a valued member of the monastery. Most strikingly of all,
Joan gains 'the Fisherman's throne' ('Piscatoris cathedram', p. 439),
the 'highest apostolate' ('apostolatus culmen', p. 439). Seen in this
light, the reminder of their female bodies acts as counterbalance
to the image of these women passing as male, much as Iphis's apparently thwarted desire, the unjust punishments of Maurine and
Theodore and the public exposure of Joan act as a counterbalance
to their social gains. The emphasis on the naked, female body nar-
ratively castrates their performance of masculinity, containing its
potential to unsettle power relations.

It perhaps also reflects an anxiety about women usurping not
just the outward manner of men, but their sexual role too. Although
fewer than ten cases survive of prosecutions of female homosexuality from before the French Revolution for the whole of Europe, those
that do suggest that the women who were punished were those who
passed as men *and* used dildos. 'Since the definition of sexuality was
phallic, criminal lesbian sexuality could only be phallic, which led
ultimately to the definition of a lesbian act punishable by death ...
as one in which a woman has sexual relations with another woman
by means of "any material instrument".'[24] For instance, Katherine
Hetzeldorferin of Nuremberg was put on trial in Speyer in 1477 for
presenting as a man and fabricating a dildo. She was found guilty
and drowned, while her partners were banished, making a 'distinction between the "guilty" manlike woman and her "innocent" partners'.[25] Such historical examples suggest that these tales' emphasis
on the uncovered, implicitly unsupplemented female body works to
position their central figures' transgression as acceptably limited by
excluding the possibility – according to medieval understanding –
of them engaging in sex with other women. Since they make no
attempt to 'pack', that is, to create a phallus for themselves,[26] their

sexual ability is presented as unsatisfactory in the case of Iphis or denied in the case of the saints, where pregnancy is used as proof of sex, focusing the readers' attention exclusively on sex that is simultaneously phallic *and* procreative. These women passing as men can be recuperated by divine transformation into either men or saints not just because 'a transformation from female to male could only be seen as an improvement' but because their bodies remain stable beneath their clothes. Iphis's, Maurine's and Theodore's portrayal as needing to disguise themselves for safety's sake – because of their social isolation or to atone for sin – and the final images of female nakedness deny that any claim is being made to full male 'potency'.

The idea that the performance of another gender could be learned was not restricted to those retelling fabulous stories, even if it was not widespread. A contemporary of Chaucer's, John or Eleanor Rykener, exemplified this possibility. In 1384, the aldermen of London heard the trial of 'John Rykener, calling [himself] Eleanor' who had been arrested 'having been detected in women's clothing' having sex with John Britby, who claimed he had no idea that Eleanor was not a woman.[27] The record states that Britby 'accosted John Rykener, dressed up as a woman, thinking he was a woman, asking him as he would a woman if he would commit a libidinous act'.[28] This formulation emphasizes both the outward appearance of Rykener and its persuasiveness. Moreover, the records reveal that Rykener was also 'living and doing embroidery as a woman in Oxford'[29] under the tutelage of Elizabeth Brodeurer, who 'first dressed him in women's clothing'. As the editors of the record point out, it 'stands practically alone for medieval England as a description of same-sex intercourse and male transvestism',[30] and the questions it raises about the 'performative nature of the medieval understanding of gender and the issues of "passing" that arise from it ... are a heavy burden for John/Eleanor Rykener to bear alone'.[31] Nevertheless, in combination with Gower's tales of Iphis and Achilles and the lives of Maurine, Theodore and Joan, it suggests that Chaucer and his contemporaries would have been acquainted with the idea of passing.

If texts in which women passed for men were familiar to Chaucer's contemporaries, they must still have raised questions for them: did those around Iphis, Theodore or Maurine *really* never notice a difference, or to put it another way, *how* were they able to pass? In the narrator's description of the Pardoner, Chaucer playfully suggests an answer to this conundrum: the viewer is conscious of doubt but for some reason allows himself no more than a passing speculation over the smooth face and high voice. Nevertheless, though suppressed, the doubt remains implicit in the way the narrator keeps returning his eye to the Pardoner's lap, drawing the reader's attention there too. Having described the Pardoner's long, lank hair that 'his shuldres overspradde' (GP l. 678),[32] he adds that 'he' did not wear a hood, but rather 'it was trussed up in his walet' (l. 681). Five lines later, the narrator again mentions 'his walet, biforn hym in his lappe / Bretful of pardoun' (ll. 686–687) and three lines after describing the small voice and smooth cheeks of the Pardoner, refers to how in 'his' pouch or 'male he hadde a pilwe-beer' (l. 694). Unless we are to imagine a Pardoner festooned with bags, Chaucer seems to be giving us a wry image of a person who lacks some signs of adult masculinity with a lap or crotch area stuffed with a hood, a bundle of pardons *and* a pillowcase purporting to be Our Lady's veil. Indeed, the use of the homonym 'male' for wallet, with its latent connotations of masculinity, seems deliberate in this context. If we approach this image from the starting point that the Pardoner has a male body, we might see this only as a joke about an emasculated man – congenital or otherwise – overcompensating for his lack. But if we approach the image open to the alternative that the Pardoner is a woman passing as a man, then there are ideas in play not only of lack but also of substitution through the allusion to packing – the stuffing of the lap or the fashioning of a 'material instrument' in emulation of a male crotch – and this in turn offers a rich comparison with the relics the Pardoner says 'he' has and the way 'he' uses them:

> ... a gobet of the seyl
> That Seint Peter hadde, whan that he wente
> Upon the see, til Jhesu Crist hym hente.
> He hadde a croys of latoun ful of stones,
> And in a glas he hadde pigges bones. (ll. 696–700)

The narrator describes how the Pardoner offers these manufactured relics to the flock of 'a povre person dwellynge upon lond' (l. 701) in return for 'moore moneye / Than that the person gat in monthes tweye' (ll. 701–704). In this way, there are a series of substitutions: replacing the 'povre person', the Pardoner acts the part 'in chirche [of] a noble ecclesiaste' (l. 708); replacing Our Lady's veil, 'he' offers a pillowcase; in place of a reliquary, 'he' offers pig's bones encased in glass.[33] However, at each stage others accept what 'he' offers and the claims 'he' makes for these objects.

Robyn Malo persuasively argues that the Pardoner is successful in cozening the parishes because of 'his' manipulation of relic discourse. 'Before he brings out his supposedly holy objects, he predisposes his audience, by his rhetorical strategies, to believe the relics he will show them are real.'[34] However, for such strategies to be convincing there has to be a degree of cooperation on the part of the listener, and this is secured for the Pardoner by 'his' listeners' desire to have access to these lesser relics. Since the most notable relics, like those at Canterbury, were 'often jealously guarded and rarely exposed to the public-at-large',[35] less notable relics offered greater access to spiritual power than was usually available to the laity. As Malo argues, in the 'Pardoner's Tale' the laity's desire to have access to what is usually inaccessible encourages them to suspend their doubts, since to admit or voice them would be to acknowledge and accept the carefully controlled distance between them and more notable sacred objects. Enquiring too deeply into the veracity of the Pardoner's claims would also require the consistent doubter to question claims made by more reputable relic custodians, since they rely upon the same strategies. The pig's bones and sheep's jaw are accepted, therefore, not just because of the way they are presented, but because of the willingness of the viewers to collude with the idea that presentation verifies what lies beneath.

There is a parallel then between the experience of looking at the Pardoner and looking at a relic, where the viewer can never really know what lies beneath, whether it is a portion of a saint's skeleton or just 'pigges bones'. Unlike Gower or the translator of the *Gilte Legende*, Chaucer refuses the reader confirmation of an underlying anatomical 'truth'. Instead of stripping the Pardoner bare, he teases the reader by successively placing more material layers over the Pardoner's genitals, making it impossible to know what lies beneath: complete male genitals, male genitals that lack something, unadorned female genitals, or female genitals that have been supplemented? The viewer must choose whether to suppress or voice their doubt and take the attendant risk of bringing into question the very idea that the performance of gender is underpinned by the body underneath. Thus, the Pardoner's 'bretful' lap offers a fuller parallel to 'his' cynical supplanting of parish priests and replacing of relics if both the meaning of 'gelding' and 'mare' are allowed to play, as it suggests not only a deliberate deception on the part of the Pardoner but both the complicit acceptance on the part of those looking and the motivation for it. This reading abolishes the division the narrator places between himself and those he sees as the Pardoner's 'apes' (l. 706), the 'povre person and the peple'. In recognizing that the Pardoner might be a 'gelding or a mare', but continuing to call the Pardoner 'he' and refraining from any challenge, the narrator's response to this ambiguous gender performance echoes contemporary responses to relics and suggests why the Pardoner's fakes are successful.

By the time, then, that Chaucer's audience encounter the 'Pardoner's Tale', they have been primed to question the relationship between surface and underlying reality. This way of thinking is further encouraged when the Pardoner begins 'his' preaching by helping the audience (pilgrim and real) to understand the world of the 'younge folk that haunteden folye' (l. 464) allegorically. They eat and drink 'thurgh which they doon the devel sacrifise' (l. 469) in 'stywes' and 'tavernes' (l. 465) that are the 'develes temple' (l. 470), and enjoy the company of 'tombesteres ... frutesteres, / Syngeres ... baudes, wafereres' (ll. 477–479) who are 'the verray develes officeres' (l. 480). Like Lot, '[they] nyste what [they] wroghte' (l. 487). As part of this introduction to 'his' exposition on sin, the Pardoner gives a particularly gruesome example of how language (and not just actions) might be conceived of as doing more than is immediately apparent:

> Hir othes been so grete and so dampnable
> That it is grisly for to heere hem swere.
> Oure blissed Lordes body they totere
> Hem thoughte that Jewes rente hym noght ynough. (ll. 472–475)

It was a commonplace of medieval sermons that swearing by 'Goddes precious herte ... his nales ... the blood of Crist ... Goddes armes' (ll. 651–654) renewed Christ's wounds. Such rebukes were meant to arouse the listener's pity for Christ's suffering and make them think twice about using this language by emphasizing its callousness and their lack of reflection on the purpose of the wounds they invoked through a comparison with the cruelty and lack of understanding of those who were at the Crucifixion. They were meant to convey that swearing was a sin that devalued Christ's sacrifice by the invocation of his pains for expressive effect. As the Parson puts it: 'semeth it that men that sweren so horribly by his [Christ's] blessed name, that they despise it moore booldely than dide the cursede Jewes or elles the devel, that trembleth when he heereth his name' (l. 598). These admonishments also drew on the notion that Christ died for mankind's sins, even those not yet born, and so every Christian's sins were impetus to his suffering.

Yet this complex use of the physical tearing of Christ's body as a metaphor for the way in which swearing both devalued the meaning of the Crucifixion and – through a theology of the Cross that emphasized Christ making satisfaction for man – necessitated his suffering was often flattened into the simplistic idea that swearing *actually* wounded Christ anew. We can see this blurring in the lines quoted above and in the 'Parson's Tale' where the language hovers between the metaphorical and literal: 'ne swereth nat so synfully in dismembrynge of Crist by soule, herte, bones, and body. For certes, it semeth that ye thynke that the cursede Jewes ne dismembred nat ynough the preciouse persone of Crist, byt ye dismembre hym moore' (ll. 590–591). But as 'his' Tale progresses, the Pardoner repeats this notion in a form that entirely obscures its complexity: 'And many a grisly ooth thanne han they sworn, / And Cristes blessed body they torente' (ll. 708–709). In these lines, the oaths are explicitly presented as doing something, moving from being 'grisly for to heere' to being described simply as 'grisly', as if the words were material and could enact torture, becoming besmirched with the blood of Christ's torn body. Far more is going on than is immediately apparent from the oaths' surface meaning. By beginning the tale in this manner – with an allegorical reading of the rioters' feasting and swearing – Chaucer focuses attention on trying to discern truth from surface detail and raises the question of what some speech does beyond communicate. This is an important prelude to a tale with oaths at its heart.

Modern linguists would describe the swearing of oaths as performative speech. John L. Austin originally defined such speech acts as meeting two conditions: 'A. they do not "describe" or "report" or constate anything at all, are not "true or false"; and B. the uttering of the sentence is, or is part of, the doing of an action, which again would not *normally* be described as, or as "just", saying something'.[36] An example of this would be '"I name this ship the *Queen Elizabeth*" – as uttered when smashing the bottle against the stern'.[37] Although Chaucer lacked the theory and vocabulary of modern linguists, he seems to have been particularly intrigued by this notion that saying something *did* something.[38] William Orth, for instance, has argued that 'we can ... trace a proto-awareness of *performativity*' in the 'Prioress's Tale' which hinges on the 'misperformance of the *Alma redemptoris mater*'[39] by the schoolboy, who sees it as merely a *representative* utterance – to use John Searle's term – that praises Mary's virtuous qualities, as opposed to a *directive* utterance that requests something of her.[40] Similarly, Mary Godfrey has proposed that the old woman's curse in the 'Summoner's Tale' allowed Chaucer to explore how cursing 'exists as not merely the speech act, the enunciated words, but at the beginning of the promised act – the outcome of the curse'.[41]

As the Pardoner progresses in his discussion of swearing, Chaucer adds to this idea that language might *do* something:

> Gret sweryng is a thyng abhominable,
> And fals sweryng is yet moore reprevable...
> 'Thou shalt swere sooth thyne othes, and nat lye,
> And swere in doom and eek in rightwisnesse';
> But ydel sweryng is a cursednesse. (ll. 631–638)

The distinction made by the Pardoner is between the swearing of oaths in confirmation of a truth, which might be classed as *representative* utterances, and swearing casually as an *expressive* utterance. Although Chaucer did not have such terms available, the Pardoner makes a similar division between oaths that have a role within 'doom and ... rightwisnesse', and 'gret' or 'ydel' swearing. The Parson expands on this at more length: 'Thou shalt sweren eek in doom, whan thou art constreyned by thy domesman to witnessen the trouthe. Eek thow shalt nat swere for envye, ne for favour, ne for meede, but for rightwisnesse, for declaracioun of it, to the worshipe of God and helpyng of thyne evene-Cristene' (l. 594). The Pardoner's use of Jeremiah 4.2 in lines 635–636 thus reminds the reader that well-made oaths perform a range of actions: they witness, declare justice and worship God. At the same time, the allusion to 'fals sweryng' introduces the notion that while oaths have this immense potential, they can also be deceptive or misleading, failing to bear true witness, establish justice or praise God. In other words, that the words of an oath are not enough to bring about such effects, or as Austin put it:

> The uttering of the words is, indeed, usually a, or even the, leading incident in the performance of the act ... but it is far from being usually, even if it is ever, the sole thing necessary if the act is to be deemed to have been performed. Speaking generally, it is always necessary that the circumstances in which the words are uttered should be in some way, or ways, appropriate...[42]

Austin called these necessary circumstances 'felicity' conditions and went on to outline them:

> (A.1) There must exist an accepted conventional procedure having a certain conventional effect, that procedure to include the uttering of certain words by certain persons in certain circumstances, and further,
>
> (A.2) the particular persons and circumstances in a given case must be appropriate for the invocation of the particular procedure invoked.
>
> (B.1) The procedure must be executed by all participants both correctly and
>
> (B.2) completely.
>
> (Γ.1) Where, as often, the procedure is designed for use by persons having certain thoughts or feelings, or for the inauguration of certain consequential conduct on the part of any participant, then a person participating in and so invoking the procedure must in fact have those thoughts or feelings, and the participants must intend so to conduct themselves, and further
>
> (Γ.2) must actually so conduct themselves subsequently.[43]

When conditions A-B are not met, he called the performative utterance a 'misfire', but he termed failures to meet Γ-conditions as 'abuses'.[44] So in the case of 'fals sweryng' there is an abuse in that the person's thoughts or feelings do not match what they say and so they deliberately mislead their hearers. The reference to such a familiar abuse of performative language as swearing at the start of the 'Pardoner's Tale', as well as other references in the tale's opening to 'lesynges ... deceite, and cursed forswerynges' (ll. 591–592), foregrounds an anxiety that apparently solemn performative utterances may be void.

It is not just the extended discussion of oaths that achieves this. The Pardoner also uses language associated with transubstantiation to decry cooks in the lines that began this article, bringing to the reader's mind the declarative utterance that would usually transform the 'substaunce' of bread into the body of Christ, leaving only the 'accident' or appearance of bread.[45] It is hard to disagree with Robinson's assertion that 'Chaucer can hardly have used this phrase without thinking of the current controversy about the Eucharist',[46] which centred in part on Wyclif's objection that a priest does not '"make" the body of Christ daily by saying mass ... he simply "makes" in the host a sign of the Lord'.[47] Contemporaries persuaded by Wyclif's arguments did not see the priest's words over the bread as performative. More importantly, even those who did believe in transubstantiation might be concerned about the words of the mass being void. As Niamh Patwell points out, the Lollard text *Of Prelates* argued that 'þe preiers of cursed prestis in þe masse ben cursed of god & his angelis, & certis a prest may be so cursed 7 in heresie þat he makeþ not þe sacrament'.[48] The regularity with which conservative religious writers assured their readers that, on the contrary, the spiritual state of the celebrant did not affect the efficacy of the sacrament suggests that Chaucer's contemporaries had some notion that there were felicity conditions for the Eucharist to be transformed:

> ...What man hath takyn the ordyr of presthode, be he nevyr so vicyows a man in hys levyng, yyf he sey dewly tho wordys ovyr the bred that owr Jord Jhesu Criste seyde ... it is hys very flesch and hys blood and no material bred...[49]

Although writers such as Margery Kempe tried to assuage such doubts, even while asserting their own orthodoxy, the fact that such assertions continued to be made until the sixteenth century suggests that they were unsuccessful in convincing the laity that the only felicity conditions for the offering of the Eucharist were that there be a priest, that he say the words Christ said and that there be bread. The combination of the references to swearing and transubstantiation at the start of the 'Pardoner's Tale' focuses attention on the way in which the effect of a performative utterance might not match what it purported to do. Thus, the concerns of the General Prologue and the Pardoner's Prologue with the ways in which surface presentation can occlude or misrepresent an underlying reality are extended to encompass language at the very start of the tale.

Indeed, the ability of performative utterances to misfire or be abused is what gives the tale its dramatic tension. The listener's pleasure in following the tale as it unfolds lies in the heightened awareness that the rioters' fraternal oaths do not offer them the safety they assume. The rioters in the tale make a *declarative* utterance when they swear to be brothers: 'Lat ech of us holde up his hand til oother, / And ech of us bicomen otheres brother' (ll. 697–698). In doing so, they meet Austin's A-B conditions: the clasping of hands and the swearing of familial ties was accepted as creating a special bond between unrelated people (A.1); as men, they are appropriate people to invoke the procedure of swearing brotherhood (A.2); and they all raise their hands and swear the oath correctly (A.3–4), allowing one to assert later, 'Thow knowest wel thou art my sworen brother' (l. 808). Yet it swiftly becomes apparent that even if the men did initially have fraternal and loyal feelings towards each other (Γ.1), they do not conduct themselves accordingly but become murderously rivalrous (Γ.2), resulting in an abuse of the performative utterance.

There are other speech acts in the 'Pardoner's Tale' that also clearly lack efficacy because the felicity conditions are not present. For instance, the old man in the tale makes three declarative utterances when he blesses the 'riotoures' (l. 661):

'Now, lordes, God yow see!' (l. 715)
'And God be with yow, where ye go or ryde!' (l. 748)
'God save yow, that boghte agayn mankynde, / And yow amende!'
(ll. 766–767)

In doing so, he appears to meet at least conditions A.1 and B.1–2, competently uttering customary words of benediction appropriate for any layman to offer. However, there is a *misfire* because the people he blesses are inappropriate subjects for a blessing (A.2). They are immersed in the sin of gluttony, committed to doing 'the devel sacrifise / Withinne the develes temple' (ll. 469–470), and resolutely suppressing any contrition that would allow God to look after them, accompany them in their actions or save them from damnation. Similarly, in his final address to the listening pilgrims, the Pardoner repeats the declarative utterance that he would use to forgive a sinner, which relies on the extra-linguistic institution of absolution: 'I yow assoille, by myn heigh power' (l. 913), but it is not at all clear that the Pardoner has the power to offer this under the terms of his office (A.2).[50]

What all these examples draw attention to is the way in which medieval life was patterned by speech acts that were meant to offer consolation through the idea that with words truth could be verified, brotherhood and loyalty created, bread transformed, blessing bestowed and absolution offered. Yet the desire for such speech acts to be effective – and their repeated citation is evidence enough of this – coexisted with a persistent anxiety that they would not be, or even *could* not be. In the 'Pardoner's Tale', the reader is gradually made to question the potential effect of performative speech even as the tale's figures curse, swear fraternity and bless others. In this way, the tale has the potential to reveal the reader's own investment in, and compulsion to uphold, a belief that words can change reality because what is at stake in paying too much attention to felicity conditions is a crumbling of a whole edifice of consolation. In much the same way that the coexistence of a relic cult with doubt about the veracity of relics can only be explained in terms of complicity, a belief in the efficacy of performative speech acts is only possible by turning away from too close a consideration of their felicity conditions. Through the figure of the Pardoner and his Tale, Chaucer made his readers newly aware of the delicate balance required by their faith between opposing ideas. As Wendy Love Anderson put it, 'otherwise unremarkable laypeople perform[ed] relatively sophisticated mental operations in order to integrate doctrinal tensions ... into their daily lives'.[51]

To return then to the tale-teller, we can see a rich parallel in the narrator's suppressed doubt over the Pardoner's gender and the ways in which the congregations in the Prologue accept 'his' relics and the tale's figures continue to believe in their speech acts. The narrator cannot question the Pardoner too closely because that would be to acknowledge that what is declared – either by speech or outward symbol – is no good predictor of what is true. A whole system of structuring the world by male and female is at stake in the instance of gender. Similarly, to challenge one relic's value is to open the door to doubting all relics, along with the idea that they might not be efficacious, and to doubt the ability of solemn performative utterances to transform reality is to challenge a whole religious system. Yet to stay silent is to become complicit, whether in the masquerading of a woman within the lower orders of the Church, the passing off of animal refuse as relics or the abuse of speech acts. In this way, the Pardoner's passing (and others' response to it) matters because it allows the reader to begin to think through the implications of ignored doubt long before the more serious questions of relic veracity or Eucharistic transformation are introduced. Ultimately, the reason why the Pardoner offers fellow pilgrims 'his' 'relics' even after revealing 'his' tricks is because 'he' is cynically conscious of this desire to affirm their veracity; this compulsion to avoid thinking too deeply about the relationship between reality and outward appearance. The reason why the Host reacts angrily is because in rejecting the relics, he is – against his will – forced momentarily to call into question the whole basis of the pilgrimage.

Alex da Costa is a Senior Lecturer in the English Faculty, University of Cambridge. Her research focuses on incunabula and early printed books meant for an English readership.

Notes

I am very grateful to Jacqueline Tasioulas and Lucy Allen for their comments on an earlier version of this article.

1. Carolyn Dinshaw, *Getting Medieval: Sexualities and Communities, Pre- and Post-modern* (Durham, NC: Duke University Press, 1999), 114.

2. Robert Sturges, 'The Pardoner Veiled and Unveiled', in *Becoming Male in the Middle Ages*, ed. Jeffrey Cohen and Bonnie Wheeler (London: Routledge, 1997), 262. Donald Howard has come closest to emphasizing both the feminine and masculine possibilities of the Pardoner, describing him as '*feminoid* in a starkly physical way – his voice, his hair, his beard are involved ... He is a mystery, an enigma – sexually anomalous, hermaphroditic...'. Donald R. Howard, *The Idea of the Canterbury Tales* (Berkeley, CA: University of California Press, 1976), 344–345.

3. 'Passing' can be defined as 'being accepted, or representing oneself successfully as, a member of a different ethnic, religious, or sexual group'. The first recorded use of this word with this sense was in 1926 but the meaning of the word has broadened to encompass ideas of gender and when used in such a context it means being accepted, or representing oneself successfully as, a different gender from the one assigned at birth. See 'pass, v.', *OED Online*, http://www.oed.com/view/Entry/138429?rskey=Qwcr0S&result=6&isAdvanced=false (accessed 4 September 2014).

4. Jeffrey Rayner Myers, 'Chaucer's Pardoner as Female Eunuch', *Studia Neophilologica* 72, no. 1 (2000): 54. Although I am concerned with a fictional character's gender representation here, Nancy Partner offers a complex analysis of how 'sex and gender offer an inadequate conceptual framework' for understanding past people. Nancy F. Partner, 'No Sex, No Gender', *Speculum* 68, no. 2 (1993): 442.

5. Walter Curry, 'The Secret of Chaucer's Pardoner', *Journal of English and Germanic Philology* 18, no. 4 (1919), 593–606; Robert Miller, 'Chaucer's Pardoner, the Scriptural Eunuch, and the Pardoner's Tale', *Speculum* 30, no. 2 (1955): 185.

6. Monica McAlpine, 'The Pardoner's Homosexuality and How It Matters', *PMLA* 95, no. 1 (1980): 11.

7. Dinshaw, *Getting Medieval*, 113–114.

8. For a critique of criticism on the Pardoner, see Gregory Gross, 'Trade Secrets: Chaucer, the Pardoner, the Critics', *Modern Language Studies* 25, no. 4 (1995), 1–36. See also Steven Kruger, who acknowledges that claims of the Pardoner as gay, 'though "historical" in that they participate in writing a certain gay history, are not necessarily "historicist"'. Steven Kruger, 'Claiming the Pardoner: Towards a Gay Reading of Chaucer's *Pardoner's Tale*', *Exemplaria* 6, no. 1 (1994): 119.

9. The *Middle English Dictionary* records two primary meanings for *gelding*: '(n.) 1(a) A gelded horse, gelding', e.g. 'Geldynge or gelde horse: Canterius' (*Promptorum Parvulorum*) and '2(a) A castrated man, a eunuch, a naturally impotent man', e.g. 'Deut.23.1: A geldynge, þe ballogys brusyd or kut off, & þe yarde kut awey,

shal not goon yn to þe chirche' (*Wycliffite Bible*). For *mare*, it offers the meaning '1. A riding horse, a steed ... any beast of burden', specifically a female horse and '*fig.* a bad woman, a slut', e.g. 'A, Lechery, thou skallyd mare!' (*Castle of Perseverance*). *Middle English Dictionary*, http://quod.lib.umich.edu/cgi/m/mec/med-idx?type=id&id=MED18336 and http://quod.lib.umich.edu/cgi/m/mec/med-idx?type=id&id=MED27420 (accessed 12 September 2016).

10. Myers, 'Chaucer's Pardoner as Female Eunuch', 55.

11. Beryl Rowland, 'Animal Imagery and the Pardoner's Abnormality', *Neophilologus* 48 (1964): 59.

12. Even Donald Howard, who labelled the Pardoner '*feminoid*' and refused to 'soften this unnerving fact into "feminine" or "effeminate"', argued that 'he *lacks* something: like a gelding the physical equipment, or like a mare the male gender-identity'. Howard, *The Idea of the Canterbury Tales*, 344, 343.

13. Carolyn Dinshaw, *Chaucer's Sexual Poetics* (Madison, WI: University of Wisconsin Press, 1989), 184. Emphasis mine.

14. Sturges, 'The Pardoner Veiled and Unveiled', 267. Emphasis mine.

15. I am grateful to Jacqueline Tasioulas for drawing my attention to Boccaccio's depiction of Pope Joan.

16. Myers, 'Chaucer's Pardoner as Female Eunuch', 54; *Sir Thomas Malory, Le Morte Darthur*, ed. Stephen Shepherd (New York: Norton & Company, 2004), 398.

17. Judith Butler, *Gender Trouble: Feminism and the Subversion of Identity*, 2nd edn (New York: Routledge, 1990; repr. 2007), vii–xxxvi, here xxiii.

18. Ibid., xxiv.

19. All line references are to *The English Works of John Gower*, ed. G. Macaulay (Oxford, 1900).

20. *Gilte Legende: Vol. I*, Early English Text Society, O.S. 327, ed. Richard Hamer (Oxford: Oxford University Press, 2006), 371. Hereafter all page references for the Lives of St Maurine and St Theodore are to this volume.

21. *Giovanni Boccaccio: Famous Women*, ed. and trans. Virginia Brown (Cambridge, MA: Harvard University Press, 2001), 439. All further references are to this text and from this edition.

22. Diane Watt, 'Gender and Sexuality in *Confessio Amantis*', in *A Companion to Gower*, ed. Siân Echard (Cambridge: D.S. Brewer, 2004), 192–213, here 207.

23. Ad Putter, 'Transvestite Knights in Medieval Life and Literature', in Cohen and Wheeler, *Becoming Male*, 279–302, here 286.

24. Edith Benkov, 'The Erased Lesbian: Sodomy and the Legal Tradition in Medieval Europe', in *Same Sex Love and Desire among Women in the Middle Ages*, ed. Francesca Canadé Sautman and Pamela Sheingorn (New York: Palgrave, 2001), 101–122, here 116.

25. Ibid., 116.

26. 'Packing' is a usefully succinct modern term for the strapping on of a soft or hard dildo to emulate the look of a male crotch and/or for sex.

27. David Lorenzo Boyd and Ruth Mazo Karras, 'The Interrogation of a Male Transvestite Prostitute in Fourteenth-Century London', *GLQ: A Journal of Lesbian and Gay Studies* 1 (1995): 482. Requoted in Dinshaw, *Getting Medieval*, 101.

28. Boyd and Karras, 'The Interrogation', 483.

29. Dinshaw, *Getting Medieval*, 109.

30. Boyd and Karras, 'The Interrogation', 479.

31. Ibid., 481.
32. GP refers to the General Prologue here. Hereafter line references are incorporated in the text.
33. Melvin Storm draws attention to how the Pardoner also functions within the structure of the *Canterbury Tales* as a 'meretricious surrogate for what the other pilgrims seek'. Melvin Storm, 'The Pardoner's Invitation: Quaestor's Bag or Becket's Shrine?', *PMLA* 97, no. 5 (1982): 810.
34. Robyn Malo, 'The Pardoner's Relics (and Why They Matter the Most)', *The Chaucer Review* 43, no. 1 (2008): 94.
35. Ibid., 86. Malo defines the types of relics: 'Notable relics must always consist of a body part, and, as a rule, they must be bigger (and better) than their non-notable counterparts. Non-notable relics extend to include the smaller or less important body parts of saints, as well as the material objects associated with the saints'. Ibid., 85.
36. John L. Austin, *How to Do Things with Words: The William James Lectures Delivered at Harvard University in 1955* (Oxford: Oxford University Press, 1955), 5.
37. Ibid., 6. Austin later abandoned the distinction between constatives and performative utterances, since even statements perform the act of stating, in favour of a distinction between 'explicit' and 'implicit' performatives.
38. Bruce Holsinger, 'Analytic Survey 6: Medieval Literature and Cultures of Performance', *New Medieval Literatures* 6 (2003): 271–311.
39. William Orth, 'The Problem of the Performative in Chaucer's Prioress Sequence', *The Chaucer Review* 42, no. 2 (2007): 198, 203.
40. John Searle refined Austin's approach by categorizing different performative utterances: '1. Representatives, which commit the speaker to the truth of the expressed proposition (paradigm cases: asserting, concluding) 2. Directives, which are attempts by the speaker to get the addressee to do something (paradigm cases: requesting, questioning) 3. Commissives, which commit the speaker to some future course of action (paradigm cases: promising, threatening, offering) 4. Expressives, which express a psychological state (paradigm cases: thanking, apologising, welcoming, congratulating) 5. Declarations, which effect immediate changes in the institutional state of affairs and which tend to rely on elaborate extra-linguistic institutions (paradigm cases: excommunicating, declaring war, christening, marrying, firing from employment)'. Geoffrey Finch, *Linguistic Terms and Concepts* (Basingstoke: Macmillan, 2000), 182.
41. Mary Godfrey, 'Only Words: Cursing and the Authority of Language in Chaucer's Friar's Tale', *Exemplaria* 10, no. 2 (1998): 324.
42. Austin, *How to Do Things*, 8.
43. Ibid., 14–15.
44. Ibid., 16.
45. For the fullest discussion of these lines, see Paul Strohm, 'Chaucer's Lollard Joke and the Textual Unconscious', *Studies in the Age of Chaucer* 17 (1995), 23–42.
46. *The Works of Geoffrey Chaucer*, ed. F.N. Robinson, 2nd edn (London: Oxford University Press, 1957), 730. For further Eucharistic and Passion parallels, see Niamh Patwell, '"The venym of symony": The Debate on the Eucharist in the Late Fourteenth Century and *The Pardoner's Prologue and Tale*', in *Transmission and Transformation in the Middle Ages: Texts and Contexts*, ed. Kathy Cawsey and Jason Harris (Dublin: Four Courts, 2007), 115–30; Rodney Delasanta, 'Sacrament and

Sacrifice in the *Pardoner's Tale*', *Annuale Mediaevale* 14 (1973), 43–52; Clarence H. Miller and Roberta Bux Bosse, 'Chaucer's Pardoner and the Mass', *Chaucer Review* 6 (1972), 171–84; and Robert Nicholls, 'The Pardoner's Ale and Cake', *PMLA* 82, no. 7 (1967), 498–504.

47. Paraphrased by Nicholls, 'The Pardoner's Ale and Cake', 502.

48. *Of Prelates: Unprinted English Works of Wyclif*, Early English Texts Society, O.S. 74, ed. F.D. Matthews (London, 1880), 102, quoted in Patwell, 'The Debate on the Eucharist', 127.

49. *The Book of Margery Kempe*, ed. Barry Windeatt (Harlow: Longman, 2000), 234–235.

50. Robert W. Shaffern, 'The Pardoner's Promises: Preaching and Policing Indulgences in the Fourteenth-Century English Church', *The Historian* 68, no. 1 (2006): 57–58.

51. Wendy Love Anderson, 'The Real Presence of Mary: Eucharistic Belief and the Limits of Orthodoxy in Fourteenth-Century France', *Church History* 75, no. 4 (2006): 749.

Chapter 11

'Double Sorrow'

The Complexity of Complaint in Chaucer's *Anelida and Arcite* and Henryson's *Testament of Cresseid*

Jacqueline Tasioulas

Robert Henryson defines his *Testament of Cresseid* as a companion piece to Chaucer's *Troilus and Criseyde*. The narrator tells us how, unable to sleep one cold spring night, he takes a copy of Chaucer's poem from the shelf and reads the tale of 'fair Creisseid and worthie Troylus' (42), and of the sorrow which the Trojan prince endures when his lover fails to return to Troy.[1] The author is heralded as 'worthie Chaucer glorious' (41), and yet Henryson's narrator never-theless casts doubt upon *Troilus and Criseyde*'s veracity, uttering the immortal line: 'Quha wait gif all that Chauceir wrait was trew?' (64). It is a forceful demand that places the work of the earlier poet under scrutiny right from the outset. This is not the 'reverend Chaucer' of Lydgate's verse, but rather an author whose work is being chal-lenged, either as somehow erroneous or else as in some way de-ceitful. It is, no doubt, a playful challenge, but the key question of truth is still being laid before us in order that we should consider

Notes for this section begin on page 245.

it as a fundamental theme in the work that will follow. Nor does the question limit itself to literary truth. What is being scrutinized is the more complicated question of the possible knowledge of truth – 'Quha wait?' – placed within the context of the dubious conveyance of truth in literary form. It is a Russian doll effect that Henryson presents at key moments in the narrative, as he embeds uncertainty within uncertainty, and sometimes lies within lies. The question of truth pervades the entire narrative of the *Testament* and lingers in the sources to which Henryson draws attention, for he employs not just one of Chaucer's explorations of falsity in love, but two. Beyond *Troilus and Criseyde* lies the love story of *Anelida and Arcite*. It is to this text that Henryson reaches at the climax of the *Testament* in order to explore the complexity of knowledge and the embedded layers of what constitutes 'truth', whether for the lover, the author or the reader.

Before that point, however, there is the matter of Henryson's teasing acrostic, 'O FICTIO' (57–63), placed just at the point where the narrator puts down his volume of Chaucer and selects another book, the inspiration for the *Testament* itself. The acrostic has engaged critics intent on establishing the existence or non-existence of the 'vther quair' (61) that Henryson's narrator claims as his source:

> Of his distres me neidis nocht reheirs,
> For worthie Chauceir in the samin buik,
> In gudelie termis and in ioly veirs,
> Compylit hes his cairis, quha will luik.
> To brek my sleip ane uther quair I tuik,
> In quhilk I fand the fatall destenie
> Of fair Cresseid, that endit wretchitlie. (57–63)

However, the verse at this point is not solely concerned with the 'other book'. More than half of the stanza is given over to Chaucer's text, and to the sorrows of Troilus. Critical emphasis is traditionally placed on the 'other book', which may be 'fenyeit' (66), but this only partially accounts for the acrostic.[2] The truth of Chaucer's verse is being explicitly called into question; indeed, its validity is being measured against that of a source that, like Chaucer's Lollius, in all likelihood does not exist at all. What becomes clear is that nothing is certain, least of all the words crafted by poets and makars. After all, this is a work in which we will encounter Mercury, that patron deity of liars, with a book in his hand, dressed 'Lyke to ane poeit of the auld fassoun' (245). All of this points to an interest in fiction, truth and lies that pervades the poem.

Furthermore, the very existence of the acrostic is proof of the poet's interest in what is occluded. By its nature, the acrostic can only be perceived visually rather than aurally, and as such it is the privileged knowledge of a sole reader rather than multiple listeners.[3] That is, of course, assuming a vigilant reader, for the acrostic reads against the main poem: the eye must be led away from the narrative to the alternative, perpendicular text. Unless signalled in some way, by a change of colour or by indentation, the majority of readers will pass over it, oblivious to the possibilities it offers.[4] None of the surviving sixteenth-century copies of the *Testament* signal the acrostic. The setter of the important Charteris witness, for example, is likely to have been completely unaware of its existence, the last two lines of the acrostic being interrupted and carried to the following page.[5] The mind at this point is forced towards division, suspending its engagement with the poem at one level in order to interpret the counter-text. Indeed, the doubleness is compounded by medieval attitudes towards lexical anticipation itself. The mind's action in anticipating words and interpreting them was, in medieval terms, both an imaginative and memorial process. Not just words, but syllables of words cease to exist as soon as they have been uttered; the forms of letters that are not currently before us similarly are non-existent to the mind, except insofar as it has already received both sounds and images, imprinting them upon the imagination, and retrieving them. As Augustine explains: 'unless the spirit immediately formed in itself the image of a voice heard by the ears, and stored it in the memory, you would not know whether the second syllable was the second, since the first would now no longer exist, having vanished after striking the ear'.[6] Remembered words, spoken or written, are already copies of utterances, suspended and arranged as the mind attempts to make sense of what it sees and hears. An acrostic is an exaggerated double form of this process, compelling the reader to suspend the main text while dealing with the puzzling counter-text, both, therefore, occupying space in the divided mind of the reader.

This cognitive doubleness is one of the key concerns of the narrative. Critical attention has been, rightly to some extent, focused upon the possibly non-existent other book, and the authorial fiction surrounding it. All texts can be, and are, challenged, including, explicitly, this one. The questioning of Chaucer's veracity is closely followed by doubts about the 'other book', which is, of course, the source of the work he proceeds to narrate, making the *Testament* itself a potentially 'feigned' text:

> Nor I wait nocht gif this narratioun
> Be authoreist, or fenyeit of the new
> Be sum poeit, throw his inventioun (65–67)

Indeed, this is the first recorded instance of 'invention' being used in English in a literary context to refer to the 'making-up' of a story (the term goes back to the Latin rhetorical term *inventio*).[7] Moreover, these three striking lines of profound doubt about the veracity of the *Testament* refer to Henryson's own text, delivered by a narrative voice whom he himself has created. The implications of the '*fictio*' acrostic, therefore, travel well beyond a hint that the 'other book' may not be what we expect, and open up the whole matter of knowledge, doubt and double thinking to scrutiny.

Of course, well beyond the *Testament*, the whole history of Trojan narratives is steeped in unreliability and conflicting accounts. When Chaucer cheerfully gathers Homer, Dares and Dictys – 'Whoso that kan may rede hem as they write' (I.147) – he is mustering the ultimate authorities on the Trojan War.[8] However, as is often the case when he refers us directly to sources, they do not say exactly what we expect. Chaucer's own source, Benoît de Sainte-Maure's *Roman de Troie*, calls into question Homer's version of events, and Dares and Dictys differ in their accounts. Throw into this mixture Chaucer's invented source, Lollius, and it is clear that both authors are keenly aware of the difficulties of recording what we see, or even of seeing what we see.[9] Henryson's questioning of Chaucer's veracity would, therefore, have been music to the earlier poet's ears: the difficulty of truth is the point. Nor does this simply refer to historical narratives, for it is a principle that extends to the core of *Troilus and Criseyde* and the reaction of the lovers to one another, and which lies at the heart of Chaucer's *Anelida and Arcite*, the other work of Chaucer's that infuses the *Testament*, its shadow stretching across the climax of Henryson's poem.

Anelida too begins with an intriguing, probably obfuscatory, reference to its own source material. Having called upon Polyhymnia, the narrative declares its intention to, 'folowe... Stace, and after him Corynne' (21). There is no known parallel to the story in any Statius that has come down to us, and the name of Corinna has prompted a great deal of speculation without ever delivering a definitive text and poetess.[10] It would appear that in *Anelida* we are playing the same game that we find in *Troilus and Criseyde*, the game that Henryson recognizes and develops in the *Testament*. Memory is invoked twice within five lines, in both cases in the context of fear of loss: of thoughts and stories fading, or of them being eaten away. The opening stanza's call to Mars is an appeal for defence against time, the great beast that attacks vulnerable memory. The muse invoked is Polyhymnia, she who is, by definition, the muse of many songs and voices, and the daughter of Mnemosyne (Memory) herself.

Towards the end of the *Paradiso*, Dante also invokes Polyhymnia. However, he does so in the context of struggling memory and poetic inadequacy. Having previously been unable to endure gazing upon Beatrice's smile, he is now offered the opportunity again. His description of the moment presents a clearly divided mind, a mind in which the conscious thought struggles with both imagination and memory:

> Io era come quei che si risente
> di visïone oblita e che s'ingegna
> indarno di ridurlasi a la mente
>
> [I was like one who comes to himself from a forgotten vision and struggles in vain to draw it back to his mind][11]

The smile itself, when it comes, defies all efforts of that same mind to describe it:

> Se mo sonasser tutte quelle lingue
> che Polimnïa con le suore fero
> del latte lor dolcissimo più pingue
> per aiutarmi, al millesmo del vero
> non si verria cantando il santo riso
>
> [If now were to sound all those tongues which Polyhymnia and her sisters with their sweetest milk made richest to help me, we could not come within a thousandth of the truth, singing her holy smile][12]

The impossibility of approaching the truth, or even one thousandth of the truth, is here made plain, as the mind confronts its own divided inadequacies and, for the first time in Dante's poem, acknowledges its inability to recount what it has seen. Polyhymnia, in lines that would have been well known to Chaucer, is associated with this failure. To call upon her at the opening of *Anelida and Arcite* is, therefore, to build upon a notion of myriad voices, none of which is able to capture the truth of experience. It is not that Polyhymnia lies, merely that assembling and maintaining constant, unequivocal truth is beyond the capacity even of the muses. For Wolfgang Clemen, the poem is straightforward in one respect at least, for he sees it as 'full of promises that are not kept and statements that are not true'.[13] T.S. Miller goes further and claims that critics have 'remained hesitant to call Chaucer what he is in the poem: a liar'.[14] There is a strong interest in truth and lies here, certainly, but that interest engages too with half-truths, with the subtleties of deception, with self-deception, with the ultimate impossibility of knowledge of another's self, or even of one's own self. Henryson's 'Quha wait gif all that Chauceir wrait was trew?', with its embedded self-doubt, is an acknowledgement by the Scots poet of the subtleties and uncertainties to be found, not just in the *Troilus*, but also in *Anelida and Arcite*.

The narrative voice of Chaucer's *Anelida* deals in dichotomies. Anelida, surpassing Penelope and Lucrece in virtue, is described from the outset as unequalled in 'trouthe' (76). As for Arcite, he is rarely mentioned without the epithet *fals*, the term being applied to him, in some form, fourteen times before Anelida's *complaint*. The way in which Chaucer chooses to describe the knight's falseness, however, defines his self-serving attachment as complicated and difficult, for Arcite is 'double in love and no thing pleyn' (87). Most of the critical attention given to the poem focuses on its intricate verse form, but it is also a sensitive and impressive analysis of unhappy love, at the centre of which is the far from emotionally 'pleyn' Arcite. The narrator constructs what is for him an easy division between false and true, but this is too stark a contrast even for Arcite. Henryson's Cresseid attempts to apply the same epithets at the end of the *Testament*, a triple refrain of, 'O fals Cresseid and trew knicht Troylus!' (546) jingling through the stanzas prior to the writing of her will. But it is too simple a dichotomy to encapsulate the truth of what it means to be Cresseid or Troilus, and too simple even for the wholly unlikable Arcite.

When he announces his intention to leave Anelida and replace her with another woman, Arcite's declared reason is that Anelida herself has been false. He condemns her 'doublenesse' (159) in what is interestingly the first recorded instance of the word being used in the context of character.[15] There is no justification for his claim: he simply wants to 'feyne' something in order to conceal his own treachery. What is not clear is whether this is a feigned reason with which he consoles himself and justifies his own behaviour, or whether it is merely an excuse intended for public consumption. It is a clear lie, but the extent to which Arcite admits to himself that it is a lie, before 'forth his way he wente' (161), is not at all clear. Being 'no thing pleyn' he chooses to 'pleyne' (157) about the woman who has offered him her love, and so leave her. The words for honest clarity and groundless accusation should not come together in this way, but this is a poem in which they do.[16] Arcite is poised between the truth and the fiction that is also his truth, the distance of the narrative report maintaining the delicate balance between the two.

The poem's exploration of doubling of many kinds, crucial in terms of 'both inspiration and structure', has been shown by Lee Patterson.[17] For Patterson, Anelida's complaint vividly conveys her self-division in the way in which it 'aspires to the self-possession of understanding – to recollection as self-collection'.[18] The notion of a divided self can be said to apply equally to Arcite, and it is one of the themes that Chaucer explores elsewhere in his work, perhaps nowhere more so than in the divided mind of Criseyde. When Criseyde sees Troilus for the first time, her response is such that the narrator rushes to assure the audience that her falling in love was not precipitous, that it was not in fact a 'sodeyn love' (II.667) in 'sodeyn wyse' (II.679). His need to defend her is the result of her own metaphor. Seeing Troilus from her window, a young prince fresh from victory on the battlefield, we are told that,

> Criseÿda gan al his chere aspien,
> And leet it so softe in hire herte synke,
> That to hireself she seyde, 'Who yaf me drynke?' (II.649–51)

The narrator responds to the notion of amorous intoxication with enthusiasm, as a conventional piece of lover's rhetoric that should not be allowed to impugn Criseyde, but which he nevertheless knows how to handle: Criseyde can be claimed to be in love and should not be criticized for it. He passes over, however, the preceding act of volition. The softness with which the image of Troilus sinks into Criseyde's heart aids the narrator in quietly allowing it to pass, but the quality of that little word, 'leet', is crucial. There is no violence done to Criseyde. Indeed, nothing is done to Criseyde. She looks upon Troilus in all his glory and chooses to allow the image of him to enter her heart. That she then chooses to present herself to herself as an intoxicated victim of love is significant but does not adequately describe events as we have seen them unfold, nor is it borne out in the careful enumeration of Troilus' virtues that follows. It is a desire to see herself as a giddy lover who can do nothing but succumb to love's power. Her blush is similarly indicative of what Windeatt calls her 'disconcertingly double perception'.[19] We are told that 'of hire owen thought she wex al reed' (II.652). She is not responding to something outside herself but to something within: it is her own thought that makes her blush, for there is a gap between the appraising Criseyde and the Criseyde she herself creates who claims to be amorously intoxicated. What is at stake here is the idea that what we think, and what we admit to ourselves that we think, are not necessarily the same thing. This is a crucial distinction for both Chaucer and Henryson.

Henryson's Cresseid is no less complex a character than Criseyde. One of the ways in which the Scots poet achieves this complexity is by assigning to her the language of conventional love poetry. Her stricken response to the news of Troilus' charity is portrayed in terms traditionally used to describe the grief of the woman forsaken by her lover. Denton Fox suggests that this is 'intentional irony' on Henryson's part,[20] but there is no need to suspect irony. Their case is a complicated one, but in its essence Cresseid *is* about to be abandoned by Troilus. In her dead faint, wails and sighs, she could be any woman in the *complaint d'amour* tradition, but there is particular reason to associate her with Chaucer's Anelida.

Having been deserted by the faithless Arcite, Anelida

... wepith, waileth, swowneth pitously;
To grounde ded she falleth as a ston;
Craumpyssheth her lymes crokedly;
She speketh as her wit were al agon. (*Anelida and Arcite*, 169–72)

The similarities between the two women extend beyond the physical in that both Chaucer's poem and the *Testament* unusually consist of a combination of rime royal and nine-line stanza.[21] In both cases, the nine-line stanza is reserved for the complaint of the female protagonist, with an identical *aabaabbab* rhyme scheme being employed by both poets. It is, as generations of critics have pointed out, a very distinctive and highly complex verse form, there being nothing quite like it in either medieval French or Latin. *Anelida*'s distinctiveness is signalled by the fact that reference works simply refer to it as the 'Anelida verse form'. Its difficulty no doubt partly accounts for its rare occurrence after Chaucer, and the *Testament* is the only occasion on which it is employed by Henryson.[22] It seems likely, therefore, that in using the distinctive *Anelida* form within a poem about a woman's suffering, a poem in which he has already drawn attention to the work of Chaucer, Henryson was intending some link to be made between the two women. That is not to say that Cresseid is faultless, merely that the form of the poem at this point opens up the possibility of a greater degree of complexity in her situation than might occasionally be acknowledged.

Cresseid's abandonment is more complete than Anelida's, her leprosy having estranged her from society as a whole. Her complaint comes in her first night in the leper house, when she retreats to a dark corner 'allone' (405). What is perhaps initially striking about her complaint, however, is that it is a complaint against fortune rather than strictly a *complaint d'amour*. There is no mention of Troilus, nor of Diomede, for that matter. Whereas Anelida speaks only of the loss of Arcite and the pain he has caused her, Cresseid's focus is on the loss of material things, the transience of beauty and of life itself. A proportion of the seven stanzas is given over to a catalogue of lost delights and comforts in the *ubi sunt* vein: 'Quhair is thy chalmer wantounlie besene ... Quhair is thy garding with thir greissis gay...' (416, 425). She dwells lovingly on the possessions of her past life, even down to the detail of her 'lawn' (423), her fine linen, pinned with a golden brooch. It is a catalogue of decadence, its lingering detail pulling against its general admonitions. The later stanzas see Cresseid herself become the fading flower (461), the focus being on death and the decay of the body, and ultimately she offers herself as a mirror to all the 'ladyis fair of Troy and Grece' (452). It is a conventional move. The fifteenth century abounds with verse and images in which beautiful youth is confronted with death and decay and is asked to reflect upon mortality, that 'reflection' sometimes taking the form of a literal mirror. One of the Harley lyrics, for instance, supplies a title of sorts for a short piece urging young women to gaze upon death, that makes its notion of mirroring clear: 'Cest le myrroure pur lez Iofenes Dames a regardir aud maytyne pur lour testes bealment adressere' ('This is a mirror for the young ladies to look upon in the morning in order to arrange their hair prettily'). Less obviously, the poem contains an acrostic – Mors Solvit Omnia – that offers, like Henryson's acrostic, an alternative perspective, a secret for the reader who knows how to look upon it.[23]

Cresseid's 'And in your mynd ane mirrour mak of me' (457) is similarly intriguing. It is too straightforward in this poem of doubts, cross-texts, possibilities and mirrors to allow her to dismiss herself as a still breathing *memento mori*. Furthermore, the distinctive structure of her complaint cannot help but evoke Anelida. As such, Cresseid, whose name will, of course, become a sixteenth-century by-word for infidelity, occupies a position of complexity that should not be overlooked. Partly, this is due to the fact that Anelida herself is almost a by-word for faithful love, and partly it is due to the fact that Chaucer creates in her a troubling and complex exploration of faithful devotion. If Chaucer's Criseyde is pared down over time until she becomes simply 'false', then the same process of oversimplification focuses only on the fact that Anelida is 'true', without contemplation of what that 'truth' involves. That Anelida is faithful to Arcite is not in doubt. However, her fidelity goes beyond the bounds of what is admirable and descends into morbid obsession. The love affair that is instigated by Arcite is wholly conventional:

> But nevertheless ful mykel besynesse
> Had he er that he myghte his lady wynne,
> And swor he wolde dyen for distresse
> Or from his wit he seyde he wolde twynne (99–102)

His entire effort is summarized in four lines of expected rhetoric. Anelida, on the other hand, gives herself entirely and exceptionally to her knight. Insofar as her behaviour is conventional, those conventions are intensified and surpassed by her. She weeps copiously during his absence, can scarcely eat for thinking about him, speaks only to those of whom he approves. Not only does she destroy the letters of any would-be lovers, but she insists that Arcite should read them before they are burned (113–15). There is an element of display in this, for which she is rewarded by a jealous performance. It is customary to condemn Arcite's possessive rage at this point. However, it should be noted that Arcite does not demand to see the letters; rather, he is confronted with them by Anelida, and his response is 'nas but sleght and flaterie; / Withoute love he feyned jelousye' (125–26). In the midst of a display of jealous ranting, it is easy to overlook the word 'flaterie'. It belongs with cunning 'sleght', of course, in the sense that it is not honest, but flattery is nevertheless the giving of words or performance that is desired by the recipient. It is further evidence of falseness and duplicity, but it is not so much spontaneous abuse by Arcite, as the provision of the expected response, the response that Anelida desires from her knight as she places the love letters of others before him. Condemned by the critics for controlling a loving woman who is fearfully attempting to anticipate his desires, Arcite is, in fact, a far more complicated case. His 'commands' are, for instance, not necessarily given by him. Instead, we are told that, 'Withoute bode his heste she obeyde' (119). The Riverside Chaucer would like us to interpret 'bode' as 'delay', but it might equally be 'bode' as in 'bidding', in the sense that she does what he wants without even having to be asked.[24] The chilling phrase of the *Testament* comes to mind in which Diomede had all he wanted from Cresseid, 'And mair' (72). Excess is demanded by the courtly love tradition, but sometimes excess itself is excessive. This is the point of the rhyme scheme Chaucer bestows upon Anelida. It has, as already stated, a complex stanzaic structure, with *aabaabbab* as its basic pattern. However, Anelida only stays with this for twenty-five lines before increasing the pressure and creating a stanza of sixteen lines with a rhyme scheme of *aaabaaab* and its mirror image *bbbabbba* (256–71). There is, in addition, lavish employment of internal rhymes, together with a fondness for homophones and echo rhymes. The crescendo comes at the end of the so-called *Strophe* in a stanza of fevered rhetorical questions, each line containing two internal rhymes as well as maintaining the usual end rhyme structure:

> My swete foo, why do ye so, for shame?
> And thenke ye that furthered be your name
> To love a newe, and ben untrewe? Nay!
> And putte yow in sclaunder now and blame,
> And do to me adversite and grame,
> That love yow most – God, wel thou wost – alwey?
> Yet come ayein, and yet be pleyn som day,
> And than shal this, that now is mys, be game,
> And al foryive, while that I lyve may. (272–80)

The verse form, like Anelida, is relentless. Furthermore, as she reaches a realization that Arcite neither loves nor pities her, there is a *tour de force* stanza in which the *a* and *b* rhymes are all *-ede* (299–307), visually the same, but different in pronunciation, the a-lines rhyming on [ɛ:] and the b-lines on [e:]. It is a completely contained performance of grief-stricken, obsessive love, hitting the same notes again and again.

The image of the dying swan with which Anelida ends her complaint (346–48) would have been familiar from Ovid's *Heroides*.[25] It is the image with which the great Carthaginian queen, Dido, begins her own letter, beseeching Aeneas not to take ship. The two queens and the two letters are, therefore, before us. There is, however, nothing of Dido's greatness in Anelida; nor is there anything of the heroism and self-sacrifice of Aeneas in Arcite. Chaucer's pair are simply further diminished by the comparison. Dido's suicide becomes figurative in Anelida's, 'Myself I mordre with my privy thoght' (291), as her own mind and morbid imagination sicken her. The sword of Aeneas upon which Dido throws herself is replaced in Chaucer's text by a metaphorical 'poynt of remembraunce' (211 and 350) that is cited at the beginning and at the end of the complaint, enclosing Anelida's already tightly contained narrative.[26] Memory itself has become the weapon as the mind turns upon itself. The memory of what has been lost, and the mourning over those things which do not deserve our attachment or our grief, links Anelida's complaint to that of Cresseid. The well-seasoned saffron sauces and the spiced wine of the later poem are not fit stuff for a true complaint, but nor is Arcite. Indeed, four of the twelve surviving manuscripts contain only the complaint, the poem's early editors having detached Anelida's words from their unworthy object.[27] Caxton's edition of 1477, however, would have circulated in full, with Arcite – shallow, duplicitous, possibly self-deceiving – present for the world to see.

Henryson's choice of Anelida's verse form for Cresseid's complaint, therefore, has implications not just for the way in which we regard her, but also for the way in which we regard Troilus; the verse's cadence of abandonment and loss providing an overture for his entrance, an entrance that occurs only two stanzas later. This is not to say that Troilus is to be simply equated with Arcite, rather that the distinctive background music of Chaucer's poem is employed by Henryson to sound a note of caution. Neat dichotomies of 'false' and 'true' are to be resisted in the *Testament*. What Chaucer, in fact, reveals in Anelida is a spirit misguided and self-deceived: what she values is not worth valuing, and the emotion that it prompts, while true in itself, can be nothing except debased by its object. Far from being an exercise in irony, therefore, the employment of Anelida's rhyme scheme for Cresseid's complaint provides further refraction within the text. It is, at surface level, the verse form of embodied truth, and to have Cresseid assume it along with her leprosy and reach the realization that earthly things pass away, is one truth. But, as Chaucer's text shows, what constitutes truth for lovers, in the midst of their self-deception and self-regard, is difficult and complex. The *Testament of Cresseid* is Henryson's exploration of the same theme, reaching its height as Cresseid is wrapped in Anelida's verse form and left behind by Troilus. Lovers' truth is, in the end, unstable and ungraspable. To bind Anelida and Cresseid together is to acknowledge this.

Dr Jacqueline Tasioulas is University Lecturer in Medieval English Literature at the University of Cambridge and a Fellow of Clare College.

Notes

1. All references to the works of Henryson are to *The Makars: The Poems of Henryson, Dunbar, and Douglas*, ed. J.A. Tasioulas (Edinburgh: Canongate, 1999).

2. For the acrostic and discussion of the 'uther quair', see William Stephenson, 'The Acrostic *Fictio* in Robert Henryson's "The Testament of Cresseid" (Lines 58–63)', *The Chaucer Review* 29, no. 2 (1994): 163–65.

3. For an exploration of the gap between the reception of a poem that is heard and its life as a text that is read, see C.W.R.D. Moseley, '"Tu Numeris Elementa Ligas": The Consolation of Nature's Numbers in *Parlement of Foulys*', *Critical Survey* 29, no. 3 (2017): 86–113.

4. As John L. Cutler states, 'Acrostics are not abundant in Middle English', but as Cutler himself shows, there are some that have been simply overlooked, due to their very nature. See John L. Cutler, 'A Middle English Acrostic', *Modern Language Notes* 70, no. 2 (1955): 87–89.

5. Both Thynne's edition of 1532 and Anderson's 1663 edition preserve the stanza intact.

6. For Augustine on the imaginative process involved in recognizing words, and of the mind's ability to imagine the other part of a word when presented with one section of it, see Augustine, *De Genesi ad litteram*, XII.16, *CSEL* 28.1:402. For a translation, see St Augustine, *On Genesis*, ed. John E. Rotelle, O.S.A., trans. Edmund Hill O.P. (New York: New City Press, 2002), 482.

7. The point is made by John MacQueen, *Robert Henryson: A Study of the Major Narrative Poems* (Oxford: Clarendon Press, 1967), 55. The idea is developed in A.C. Spearing, *Textual Subjectivity: The Encoding of Subjectivity in Medieval Narratives and Lyrics* (Oxford: Oxford University Press, 2005), 22–23. The word 'inventioun' appears earlier than Henryson, notably several times in Lydgate's *Fall of Princes*, in order to refer to poetic creativity, but these references are to rhetorical invention rather than to the creation of a literary work *ab initio*.

8. All references to the works of Chaucer are to *The Riverside Chaucer*, ed. Larry D. Benson (Boston, MA: Houghton Mifflin, 1987).

9. For Chaucer's relationship to the classical texts, see Barry Windeatt, *Oxford Guides to Chaucer: Troilus and Criseyde* (Oxford: Clarendon Press, 1992), 37–44, 72–77.

10. For a history of scholarship on the subject, see Vincent J. DiMarco's note in Benson, *The Riverside Chaucer*, 991. For further development of the debate about Corinna, see Lee Patterson, *Chaucer and the Subject of History* (London: Routledge, 1991), 63n59.

11. Dante Alighieri, *Paradiso*, ed. and trans. Robert M. Durling (Oxford: Oxford University Press, 2011), xxiii, 49–51.

12. Ibid., xxiii, 55–59.

13. Wolfgang Clemen, *Chaucer's Early Poetry*, trans. C.A.M. Sym (London: Methuen, 1963), 199.

14. T.S. Miller, 'Chaucer's Sources and Chaucer's Lies: *Anelida and Arcite* and the Poetics of Fabrication', *Journal of English and Germanic Philology* 114, no. 3 (2015): 373–400, here 375.

15. See *OED*, s.v. 'doubleness' (n.(2)); *MED*, s.v. 'doublenesse' (n.).

16. For an exploration of the idea that a man betraying a woman in *Anelida and Arcite* is an allegory for poetic language betraying literal meaning, see Dale A. Favier, '*Anelida and Arcite*: Anti-feminist Allegory, Pro-feminist Complaint', *Chaucer Review* 26, no. 1 (1991): 83–94.

17. Patterson, *Chaucer and the Subject of History*, 63.

18. Ibid., 66.

19. Barry Windeatt, *Oxford Guide to Troilus and Criseyde* (Oxford: Clarendon Press, 1992), 282.

20. Robert Henryson, *Testament of Cresseid*, ed. Denton Fox (London: Nelson, 1968), 125.

21. *Anelida and Arcite* also has two sixteen-line stanzas, one in the *Strophe* and the other in the *Antistrophe*. These have a rhyme scheme of *aaabaaab*, and its inverse *bbbabbba*. Chaucer's short poem, 'Womanly Noblesse', has a nine-line stanza form identical to that found in *Anelida*, but with a medial stanza of eight lines and a final stanza of six.

22. For analysis of the form, see Paull F. Baum, *Chaucer's Verse* (Durham, NC: Duke University Press, 1961), 99–101. Similar schemes in the French love complaint tradition are explored by James I. Wimsatt, *Chaucer and the French Love Poets: The Literary Background of the Book of the Duchess* (Chapel Hill, NC: University of North Carolina Press, 1968). For similarities with Machaut's 'Amis, je t'ay tant amé et cheri', see James I. Wimsatt, *Chaucer and His French Contemporaries: Natural Music in the Fourteenth Century* (Toronto: Toronto University Press, 1991), 124–26.

23. Carleton Brown, *Religious Lyrics of the XVth Century* (Oxford: Clarendon Press, 1939), 241. Brown entitles the lyric (no. 152), 'A Mirror for Young Ladies at their Toilet'. As Cutler notes, Brown has failed to spot the acrostic, and thus his text needs to be emended in two places: line 8 should begin with *vche* and line 13 should begin with *ne*. See Cutler, 'A Middle English Acrostic', 89.

24. See *MED*, s.v. bod (n.(2)). The *MED* also offers a more anticipatory definition of 'heste' as 'inclination' or 'intention', rather than the more declarative 'command'. See *MED*, s.v. hest(e (n.(1))).

25. In addition to Anelida, Chaucer uses the image for his own Dido. See the *Legend of Good Women*, 1355–56. For Chaucer and Ovid's *Heroides*, see Edgar F. Shannon, *Chaucer and the Roman Poets* (Cambridge, MA: Harvard University Press, 1929), 38–43.

26. Anelida's metaphor is taken from Dante's *Purgatorio*, XII, 20. For discussion, see Howard H. Schless, *Chaucer and Dante: A Revaluation* (Norman, OK: Pilgrim Books, 1984), 87–88.

27. See Benson, *The Riverside Chaucer*, 1144.

Index

A

accident, 211, 212, 225
Achilles, 214–15, 217, 219
acrostics, 126, 234–36, 241
Adams, Douglas, 206
Aeneid, 107, 116
Aers, D., 126
aesthetic, constructionist, 107
affirmative adverbs, 70
Alain de Lille, 107, 110, 127, 129f.,
    186
Albertanus of Brescia, 159f.
Alberti, Leon Battista, 127
Alcyone, 84, 95
Alexander the Great, 48
Alexandrian school, 107, 126
allegory, 161, 169, 222–23
Allen, Elizabeth, 208
anaphora, 63, 72
Anticlaudianus, 107
Antiochus, 51
antiphrasis, 160, 162
apostrophe, 170, 171, 198
Aquinas, 107
Aristotle, 8, 165, 166, 186
ars lacrimandi, 35, 52
ars poetica, concepts of, 108
Art of Courtly Love, 141
Arundel Constitutions, 80, 95
aspectuality, 5, 12n17
Astell, Ann W., 147, 153, 158, 208
Attridge, Derek, 59, 74n24
Auchinleck manuscript, 60

audiences, 104ff., 118ff.,
Augustine, St, 8, 105, 107, 124, 126,
    132, 135, 149, 175, 176, 178,
    181, 187, 189, 245
author, resurrection of, 5, 12n16
authority, 7ff.

B

Bahr, Arthur, 126
Bale, John, 11n5
Barddoniaeth, 87
Bate, Jonathan, 12n17
Batts, M. J., 129
Baum, Paull F., 73
Bazak, J., 127
Beaufort, Cardinal Henry, 93
Bennett, J. A. W., 126
Benoît de Sainte-Maure, 48, 236
Benson, C. David, 207
Benson, L. D., 145
Bernard the Chancellor, 107
Bernardus Silvester, 196
Bertran de Born, 86, 100
Bible
   Ecclesiasticus 22v.6, 53
   Genesis, 164, 166, 167, 179, 180
   John, Gospel of, 35, 36
   Philippians 3v.18, 41
   Proverbs, 172
   Romans, 35, 39
   Revelation of St John, 110
   Song of Songs, 166, 176, 188
Black Knight, 85, 96

Blake, Norman, 90, 95, 96, 103,
    207–8
Blanche, Duchess of Lancaster, 2,
    3, 81, 82, 83, 84, 88, 89, 91, 98
Bleeth, Kenneth A., 188, 189, 190,
    191
Blessed, number of, 110
blessing, 227
Bloom, Harold, 4
Boccaccio, Giovanni, 22–26 *passim*,
    124, 127, 132, 142
  Filostrato, 39, 43, 47, 48, 49, 50, 54
  Teseida, 40, 106, 130n40
  Decameron, 214
  De mulieribis claris, 214
Bodleian Library MS638, 89, 95
Bodleian Library MS Fairfax16, 89,
    91, 92, 94, 95, 101, 102, 103
Bodleian Library MS Tanner346,
    90, 95
Boece, 14, 25, 27, 29, 136–43
Boethius, 9, 47, 48, 49, 50, 51, 107,
    126, 127, 129, 134ff., 193, 207
Boffey, Julia, 102
Boitani, P., 126
Bovair, Simone, 9
Breeze, Andrew, 102
Brewer, D. S., 3, 11n, 98, 99, 126,
    128, 129
Bright, Timothie, *A Treatise of
    Melancholie*, 52
Brook, G. L., 72
Brooks, Cleanth, 104, 125
Brown, Carleton, 207
Brusendorff, Aage, 78, 90, 101, 103
Burnley, J. D., 184, 186, 187, 190
Burne-Jones, Edward, 3, 11n8
Burrow, John, 86, 100
Butterfield, Ardis, 85, 100
Byrne, Aisling, 102

C

Cade, Jack, 93
Caie, Graham D., 208
Calin, William, 102
Calkin, Siobhain Bly, 209

Camargo, Martin, 151
Cambridge, 4
Campbell, Bruce, 11n2
Canterbury Tales, musical, 3
Capellanus, Andreas, 141
Carlson, David, 101
Carruthers (Schroeder), Mary, 53,
    185, 188, 192
Cartier, 83, 99
Castiglione, Baldassare, 9
Castor, Helen, 82n, 99
catalogues, 66–68, 72
Caxton, William, 90, 206, 244
chain of love, 134–41, 148f., 153n15
charity, 138, 148, 150
Charles d'Orléans, 93
Chastising of God's Children, The,
    45, 46
Chaucer, Alice, 93–97
Chaucer, Geoffrey, 77–103
  ABC, 27, 30, 108
  Anelida and Arcite: 80, 233–45
  Book of the Duchess 2, 58–71, 79,
    80, 81, 82, 83, 118, 124
  Fortune, 25, 29–31
  Canterbury Tales, 3, 8, 80, 104;
    'Canon's Yeoman's T.', 175,
    160; 'Clerk's T.', 42, 43, 135,
    142, 167, 169, 171, 172, 174,
    178, 179; 'Franklin's T.', 10, 39,
    51, 144, 165, 177; 'Friar's T.',
    180, 190; 'General Prologue',
    8, 28, 43, 51, 75, 162, 194;
    'Knight's T.', 7, 8, 9, 22–23,
    25, 26, 27, 29, 40, 41, 43, 45,
    58, 61, 62, 65, 75, 135, 169;
    'Manciple's T.', 133, 172, 179;
    'Man of Law's T.', 9, 142,
    193–210; 'Merchant's T.', 8, 135;
    'Miller's T.', 4; 'Monk's T.', 22,
    25, 26; 'Nun's Priest's T.', 64,
    131, 159, 161, 170; 'Pardoner's
    Prol. and T.', 9, 12n, 25, 76, 185,
    211–232; 'Parson's T.', 163, 168,
    223; 'Prioress' T.', 159, 160,
    223; 'Reeve's T.', 177, 179;

'Second Nun's T.', 142, 159, 160, 161; 'Squire's T.', 30, 45, 46, 147; 'Summoner's T.', 224; 'Melibee', 35, 159, 161, 162, 164, 165; 'Wife of Bath's Prol. and T.', 142, 145f., 163, 167, 180
Complaint of Mars, 62, 80
House of Fame, 2, 7, 8, 9, 57–60 80, 89, 90, 93, 94, 101, 116, 162
Legend of Good Women, 78, 83, 84, 98, 101, 131, 134; *Prologue,* 10, 161, 195
Parliament of Fowls, 2, 6, 9, 104ff., 109
Retracciouns, 78, 81
Troilus and Criseyde, 4ff. *passim,* 23–24, 25, 31, 60, 104, 108, 112, 134ff., 159, 177
Chaucer, Philippa, 84
Chaucer, 'Progenie of', 2
Chaucer, Thomas, 94
chiastic patterns, 108ff.
Christine de Pizan, 94
Cicero, 114, 131
Clasby, Eugene, 209
Claudian, *De raptu Proserpinae,* 191
Clemen, Wolfgang, 238
Coghill, Neville, 3
Coleman, Joyce, 101, 126
'common profit', 117f.
complaint d'amour, 240
Condren, E. I., 98, 128
Confessio Amantis, 56, 73, 79, 115
Connolly, Margaret, 210
Consolation of Philosophy, 134ff.
Cooper, Christine, 209
Cooper, Helen, 1, 5, 7, 193, 207, 209, 210
Conrad, Joseph, 7
contemptus mundi, 137f., 143, 146, 149
Corinna, 236
Crisis, General, 1, 11n
Crow, Charles Langley, 60, 66, 67
Crosby, Ruth, 126
Coward, Barry, 102

Cursor Mundi, 58, 60, 65, 66, 68, 73, 75, 76
Curtius, E. R., 126

D
Da Costa, Alexandra, 9
Dante, 9, 37, 107–8, 124, 127, 128, 131, 161, 237
　Convivio, 108, 132
　De Volgari Eloquentia, 108
Dares, 236
Darwin, Charles, 53
David, Alfred, 136, 140, 146, 148, 152ff.
Davis, Norman, 75
debate, 113ff., 167
decasyllable, 59
decorum, 9
De Hamel, Christopher, 98
Delasanta, Rodney, 208
Delany, Sheila, 209
de la Pole, Edmund, 2
de la Pole, William, 93
delivery, oral, 104ff.
Deschamps, Eustache, 88, 97, 101, 168
Dickerson, 90
Dictys, 236
Dido, 244
dildos, 218–19
Dinshaw, Carolyn, 197, 208
disyllabic prepositions, 58–59
Donaldson, E. Talbot, 135, 144, 146, 169, 181
doubt, 211–12, 217, 219–21, 226, 228
Doyle, A. J., 98
Drimmer, Sonia, 11n3
Dryden, John, 4, 12n, 69, 73n
Duffell, Martin J., 73n2
Duncan, Thomas G., 72n1
Dunning, T. P., 140, 153, 154

E
Eade, J. C., 208
Eberle, Patricia J., 196

Edwards, A. S. G., 207, 208
Edwards, Robert, 182
Edward III, 87
-e final, 58, 74, 75
effeminate masculinity, 213
Eleanor of Aquitaine, 86
Ellesmere MS., 65, 79, 160, 161, 163, 170
Empson, William, 12n17
enjambement, 61, 68–70, 76
Entrelace, 5
equivocation, 160
Eriksen, R. T., 126, 129
eunuch, 212–13
euphemism, 166, 179, 181
Ewelme, 94

F
Fabliaux, 172, 180
fashions, critical, 5
fear, 148
felicity conditions, 224–25
Fellowes, Jennifer, 131
Fichte, Joerg O., 209
figura, 107
Filostrato, 143, 150
Fleming, John V., 182
Flood, Victoria, 102
form, 6
Fortune 1, 7, 135, 137
Four Loves, 135, 148ff.
Fowler, A., 128
Fox, Denton, 240
Fradenburg, Louise, 99
Frankis, J., 140
fraternal oaths, 226–27
Freed, E. R., 128
Freudenberger, Markus, 57
Froissart, 83, 85, 86, 87, 88, 97, 101
Furnivall, F. J., 78
Fyler, John, 8, 99

G
garden, allegorical, 111ff.
Gawain poet, 108, 109, 129

'gay ancestor', 212
gender, 9
gentilesse
    concept, 135, 141f., 144f., 148, 156n, 172
    poem, 145
Geoffroi de Vinsauf, 108, 127
Gilte Legende, 214–15, 217, 221
Given-Wilson, Christopher, 99
Goodman, Anthony, 82, 99, 101
Gower, John, 21, 25, 27, 29, 56, 79, 108, 115, 214–15, 217
    Confessio Amantis, 56, 73, 79, 115
    'In Praise of Peace', 56
Groves, Peter, 75n39
Grandson, Oton de, 85
Green, D. H., 126
Green, Richard Firth, 207, 209
Griffiths, Ralph, 77, 102, 103

H
Hainault, 86
Hammond, Eleanor Prescott, 90, 101
Harley Lyrics, 241
harmony, 124
Harrowing of Hell, 60, 75
Hart, T. E., 129
Hartman, Geoffrey, 160
Hawkins, John, 3
headless lines, 56–71
hendecasyllable, 59
Hengwrt MS, 65f., 79, 98, 160
Heninger, S. K., 128
Henry II, 86
Henry of Lancaster (Henry IV), 82, 89
Henry VI, 2, 92, 93
Henry VII, 2
Henryson, Robert, 6, 118, 128, 130, 233–45
Herbert, George, 127
hermaphrodite, 212
heterosexual, 212
Hill, John, 140, 152, 154, 158
Hill, Richard, 3

Hoccleve, Thomas, 78, 83, 101
Holt, Anne D., 92, 102
Homer, 236
homosexual, 212–13, 218, 229
Hopper, V., 129
Hrabanus Maurus, 105
Hugh of St Victor, 129
Hume, Cathy, 209
Hurst, A., 126, 129

I
iambic pentameter, 56–71
iambic tetrameter, 56–71
Ianthe, 215, 217
imperatives , 61–62, 72, 74
Innocent III, Pope, 197
interrogatives, 61–62, 72
invention, 236
Iphis, 214–15, 217–19
Isidore of Seville, 31, 35, 40, 129, 160, 163
Italian influence on Chaucer, 59, 74

J
Jansen, J. P. M., 102
Jean de Meun, 32
Jerome, St., 163, 165 163
Jesus Christ, 36, 39, 201, 205, 209
John of Gaunt, 2, 16, 80, 81–87, 93, 94,
Johnston, Arthur, 98
John the Baptist, 201, 209
Jordan, R. M., 99, 126
Julian of Norwich, 39, 42

K
Kantor, Norman, 81, 98
Kasmann, H., 128
Kelley, M. R., 126
Kemp, C. E., 3
Kempe, Margery, 39, 45, 52
Kierkegaard, Søren, 152n6
Kirk, G. S., 132
Kittredge, George Lyman, 199
Knight, Stephen, 99

L
Ladd, Roger A., 208
La Manekine, 209–10
Landino, Cristoforo, 127
Langland, William, 137f., 150
Langton, Stephen, 123
Lawrence, M., 126
Lazarus, 35, 36
Lee-Meyers, Robert, 207
Leprosy, 240
Lewis, C. S., 135f., 148ff.
Livy, 37
Lollards, 11n
Lollius, 234, 236
love, 9, 110ff.
    divine and romantic, 134ff.
Lucrece, 238
Lucretius, 193
lust, 140, 142
Lydgate, John, 83, 94, 101, 102, 112, 233
Lynch, Kathryn L., 99, 208

M
Machaut, Guillaume de, 109
MacCracken, H. N., 102
Machaut, 85, 97, 100
Macqueen, J., 128
Macrobius, 126, 131
Magdalene College, Cambridge Pepys MS 2006, 89
Magoun, F. P., 132
Malory, Thomas, *Morte Darthur,* 214, 217
Marlowe, Christopher, 65
Mandeville's Travels, 132
Mann, Jill, 125
Manning, Stephen, 208–9
Marenbon, John, 151
Marie d'Oignies, 52
Mars, 40, 41, 54
Martianus Capella, 107, 166
Mary Magdalene, St, 36, 37
manuscript, 195, 205
Mathew, Gervase, 102
Matilda, d. of Henry II, 86

Maud, Countess of Leicester, 82
Maurine, St, 215–19
McLaughlin, Mary Martin, 186
Meale, Carol, 94, 97, 103
Medieval Scribes Project, 79
Meecham Jones, S., 2
memento mori, 242
memory, 237, 244
Mercers' Company, 197
Mercury, 234
Miller, T. S., 238
Milton, John, 4, 59, 66, 76, 105,
    110, 117, 128
Minkova, Donka, 72n2
Minnis, Alastair, 128, 209
mirror, 85, 241–42
misogyny, 9, 183
Modernism, 5
Mooney, Linne, 98
Morgan, G., 130, 140
Morpheus, 84
mulier fortis, 159, 172
Muscatine, Charles, 86, 87, 100
Muses, 47
music, 7, 107, 108, 117, 118, 120,
    122, 123
Myrra, 49

N
Nahm, M. C., 127
Nature, 111ff.
Near, M. R., 132
Nebuchadnezzar, 37
Neilly, Mariana, 102
neophilia, 4
Nolan, Maura, 208
Norton-Smith, John, 89, 90, 95, 101
number, 106ff.
numerology and number symbol-
    ism, 107ff.
Nyobe, 49

O
oaths, 211, 212, 223–26
Occitan, 86
O'Connell, Brendan, 209

oral poetry, 123. *See also* reception
Orpheus, 49
Ovid, 35, 37, 47, 49, 84
    Heroides, 244
Oxford Group MSS, 90, 95

P
packing, 220, 230n
Paden, William, 100
Palmer, J., 98
Pandarus, 9, 108
Panofsky, E., 129
Paradise, 130, 162, 176, 178, 180
paraphs, 65
Pardoner, 9
Parker, G., 11n1
Parker, Patricia, 161
Parkes, Malcolm, 98
Parry, Milman, 132
Parry, Thomas, 87n, 101
Parson, 6
passing, 212–16, 218–20, 228n
Paston family, 94, 103
past participle, 70
Paterson, Lee, 98, 239
pattern, 107ff., 135, 152
Paul, St, 39, 41
Pearsall, Derek, 57, 77, 97, 98, 102
Penelope, 238
perception, difficulties of, 121
Percy Folio, 92
performance, 105ff., 215, 217–19,
    221–24
performativity, 9
persona 2, 5, 12n, 106, 120, 121,
    122, 125, 130 and *passim*
Petrarch, 43, 108, 124, 128
Philippa of Hainault, 88, 101
Philippa of Lancaster, 101
Pierides, 197
Piers Plowman, 11n, 137f., 150
Plato, 131, 137, 151
Plowman's Tale, 2
Poetry and philosophy, relationship
    between, 149ff., 158n
Poirion, Daniel, 102

Polyhymnia, 236–37
Pope Joan, 214, 216–17
Pope, Alexander 3, 56
  Essay on Criticism, 59
Powrie, S., 127
Pratt, Robert A., 161
Prelude, 3
present participle, 70
pride, 141, 143
Prioress, 10
pronuntiatio, 163
proportion, 107
prudence, 148
Pseudo-Origen, *De Maria*
  Magdalena, 36, 37
Puttenham, George, 122, 127
Putter, Ad, 4
punctuation, 64, 68–70
Pynkehurst, Adam, 78

Q
quaestio, 115
Quinn, William, 9, 126

R
Rayner, Samantha, 100
readers, 104ff., 119f., 132
reading
  private, 123, 129
  aloud, 7, 13, 105
Reason and Sensuality, 112
reception, oral, 104ff., 119f.
reception, linear and panoptic, 106
Regalado, N. F., 126
relics, 211–12, 220–22, 228, 231n35
Richard II, 88
Richard of St Victor, 107
rime royale, 108, 240
Roberts, Jane, 98
Robertson, D. W., 140, 152
Robertson, Elizabeth, 207
Rogation Days, 216
Roman de la Rose, 32, 100, 112, 166,
  180, 186, 191
Roman de Troie, 236
Rosenfeld, Jessica, 149

Røstvig, M.-S., 127, 128, 129, 131
Rothschild, V., 127
Roundel, 109, 110, 118, 122, 127
Ruggiers, Paul, 98
Ryding, W., 129
Rykener, John or Eleanor, 219

S
Sacrifice of Isaac, 202
St Valentine's Day, 110
Samson, 37
Saturn, 41
Saul, Nigel, 99
Scaliger, J. C., 127
Scheps, Walter, 208
Schibanoff, Susan, 168
Schless, Howard H., 161
Seasons, cycle of, 118
Shakespeare, William, 56, 59, 65,
  71, 75, 76
Shannon, Edgar, 58
Shippey, T. A., 128
Shirley, John, 78
Sir Dinadan, 214, 217
Sir Gawain and the Green Knight, 92
Sir Lancelot, 214, 217
Skeat, W. W., 57, 78, 109, 194
Skelton, John, 11n5
Sklute, L. M., 126
Slaughter of the Innocents, 202
Smith, Lesley M., 11n1
Sobecki, Sebastian, 6, 98
Somnium Scipionis, 114, 115, 116ff.,
  121, 131
Spearing, A. C., 12n18, 198, 208
Speculum Christiani, 53
speech acts, 223–24
Speed, John, 2
Speght's edition, 2, 78, 90, 98
Spenser, Edmund, 4
Spurgeon, Caroline, 3, 11n
Stabat Mater, 202
Staley, Lyn, 82, 88, 98, 99, 101
Stanbury, Sarah, 209
Stanley, John, of Lathom, 91, 103
Stanley, Sir John, 91

Stanley, Peter Edmund, 102, 103
Stanley, Thomas, 103
stanzaic form, 106ff.
Statius, 236
sterility, 213
Stowe, 78, 95
Strohm, Paul, 98, 99
structure, 6, 106ff.
Stubbs, Estelle, 98
subjunctives, 61–62, 72
substance, 211, 212, 225
Suffolk. *See* de la Pole
Suger of St Denis, 127
swearing, 222–23
Swift, Jonathan, 190
Swynford, Katherine, 84, 93

T
Tasioulas, Jacqueline, 8
Tatlock, J. S. P., 32, 98, 184, 189
Ten Brink, Bernhard, 57, 74
Teseida, Ch.'s use of, 106, 130n40
Testament of Cresseid, 6, 8, 130,
    233–45
Theodore, St, 215–19
Theophrastus, *The Golden Book of
    Marriage*, 163
Thompson, J. W., 132
Thynne's ed. of Chaucer, 2, 90, 95,
    206
Timaeus, 137
Tolkien, J. R. R., 10
transubstantiation, 225–26
Trevet, Nicholas, *Cronicles*, 38, 42
Trevisa, John, 40
trochaic inversion, 56–71
Troilus's death, 146–49
Troilus's hymn (III.1744–71),
    138–40
Trojan War, 236
'trouthe', 7f., 9, 10, 135, 144f., 156n
Troy, 233

trust, 211
truth, 106
typology, 107

U
utterance, imprecision of, 106ff.,
    120f.

V
Venus, 40, 41, 111ff.
verse, technicalities of, 7
Virgin Mary, 44, 53
Virtues, Cardinal, 109
Vita Nuova, 108
Vitz, Evelyn B., 126

W
Watts, Cedric, 12n16
Watts, John, 102
Wedgwood, Josiah C., 92, 102, 103
Weisberg, David, 209
Weyden, Rogier van der, 123
Wife of Bath, 6
Wild, Friedrich, 74
Williams, Bernard, 151
Williams, Deanne, 82, 99
Wimsatt, W. K., 66–67, 83, 87, 99,
    100, 101
Wind, E., 128
Windeatt, Barry, 10, 139, 140, 146,
    149, 240
Wisdom of Solomon, 107, 126, 127
Wolffe, Bertram 102
Wood, Chauncey, 208
Woods, William, 209
Wordsworth, Dorothy, 3
Wordsworth, William, 3, 59, 84, 89

Y
Yates, Frances, 126
Yeager, R. F., 101, 128
Yeats, William Butler, 190